POTS AND PALACES

VIJAYANAGARA RESEARCH PROJECT MONOGRAPH SERIES

GENERAL EDITORS

John M. Fritz
George Michell
M.S. Nagaraja Rao

Vol.1. Pots and Palaces by Carla M. Sinopoli
Vol.2. The Ramachandra Temple at Vijayanagara by Anna L. Dallapiccola, John M. Fritz, George Michell and S. Rajasekhara
Vol.3. The Vijayanagara Courtly Style by George Michell

POTS AND PALACES

The Earthenware Ceramics of the Noblemen's Quarter of Vijayanagara

Carla M. Sinopoli

MANOHAR
AMERICAN INSTITUTE OF INDIAN STUDIES
NEW DELHI
1993

ISBN 81-85425-28-0

First Published 1993

Published by Ajay Kumar Jain, Manohar Publications,
2/6 Ansari Road, Darya Ganj, New Delhi 110002 for
American Institute of Indian Studies,
D-31, Defence Colony, New Delhi 110024.

Photoset by Phoenix Phototype Setters
708, Dalamal Tower, Nariman Point, Bombay 400021
and printed at Pauls Press,
E44/11, Okhla Indl. Area II, New Delhi.

Contents

Preface

During the past 20 years world archaeologists have rediscovered "variation." We all knew, of course, that pots differed from palaces; we even knew that there were different kinds of pots, and that often they had different kinds of uses. But the rediscovery concerns the way that we think about pottery types.

We used to believe that a particular type of pot embodied a particular ideal form, and that different types of pots could be precisely differentiated. These assumptions seemed to work when we distinguished objects resulting from techniques of mass-production. However, when we examined the products of economies where individuals or small workshops were the primary producers, our assumptions did not work so well. When sorting pots (or, more frequently, the shards of broken pots) which we had excavated, we discovered that no two were precisely alike. The pots within "a type" varied in their formal attributes; that is, in size, shape, colour, material and decoration. Often the defining attributes of one type seemed to overlap with those of another. To add to the confusion, pottery shards sometimes could be assigned to one type on the basis of certain attributes, but to another type on the basis of other attributes.

Archaeologists generally attributed variation from the "ideal" to "error" on the part of the craftsmen. But eventually we realized that it was we who were mistaken. Variation in ceramic form was not simply due to the more or less successful adherence to an ideal on the part of potter. Rather, the form of each pot was the product of a complex interaction of learned, invented and imposed patterns as well as numerous economic and social factors. Ceramic variation is now seen as a means by which archaeologists can observe the complex influences on past production and, indirectly, to understand the workings of past societies.

Dr. Carla Sinopoli's work represents an innovatory approach to the study of variation in pottery. She uses multivariate statistical techniques to analyse variation at two scales—pots and space. She precisely measures variation in the forms of shards from the rims and bodies of several thousand earthenware pots used at Vijayanagara. Her analysis defines many different clusters or patterns of association of pottery attributes. These, she suggests, indicate different "primary uses", such as storage of water, cooking or lighting; the production of different workshops; or, the selection of pots by different consumers. Sinopoli then analyses the distribution of these attribute clusters in the "Noblemen's Quarter", a zone containing the basements of severaly palace buildings. This area has been excavated by the Directorate of Archaeology and Museums, Government of Karnataka, and the shards uncovered by the archaeologists were graciously made available to her for study. Sinopoli's spatial analysis aims to discover those patterns of variation that indicate the changes in the forms of pots over time, as well as changes in the distribution of activities and consumers. We refer readers to Dr. Sinopoli's lucid text for a detailed exposition of research questions, techniques and results.

It is with considerable pride that the editors acknowledge the profound contribution to Vijayanagara studies made by Dr. Sinopoli. It is fitting that the innovative work of this younger scholar should begin this series of monographs. We hope that her work will encourage other scholars to use multivariate techniques to investigate similar questions at other medieval cities in South Asia and elsewhere in the world.

John M. Fritz, George Michell
and M.S. Nagaraja Rao
General Editors
Vijayanagara Research Project,
Monograph series

Acknowledgements

This work is the result of three years of fieldwork at Vijayanagara, and many months of sitting in front of a computer screen and drafting table. A great many individuals provided support, encouragement, and assistance during the course of this research, and I am grateful to each of them. The Archaeological Survey of India under the direction of Dr. Debala Mitra, Dr. M.S. Nagaraja Rao, and Dr. J.P. Joshi have graciously granted me permission to carry out work at Vijayanagara, in 1983, 1984, 1986, and 1988, and I am most grateful to each of these individuals, to the Archaeological Survey, and to ASI personnel at Vijayanagara. I would also like to thank Mr. L.K. Srinivasan, of the Archaeological Survey of India, for his interest and encouragement in support of my work.

As Director General of the Archaeological Survey, and as Director of the Karnataka Directorate of Archaeology and Museums, Dr. M.S. Nagaraja Rao first invited me to work on the Noblemen's Quarter ceramics in 1983 and has provided continued encouragement throughout. I am most grateful to him for his support and friendship. The staff of the Directorate of Archaeology and Museums, particularly Mr. C.S. Patil and Balasubhramanyam, provided comfortable accomodations and assistance in all aspects of the work. I am grateful to them, as well as to the other employees of the Karnataka department, T.S. Ganghadar, M.P. Kumar, Manjunataiah, and Shivappa.

I would also like to thank the Ministry of Education and Culture of the Government of India for permission to carry out this research. I especially thank Dr. S.K. Sengupta, Under Secretary in the Ministry for his support. Dr. Kapila Vatsyayan, director of the Indira Gandhi Centre for the Arts, has been particularly supportive of my work; I am grateful to her for her help and kindness.

The American Institute of Indian Studies has provided much appreciated support in all stages of the permission process, as well as institutional affiliation during my work in India. I am especially grateful to Dr. Pradip Mehendiratta for his generous help and wise advice. I also thank Mr. Suri and Mrs. Raghavan for their kind support and assistance to me in Delhi.

Large numbers of people have helped with the monotony of ceramic collection and analysis, and I am grateful to each of them. Anuradha Subhramanyam, T. Richard Blurton, John Fritz, Kathleen Morrison, Louann Wurst, Mark Cassell, Michael Sutherill, and Laura Junker helped to collect ceramics from the East Valley and Islamic Quarter, and I thank them for their assistance. I would particularly like to thank Laura Junker, who joined me in India in 1984, and aided in all aspects of the ceramic analysis. This project would not have been nearly as successful without her help, and her presence made the often monotonous tasks of collecting, sorting, and measuring many thousands of sherds much more pleasant.

The work of Laura Junker, Richard Blurton, and myself at the pottery workshop in Kamalapuram provided an important adjunct to our archaeological work. I would like to thank Mahadevappa and his family for patiently answering our many questions and for permitting us to intrude on their privacy. Several people served as interpreters during these ethnographic forays. I would like to thank: Mr. C.B. Patil, Mr. U.V. Srinivas, Sudarshan Holla, and Stephen Huyler and Naidu for their assistance.

The contributions of John Fritz and George Michell to this research are many, all deeply appreciated. John Fritz first invited me to join the joint Government of Karnataka University of New Mexico Research Project in 1981. Since then, he has provided me with advice, encouragement, financial support, and friendship; I am grateful for all of these.

This work began as a Ph. D. Dissertation at the University of Michigan, which was expanded upon by additional fieldwork. I would like to thank my thesis committee, and particularly Henry Wright, for their help. Dr. Susan A Gregg wrote the computer program used in the analysis of ceramic chronology, and I am most grateful to her for making it available to me. This manuscript was largely written during a Weatherhead Fellowship at the School of American Research in Santa Fe; I am most grateful to the staff and my fellow Resident Scholars at the School for providing such a pleasant and tranquil environment in which to prepare this text.

Carla M. Sinopoli

Acknowledgements

I. Introduction

I arrived at Vijayanagara in January of 1983 in order to undertake a study of the ceramics of this great imperial city. Prior to that time, medieval ceramics had not been systematically studied in India. Rim profiles appeared occasionally in the reports of archaeological surveys and excavations, but no systematic attempt had been made to recover, classify, and interpret the vast ceramic remains that litter the surface of medieval sites throughout the subcontinent. I will argue in this work that the lack of attention to artifacts of everyday use, of which ceramics are the most common, has denied researchers a valuable source of evidence on the lifeways, economy, social organisation, and chronology of the historic towns and cities of medieval India.

The general lack of interest in ceramics, in India and elsewhere, is readily understandable when one considers the scale of many medieval sites — their spatial extent, the complexity of their architectural remains, the availability of literary texts and inscriptions, and their rich artistic heritage of sculptures, paintings, jewels and other valuable and beautiful works of art. Most ceramic remains, particularly from Hindu sites such as Vijayanagara, are, in contrast, simple, plain, and taken individually, quite uninspiring.

In this chapter I will present some reasons why ceramic analysis is valuable to our studies of medieval sites and societies, and some of the research questions we can pursue using ceramic data. As in all archaeology, historic and prehistoric, the usefulness of any class of materials depends on the sorts of questions we are asking of the past, or better, of the contemporary remains of past activities. If, for example, we are interested in examining the development of architectural styles, or of iconography, then the study of domestic ceramics will be of little use in answering these questions. Ceramics are useful, though, for examining a variety of other questions — concerning chronology, the definition of activities which occurred across a site, the spatial distribution of elite and non-elite social groups, and information on a number of aspects of economic organisation, including craft production and distribution, and trade. Each of these concerns is abundantly treated in the archaeological literature (see Bibliography, also Sinopoli n.d.a), and for present purposes each topic will be only briefly outlined.

The analysis of the ceramics of the Noblemen's Quarter of Vijayanagara, which comprises the bulk of this work, provides an illustration of a number of methods and approaches to ceramic analysis, and presents a detailed typological description of the ceramic inventory of the medieval city of Vijayanagara.

USING CERAMICS TO ANSWER QUESTIONS

In order to effectively address any of the questions presented below certain basic requirements must be met. The ceramic samples used in these studies must be: (1) sufficiently large as to encompass the total range of variation in the ceramic repertoire of the site or region under study; (2) collected in such a way as to be a representative sample of the sites, strata, or areas under study; and (3) organised into a classificatory system that records information on ceramic variation relevant to approaching particular research questions. This last point is of extreme importance as the system of ceramic classification employed provides the basis for all subsequent analyses.

As noted above, the first step in any study of archaeological materials is, necessarily, ordering the material into some sort of classificatory system. A pile of undifferentiated sherds tell us nothing about their producers other than that they made pottery. In order to learn something more from the sherds, about, for example, their chronology, use, or production, we must be able divide that pile into groups or *classes* which encode the form and structure of ceramic variation relevant to temporal change (i.e., were certain rim shapes used in certain chronological phases?), vessel use or function (i.e., does a certain form show evidence of being a cooking pot or water jar?), or production techniques (i.e., can we identify marks from the potter's wheel, or traces of coils, or paddle and anvil impressions?). As these examples demonstrate, approaches to ceramic typology are, and should be varied. An archaeologist studying changes in ceramic technology will record very different sorts of information than one studying ceramic decoration. The *variables*, or characteristics, of vessels which we choose to focus on should largely depend on what we ultimately wish to learn from our ceramic sample (Hill and Evans 1972).

Along with defining relevant variables, we must also consider how we will measure and record them, and how our measurements will ultimately be used to construct our typology. Numerous publications discuss the merits of descriptive or qualitative variables vs. numerical or quantitative variables, and both certainly have their place in ceramic analysis (for discussions of these issues see Whallon and Brown 1982). If we are examining vessel size through the variable rim diametre, for example, we may record the variable qualitatively by coding vessels as belonging to small, medium and large rim diametre classes, or we may take a quantitative approach by measuring rim diametre to the nearest centimetre, and then identifying size groups or classes from our numerical measurements. Once we have recorded information on this and other aspects of a vessel (e.g., surface colour, wear traces, height, shape, decoration, and so on), we can use this information to construct a typology of the vessels, by grouping similar vessels into types or classes which share one or more defining characteristics. As with our choice of variables, our approach to typology can be qualitative — "large red bowls with black painted designs" or quantitative — "vessels with heights of 20—25 cm., and rim diametres of 10—15 cm., neck diametres of 5—8 cm., and maximum diametres approximately twice the value of the rim diametre". Most often our typology will rely on some combination of qualitative and quantitative characteristics.

A number of approaches may be used for constructing a ceramic typology: (1) traditional typology involves laying out sherds on a table and grouping them into coherent groups that look alike and then assessing their defining characteristics retrospectively (see Whallon 1972); (2) the type-variety method, pioneered by Wheat, Gifford, and Wasley (1958) in which qualitative variables are used hierarchically to sort and subdivide vessels from a region; or (3) statistical approaches, where we examine the relations between groups of variables, and the distributions of individual variables using statistical techniques in order to subdivide the sample into meaningful and consistent classes. A statistical approach to ceramic classification was used in the development of a classification system for the Vijayanagara ceramics. This approach and its results will be presented in considerable detail in Chapter IV.

Establishing a ceramic classification, while critical, need not be the end of our analysis. A classification in and of itself tells us little about the society which produced the ceramics. While we may be able to say, for example, that the Vijayanagara potters produced a large number of vessel form variants, we cannot consider the significance of this fact until we use our classified sample to examine other factors or conditions of Vijayanagara society which may have contributed to the form and structure of the ceramic inventory. Such factors may include, among other things, temporal change, social selection, or differences among pottery making workshops. A ceramic classification, then, organises our data base, the piles of sherds recovered in excavations and survey, in such a way that we can ask and seek to answer a variety of questions about the society and culture which produced the ceramics we collect. Some of these questions will be discussed in the remainder of this chapter.

Using Ceramics to Study Chronology

The use of ceramics in the construction of chronologies has a long history in archaeological studies, extending back to the late 19th century. The association of certain classes of vessels in stratigraphic levels provides one means for constructing ceramic chronologies based on the principles of stratigraphy. When such sequences are repeated in part or in whole across a number of sites it is possible to build up broad regional sequences. Recently, the availability of absolute dating techniques, such as carbon 14 dating and dendrochronology, has allowed the dating of associated materials, including ceramics, with increasingly fine precision.

In many archaeological situations, however, archaeologists deal with single phase sites or sites with disturbed stratigraphy and a paucity of materials which can be dated using absolute techniques. In such cases, alternative techniques must be employed to develop chronological sequences. One such method is seriation, defined as "the procedure of working out a chronology by arranging local remains of the same cultural tradition in the order which produces the most consistent patterning of their cultural traits" (Rouse 1967: 157).

Seriation entails a basic assumption on the nature of artefact change. This is that a class of objects is slowly introduced into a social system, gradually increases in popularity, and eventually declines in use and disappears. A new pottery class, for example, may first be adopted by only one or two members of a community. As it becomes better known and more accepted, more and more people may begin to use it, until eventually that class of pottery becomes very common. Eventually, new classes will come into vogue and the first class will decline in popularity and eventually disappear. Seriation uses this assumption to examine the percentages of different pottery classes in strata, within a site, or between a set of sites. Seriations can be constructed using a variety of techniques, from plotting frequencies on graph paper, to computer assisted techniques such as the Brainerd Robinson similarity matrix (Doran and Hodson 1975: 272-274) and multi-dimensional scaling (Cowgill 1972; Doran and Hudson 1975: 213-216; Pollock 1983b: 94-96; Steponaitis 1983). A seriation using Brainerd-Robinson similarity matrices was conducted on the Noblemen's Quarter ceramics, results of which are presented in Chapter V.

Using Ceramics to Study Activity Distribution

Ceramic vessels are tools — objects used in specific activities to serve specific ends (Braun 1983: 107). The intended use of a vessel affects the final form the vessel will take in a number of ways, including the vessel shape and types of clays and tempers used in vessel construction.

Cross-cultural studies of relations between vessel form and vessel use have revealed pronounced regularities over time and space (Smith 1985; Henrickson and McDonald 1983). Factors such as the size of the opening, ease of access to a vessel's contents, volume (and weight when full), location of the center of gravity, and vessel stability, all seen to be partially determined by the intended function of a vessel. For example, narrow-necked vessels are likely to be used for transporting water because less will spill from their openings than from wide-mouthed vessels. Round bases are advantageous on cooking vessels because they transmit heat easily and are less susceptible to breakage from thermal stress than flat-based vessels. The material constituents of the vessel may also be determined by the intended use of the pot; certain tempering materials or clays may be favored for cooking pots, while others are favored for water storing vessels, based on their ability to conduct heat, their transpiration rate, and their rate of expansion and contraction in response to heating (see Steponaitis 1984: 86-108).

This does not mean, however, that all vessels are ideally suited to their intended use. Vessel shape is also determined by normative ideas, fashion, and the technology of ceramic production. Nor is it the case that vessels are always used for the purposes for which they were originally intended. Additional evidence of ceramic use may be attained through wear traces found on the vessels. Cooking vessels may be charred on the exterior; vessels traditionally covered with lids may be abraded on the rim top; and residues of materials held in vessels may remain on their surfaces. Given these differing lines of evidence — morphology, technology, and use wear — it is frequently possible to make some inferences about the range of activities in which particular vessels were 'most likely' used.

Under certain circumstances it may be possible to consider the precise spatial location of activities across a site using ceramic data. Such circumstances occur when vessels enter into archaeological deposits in the same area in which they were used. Much attention has been devoted, particularly in prehistoric studies, to the identification of activity areas (see Binford 1976; Binford et al. 1970; Yellen 1977). An activity area is, simply, an area where specific past activities occurred which can be identified from archaeological data. Most types of activity areas are seldom identifiable in the archaeological record. Behaviors such as clearing the refuse of activities, and depositing it in trash middens or dumps destroys traces of many past activity loci. Site formation processes can also lead to the displacement of materials once they have entered into the archaeological record (Schiffer 1976).

Under certain conditions, ceramics may enter the archaeological record in the locations where they were used; the analysis of materials deposited in such contexts can provide a tremendous amount of information on the distribution of activities across a site. Vessels might be deposited where they were used in contexts such as at water-collecting locations, such as wells or tanks, where a certain number of vessels are inevitably dropped and broken. A more important context in which activity loci might be preserved archaeologically arises when a site or part of a site is suddenly abandoned or destroyed through natural or cultural disaster. Such events might include fire, flood, warfare, or volcanic eruptions. In such an event, and assuming limited post-depositional disturbance, materials should be found in the areas in which they were last used. Ritual or votive deposits or caches represent another sort of activity-specific deposit in the archaeological record.

Even when we cannot use ceramic distributions in the identification of specific activity areas, in many contexts the spatial distribution of ceramics across archaeological sites can reveal much information. It can often be assumed that middens or trash deposits are located relatively close to occupation areas, e.g., in abandoned rooms or buildings, against the back wall of a house or house compounds, in a neighborhood dump, and so on (Boone 1987). In the case of ceramics, sherds may often be incorporated into walls or roof of a house or other structures in later construction phases. The assumption that materials tend to be deposited relatively near to where they were used underlies many of the attempts to use ceramics to examine intrasite social, economic, or political organisation (see for example, Hill 1970, 1972; Deetz 1965; Longacre 1968). As will be discussed in later sections of this work, the ceramics from the Noblemen's Quarter of Vijayanagara, where a series of burnt palaces have been excavated (presumably burnt at the end of the city's occupation), provide a good case for using ceramics to examine the distribution of activities within that area.

Using Ceramics to Study Social Organisation

The use of ceramics in studies of social organisation is predicated on basic concepts concerning the transmission of knowledge on ceramic production techniques and the communicative nature of material culture. Ceramics, like all material products of human activity, are used and produced in a social context. Ethnographic studies of the transmission of the pottery craft in societies where pottery making is a household industry, have demonstrated that potters absorb influences from many sources and learn from many individuals (see Friedrich 1970; Hardin 1979, 1984; Stanislawski 1969, 1973). While certain aspects of pottery manufacture and decoration may be conditioned by learning contexts (as, for example, how one holds a brush or other tools, or micro-characteristics of design application and form), potters are typically very conscious of the form their products take and are very much in control of their products. Potters can readily alter the form and style of their products when circumstances encourage such changes. Potters should therefore be viewed as active transmitters and transformers of their craft, rather than as passive recipients of traditional knowledge.

Potters produce for consumers and make vessels in accordance with the demands of their users — demands for functionally effective and formally appropriate vessels. Culturally conditioned opinions on the appropriate form of ceramics or other goods ultimately determine whether new forms will be accepted or rejected, and contribute to the historic continuity of particular forms over multiple generations. Goods, then, are produced in a system of meaning, which governs definitions of appropriate form, techniques, and use, as well as the assignment of value.

"Goods", write Douglas and Isherwood, "are needed for making visible and stable the categories of culture" (1979: 59; see also Appadurai, ed. 1986; Miller 1985). The symbolic importance of goods is readily recognisable in contemporary contexts; clothing styles, house forms, jewellery, the foods one eats, and numerous other categories of goods convey information on the social or economic position of their user, or on the status that the user wishes to present. Even the simplest of cultures has, of course, a great many social categories, with a large number of multi-layered sets of social relations. It is therefore, not adequate to say simply that material culture participates in the definition and reinforcement of social relations. Different classes of goods and their specific contexts of production, distribution, use, and valuation, must be considered independently in order to assess at what level they might be expected to convey and represent social relations, and what sort of relations they might convey, or, possibly, obscure.

Turning specifically to ceramics, consideration of the symbolic or significatory role of ceramics in specific contexts must entail the examination of: (1) how they were used and the importance of such activities to the society; (2) who would have seen them while they were in use; (3) contexts of production and distribution; and (4) the valuation of ceramic classes in themselves, and relative to non-ceramic equivalents of metal, basketry, cloth, etc. Different classes of ceramic vessels, such as utilitarian storage pots, plain serving vessels, and fancy serving wares are used in very different contexts, and their forms, as well as their occurrence and distribution within and between settlements could be expected to convey very different sorts of social information. Types of information which may be conveyed through ceramics include social status — through distinctions between elite and non-elite wares, and group identity — such as variations in ceramics used by different kin groups or clans in egalitarian societies, or by equivalently ranked social groups in more complex societies.

Vessel use and the context of use are very important to evaluating the potential and level of social variation in ceramics, and their possible potential symbolic content (Pollock 1983a). While ceramic vessels may be put to a wide variety of uses, the major use of ceramics involves food — its storage, cooking or serving. Ceramic forms are consequently associated with, and meaningfully linked to, the specific foods used by members of a society (and these may vary significantly between individuals and groups within that society), their means of preparation, and the cultural significance of food consumption and sharing.

The involvement of vessels in the highly ritualised and meaning-laden food system of a culture (see Goody 1982; Levi-Strauss 1969; Douglas 1974) contributes both to the conservatism of vessel forms, and to the association of symbolic significance with vessels and their use. Thus, royalty may eat off of plates of gold and commoners dine on wooden slabs or banana leaves, the 'good china' may be used only on special feast days or to entertain the boss, and disposable plates are appropriate for outdoor picnics. The association of vessels with foods and contexts of use and with the user's status does not only apply to serving vessels, but to food preparation vessels as well. Even in the context of food preparation and/or consumption, the types of information conveyed by these vessels may vary considerably. In the examples presented above, gold or wood plates express rank or status, the use of the 'good china' denotes a specific time in the annual cycle, and disposable plates signify a particular kind of meal and dining context.

While in the examples presented above vessel raw material is considered, similar differences may be expressed through vessel shape or decoration within a single material class. Ceramics must, however, always be considered as only one of many possible materials for vessel construction. The 'status' of ceramics relative to alternative materials is perhaps nowhere made more explicit than it is in traditional India where, because of their vulnerability to ritual impurity, the precious metals are most highly rated, followed by other metals (copper, bronze), below which is ranked earthenware. As with rules concerning food sharing and food preparation, the relative ranks of different materials and different ceramic wares (e.g., porcelains vs. earthenwares) may vary contextually. However, I would expect the valuation of such goods to be subject to some generally applicable rules involving the "cost" of their acquisition or production. Following Pollock (1983b: 19-20), more 'costly' goods may result from (1) the use of materials which are in limited supply locally or are non-local, (2) the care and elaboration involved in the production of the object, and (3) the abundance of the good or some dimension of it (e.g., size).

I have considered thus far only ceramics used in activities involving foodstuffs. Ceramics may be used in a number of other contexts as well —as ritual vessels, perfume holders, well-linings, water pipes, dove cotes, and so on. Functional interpretations of such vessels may be approached through a consideration of their morphology and depositional contexts. A consideration of the role of varying vessel forms in symbolising and defining social relations must take into account the nature and significance of the activities in which they were used. For example, the importance of ritual in formally and often publicly expressing social positions of various types (gender, rank, and so on; see Rappaport 1971), likely extends to the material paraphernalia associated with ritual events. Other functional classes of vessels must be similarly considered with respect to their specific contexts of use.

The analysis of ceramic data in studies of social organization involves, as do all archaeological studies, the recognition of patterns —consistent associations of ceramic classes, spatial clustering within sites, and so on. The assignment of specific meanings to these patterns operates on two levels. The first is an analytical meaning: ceramic cluster A is found in area C, while ceramic cluster B is found only in area D. Differences between ceramic clusters A and B do not appear to be functional (i.e., the same array of general vessel-use forms are found in each cluster, indicating a similar array of activities in each area) or chronological. They can therefore be interpreted as representing meaningful social variation between the occupants of areas C and D.

The second level of meaning is much more difficult, and often impossible for archaeologists to deal with—that is, the meaning that the pottery makers and users assigned to specific symbols, colours, or forms. We can look at the archaeological contexts of material deposition and use and temporal changes in artefact occurrence and distribution, and can develop some abstract framework of 'value' and access to and categorisation of goods. Such information can then be used to infer much about the social system in which the goods were produced. We cannot, however, precisely define why some symbols were chosen over others, or what they signified to their makers and users.

Most studies of ceramics and social organisation have focused on painted vessels and design form and structure (see Washburn 1977; Kintigh 1985; Plog 1980). The reasons for this are readily apparent. Ceramic decoration is typically highly structured and easily recognised and decodable (see Washburn 1977). Unlike other dimensions of ceramic variability, such as vessel form, decoration belongs solely to the realm of expressive treatment. However, within the technological constraints imposed by raw materials and pottery making techniques, ceramic form is also highly flexible. It is reasonable to expect, therefore, that micro-variation in rim form, vessel shape, and other morphological characteristics, within broad functional groups of vessels, might also exhibit meaningful variation between social groups.

Because the assignment of meaning to particular attributes is an historical and, to some extent, arbitrary process (or at least one that we don't have direct access to), there can be no exact formula for determining which attributes to study and how to define them in an analysis of social variation in ceramics. While we can develop some general expectations based on criteria of context of use and visibility, value, and so on, we must also engage in an analytical process which involves intensive feedback between pattern recognition and interpretation. Analysis should involve a process of: (1) developing a theoretical framework in which to view ceramic variability in general and in specific archaeological contexts; (2) identifying patterns or structure in a body of data; (3) evaluating the occurrence of these patterns over space and time, and with respect to the underlying analytical framework, and (4) reevaluating and revising, when necessary, both interpretations of the data and the underlying theoretical perspective.

Using Ceramics to Study Economic Organisation

Included under the heading 'economic organisation' are a number of issues which we can study with ceramic data. We can examine, first of all, the organisation and techniques of ceramic production—whether ceramics are produced by their users, in small neighbourhood workshops, or in large 'industrial workshops', Each of these implies very different things about the scale of production and equally important, about the nature and scale of the distribution systems. In examining the organisation of ceramic production we can also learn about the political setting in which ceramic producers operated—were materials produced by independent potters, or by potters attached to and regulated by higher authorities, such as chiefs, temples, or states? Third, we can use ceramic data to examine local and long-distance trade. Vessels can be sourced to their production locale through chemical or petrographic analyses, through workshop marks, or regional styles, and we can ask questions about how far they travelled from their locus of production and how the trade was structured.

Ceramic Production. Van der Leeuw (1977) has presented a useful typology of the organisation of ceramic production, ranging from simple to complex productive systems. At the simplest level is *household production,* in which members of each household produce vessels for their own use. Household production was probably characteristic of the earliest pottery producers and may have held for many 'neolithic-level' non-hierarchical sedentary agricultural societies throughout the world. In household production, pottery is typically handmade and fired in the open, a relatively simple technology with little investment in raw materials, tools, or permanent facilities. Pottery manufacture is periodic; the yearly needs of the household for ceramic vessels can be satisfied in a relatively short period of time. Even in such a system, it is likely that pottery moves beyond the boundaries of the household, as gifts, parts of dowries, or in exchange for other goods.

The second level of production described by van der Leeuw is the *household industry.* In this system, ceramics are still produced at the level of the household, though much production is oriented towards trade or sale beyond the household. Potters are not full-time specialists, and pottery making generally supplements agricultural activities or other sources of income. However, pottery is produced in larger quantities than in the first level, and pottery production takes place more frequently. The technology of ceramic production remains relatively simple, and time-consuming. Household industries may emerge under a number of conditions. Widows or non-married women may become part-time specialists in order to generate necessary income (see Balfet 1981), or members of households which lack access to sufficient good agricultural land may specialise to some extent in pottery production in order to supplement limited agricultural returns (see Arnold 1985: 226).

The third level of ceramic production defined by van der Leeuw is marked by the emergence of specialists who work virtually full-time at pottery production. This is a *workshop industry,* characterised by increased scale and efficiency of production, typically involving major changes in ceramic technology. Vessels may be wheel- or mould-made. Both technologies permit the production of large quantities of vessels in a short period of time. Firing technology is also improved with the introduction of permanent ovens or kilns. Pottery is produced more or less year round, except during rainy periods, and is distributed through markets, middlemen, or directly from the workshop. Because pottery making is a regular activity and there is incentive to produce many vessels, vessels can be expected to become increasingly standardised, as potters attempt to minimise time and energy invested per vessei.

Workshops are typically family enterprises; potters include both male and female members of a nuclear or extended family. While females were the major ceramic producers in the household production and household industries, males typically are the primary labourers in workshop industries, particularly as regards work on the potter's wheel. Contemporary ceramic production throughout rural India is organised at the level of the workshop industry (see Saraswati and Behura 1966; Saraswati 1978; Behura 1978; Sinopoli and Blurton 1986; Junker 1985; Miller 1985).

The last level in van der Leeuw's framework is the *large-scale industry*. This system of ceramic production is characterised by workshops or factories which employ large numbers of people. Production is full-time and large scale investment in drying chambers and kilns minimises the effects of rainfall and climate on production. Ceramics are extremely standardised and productive technology is highly refined and highly specialised.

The broad classification of scales of organisation of ceramic production is a useful framework in which to view ceramic manufacture. Other productive systems may exist, and van der Leeuw has discussed itinerant potters as one example. Nonetheless, the classification of ceramic production does seem to describe the most common modes of organisation of ceramic production, as known from world-wide ethnographic studies (see Kramer 1985), and provides a general framework for viewing pre- and protohistoric and historic systems of ceramic production.

The organisation and scale of ceramic production has very important implications for the nature of the finished products which we recover archaeologically. When pottery production is at the level of the household, vessels are typically simple in form, produced by coiling or other hand-building methods, and fired in open fires at relatively low temperatures. Since pottery manufacture in such industries is periodic, with vessels produced at certain times of the year or when needed by the household, there is a fair amount of variation in vessel shape and other characteristics from year to year. In addition, the clays and tempering materials used are likely to be those locally available at little or no cost to the potters.

As the scale and frequency of ceramic production increases, so will the impetus for more sophisticated techniques for vessel production and firing. The introduction of potters' wheels or moulds will lead to increased standardisation of the final products. Increased frequency of manufacture will also encourage standardisation, as it is more efficient to produce many identical or nearly identical vessels, than to make each vessel unique. In addition, the range and variability of these standardised types may increase, as ceramics come to play increasingly important roles in daily life, and as market or other demands become important to workshop survival and success. In order to fire larger numbers of vessels more efficiently, permanent firing facilties such as kilns or ovens may be introduced. Such facilities, in turn, generate higher firing temperatures and more efficient transmission of heat, which lead to well fired vessels.

Innovations in production and firing techniques place constraints on the raw materials which can be used in vessel manufacture. The introduction of the potters' wheel, in particular, imposes limitations on the quality of clays and tempers which can be used. The potters' wheel is an efficient tool, with which a proficient potter can form vessels in just a few minutes. Not all clays are suited to wheel-throwing, however, and potters must become more selective in the materials they use. In addition, more attention must be devoted to clay and temper preparation, as the presence of large non-plastic inclusions in a vessel wall can result in the vessel being torn apart on the wheel, due to the friction of the force of the wheel against the potter's hands. Successful kiln firing requires the use of good quality, hot burning fuels, i.e., wood or coal, which must also be acquired by the potters. In contrast, low burning fuels such as dung or brush are quite effective in open or pit firing. The effects of higher firing temperatures on finished vessels are readily observable in vessel hardness, chemical transformations of clay and tempering minerals, degree of oxidation, and so on (see Rye 1981).

Even in the absence of direct archaeological traces of pottery manufacture, such as firing or workshop facilities and implements, it may therefore be possible to argue back from the vessels themselves to the techniques which produced them, and in turn, to develop some reasonable expectations concerning the organisation of ceramic production. The organisation of ceramic or other craft production is not independent of the socio-political and economic contexts of the society in which the vessels are produced. The emergence of full-time craft specialisation, for example, has been linked to the ability of a society to produce an agricultural surplus to support non-agricultural segments of the population (Arnold 1976; Rice 1981). It has been argued by Foster (1960), Arnold (1985), and others, that specialised production emerges in agricultural societies under conditions of population pressure. In such cases, it is proposed that specialists come from groups which occupy marginal agricultural lands, and use supplementary income to meet their subsistence needs. Other factors, such as the size and density of the consuming population, the nature and regulation of distribution and transportation channels, the valuation of ceramics and alternative vessel materials, as well as social, ideological, and political factors, may also condition or determine the nature and organisation of ceramic production systems.

Ceramic production, as we have seen, can be organised in many ways and at a variety of scales. It should be noted that different scales and systems of production can coexist in a single society (Balfet 1981). The coexistence of multiple production systems can endure at more or less constant levels for long periods of time, as seen in North Africa. In addition, the relative importance of one or another system of production can change over time. If, for example, trade routes or traditional market systems are disrupted and products of specialists can no longer be distributed, household production and household industries may become increasingly important. The coexistence of multiple modes of ceramic production, then, provides a highly flexible and adaptive system of ceramic production.

Archaeological studies of ceramic production can call on several lines of evidence. Including among these are direct traces of pottery manufacture (Stark 1985). Such traces include remains of kilns or ovens. Materials frequently associated with firing areas include large numbers of misfired or over-fired vessels, or 'wasters', often blistered or warped; kiln furniture—pieces of shaped clay placed between vessels to prevent them from sticking together during firing and which permit the flow of air between vessels in the firing chamber. Large deposits of ash from firings may also be present. The discovery of firing areas is most likely to occur when pottery production was at a fairly large scale, such as in workshop industries or large-scale industries. In household production, firing usually takes place in the open without permanent facilities, and leaves little easily identifiable trace in the archaeological record.

Probable areas of vessel forming are more difficult to identify than large-scale firing areas. Recovery of moulds, large deposits of raw materials, or pottery-making tools, such as stone anvils, wheel sockets or axles, and decorative stamps, may be used to identify production areas. As noted earlier, additional indirect evidence on the organisation of ceramic production may be inferred from the vessels themselves, including evidence for production techniques, firing temperature, standardisation, and so on.

Ceramic distribution. Along with variation in the organisation of ceramic production, considerable variation can exist in the ways in which ceramics are distributed, and the distances over which they are transported. The study of distribution systems is of great interest to archaeologists concerned with the nature of interaction between different cultural groups, including diffusion and long-distance trade, as well as with distribution systems internal to a single cultural system, including such issues as the development of market systems. The study of ceramic distribution involves, first, identifying the source of the vessel, either the workshop or region in which it was produced, and second, examining mechanisms by which it may have reached its ultimate destination. Sourcing ceramics may be accomplished on stylistic grounds or by studying technological attributes, including clay and temper mineralogy. Methods such as neutron activation or x-ray spectroscopy can be used to characterise clays from various regions and to identify the probable sources of vessels, providing that sufficient regional variation in clays and tempers exists (see Rye 1981). Macroscopic variation in ware colour and paste consistency may also be used to identify probable locations of ceramic production.

The identification of distinctive regional ceramic styles may also provide evidence on the general location of pottery production. Both decorative treatment and vessel form may be distinctive to a particular region or 'culture' and their presence outside of their core area indicates some sort of contact between regions. This contact may take the form of trade or gift-giving, or local imitation of non-local or exotic wares. Imitations of exotic wares may be identified through microscopic or macroscopic studies of raw materials and construction techniques.

Within their region of production ceramic vessels

may be: (1) used where they were produced; (2) sold or traded directly from production sites for use within the community in which they were produced; or (3) transported to and sold at weekly markets by the potters themselves, by middlemen, or by merchant groups. Because ceramics are both bulky and breakable, transportation of large numbers of vessels over long distances is not very common. Foster has suggested that 150 miles is the maximum distance which pots will be transported in traditional economies (1965: 56), and typically the distance is far less than that. Where water transportation is possible, pots may travel greater distances than when they must be moved overland on the backs of draft animals or humans (Nicklin 1971; Ellen and Glover 1974).

Ceramic vessels, however, sometimes travel considerably beyond the bounds of their immediate area of production and primary use. It probably is relatively rare for vessels themselves to be objects of long distance trade, except in contexts where the vessels are indicators of status or are required in rituals or other special purpose activities. Ceramic vessels, however, serve as containers for materials which are objects of long-distance trade, such as oils, spices, wine, and so on. In such cases, vessels containing these materials may travel considerable distances; witness, for example, the Roman amphorae which are found throughout the extent of the Roman empire and beyond its bounds, in South Asia and the Near East (Wheeler 1946; Williams 1981).

As will be discussed in more detail in later chapters, present evidence for Vijayanagara ceramic production indicates that, like contemporary South Indian pottery production, ceramic manufacture was a household industry, conducted by full-time specialists. Production involved the use of a potter's wheel, as well as hand-building techniques including moulds, paddle and anvils, and slab building methods. It appears that ceramics were not traded over long distances during the Vijayanagara period, and vessels used within the city were probably produced within the greater metropolitan area of Vijayanagara (see Sinopoli n.d.c).

The Ceramics of the Noblemen's Quarter of Vijayanagara

With this background on some of the problems that ceramic analysis may consider, the remainder of this work will examine the ceramics of the medieval south Indian city of Vijayanagara, and in particular the ceramics of eleven palace complexes recently excavated by the Government of Karnataka, Directorate of Archaeology and Museums in an area known as the Noblemen's Quarter. Many of the questions addressed in this chapter will be examined with the Noblemen's Quarter (NMQ) ceramics. A typology of Vijayanagara ceramics is developed, and analysis of the NMQ ceramics will consider activity distributions, social organisation, and chronology of the Noblemen's Quarter. Before presenting the ceramic analysis, a description of the plan and structure of the Noblemen's Quarter will be provided in Chapter II. Two other areas of the site from which ceramics were examined—the East Valley, and the city's main Islamic Quarter—will be briefly discussed.

Chapter III presents information on the ceramic sample analysed from the Noblemen's Quarter: how it was collected, where it was collected from, and its size. The goals of the Noblemen's Quarter ceramic analysis will be presented in greater detail. The Vijayanagara ceramic typology will be examined in Chapter IV. Definition of relevant variables, techniques employed, and the final ceramic classification will be presented. Chapter V will examine the spatial distribution of ceramics in the Noblemen's Quarter, looking at distributions within and between the sampled compounds. Ceramic distributions will be used in interpretations of activity distributions and social variation in the NMQ area. In Chapter VI, the Noblemen's Quarter ceramics will be compared to ceramics from the East Valley and the Noblemen's Quarter to examine differences in production, ceramic use, and social organisation across the city. Chapter VII will summarise what we have learned from the analysis of the Noblemen's Quarter ceramics: about Vijayanagara period ceramics, about the Noblemen's Quarter in particular, and about the city and empire of Vijayanagara in general.

II. The Noblemen's Quarter Described

The capital of the Vijayanagara empire was located on the southern bank of the Tungabhadra River (Figure 2.1), an area sacred in local religious beliefs as the birthplace of Hanuman the monkey god and the resting place of Rama, the avatar of Vishnu as ideal king. Vijayanagara the city was in every sense an imperial capital—in scale, architecture, and wealth. Records of the city from the time of its occupation come from court poets and musicians, as well as from foreign—Persian and European—visitors. A further source of information on the city of Vijayanagara comes from photographs, drawings, and descriptions of the city composed several centuries after its destruction, by British surveyors, scholars, and government officials (Michell 1985a: 196-198).

Architectural, epigraphic, and archaeological work at the site provides an additional source of information on the medieval capital (Nagaraja Rao, ed. 1983, 1985; Fritz and Michell 1984; Fritz, Michell and Nagaraja Rao 1985). Thorough descriptions of the city are available in Fritz, Michell, and Nagaraja Rao (1985; see also Dallapiccola, ed. 1985; Nagaraja Rao, ed. 1983, 1985). In this chapter, I will focus only on those areas from which ceramics were examined: the Noblemen's Quarter, the East Valley, and the city's main Islamic Quarter.

THE NOBLEMEN'S QUARTER

The area located to the north and west of the areas of royal residence of Vijayanagara has been designated as the "Noblemen's Quarter" and has been the focus of large scale excavations by the Government of Karnataka Directorate of Archaeology and Museums (DAM) since 1982 (Figure 2.2). This area, which is bounded to the east and west by massive granite outcrops, contains a large number of elite stepped structures, commonly referred to as palaces. The quarter is bounded to the south by the compound walls of the royal residential area (popularly referred to as Danaiak's Enclosure and the Mint Enclosure; Fritz and Michell's enclosures VII and VIII) and a temple dedicated to Virupaksha, the tutelary deity of the Sangama rulers. To the north of the Noblemen's Quarter (NMQ) is a large gate, which has been partially excavated by the DAM team.

The architectural remains of the NMQ consist of a number of stepped platforms, typically located within walled compounds which contain one or more subsidiary structures. Other subsidiary structures are found outside of the compound walls. The NMQ structures are primarily non-religious buildings, though a number of small shrines are found within the quarter. The structures of the Noblemen's Quarter have been interpreted as palaces, or elite residential buildings (see Patil 1985). It must be noted, however, that the precise functions of these structures are unknown, nor is it clear what segment of the Vijayanagara elite utilised them. It is likely that the buildings and compounds served a variety of functions, including residential and public uses and that these uses varied between the different NMQ compounds.

Eleven excavated compounds form the basis for the present study. These are designated as NMQ1-NMQ10 and NMQ12 (see Figure 2.2). The compounds vary considerably in form, size, and their state of preservation. Some of the compounds are freestanding, surrounded only by their compound walls (NMQ1, NMQ2, possibly NMQ12). Others are contiguous and share border walls with neighbouring compounds (NMQ3-11). The architectural and archaeological remains of the NMQ compounds provide evidence of a long and complex building sequence in the area. Certain of the compounds (NMQ7-9) are in a very poor state of preservation, with only foundation walls remaining intact. It is likely that many of the faced structural elements were removed after these compounds fell into disuse, and utilised in the construction of later structures. Other compounds (NMQ6) exhibit traces of extensive rebuilding and remodeling, indicating a change in scale and, perhaps, in function. Still other compounds (NMQ1-5, 12) are in a very good state of preservation and may have been occupied up until the last days of the city. Ceramics have been examined from eleven excavated palace compounds in the NMQ area. These compounds will be described in some detail, since both their commonalities and the differences between them are a major concern of the ceramic analysis.

The Palace Compounds

Compound 1 in the Noblemen's Quarter is the largest free-standing compound in the area. The compound walls extend 64.5 m. east-west by 56.5 m. north-south, encompassing an area of ca. 3650 square metres. (Nagaraja Rao 1983b: 15; Figure 2.3). The main entry to the compound is in the north, approached by a flight of 13 stairs. A road runs along the western boundary of the compound. This road, which Fritz (1983b: 50-53) has labeled N2, passes through the northern gate of the Quarter, through a gate near the northeastern corner of the walled urban zone and on towards the canal which separates the main residential core of Vijayanagara from the city's temple zone. Within the main compound walls of NMQ1 is a three-sided inner enclosure wall, open to the north, which surrounds the main structure and related subsidiary structures. These subsidiary structures include two pillared halls located to the east and west of the compound's main building. The largest of these, the eastern hall, has column bases, a moulded basement, and one stairway still preserved. To the south of the main structure are the remnants of another platform which abuts against the inner compound wall (Nagaraja Rao 1983b: 15). Traces of water control systems in the compound include: water outlets which cut through the south wall of the inner enclosure, an aqueduct and tank, and a large well to the north of the main structure.

The central structure of the NMQ1 compound measures ca. 25 m. north-south by 20 m. east-west. This building is stepped, or terraced, built on a stone-faced platform. It has three main levels and a U-shaped plan. The two lower levels of the structure are large open areas with remains of column bases which would have supported the wooden superstructure of the building. The uppermost tier of NMQ1 contains a central chamber, surrounded by three rooms, one each to the west, south and east. Two other small chambers, possibly toilets or washrooms, are located in the southeastern corner of the building. The main platform and each landing of NMQ1 are elaborately carved with geometric and animal designs and dancing figures (Nagaraja Rao 1983b: 17). The excavators have interpreted the upper level as the main residential or domestic portion of the building, while the more open lower levels may have served as reception chambers, or other relatively public areas (Nagaraja Rao 1983b: 17). The plaster floors and stone and stucco balustrades within the building are badly charred and blackened from fire. Several of the structures excavated in the Noblemen's Quarter exhibit similar indications of burning, with the charred remains of the buildings' superstructures overlying the floor levels. It is likely that these buildings were destroyed during the sacking of the city which followed the Talikota battle in 1565. Large numbers of imported porcelain sherds were recovered in the excavations of NMQ1, and have been dated to the late fifteenth or early sixteenth centuries (personal communications, John Carswell and Margaret Medley).

Compound 2 in the Noblemen's Quarters is quite different in scale and form from NMQ1 (Figure 2.4). NMQ2 is located at the southern edge of the Noblemen's Quarter, ca. 100 m. east-northeast of the Virupaksha or underground temple and ca. 100 m. east-northeast of the zone of royal residence. The NMQ2 enclosure is significantly smaller than NMQ1, measuring ca. 37 m. north-south by 49 m. east-west. The structure has been partially destroyed by post-Vijayanagara road construction and erosion. Like NMQ1, NMQ2 contains a main central structure flanked by long narrow secondary buildings. NMQ2 is oriented east-west with the main entry of the central structure facing towards the east. This building is built on a stone platform and has four tiers. The lowest level has a central stairway, with two column bases on either side of the stairs and on the flanking walls. The remaining three platforms were approached via two flights of three steps each. Atop the highest platform is a single central chamber, with walls preserved up to almost one metre in height. The moulded exterior platform of the structure is quite ornate, as are the interior elephant shaped balustrades. The detail carvings found in NMQ1 are absent. Grinding stones, for grain or mortar, are found in both NMQ1 and NMQ2. While drains are found in NMQ2, there is no evidence of tanks or wells.

The precise function of Noblemen's Quarters Compound 2 is not clear. The single chamber, and absence of major water facilties seem to preclude a domestic function for the building. If the association, drawn above, of large open terraces with public space and the small enclosed rooms with private space, are correct, then NMQ2 is clearly most strongly associated with public activities. Nagaraja Rao has proposed that NMQ2 may have been an administrative structure, perhaps the "office of a high dignitary" in the Vijayanagara political hierarchy (1983b: 29).

Compounds NMQ3-NMQ11 present still another architectural form in the Noblemen's Quarter. While both NMQ1 and NMQ2 were freestanding structures, defined by unique compound walls, the NMQ3-11 compounds abut against each other, sharing walls and sometimes cutting into earlier walls (Figure 2.5). In fact, the westernmost wall of this area serves as the western compound wall of compounds NMQ3, 5, 6, and 7. The southermost compounds in the area, NMQ7, 8, and 9, appear to be the oldest, with subsequent compounds added to the north.

The main structure in **Compound MQ3** is oriented towards the north, and slightly west (Figure 2.5). Unlike NMQ1 and NMQ2, where structures and compound walls appear to be oriented to the cardinal directions, the northern compound walls of NMQ3 are markedly asymmetrical, perhaps to take advantage of natural stone outcrops and surfaces. The interior of the compound in front of the structure has a finely plastered surface. Substantial outlying structures are absent in this compound. To the west of the building is an area that was most likely a food preparation or kitchen area. This area is bounded by the compound wall to the west and a small rubble wall to the east and had a packed earth surface. It contained a stone mortar. Extremely high densities of ceramics were found in this provenience. A sealed doorway is located in the southern wall of the NMQ3 compound; this doorway connected to compound NMQ5.

The main structure of NMQ3 is comparatively small, ca. 15 m. long by 11 m. wide, and is built on only two levels. The lowermost level is approached by a central stairway, while the top level was reached via two stairways at either end of the platform. Like NMQ2, only one central room was present on the building's upper level. NMQ3 also has evidence of having been burnt (Nagaraj a Rao 1985: 11) Evidence for a plastered upper storey is found in collapsed debris on the floor of the main structure (Nagaraja Rao 1985:11). The comparative simplicity of NMQ3, and the evidence for food preparation in the compound seem to indicate that the structure may have served at least partly as a residential building, though again may have had public/civic purposes as well. Numerous ring-well fragments and the well itself, were found to the northeast of the compound wall.

Compound NMQ4 of the Noblemen's Quarter has yet another architectural plan, and appears to have been devoted largely to non-residential activities (Figures 2.6). The structure is oriented towards the east-southeast. The eastern wall of the NMQ4 compound is no longer preserved, if one ever existed, and soil accumulation was slight in the eastern half in general. The northern wall of the NMQ4 compound abuts the eastern wall of NMQ3, which may have been partially destroyed to accomodate the construction of NMQ4. It appears, therefore, that the construction of NMQ4 occurred after that of NMQ3 (Nagaraja Rao 1985: 12). The lack of preservation of the area in front of NMQ4 inhibits interpretations of this part of the compound, and no ceramics were recovered from that area.

The main structure within NMQ4 faces east and measures ca. 24 m. in width (north-south) by 23 m. (east-west). Like all of the Vijayanagara 'palaces', the structure is stepped, being constructed on three levels. It is unique among the excavated structures in the Noblemen's Quarter, in that its one central room is a level in itself—the topmost level of the structure. The floor of the chamber has collapsed. It may be that this chamber was an elevated platform rather than an enclosed room. The lowest level of NMQ4 is a large open space, ca. 160 m. square (16 m. north-south by 10 m. east-west), the largest open space in any of the excavated structures. The second level, approached from a central stairway, is approximately 24 m. north-south and three m. east-west, and encloses the top platform to the north, west, and south, forming a corridor around the central chamber. Another corridor encircles the structure to the north, between the first basement and the compound wall.

A small compound adjoined to NMQ4 has been excavated to the north of the main compound. This area has been designated as NMQ4A, and contains several poorly preserved walls with evidence of at least two construction phases (Figure 2.7). Contained within NMQ4A is an apparent toilet area, located against the western wall of the compound. This area consists of a finely plastered platform (ca. 1.5 sq. m.) which is approached by three stairs. On this platform are two plastered ledges, hemispherical in plan, and ca. 10 cm. in height by 40 cm. in diametre. Along the northern end of the platform is a square ledge, ca. 75 cm. on a side, which is bisected by a drain, below which are a series of drains. Adjacent to the toilet area, is a single-roomed rectangular structure, ca. 14 m. north-south by 8 m. east-west. This building has been interpreted as a gymnasium by its excavators (Nagaraja Rao 1985: 17). Whatever the precise use of this structure, it seems clear that the NMQ4A area was largely devoted to activities involved with personal hygiene. NMQ4 and NMQ4 are linked through a doorway in the northern wall of the open plaza area to the front of the main palace structure.

An asymmetrical cluster of walls is located to the east of the main NMQ4 structure. This area has been designated as NMQ4B, and is believed by the excavators to predate the construction of the central structure of the NMQ4 compound.

NMQ4, with its large lower chamber and elevated central platform, could have accommodated large numbers of people, and appears best suited for public receptions or meetings (Nagaraja Rao 1985: 13). Whether such events related to the political operations of the Vijayanagara state or the internal activities of the occupants of the Noblemen's Quarter is unknown. Areas to the west of the main structure, within the compound walls may have been the loci for more general domestic activities, as might have been the open area to the east of the compound. Unfortunately, these areas either contained very little accumulation of soil and ceramics, or had not yet been excavated when I was at Vijayanagara, so ceramic samples from them are not included in this analysis.

Compound NMQ5 (Figure 2.7) is located directly to the south of NMQ3 and is in a good state of preservation. Access to NMQ5 was from an open area to the east (discussed below). An entryway from NMQ3 may have been in use for a while, but was sealed off, perhaps at the time of the construction of the NMQ5 structure itself. The elevation of the main surface of the compound, on which the palace platform was built, is level with the uppermost tier of the structure in NMQ3. The NMQ5 compound contains a single structure which exhibits evidence of intense burning. This structure is quite similar in plan to the structure in NMQ3, though it is much smaller in size. The eastern edge of the NMQ5 structure is badly damaged at the lowest tier. This is a two-tiered building, with a central stairway leading to the lowest level, and two stairways leading to the upper level. The latter contained a single chamber, surrounded by a narrow corridor.

A small wall extends from the northwest corner of the structure to the western compound wall. This wall, only 40 cm. in thickness, clearly postdates the construction of the building and served to block off the corridor which surrounded the palace structure. A small complex of walls is found to the southeast of the structure. These walls form a roughly rectangular chamber that abuts against the compound and structure walls. It is unclear whether this chamber was in use during the occupation of NMQ5, or what purpose it might have served. Entrance to the chamber might have been from the north. Other than this single problematic chamber, compound NMQ5 contains no outlying structures, and is, overall, the smallest and simplest of the NMQ compounds.

Compound NMQ6 is, without doubt, the most confusing of the NMQ compounds (Figure 2.7). The compound contains evidence for extensive rebuilding and subdividing and the original plan of the compound's main structure is obscured by much reworking. The proposed construction sequence presented here, therefore, is tentative. It seems likely that in the first construction phase the main structure of NMQ6 faced north and extended into the area later occupied by NMQ5. The compound wall separating NMQ6 from NMQ5 is constructed of small boulders. This contrasts sharply with the more substantial compound walls found to the east and west of the main structure. In this first construction phase, the main structure of compound NMQ6 was probably quite large, with three chambers on the uppermost tier. The structure consisted of two or possibly three tiers, though differed from NMQ1-5 in that these tiers appear to have been separated by only one step, rather than the three to four steps found in the other (later?) compounds. If the structure was symmetrical at this time, as is the 'typical' Vijayanagara palace, the easternmost platform on the lowest surviving tier would not have been present and may represent a later addition to the structure.

Subsequent to the initial construction and use of the NMQ6 structure, major architectural revisions took place. The sequence of these construction events is, however, uncertain. The presumed northern entry to NMQ6 was sealed up and the compound wall separating NMQ6 was constructed. Entry to the compound subsequently was attained from the east, where the partial remains of a balustrade and stairway are found. The surface to the front of these stairs is badly eroded. A major north-south wall was then constructed, which approximately bisected the lowest (remaining) tier of the original structure. This wall runs from the northern edge of the structure to the doorway of the central chamber, effectively blocking its entry. The wall appears to have been a foundation wall, and contains five column bases. It is oriented slightly to the east of north, different than the orientation of the original building. If a substantial wall rested above this, access to the western half of the building would have been cut off. It is possible that the entire floor level of the structure's lowest tier was raised to or above the level of this wall, though no evidence of this remains. It is also not evident whether the entire western half of the original structure fell into disuse at this time, or whether some sort of access to it existed, either from outside of the building or through a doorway located in the new wall. Very little accumulated deposition overlay the surface levels of NMQ6, and much of the archaeological evidence for the uses and plan of this structure was lost through natural erosion processes.

It is difficult to come up with any interpretation for the reasons and purposes underlying the division of NMQ6. In its initial phase, the compound appears to have been a 'typical' Vijayanagara palace compound, probably serving some combination of residential and public functions. Later, however, the size of the compound was restricted (perhaps with the construction of NMQ5?) and the layout, and presumably, the function, of the compound's main structure changed dramatically. In these latter stages of use, the structure covered virtually the entire compound, with no room for subsidiary structures. It may be, in fact, that the entire compound or at least its western half, became a subsidiary structure itself, either to a residence in the eastern half of the compound, or to one of the other compounds. While in its initial phase it appears that NMQ6 was a residential compound, its functions in its later phase of existence are unknown.

While NMQ6 presents a confusing architectural problem, the remains of the main structure are generally well preserved. Plaster surfaces remain intact, and architectural elements, such as mouldings, are in good condition. The excavators identified some traces of burning in the structure (Balasubrahmanyam, personal communications). In some areas of the structure traces of red paint are visible on the plastered floors.

Compound NMQ7-9 differ dramatically from the other NMQ compounds in their condition of preservation (see Figure 2.8). While some traces of original surface levels remain in each compound, these are generally scarce, and the compounds primarily contain the remains of foundation walls. Few worked architectural elements, such as mouldings or balustrades, are present. It is possible that these are among the earliest compounds of the Noblemen's Quarter and were eventually abandoned, with architectural elements removed for use in later NMQ compounds or elsewhere on the site.

Compound NMQ7 is quite large and contains the remains of a number of features. The area designated as NMQ7 might better be conceived of as two compounds, partially separated by a major north-south wall. The westernmost area of NMQ7 is located directly to the south of NMQ6. This area contained a rectangular structure, approximately 5×10 m. in dimensions, with its long axis oriented northeast-southwest. As with other structural remains in NMQ7, the surviving walls of this structure are foundation walls, and the northernmost wall contains at least three column bases or supports. Immediately to the south of this building is a large cistern or tank. A plastered surface is found to the west of the tank, between it and the compound wall. This surface slopes down towards the wall which is cut by a drain. Residents who drew water from the tank would have stood on this surface so that the spilled water drained out through the compound wall. Three long rectangular stones overlie the opening of the tank.

Numerous traces of foundation walls are found in the eastern part of the NMQ7 compound. These are in a poor state of preservation. They appear to include the remains of an eastward facing palace structure, as well as other subsidiary structures. A ceramic ring-well or soak pit is also found in this area.

Although also consisting exclusively of foundation walls, the plan of the main structure of **Compound NMQ8** is much more readily decipherable than that of NMQ7. This compound provides valuable information on the construction techniques of Vijayanagara palace platforms. Coarsely finished foundation walls define room boundaries and additional foundation walls were sometimes placed under large open areas. The foundation walls were composed of large and small stones, and were approximately one-half to one metre in height. Large rectangular stones, presumably column foundations or some other form of support, are located along the top of the walls, spaced at distances of 1.5 to 2 metres. The gaps between the foundation walls would have been filled with earth and rubble debris, with the superstructure of the building constructed over this base.

The main structure of NMQ8 faced north, and had two, or possibly, three tiers. A central chamber, flanked by two side chambers, comprised the uppermost tier. Other wall fragments indicate the presence of outlying buildings to the east of the main structure. A large grinding stone was found there as well.

Compound NMQ9 is located to the south of NMQ4 and to the north of NMQ8. NMQ9 exhibits evidence of multiple construction phases, with a plaster surface found underlying the foundations of a later palace structure. Some areas of the NMQ9 compound have well-preserved surfaces and walls, though the plan of the central structure is not fully preserved. A large square well is found in the western end of the compound, with an associated sloping plastered surface to drain water through the compound wall. To the east of the well are the remains of a rectangular chamber. This chamber is enclosed by a wall constructed of packed mud and brick and stone fragments and surfaced with plaster. Inside of this wall are two surface levels—a central, slightly lowered surface which is lined with rectangular stones, and an upper surface or corridor surrounding the depressed area. The surface in this area is badly burnt, and large fragments of burnt beams were recovered by the excavators. To the east of this surface are the remains of large blocks of stone, probably portions of collapsed compound walls. It is unclear whether the preserved surface described above was part of a typical palace structure, or represents the remains of another structural form of the NMQ area.

To the west of the well are the remains of a partially preserved stepped palace structure. This structure abuts directly against the compound walls of NMQ4. The southern and eastern portions of the east-facing palace are poorly preserved. The structure was three-tiered, with a single central chamber on the uppermost level. The chronological position of this palace and its relation to NMQ4 are not clear.

Compound NMQ10 is located in the southeastern corner of the large architectural block containing NMQ3-10. The remains of a fairly substantial palace structure are found against the southern edge of the compound near the boulders which border the area. The structure is in a poor state of preservation, though enough remains to identify its plan. It consisted of three tiers, with no enclosed chambers. The second level is the best preserved of the three, and has a finely plastered surface. Evidence for burning is not pronounced, though some charred wood was found during excavations. A subsidiary structure is found to the east of the compound. It contains column bases and at least two rectangular chambers running east-west. The surfaces of this structure are finely plastered.

Areas to the north of the palace structure are poorly preserved. Several wall fragments are found here. A major east-west wall divides NMQ10 into two sections. The southern section contained the palace structure. The northern area contained flagstone surfaces, approximately 2 m. × 5 m. in dimensions, in the southeast and southwest corners of the area.

Compound NMQ12 is located approximately 60 metres to the north of compound NMQ4. Like compounds NMQ1 and NMQ2, NMQ12 is a freestanding compound (Figure 2.9). The structure is generally in a very good state of preservation, though areas to the north and east of the structure are eroded. The central structure faced east, and was built on three levels. The lowest level is a rectangular chamber, some 6.0×8.5 m. in dimension. Two flights of stairs led to the next level, which encloses the first in a U-shaped tier. The uppermost level contained a single central room, with well preserved walls that have traces of red paint along the finely plastered moulding. The corridor surrounding this upper chamber was also finely plastered. In the northwest corner of the structure are the partial remains of a stairway which led to a second storey or roof of the building. A small chamber is found to the south of the central chamber on the upper tier of the structure. Unlike most other palace structures, which are symmetrical, no corresponding chamber is found on the north side of the building.

In general, the mouldings are simple throughout the structure and no balustrades are associated with any of the stairways. Nonetheless, numerous stucco ornaments were recovered in excavations, indicating that the structure was elaborately decorated. To the east of the structure the excavators uncovered the remains of walls, which were found significantly below the level of the main structure. These are the remains of an earlier construction phase in the area. To the south of the structure is a plastered surface which may have been associated with a subsidiary structure.

The eleven architectural compounds excavated in the Noblemen's Quarter differ from each other in scale, size, and plan. They do, however, share some essential features. The first, is their spatial proximity within an area bounded by cultural and natural features. Second, none of these structures are clearly religious in nature; that is, none are temples, nor are any clearly administrative structures like the columned halls and major platforms found in the western part of the royal/administrative core. All are constructed within walled compounds and are stepped buildings, going from open (public) space at the lower levels, to smaller, more restricted spaces at the upper levels. All have moulded stone basements which vary in their elaboration but not in general form. These and similar stepped buildings found in the royal enclosures, Enclosures XIV (the zenana), and the East Valley (Patil 1985a, b), have been grouped together, as representative of Vijayanagara palace architecture. While this term may be somewhat misleading—as not all of the structures in this class appear to have been residential buildings (e.g., NMQ2, NMQ4)—these buildings do comprise a consistent class of elite architecture found within the royal centre of Vijayanagara.

Other Architectural Features of the Noblemen's Quarter

Several other structures are found in the NMQ area. Some of these are closely associated with the palace compounds, while others are more functionally and spatially removed. Included among these latter features are: shrines, a rectangular single-chambered structure on the hill to the west of the NMQ area, and numerous multi-chambered structures which surround the walled compounds.

One of the major shrines of the NMQ area is located to the west of NMQ1 along a road that led from NMQ2 to the gate which formed the northern boundary of the quarter. This shrine complex contains a small temple. Figures of Rama, Sita, Hanuman, and Sugriva are carved on to the surface of a nearby boulder. A small structure, no longer preserved, enclosed these carvings. Small niches for offerings are also carved into the boulder. A second well-preserved shrine is found immediately to the west of NMQ12. This shrine also incorporated the natural boulders. A beautifully executed carving of Virabhadra was produced on a large boulder, and enclosed by a small structure. On top of the boulder is a brick shikara. An inscription on an associated boulder refers to the "bastion of Hampi" (Nagaraja Rao and Patil 1985b: 99). It is not clear whether this refers to the Noblemen's Quarter area itself, or is pointing northward towards the temple centre at modern-day Hampi. Other shrines undoubtedly existed in the NMQ area—to the south of NMQ1, as well as along the north-south road. Household shrines probably also were found within each compound.

A large mandapa is found on the boulders which define the western boundary of the Noblemen's Quarter. This structure was constructed completely of granite, with horizontal slabs set between vertical posts to form the walls. The roof is also constructed of granite slabs; with triangular slabs along the narrow east-west axis. This single chambered structure conforms neither to common residential nor religious structures in form. It may have served as a guard's quarter, storehouse, meeting place, or other special function. Numerous features, such as mortars, post holes, gaming boards, stairways, horse-ties, and so on are carved into the boulders which surround the NMQ area. These areas appear to have been intensively utilised and, perhaps, permanently inhabited.

Several architectural features are associated with the NMQ3-10 block. Within this block is a 'corridor' located immediately to the east of compounds NMQ5 and NMQ6 (see Figure 2.2). This area provided entry to the compounds (see above) and contained a number of small chambers and wall fragments. A lot of wall fall from NMQ4 compound walls is found in this area, obscuring some of the original surface. In the northern end of the area is a filled-in doorway, which led into NMQ3. Two walls flank the NMQ3 entry and extend southward for approximately five metres. To the west of these walls is a rectangular platform subdivided by a large number of wall fragments. These fragments presumably represent the remains of multiple building stages. This area seems to have been some sort of public space between several of the NMQ compounds. Access was provided to some compounds from this area and other activities may have occurred here as well.

Excavated areas to the south, west, and north of the NMQ3-10 compound walls have yielded dense architectural remains. These consist primarily of small single or multichambered structures. These structures are insubstantial compared to those found within the compound walls, and are built of a mixture of large and small stones and packed mud. Large numbers of circular mortars and grinding stones are found in these areas. The outlying structures may have served as lower status residences that housed people associated with the NMQ palace complexes. They may also have served as kitchen or food preparation areas for the residents of the larger complexes. A large rock-cut well is found in the area to the south of NMQ7. This well apparently fell into disuse prior to the abandonment of the site, as it contained refuse deposits, including numerous ceramic vessels.

It should be noted that the areas which appear as open spaces in the map of the Noblemen's Quarter (Figure 2.2) are unexcavated areas. It is readily apparent upon walking over areas to the south and north of NMQ1 and between NMQ3 and NMQ12, that several more palace compounds exist in the area, and, presumably, numerous secondary structures and features are found here as well. Excavations conducted since 1986 continue to expose many of these structures and their interrelations.

THE EAST VALLEY AND ISLAMIC QUARTER

Ceramics from the East Valley and the city's main Islamic Quarter will be considered in comparison with the ceramics of the Noblemen's Quarter in order to assess differences or similarities in ceramic use between these three spatially and socially diverse areas of the site. The relative locations of the three areas are illustrated in Figure 2.1. All areas are found within the main residential zone of Vijayanagara: the city's urban core. Within the urban core, the Noblemen's Quarter and western half of the East Valley lie within a zone designated as the city's "Royal Centre" (Fritz, Michell, and Nagaraja Rao 1985). The royal centre of Vijayanagara contains large numbers of public buildings as well as palaces, and was the focus of the public and private lives of the king and court. The western half of the East Valley and the Islamic Quarter lie outside of the royal centre in the main residential district of the city. This area presumably housed individuals of somewhat lower social status than those residing in the royal centre. Places of worship, temples or mosques, were found throughout the city, as were markets (Paes, in Sewell 1900), and, possibly, manufacturing locales, such as metal workshops and other artisan workshops.

The East Valley

The East Valley was the site for an intensive surface collection of earthenware and other materials which form a significant part of the ceramic data analysed from Vijayanagara. The valley, as defined by granite outcrops, is roughly one kilometre in length and varies in width from ca. 200 to 500 m. (Figure 2.10). The valley was bisected at its narrowest point by a north-south wall, part of the enclosure wall of the city's royal and administrative center. The area to the west of the wall lies within the royal centre, and the land to the east is outside of it, but within the city's urban core. The East Road crossed the enclosure wall through a large gate, located in the middle of the valley. A secondary road, coming from the palace area of the East Valley may have entered into the East Road to the west of the gate. An inscription, dating to the first dynasty of Vijayanagara, on a boulder on a hill overlooking the gate refers to it as the Monday Gate, possibly indicating that a Monday market was held nearby (Nagaraja Rao and Patil 1985b: 96). Such periodic markets are common throughout rural and urban India today (Verghese 1971; Karve and Açharya 1970).

Marked architectural differences exist among the limited structural remains found in the western and eastern portions of the valley. Architectural remains on the west side of the valley include a number of small shrines, a palace complex, mandapas, and other elite structures. Remains of an unusual structure are found in the southwestern quadrant of the valley (Nsv/2 in Michell and Fritz' [1985] recording system). This building, of which only a limited portion remains, was quite large (ca. 20 m. east-west). At its southern edge, four pairs of carved balustrades flanking small flights of steps are found. The balustrades are similar to those known from structures excavated in the Noblemen's Quarter, and found at palace structures elsewhere in the royal centre. Judging from the scale of the building and the absence of any temple-like features, it is probable that this was a public or administrative structure of some sort. Also found in the western part of the East Valley are the remains of a large walled complex, which appears to have contained one or more stepped structures resembling the palace structures known elsewhere at the site.

The area to the east of the Monday Gate also contains the remains of a number of structures. Unlike the western part of the valley, no elite residences, or other clearly civic or high status structures are found outside of the walls of the city's royal core. Located along the East Road, approximately 100 m. east-northeast of the gate, is a well-preserved Jain temple. The remains of a number of other Jain shrines are also found in this part of the valley, in a complex located along the southeastern edge of the valley. Hindu shrines are also found within the eastern section of the East Valley, as is a large carving of Hanuman (ca. 2 m. high) the city's protector deity. A Hanuman shrine is found in the boulders at the southern edge of the valley, west of the Jain shrines (NSy/-1) nearby other Vaishnavite and Shaivite shrines (NSy/1, NSz/1,2). Few non-religious structures are found in the eastern half of the East Valley. A few small mandapas are the only other standing structures.

From the architectural remains, the eastern half on the East Valley thus appears to be quite distinct from the area to the west of the gate. No remains of elite residences or civic architecture are found, and in general fewer durable (i.e., stone) architectural remains are present. Most residential structures at Vijayanagara were built of non-durable materials such as reed, bamboo, and earth (Mahalingam 1975: 56-57). Both sides of the East Valley likely contained many such structures, and the density of ceramics, particularly from the eastern half of the valley indicates a relatively high occupation density in the entire area. On the basis of the architectural evidence it appears that the East Valley to the east of the Monday Gate was occupied by non-elite residential and occupational groups, living and working in structures which have left no visible surface remains. Members of different religious groups, Jain and Hindu, and, we presume, castes, resided together within the valley. The western half of the valley, within Vijayanagara's royal core, may also have contained economic structures or activities such as markets, but was primarily an area of elite residence and, possibly, administrative activities.

The Islamic Quarter

One other area of Vijayanagara will figure in the ceramic analysis, and this is the city's largest Islamic Quarter (Figure 2.11). This district of Vijayanagara is readily identifiable from the many small tombs found in the area, built in distinctive Islamic architectural styles. The Vijayanagara Islamic Quarter was located beyond the walls of the city's royal core in the northeasternmost part of the city's urban zone, due north of the large temple complex atop of Malyavanta Hill. Along with the tombs, the Islamic Quarter contained a pillared hall with a dated Kannada inscription. The inscription states that the building, referred to as a *Dharmashala* (rest house), was constructed by an officer named Ahmadkhan on the tench day of the bright half of the month of Asjiva during the cyclic year Siddharthi (that is, the 18th of September 1439), so that his master, Devaraya, might attain merit (Nagaraja Rao 1983a: 65). The inscription also mentions a well, built at the same time, and located to the west of the building. The building contains a niche in its northern wall (the direction of Mecca), and was probably a mosque (Michell 1985c: 282). Another inscription found in this area of the city mentions a village located below the Islamic tombs (many of which were located along a granite ridge). A second mosque is found ca. one-half kilometre southeast of the first, at the foot of Malyavanta Hill (Michell 1985d: 107).

ISSUES IN VIJAYANAGARA ARCHAEOLOGY

Recent work on the city's plan and its major buildings, has provided a great deal of information on Vijayanagara's organization and history. The architectural remains at the site are, however, largely the remains of elite activity and state operations, with the exception of some of the smaller shrines which may have been neighborhood or caste-specific. The vast majority of the city's population presumably was, however, not of the elite or twice-born castes, but were of the craft-producing, agricultural, or service groups of the shudra varna. These groups left behind very little in the way of architectural remains. Virtually nothing is known about the low status segment of Vijayanagara's population, or about how they were distributed throughout the city. Virtually, the only source of information we have on the non-elite segments of Vijayanagara are the remains of the artefacts, particularly ceramics, which they used in their daily life. The three areas described above provide the ceramic sample on which the analyses of Vijayanagara ceramics, are based and from which we will attempt to draw inferences about a number of aspects of Vijayanagara society. Each area is quite different, in plan, and in recovery procedures used to collect ceramics for analysis. The nature of the ceramic sample—its sources, size, and means of collection will be presented in Chapter III.

I have written above of different quarters or districts within the city of Vijayanagara—the Islamic Quarter, the Noblemen's Quarter, the East Valley—and have treated them as coherent, and in some sense isolable, units. The relations between and within these areas of the city, and the validity of treating them as discrete quarters are major questions concerning Vijayanagara's organization. If these, and other areas of the city, often defined by topographic boundaries, were coherent units, what were the linkages between the city's quarters? To what extent were these areas economically independent of interdependent? Were centers of domestic craft production, such as ceramic workshops, carpentry, and blacksmith shops, oriented towards meeting the daily needs of the city's population, found in each residential zone of the city, or was craft production spatially restricted to only certain areas of the city? These are not question that can be fully evaluated in the present study, although the data base of this study—ceramics used by all segments of Vijayanagara's population—represent the most numerous artefact class availabe for approaching such questions.

Although the ceramic analysis presented in this volume will deal primarily with the Noblemen's Quarter alone, ceramics from all three areas will be used to consider some of these broader questions on the overall organization of the imperial city of Vijayanagara. The distribution of ceramics between and within the three sample areas will be examined in order to consider the internal divisions and external bounds within the medieval capital of Vijayanagara.

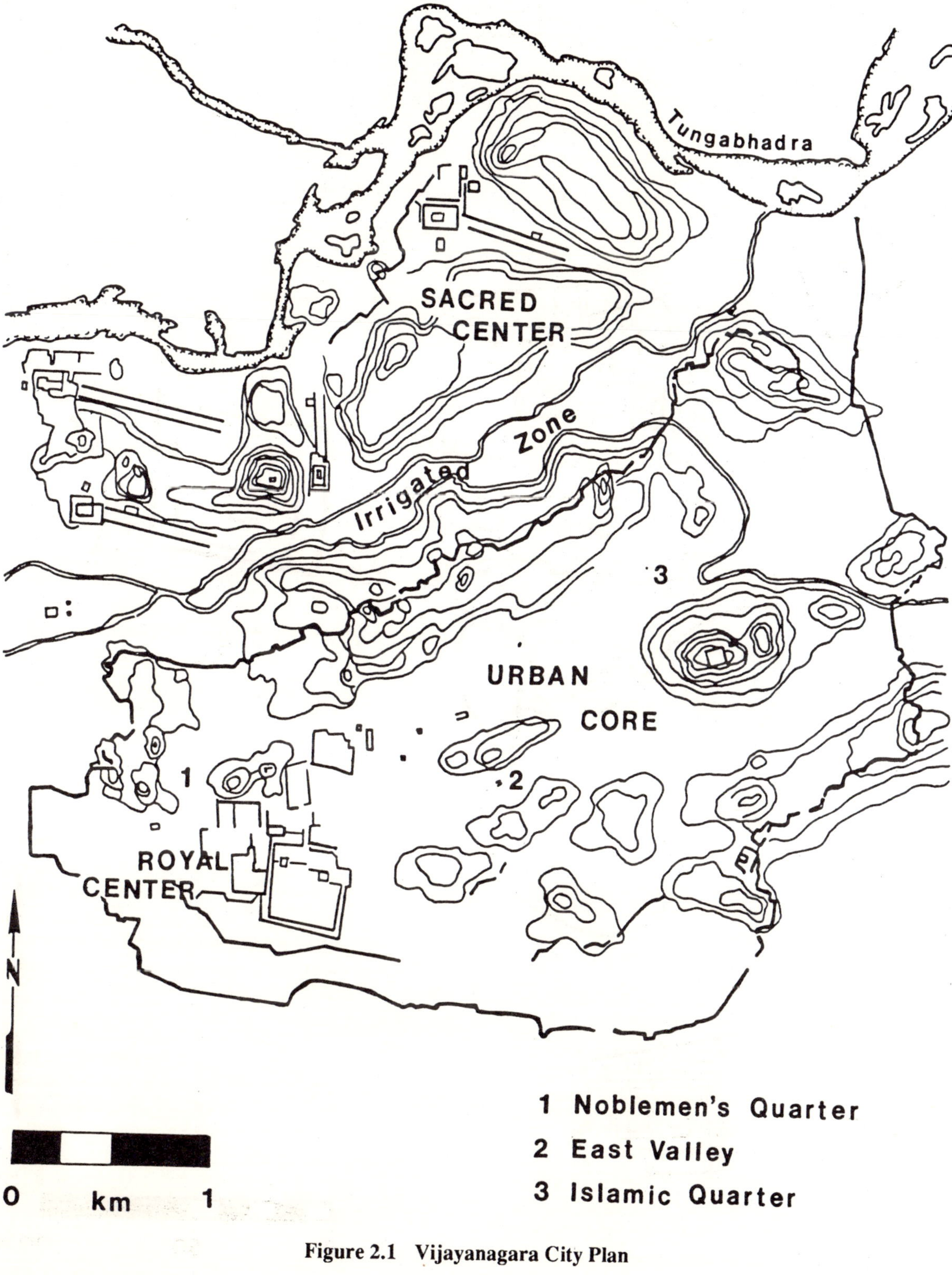

Figure 2.1 Vijayanagara City Plan

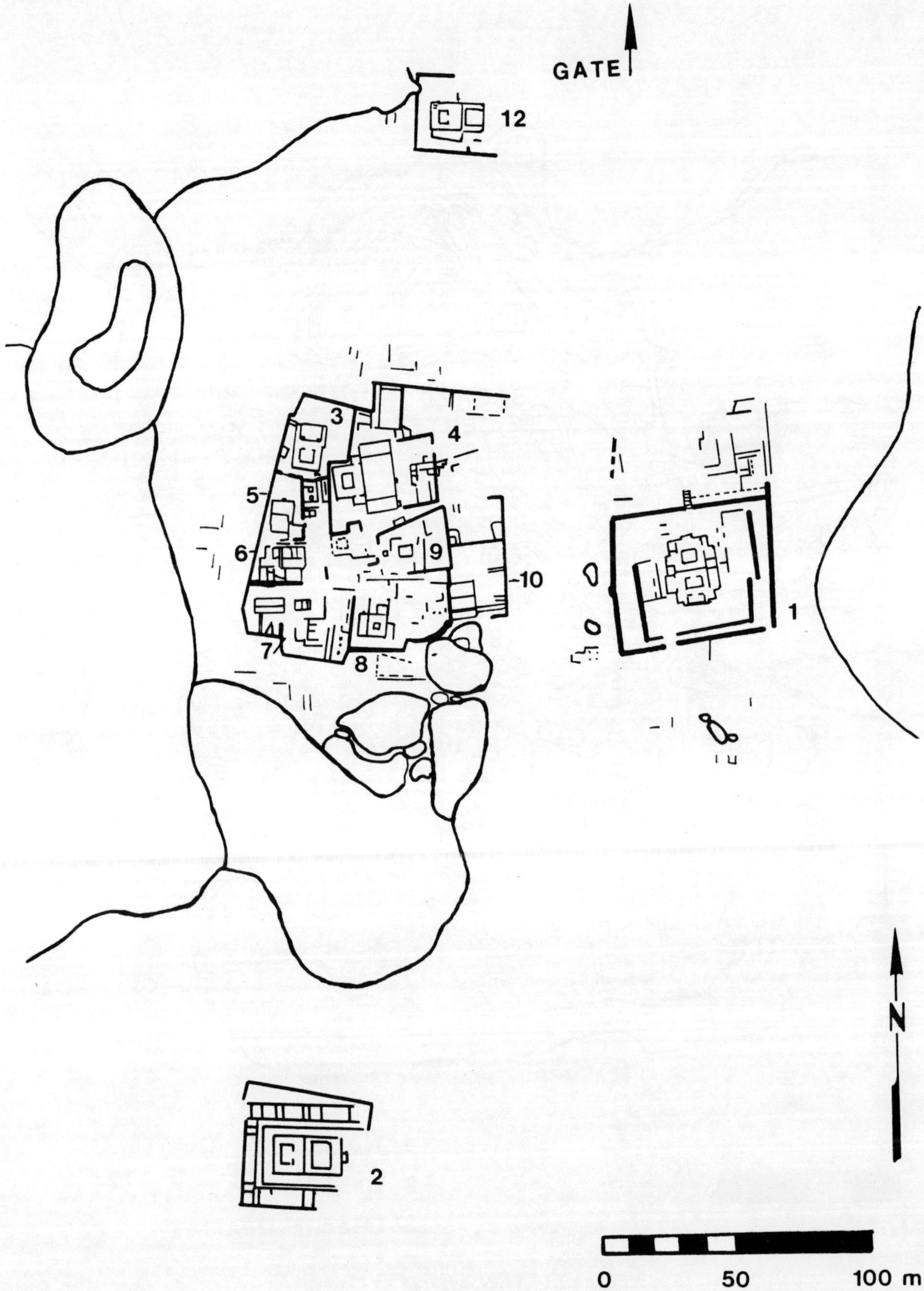

Figure 2.2 Plan of the Noblemen's Quarter

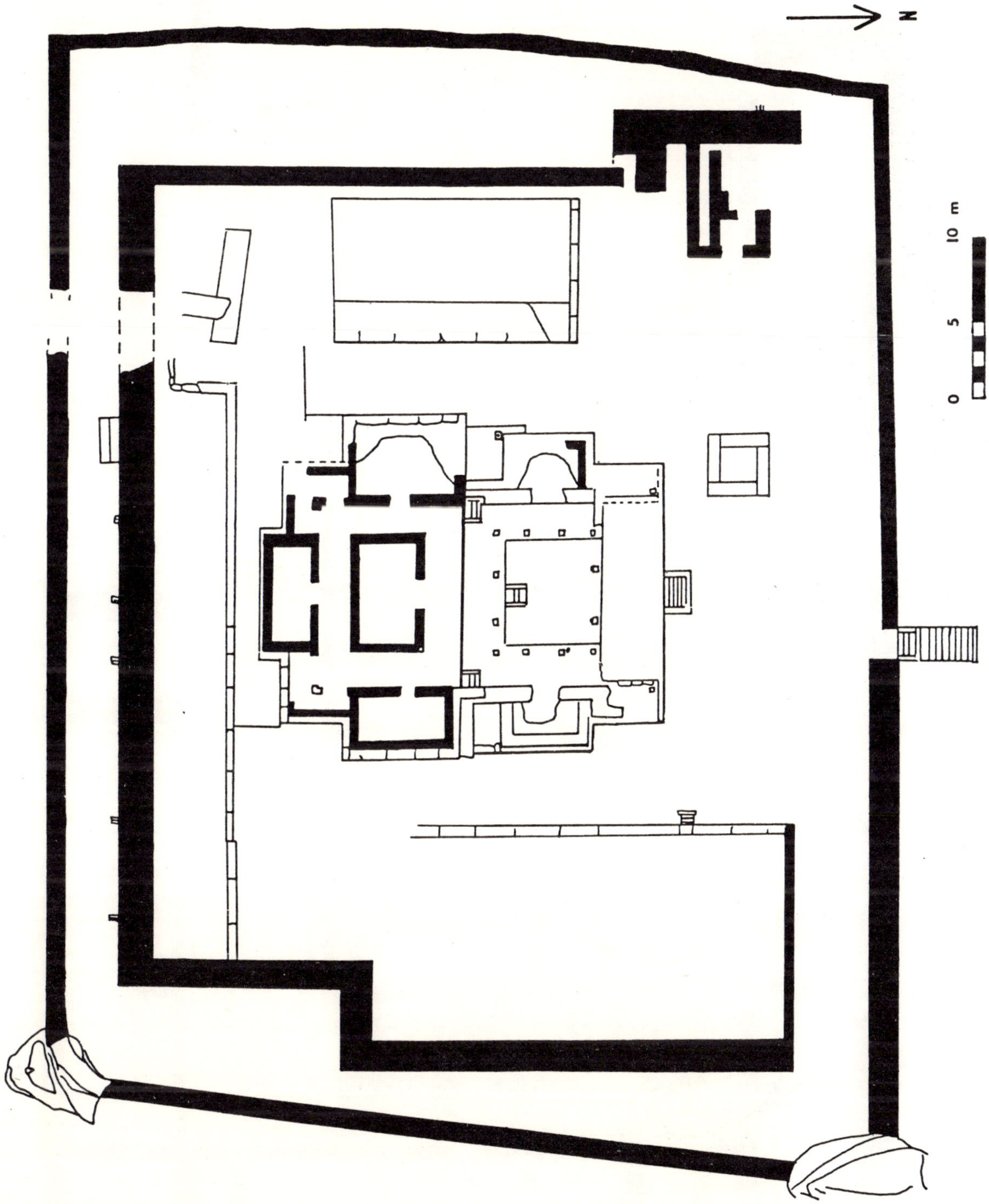

Figure 2.3 Compound 1

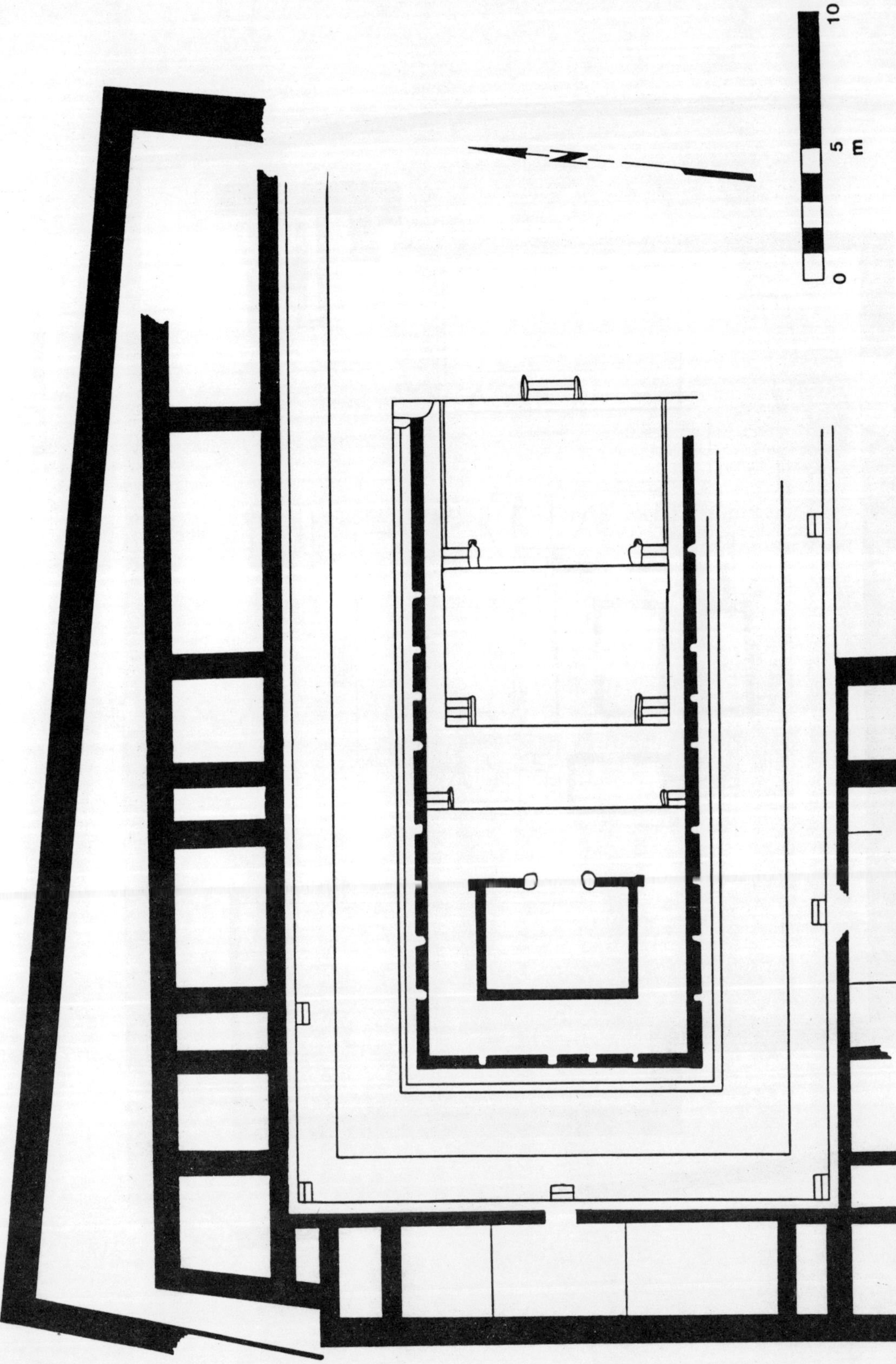

Figure 2.4 Compound 2

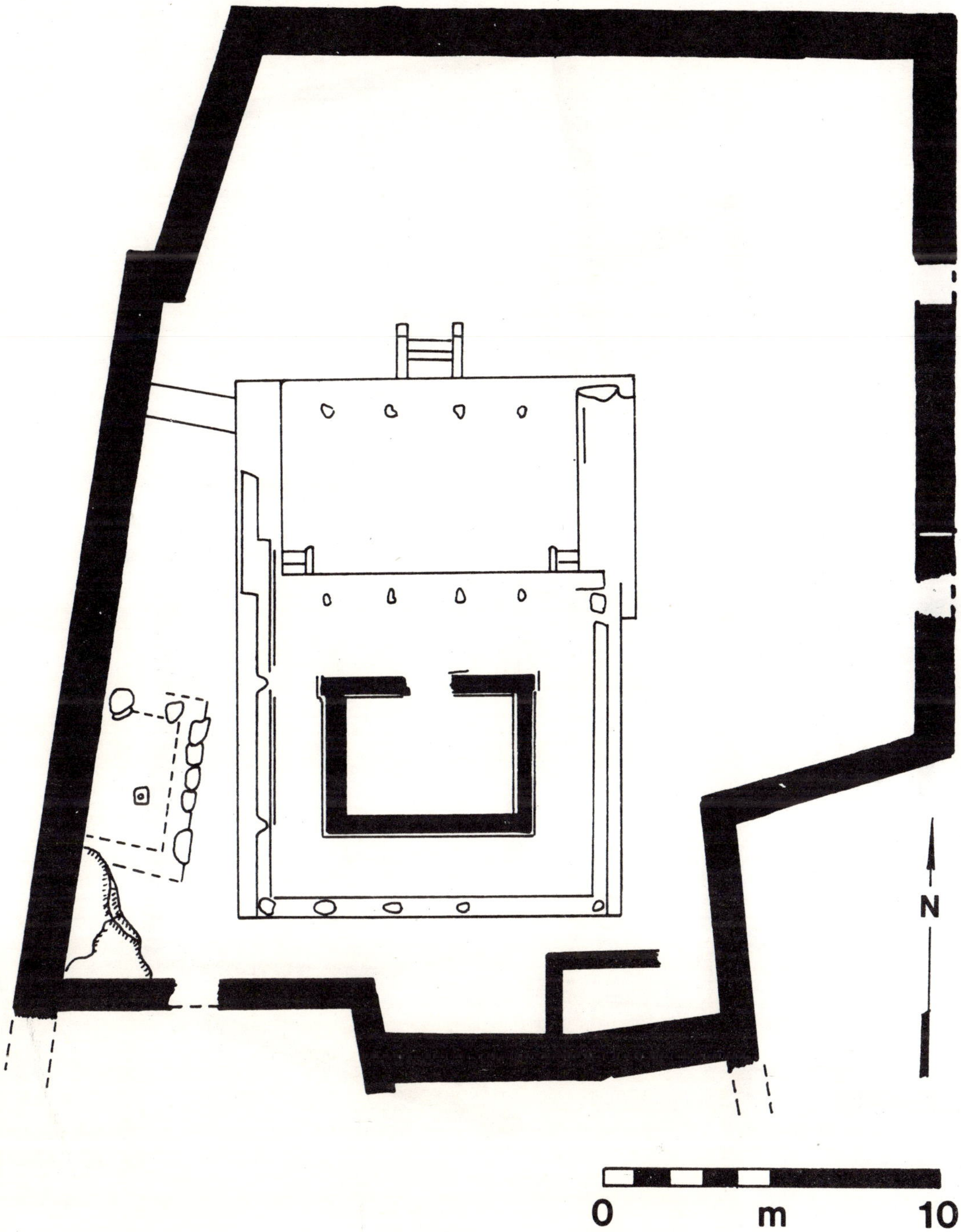

Figure 2.5 Compound 3

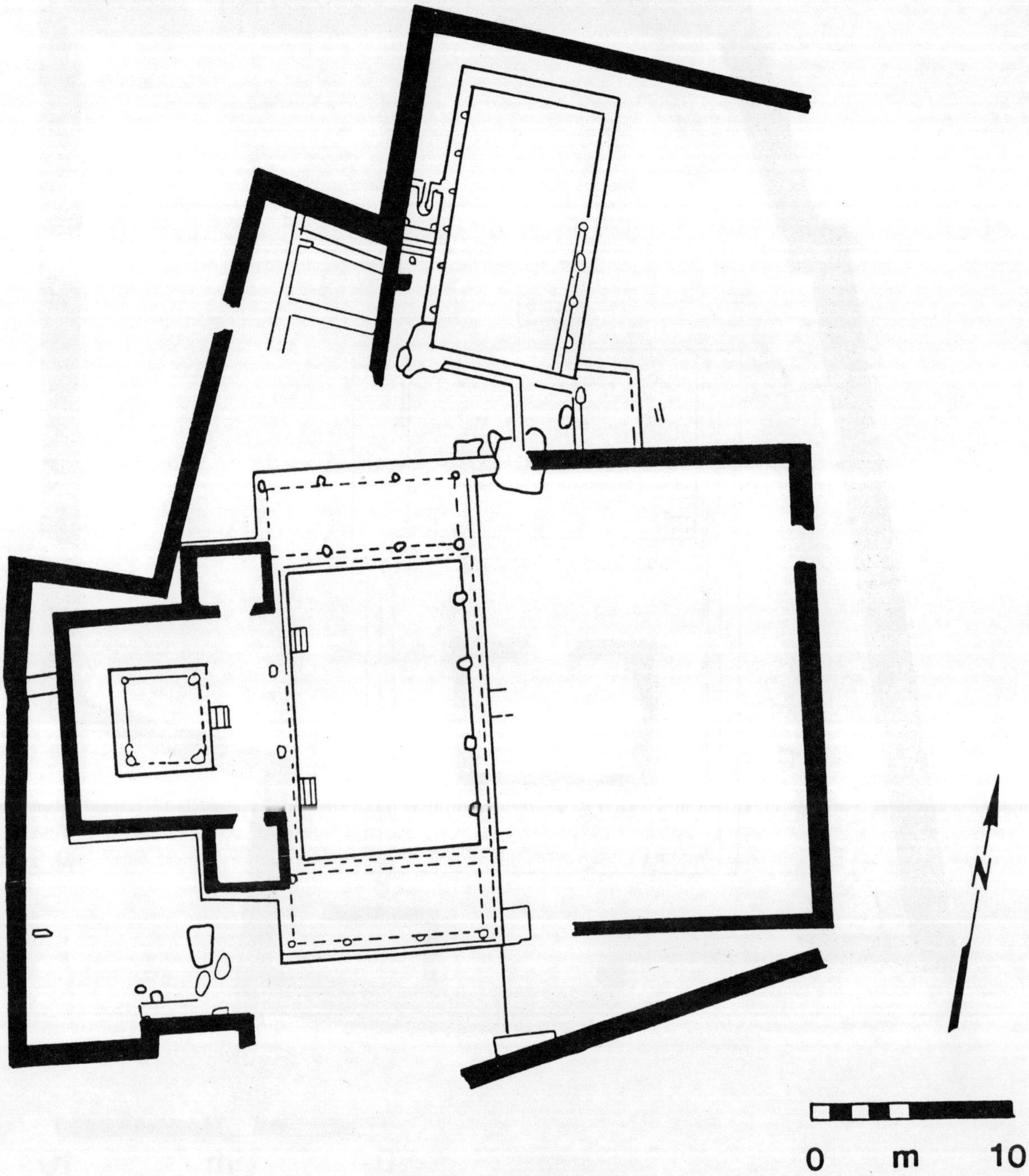

Figure 2.6 Compound 4

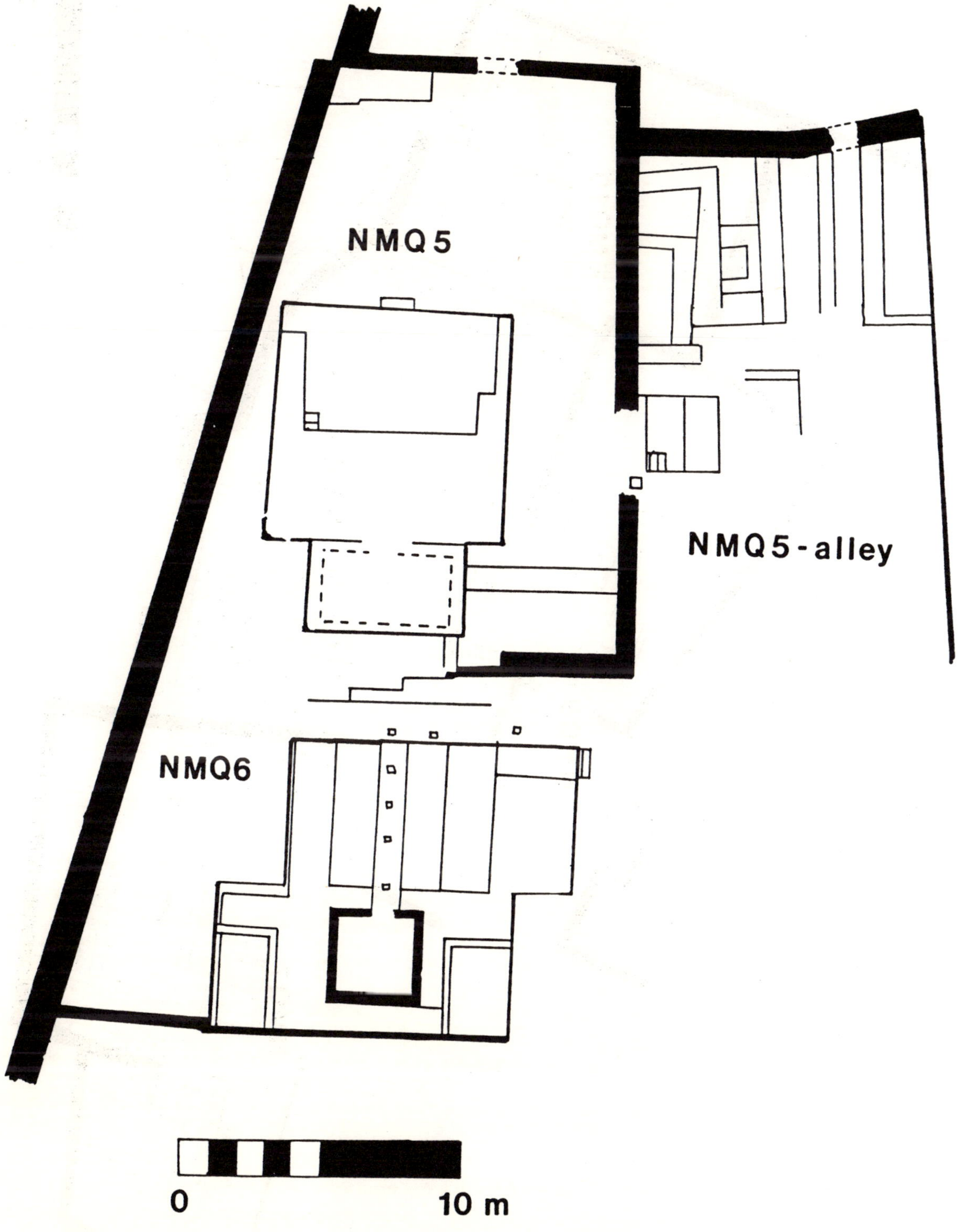

Figure 2.7 Compounds 5 and 6

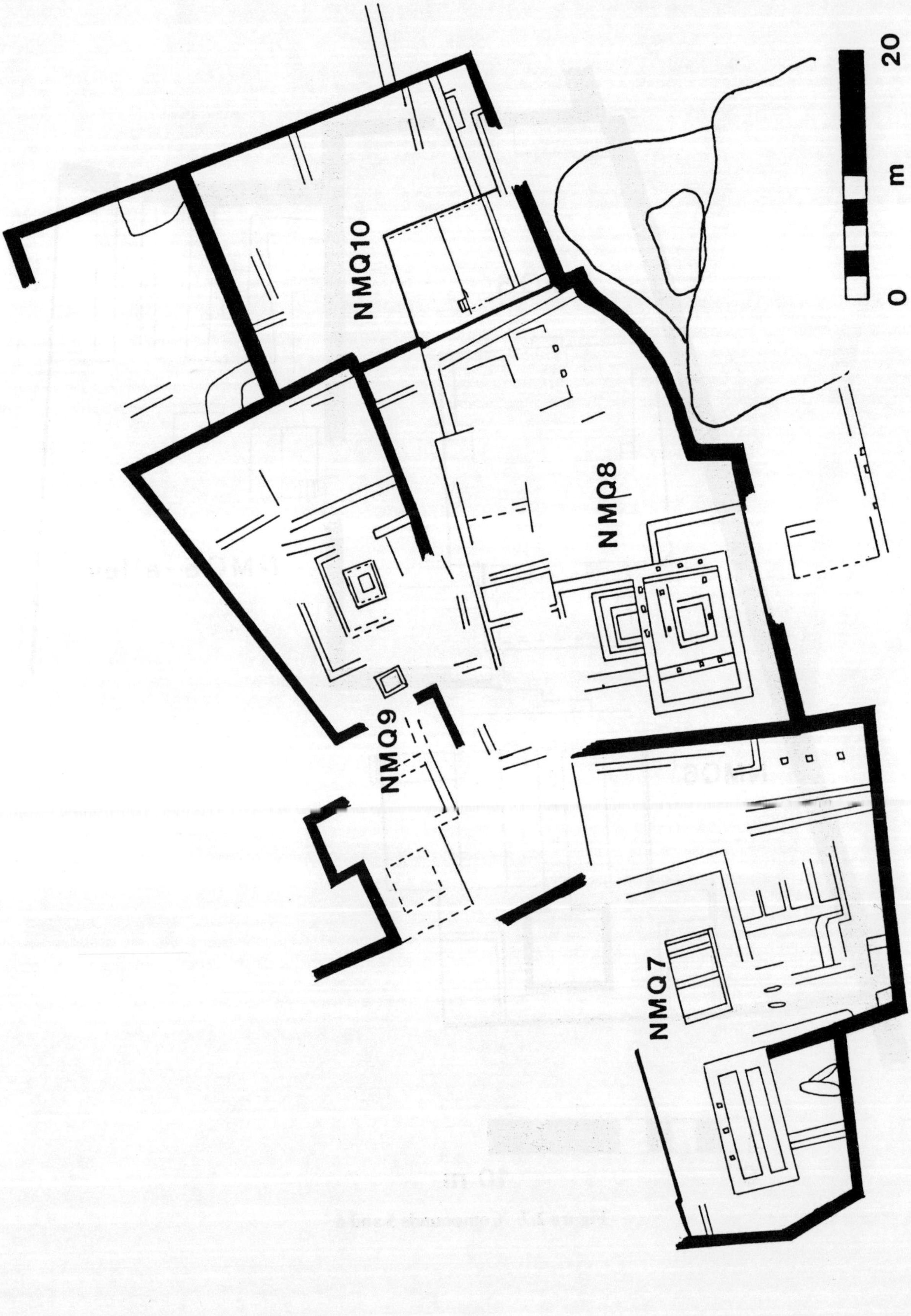

Figure 2.8 Compounds 7- 10

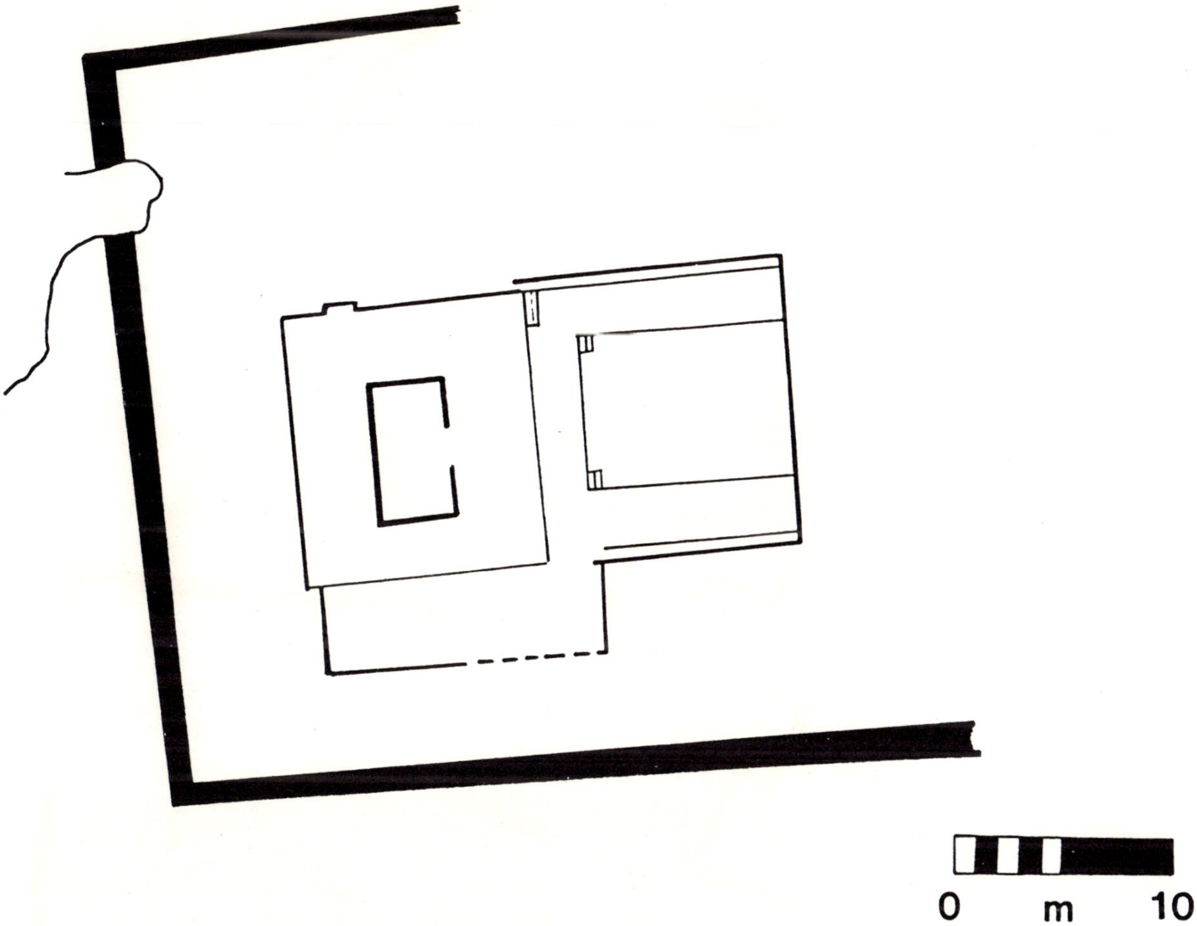

Figure 2.9 Compound 12

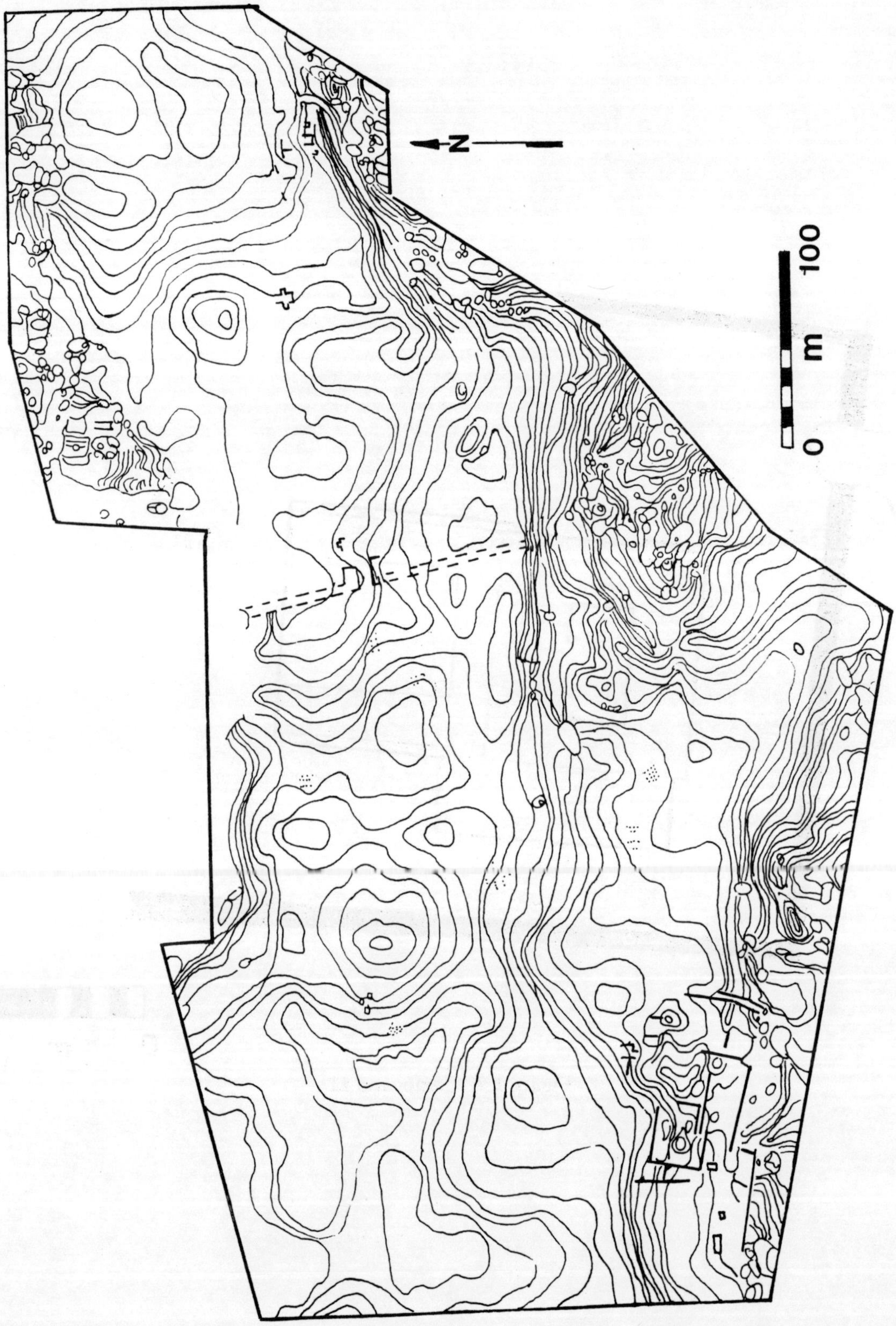

Figure 2.10 Plan of the East Valley

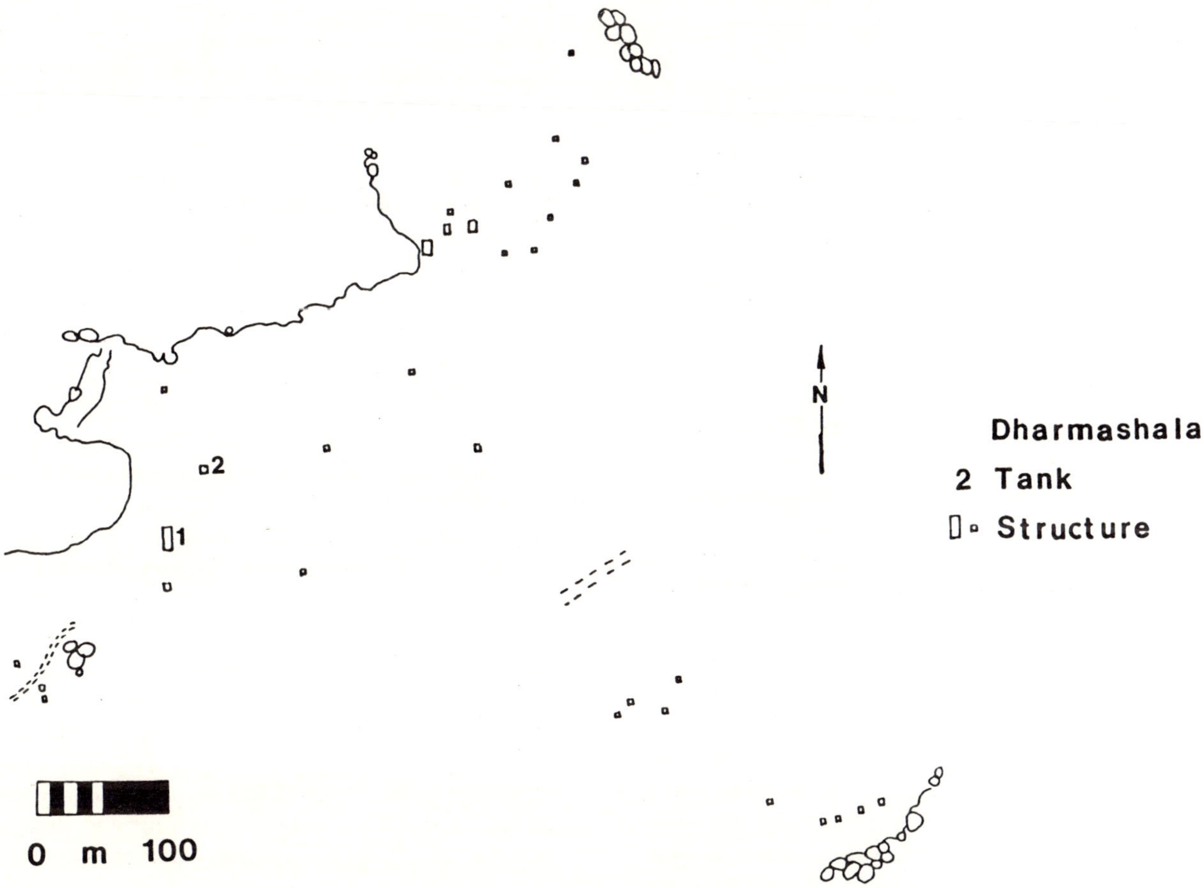

Figure 2.11 Plan of the Islamic Quarter

III. The Noblemen's Quarter Ceramic Analysis; Research Goals and the Ceramic Sample

RESEARCH GOALS

This analysis of Vijayanagara ceramics was undertaken with a number of specific goals in mind. Medieval ceramics have been little studied in Indian archaeology, where research has largely been oriented to the documentation of urban plans and architecture (Mehta 1979; Mate 1985). In the case of medieval sites such as Vijayanagara, ceramics are among the most numerous and most accessible of domestic materials. Because of the lack of knowledge on medieval ceramics from India in general, and Vijayanagara in particular, the first goal of this study is descriptive—to provide a clear and parsimonious characterisation of Vijayanagara ceramics. The ceramic classification developed and the techniques used in its development will be discussed in Chapter IV.

A second goal of this study is to develop some interpretations of vessel use, based on direct evidence (burning, residues, etc.), analogy, vessel morphology, and technological information. These interpretations can then be used to consider the definition of functional space within the Noblemen's Quarter and across the site of Vijayanagara. The identification of activity specific areas within the Noblemen's Quarter will considerably enhance our understanding of the range of uses to which the diverse class of 'palace' structures were put.

A third goal of this analysis is to examine the relation between the material data—ceramics—and human behaviour and social organisation within Vijayanagara society. The attainment of this goal entails an analysis of ceramic variation with respect to the spatial distribution of ceramic forms. As noted in Chapter II, samples analysed come from Directorate of Archaeology and Museums excavations in the Noblemen's Quarter, as well as from surface collections in the East Valley and the main Islamic Quarter of the city. Detailed information on these samples is presented below. The study of relations between ceramic data and social organisation at Vijayanagara is based in our knowledge of Vijayanagara state and society, as derived from historic and ethnographic sources.

Vijayanagara society as a caste society was one in which social distances between people were believed to be innate and immutable. Such distances were behaviorally expressed (and at times, altered) through diet, costumes, and residential proximity. The importance of diet as a caste-differentiating factor would have encouraged caste-specific variations in vessels used in food preparation and serving. Such variations in turn would play a role in reinforcing the behavior and ideological concepts which underlay them. Caste variations in ritual vessels would have similarly affected ceramic form (see Miller 1985). Variation in ceramic vessels in such contexts is expected to be minor but readily identifiable, operating within the limitations imposed by vessel function and manufacturing techniques. That potter's workshops would be responsive to a demand for highly specific formal variants by the members of the different social groups which comprised their market, is not surprising. Similar patterns have been noted by Birmingham (1975) in Nepal and by Miller (1982) in Central India.

If the proposed relations between ceramic variablity and social organisation in Vijayanagara society are tenable, then there are some major implications for the importance of ceramic analysis to an understanding of Vijayanagara social organization and urban form. Different social groups should be identifiable through more or less distinctive assemblages of vessels forms. The same general functional classes are expected to occur in all residential areas; minor, but significant differences in rim form, general vessel proportions, and vessel size, are expected to occur between groups. The implications of this approach to ceramic variation on data recording and analytic approaches will be discussed in Chapter IV.

As residential and occupational groups, castes at Vijayanagara lived in more or less discrete and more or less bounded areas within the city. While I do not expect, for example, that all of the potters at Vijayanagara necessarily lived in a single district or quarter of the city, I do expect that potters' workshops were not found in isolation. Rather, there may have been several clusters of potters' workshops or subcastes throughout the city or its metropolitan area. The same pattern is expected for other Vijayanagara subcastes and, possibly, at a broader level, for language groups and religious groups. Such patterns of settlement should be apparent in the spatial distributions of ceramic assemblages, that is, in the distribution of forms which regularly occur together in samples from distinct provenience units. Social boundaries may thus be identifiable through an analysis of Vijayanagara ceramics.

While the precise groups which resided within these boundaries can not be identified, several additional sources of information may be called upon to situate them more accurately in the social universe of Vijayanagara society. Architectural remains provide one source of evidence for hierarchichal status, as Vijayanagara elite architecture is generally easily identifiable, and materials found in or near such structures may reasonably be assumed to have been associated with elite occupation and activities. Other materials found associated with ceramics, such as: debris from manufacturing activities, including iron or ceramic slag; and imported items such as celadons and porcelains; or metals and semi-precious stones, may also provide clues for situating groups defined by ceramic complexes into a general model of Vijayanagara society.

A fourth goal of this analysis is the development of a ceramic chronology. Such a chronology would prove useful both in characterising the ceramic inventory itself, and documenting temporal changes in that inventory, as well as for approaching chronological sequences across the city and its hinterland. Ceramic sequences could, in conjunction with architectural sequences, considerably strengthen our understanding of the sequence and structure of urban growth at Vijayanagara from its founding until its abandonment in 1565.

Any analysis is only as good as the quality of the data used in it. Before turning to the substantive results of this study, I wish to briefly consider the nature of the sample examined—where it comes from, how it was collected, and its limitations and suitability to the research goals defined above.

THE CERAMIC SAMPLE

The sample of Vijayanagara ceramics comes from three primary areas of the site: the Noblemen's Quarter excavations, the East Valley, and the city's main Islamic Quarter. Architectural descriptions of the areas have been presented in Chapter II. Ceramic collection procedures will be outlined in this section. In general, the objective of the ceramic collections was to acquire a representative sample of ceramics from each of the three areas, and from a variety of locations within each area. This meant, in all cases, a focus on collecting representative samples of *all* of the ceramics present in an area in the proportions in which they occurred in that area, rather than focusing on only the whole vessels or the decorated vessels. The research goals outlined above, require large and unbiased samples. Ideally, for each selected provenience unit from which ceramics were to be examined, collections were made of all ceramics in the unit.

The Noblemen's Quarter Sample

Ceramics analysed from the Noblemen's Quarter were collected by the Karnataka Government DAM in excavations conducted between 1983 and 1986. These materials were gathered as part of an intensive project focused on uncovering the architectural remains of the Quarter. The materials analysed come from in and around the eleven palace compounds described above. The excavation of each compound was conducted in a similar manner. First, an arbitary grid of 10 metre squares oriented to the cardinal directions was marked in with stakes. NMQ1 and NMQ2 were excavated according to unique grids, while a single grid system spanned the area encompassing NMQ3-NMQ12. The units formed by the intersection of the north-south and east-west grid lines were designated by a letter-number combination. The letter referred to the unit's position on the east-west axis, with the westernmost unit designated as 'A'. The number referred to its position along the north-south grid, with '1' as the northernmost unit. Each 10 metre square was subdivided into 4 quadrants. These quadrants, separated by baulks, measured 4.25 m. on a side, and were the major units for excavation and artefact recovery. The quadrants were numbered in a clockwise fashion beginning in the northwest. In general, excavations in each quadrant were sensitive to architectural features which did not follow the arbitrary grid. That is, if a wall divided a unit into two sections, materials found on either side of the wall were usually collected separately.

As noted earlier, several compounds excavated in the Noblemen's Quarter were burnt (NMQ1, NMQ2, NMQ3, NMQ4, NMQ5, NMQ6, NMQ10(?), NMQ12). This resulted in a stratigraphic sequence in which materials on or near the floor of the structures are overlain by the charred remains of the burnt wooden super-structure. In the case of NMQ2 and NMQ3, fragments of a collapsed plastered-surface overlay the burnt debris as well; fragments which either were part of a floor of a second storey or of a flat roof, such as described by Paes and others (in Sewell 1900). Above the burnt levels in the excavated structures were upper layers of fill, produced by post-abandonment processes. Where identifiable, the excavators attempted to keep materials from floor levels separate from materials from in or above the charred levels. In unroofed areas of the compounds and in compounds which lacked evidence of burning, arbitrary levels were excavated until floor levels were reached.

If, as proposed above, some of the Noblemen's Quarter structures were burnt during the sacking of the city in A.D. 1565, it is expected that ceramic and other artifacts found on or near floor levels date to that time and that those compounds were hastily abandoned. Spatial patterns evident in ceramic materials found at floor levels should relate to the distribution of activities within the compounds. Thus, cooking areas, storage areas, house dumps, and so on, may be identifiable through the analysis of artefact forms and frequencies. In selecting samples to examine I focused largely on floor samples from well-controlled proveniences from a variety of units within each compound. Where possible, I coded samples from units found within the various platforms and rooms of the main palace structure, as well as materials from subsidiary structures, open areas within the compound walls, and areas immediately outside the compound walls.

Units sampled from palace compounds NMQ2 through NMQ12 are illustrated in Figures 3.1-3.3. NMQ1 was excavated prior to the establishment of a system for collecting ceramics, and precise proveniences could not be identified for the ceramic samples examined. Two small stratigraphic soundings (S1 and S2) were excavated by the DAM in an area to the north of NMQ1. Ceramics samples from 23 excavation units were examined from NMQ2. These can be grouped into 16 units by linking those units which are spatially contiguous and contextually equivalent. These have been numbered Units 2.1-2.16 and are illustrated in Figure 3.1. A total of 1429 diagnostic sherds were coded from NMQ2. Sherds counts by provenience unit for all NMQ compounds are listed in Chapter V, Table 5.1

Ceramics analysed from NMQ3 excavations come from eight spatial units (a total of 13 excavation units). As with NMQ2, samples were analysed from within the main structure, as well as from areas surrounding the structure, and outside of the compound walls (Figure 3.2; Units 3.7, 3.8). A total of 897 diagnostic sherds were analysed from NMQ3, with individual units containing from 33 to 289 diagnostics. The highest densities were found in unit NQ3.7 (n=229) located outside of the compound to the north, and in unit NQ3.1(n=289) located in the western end of the compound.

A total of 13 spatial units and 847 diagnostic sherds were examined from NMQ4 (7 units) and NMQ4A (6 units), with samples derived from 23 distinct excavation units. These units are designated NMQ4.1-NMQ4.13 and are illustrated in Figure. 3.2. The scarcity of deposits from the eastern end of the NMQ4 compound resulted in an under-representation of ceramics from that area of the compound. Samples from the main structure and the alley between the structure and the compound wall were analysed. Samples from NMQ4A included several units located adjacent to the plastered latrine feature described in Chapter II (Units 4.9-12), as well as units located within and beyond the compound walls (Units 4.8 and 4.13, respectively). The number of diagnostic sherds per unit range from 26 to 129. High ceramic densities are found in the alley bordering the main structure of NMQ4 (NQ4.1, n=129) and in the lowest tier of the main structure (NQ 4.3, n=118). Large numbers of sherds are also found in the northern edge of the latrine feature in NQ4A (NQ4.11, n=120).

A total of eight spatial units and 719 diagnostic sherds were coded from the NMQ5 area. These units come from three distinctive areas. Four sample units (5.4-5.7, n=390) lie within the compound and structure of NMQ5. The remaining four units (5.1-5.3, 5.8, n = 329) are in the corridor to the east of the main NMQ5 compound. No sherds were collected from inside the NMQ6 compound, due primarily to the negligible overburden in the area. Sherds were collected from three units located to the west of the compound wall (6.1-6.3, n=182), an area which contained wall fragments and a number of grinding stones.

Sherds were collected from two units within compound NMQ7 (n=177), and from 3 units to the south of the compound (n=336), with a total of 513 diagnostic sherds analysed. Six provenience units were sampled from NMQ8, with a total of 336 diagnostic sherds examined. All but one of these units (8.1) lay inside the compound walls. None came from the main structure itself, which as discussed in Chapter II, was in a very poor state of preservation. Eight units from NMQ9 were sampled, with a total of 434 diagnostic sherds. These units were dispersed throughout the compound.

Ceramics were collected from eight units in compound NMQ10. Four of these (10.1, 10.2, 10.7, and 10.8) lay immediately outside of the compound wall, while the remainder were variously placed inside of the compound. A total of 405 diagnostic sherds were examined from NMQ10. A total of 512 diagnostic sherds were examined from 9 provenience units in NMQ12. Two units, 12.6 and 12.8 (n=90 diagnostics) lay immediately outside of the compound walls, and one unit, 12.9 (n=86), was located near the early walls to the east of the main structure. The remaining units were inside of the main structure of the NMQ12 compound.

Limitations in the Noblemen's Quarter Sample. A number of limitations in the NMQ ceramic sample should be noted. Variations in sample sizes between palace compounds result both from differences in the density of materials in each compound, and from time available in the field to analyse ceramic samples. Additional limitations in the ceramic sample of the Noblemen's Quarter result from the excavation strategy itself. The major goal of the excavations was to uncover and examine the elite architecture of the Noblemen's Quarter. The excavation of the enormous areas covered by these palace compounds was oriented toward that goal, resulting in excavations conducted on a large scale, with crews of local labourers working with mattocks and small picks. Excavated units were not screened and the many artifacts that were not observed and collected were redeposited in backdirt piles. The number of sherds I examined from each unit, then, represents an unknown proportion of those actually found in the unit. In this analysis, I will assume that the relative frequencies of sherds collected and discarded in each unit were fairly constant and that sherd densities between units are proportionally correct. Biases in collection procedures would, I suspect, result in more rim than body sherds, and perhaps, a disproportionate amount of the highly burnished red ware being collected. Proveniences containing large sherds, such as a storeroom where whole vessels were kept, might be more likely to be carefully collected than those in which very small sherds predominate, such as along paths or in other heavily travelled areas.

A further problem with the Noblemen's Quarter data is with the adequacy of stratigraphic control. While an attempt was made to maintain some distinctions between floor levels and later fill levels, the excavation strategy did not lend itself to effective stratigraphic control. As a result, many of the units which I analysed as 'floor level' units probably contained materials from the floor and up to 20-30 cm. above it and, possibly, mixing from higher levels as well. While the materials analysed from floor levels mostly contain materials actually found on the floors of the structures, the samples must be assumed to *not* be entirely composed of ceramics from floor levels.

The limitations in the ceramic sample from the Noblemen's Quarter were beyond my control. While they do impose some constraints on the analysis, and on interpretations of the data, the sample from the Noblemen's Quarter has several strengths as well. The ceramics all come from spatially secure contexts with somewhat greater chronological boundedness than the East Valley samples. For compounds NMQ2-NMQ10, and NMQ12, provenience units are well-controlled, allowing a consideration of the distribution of activities within the compounds. The eleven compounds represent variants of a single architectural form, Vijayanagara palace architecture, and comparisons of materials from each compound may help to inform on differences and similarities in the nature and use of each. Finally, as an area, the Noblemen's Quarter is quite different from the East Valley and the Islamic Quarter, and fruitful comparisons may be made of ceramic diversity between the three functionally, socially, and spatially distinct areas.

The East Valley Ceramic Sample

The surface collection in the East Valley was planned and conducted with the aim of collecting a representative sample from the entire spatial extent of the valley in the brief time available. Since I was interested in studying spatial diversity throughout the valley, a sampling technique was developed to provide an even coverage of the area. The technique chosen was a stratified systematic partially-aligned random sample (Redman 1973; Hole 1980). This technique differs from a simple random sample technique in that prior knowledge of the area can be taken into account, and even coverage is assured.

A grid line was established with its origin point at the centre of the main gate which separated the western elite (royal centre) half of the valley from the eastern, non-elite, urban half. This baseline was oriented to follow, as much as possible, the Vijayanagara road which ran through the valley, identifiable through the location and orientation of structures. The orientation of the baseline differs slightly between areas west and east of the gate—on the west the line is oriented 78^0 east of north, and to the east of the gate, at 81^0 55' 20" east of north.

Using the gate as a zero point, the axis was divided into 50 m. wide units, which defined sampling strata that extended to the northern and southern limits of the valley. Seventeen strata were defined and were designated with the letters A-Q from west to east. Two points along the baseline were randomly selected within each stratum. The points defined transects which were oriented perpendicular to the main axis and extended the width of the valley. Points along the transects were randomly selected—two points every 50 m. in the west half of the valley, and three points per 50 m. in the east (Figure 3.4). When points were located on modern walls or paths, or beyond the boundaries of the valley, judgement units were defined as near to the randomly selected point as possible. The units were designated by their grid unit, A,B,C, ..., transect number, and location to the north or south of the baseline. Thus, unit A23N66 was located 23 m. from the 0 point of the A stratum (the point closest to the gate) and was 66 m. north of the baseline.

The points defined marked the centre of circular collecting units with a radius of two metres. These were collected using a 'dog-leash' strategy (Whallon 1983). Unit size was determined by experimentation on the basis of two criteria: (1) that an adequate sample of diagnostic sherds could be collected from most units (i.e., more than 20), and (2) that the samples could be collected rapidly enough to permit collection of all units. Using this system, a total of 294 units were laid in and collected in a period of two weeks, by a crew consisting of two to three archaeologists, a surveyor, and three to six local labourers. During the collection of each unit, information was recorded on the condition of the ground surface, with an emphasis on the effects that vegetation and soil conditions would have on ceramic visibility and recovery rates. These factors were taken into account in subsequent analyses of ceramic densities across the valley (see Sinopoli 1986).

The total area collected was 3700 square metres in a valley some 170,000 square metres in area. Sample size was thus 2.2% of the total area. The limitations of the small sample size must be acknowledged. Nonetheless, while interpretations of ceramic variability within the valley may not be as statistically secure as might be hoped for, the enormous quantities of materials which this collection generated do provide a sound basis for drawing inferences about ceramic and spatial variability within the East Valley.

All sherds more than 2.5 cm. on a side were collected from each unit. Materials from all units were reverse-screened through a mesh of this dimension in order to obtain comparability between samples collected by different individuals. All units collected were weighed to the nearest 50 gms. after screening. Non-earthenware materials, such as iron slag, copper, beads, figurines, and Chinese and Southeast Asian porcelains were also gathered in the surface collection. Architectural remains such as bricks or plaster were noted and weighed in the field.

The unexpectedly large quantities of diagnostic sherds recovered from most units (mean count from coded units equals 50) made it impossible for us to analyse all of the collected units. We chose instead to measure materials from one transect in each stratum. A total of 143 units from 17 transects were examined (Figure 3.4). In the analysis all body sherds were sorted into ware types and counted and weighed. Unmeasurable rims were sorted into general rim class categories and counted. All measurable rims from each unit were analysed and a sample of these were drawn. Other diagnostic pieces, such as pedestal bases, spouts, or particularly good examples of stamped or other decorations, were also drawn and measured. Nearly 7000 diagnostic sherds were measured from the East Valley surface collection.

The Islamic Quarter Sample

A small sample was collected from the main Islamic Quarter of Vijayanagara. The sample came from nine loci, which included seven 10 by 10 metre square surface collection units (IQ2, 4-9), and two areas where clearance and restoration work by the DAM resulted in the recovery of ceramics (IQ1 and 3, see Figure 3.5). Collection IQ1 was made from DAM clearance and conservation work within and around the Dharmashala. The exact original location of the ceramics relative to the building is unknown, but they all clearly were associated with the structure. Sample IQ3 comes from DAM excavations of a large well located to the west of the Dharmashala.

All of the surface collection samples were located using judgement sampling. This simply means that they were placed in arbitrary locations defined by criteria such as visibility and the presence of ceramics on the surface, and by a desire to place units over a broad area of the Islamic Quarter. Surface ceramic densities in this area of the site are quite low as compared to the East Valley, and the sherds visible are generally fairly small (thus, the large size of the collection units). It was therefore decided that a more statistically sophisticated random sampling technique would be innappropriate here, since in many areas of the Quarter virtually no ceramics were visible on the surface. In contrast, the materials from the DAM excavations are quite large and well-preserved, and appear somewhat more numerous. The relative paucity of ceramics on the surface in the Islamic Quarter area may result from a lower population density in this area, or from post-abandonment factors affecting soil accumulation and land use.

The approximate locations of the six surface collection units in the Islamic Quarter are mapped on Figure 3.5. As with the East Valley samples, all sherds visible on the surface were collected, though only sherds larger than 2.5 cm. in dimension were examined. A total of 584 diagnostic sherds were examined from the Islamic Quarter Area. The sample size from this area is clearly not comparable to that from the Noblemen's Quarter or East Valley, and is not adequate spatially or numerically to permit a consideration of ceramic diversity within this quarter of the city, or to effectively compare Islamic Quarter ceramics with materials from other parts of the site. These samples were collected primarily to discover if there are any marked contrasts with other, Hindu, areas of the site—in technology, ceramic form, or decoration.

DISCUSSION

Ceramics collections in these three areas of Vijayanagara yielded more than 15,000 diagnostic sherds for analysis. Of these, a total of 7959 diagnostics were analysed from the Noblemen's Quarter, 6717 from the East Valley, and 584 from the Islamic Quarter (ceramics analysed from the royal centre are are not considered here; see Sinopoli, n.d.b). Along with the diagnostics, more than 100,000 body sherds were sorted and counted. Although these numbers are considerable, it should be noted that the samples analysed represent only a very small percentage of the sherds present in each area, and that these areas are only a very small part of the site of Vijayanagara. Nonetheless, the collection procedures employed permit the assumption that the ceramics analysed are a representative sample of the materials in use in each area of the city during the Vijayanagara period. While expanded collections and analyses will undoubtedly expand the range of known Vijayanagara ceramic forms, we can safely assume that the classification of Vijayanagara ceramics, presented in Chapter IV and based on the total current collections, generally encompasses the range and variation of the ceramic inventory of medieval Vijayanagara.

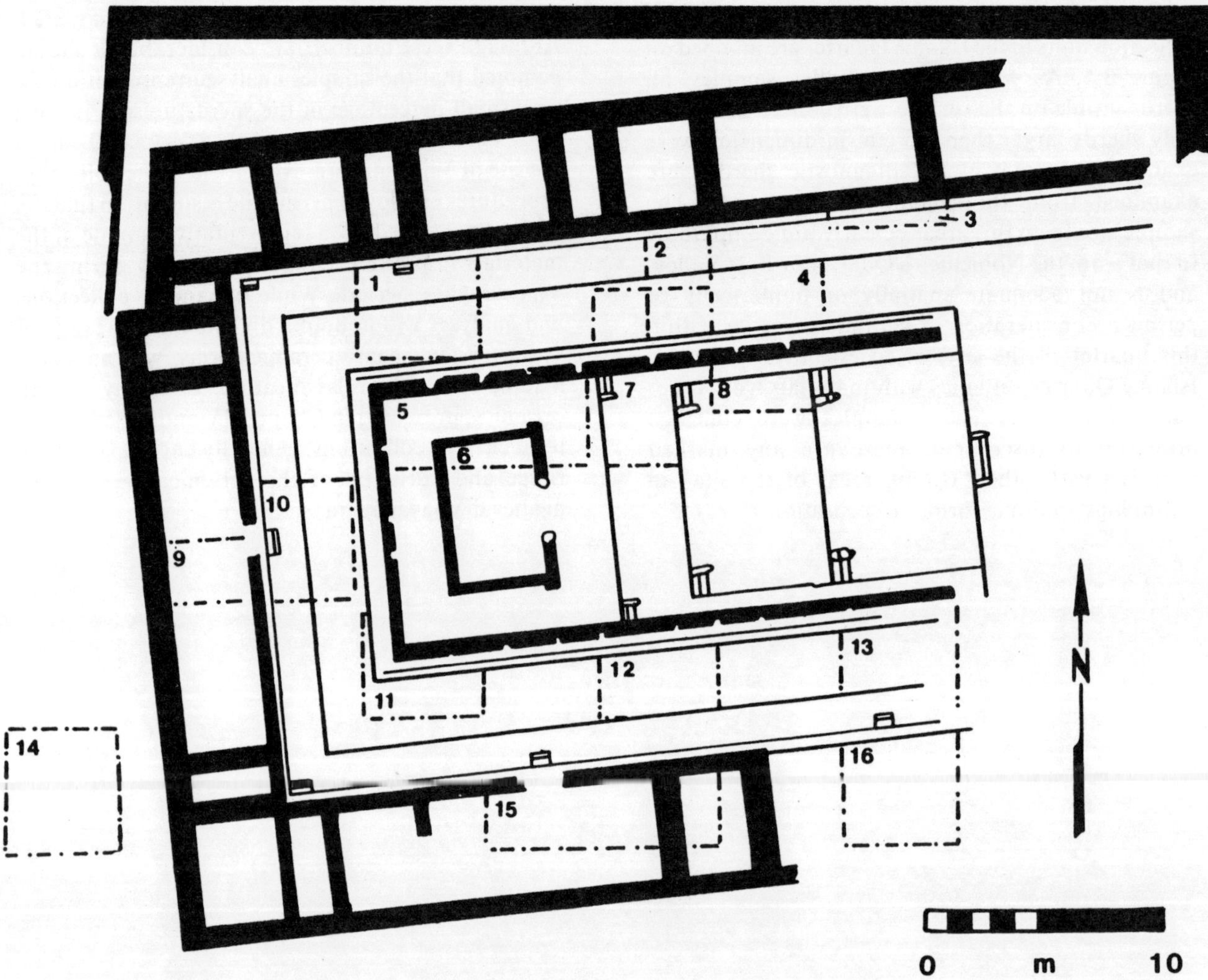

Figure 3.1 Compound 2 Sample Units

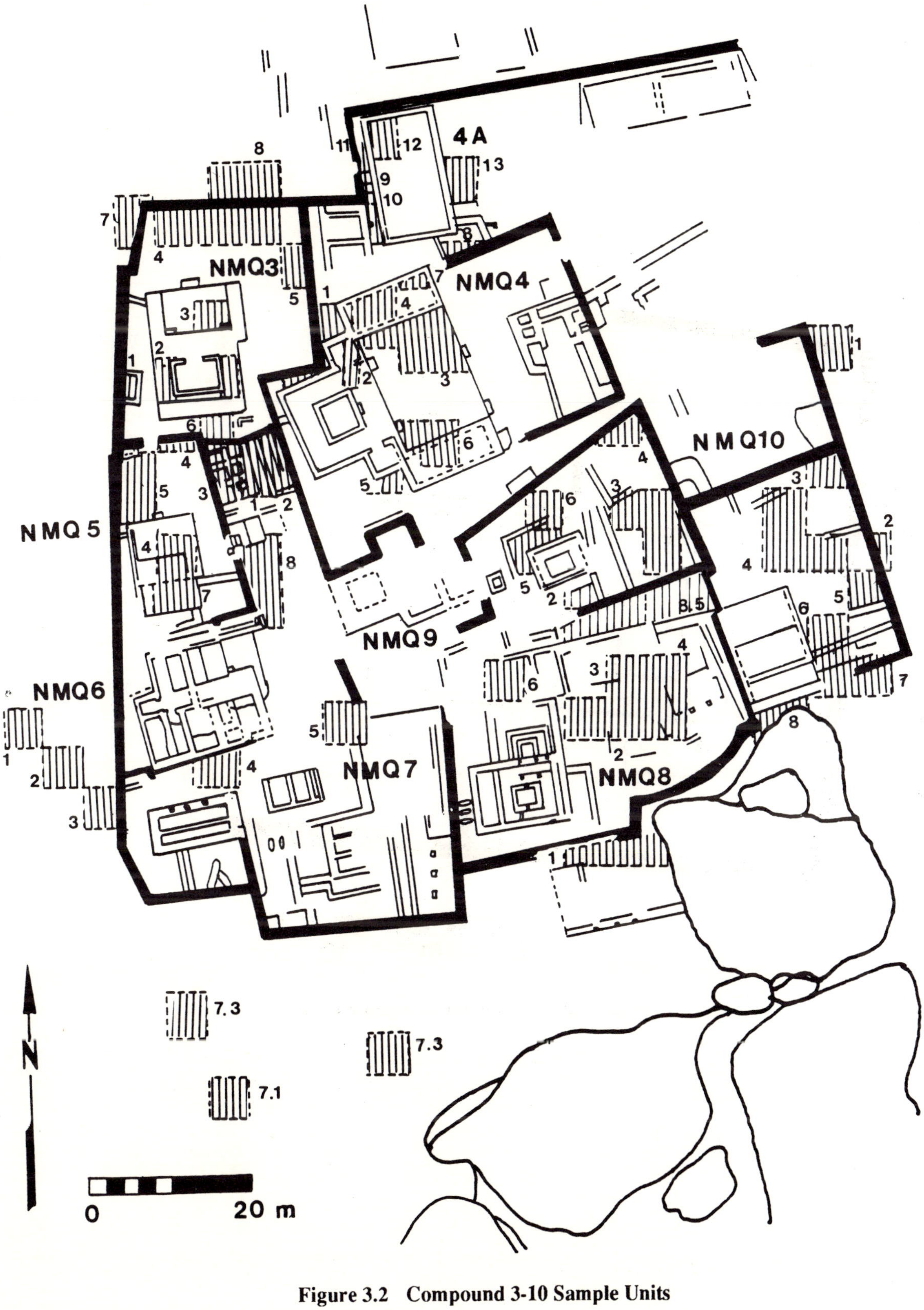

Figure 3.2 Compound 3-10 Sample Units

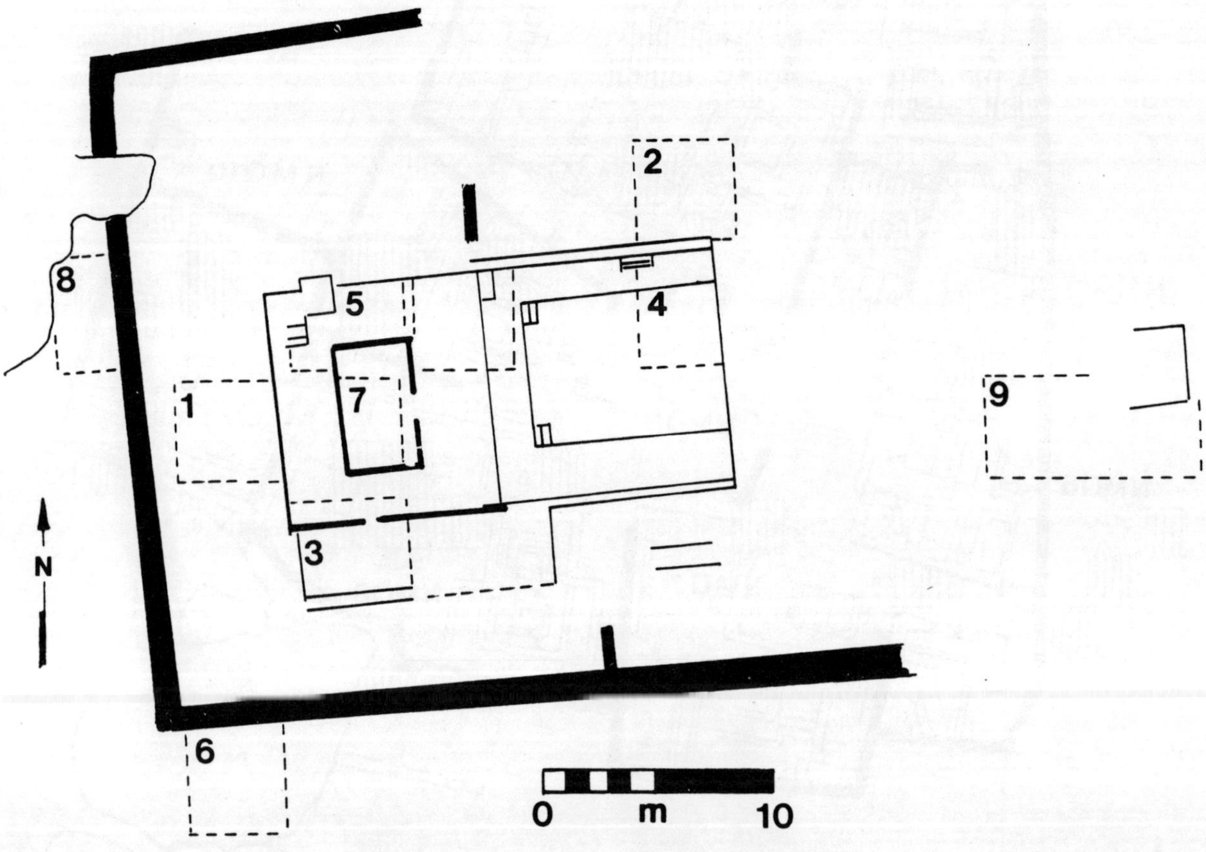

Figure 3.3 Compound 12 Sample Units

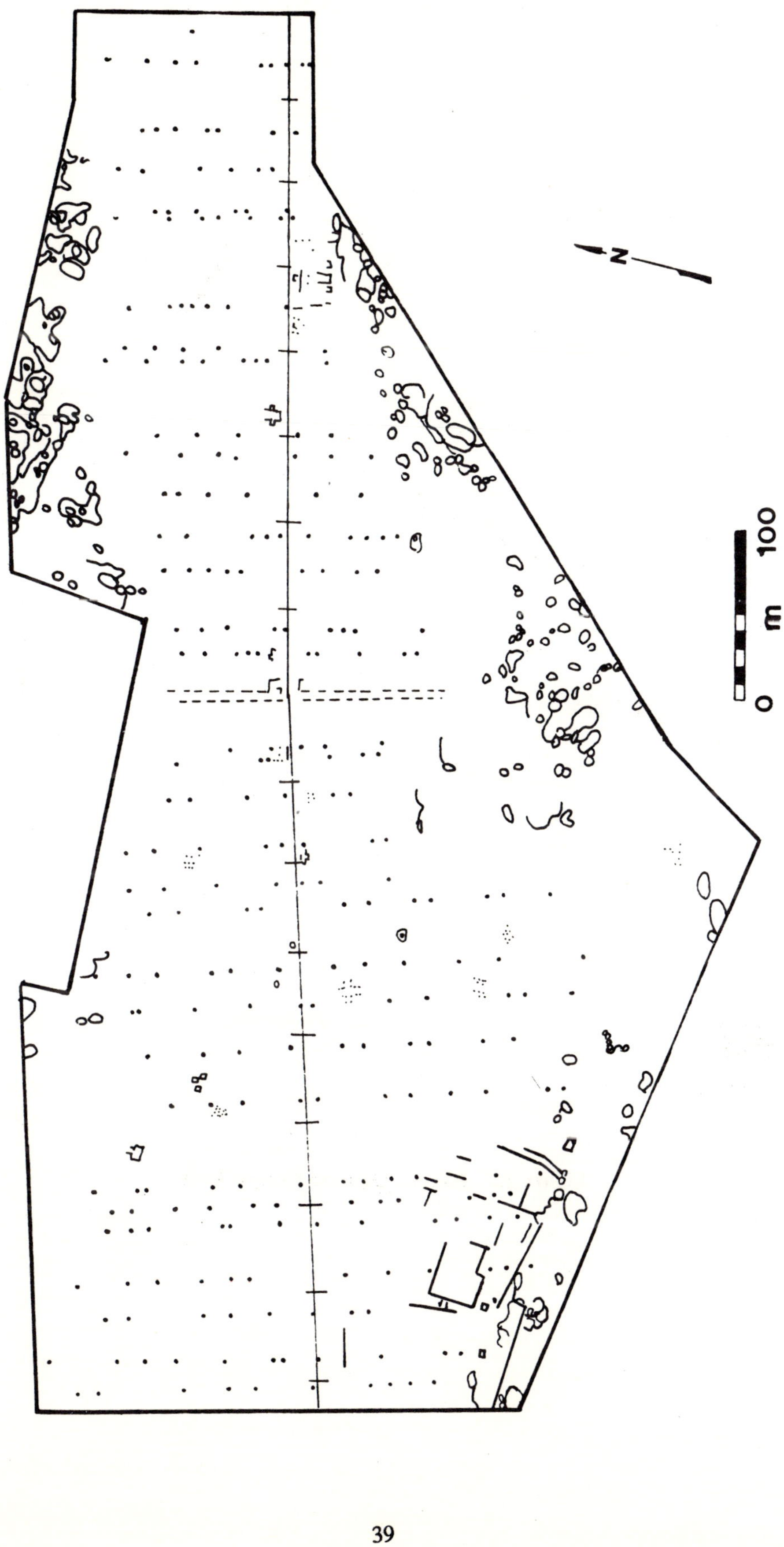

Figure 3.4 East Valley Sample Units

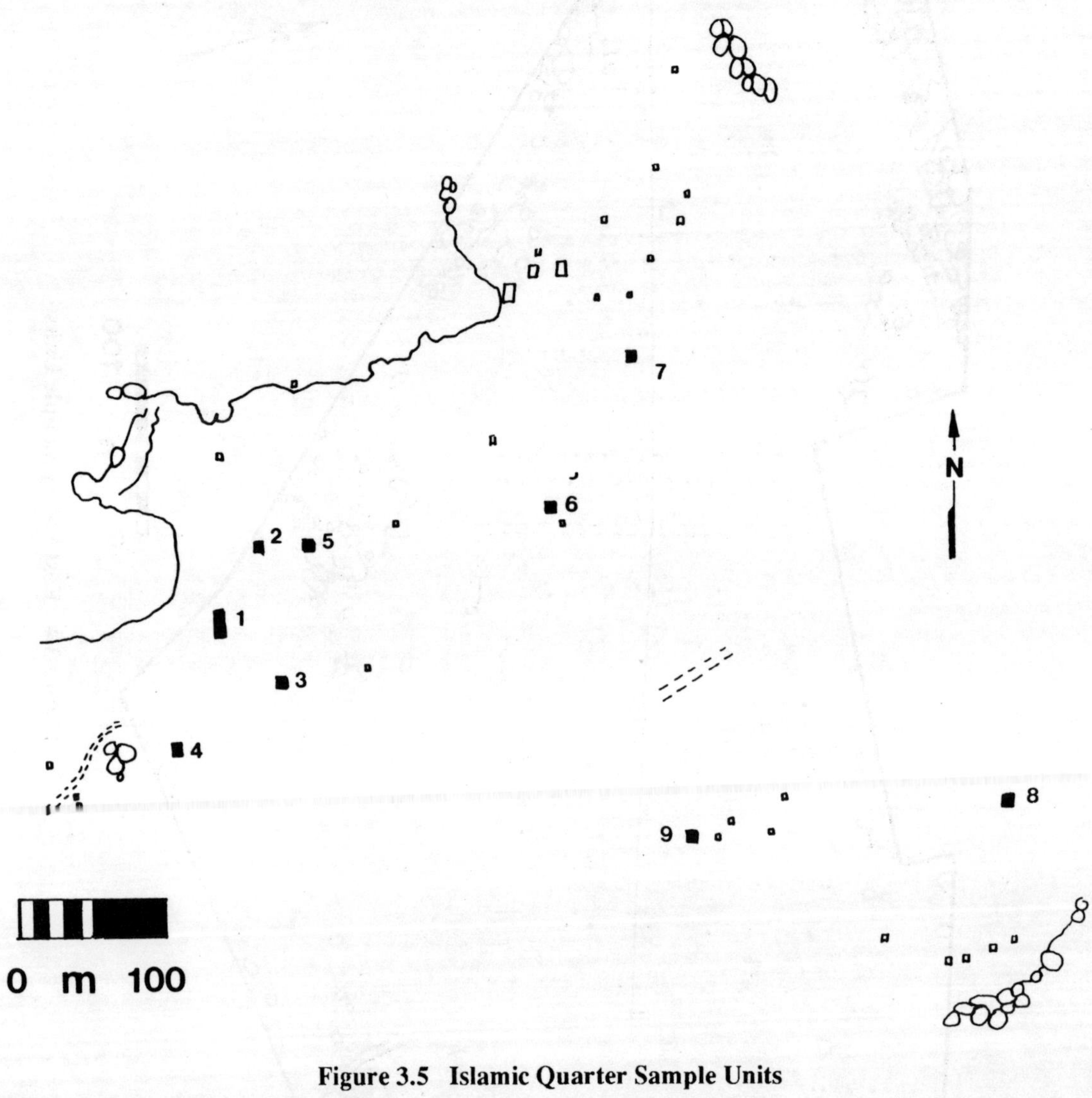

Figure 3.5 Islamic Quarter Sample Units

IV. The Ceramic Classification

In the development of the Vijayanagara ceramic classification, I chose to take a quantitative approach to ceramic typology. This approach was selected because it was best suited to the goals of the ceramic analysis, and to the nature of the Vijayanagara ceramic inventory. Given that this is the first classification attempted of medieval south Indian ceramics, I sought to develop a classification that would encompass a wide range of ceramic variation, including vessel shape, size, rim forms, decoration, and production techniques. Alternative approaches to the ceramic classification could no doubt have been taken, and yielded equally legitimate results. In this chapter, I will outline in some detail both the process of development of the classification and the final classification of the Vijayanagara ceramics which was employed in subsequent analyses, in the hopes that such a discussion will prove valuable both for the study of Vijayanagara ceramics and as a case study of systematic ceramic classification in general.

The first stage of the classification process involved recording quantitative and qualitative information on each diagnostic sherd. Approximately 16,000 diagnostic sherds from Vijayanagara were coded in the 1983, 1984, and 1986 seasons. For the most part, these were rims, though pedestal bases, stamped or otherwise elaborately decorated body sherds, and other distinctive pieces were also examined. Few whole vessels were preserved. Given the broad scope of the goals of the ceramic analysis, a broad range of variables were recorded on each diagnostic sherd. In some cases, these variables were specific to general vessel shape classes. Other variables, particularly those relating to production techniques and weres were recorded on all diagnostic sherds.

VARIABLE DEFINITIONS

Among the information recorded for all diagnostics were a number of categorical attributes (Table 4.1). These include descriptions of the non-plastic inclusions in the vessel paste, whether added as temper or found naturally in the clays. Identification of the inclusions was aided by the use of a hand lens with 10x magnification. Information on the absolute percentages of inclusions and the types of inclusions were recorded. Percentage values coded were none, trace, 5%, 10%, 15%, and so on, in increments of five percent. Inclusion percentages were assessed using a geological chart of densities (Figure 4.1). Inclusion types noted in Vijayanagara ceramics include sand, chaff or other organic materials, a soft red grit (hematite), and a soft white grit (calcite). The presence of other inclusions, such as shell, grog, and mica, was also recorded, and inclusions more than 3 mm. in dimension were noted and measured.

Body and surface colours were also recorded for each piece. In the 1983 season, Munsell measures were taken of the more than 3000 sherds coded. In 1984, I switched to a more expedient categorical recording system. Body colours recorded include: black, red, brown, red with a black core, brown with a black core, grey with a black core, white, and other. Body colour is dependent upon clay constituents, firing atmosphere and temperature, and firing time, as well as a vessel's position in the firing area. An interior core results from the incomplete oxidation of organic materials in the clay, or from the conditions under which a vessels is cooled post-firing (Rye 1981:114-118). Exterior surface colours were recorded on restricted vessels and interior surface colours were recorded on the unrestricted vessels. Surface colours noted were black or grey, red, brown (including pale brown), white, and other. Surface colour is determined by clay and slip constituents, firing atmosphere, a vessel's position in the kiln, and by vessel use. Large vessels, in particular, exhibited considerable variability in colour, often grading from brown to black, with blackened areas resulting from proximity to fuel and low availability of oxygen in the firing. In these cases, the dominant vessel colour was recorded.

Information on interior and exterior surface treatment was also recorded for each diagnostic sherd. Surface treatment is simply defined as identifiable traces of the way the potter or pottery user finished the surface of the vessel before or after firing. The range of Vijayanagara surface treatments include: traces of smoothing, polishing, burnishing, partial burnishing, paddle and anvil impressions, the application of a slip, burnishing over a slip, coarse surfaces with impressions of sand, chaff, or small pebbles, and other surface treatments. The distinction made between polished and burnished surfaces was one of degree—polished surfaces were those that had been lightly rubbed with a cloth or with a paddle in the final stages of paddle and anvil work and had a slight gloss, while the designation burnished was used to refer to only those sherds which had a high and consistent sheen, typically found on thin-walled red or black wares.

Interior surface treatment was only measured on those pieces on which a sufficient portion of the vessel interior below the rim was preserved. For restricted vessels this value was arbitrarily set at two centimetres below the neck inflection. The measure of surface treatment provides information on production techniques and treatment after the vessel was formed, and may provide information on the intended function of the vessels. Other information such as the presence of paint (very rare) or plaster on a sherd was noted in a comment. The treatment of the rim interiors of restricted vessels, whether polished or burnished, was recorded in the 1984 and 1986 seasons, as was the presence or absence of an interior ledge at the neck.

The remainder of the variables recorded were quantitative, and varied somewhat with the general form of the vessel, whether restricted or unrestricted. These two broad categories served to subdivide the vessels on the basis of general vessel shape, and permitted the definition of appropriate variables to record the range of variation present in the Vijayanagara ceramic inventory. Unrestricted vessels are, simply, defined as open vessels which do not narrow below the rim (though the vessel may slope inward at the rim itself). Restricted or necked vessels narrow below the rim and then turn outward again, creating an inflection point at the neck. Where clearly distinctive and coherent groups of vessel forms were recognisable within the two classes, these were defined as subsets of the unrestricted and restricted groups. Thus, the unrestricted vessels were divided into three categories (1) lamps, or small shallow saucers; (2) shallow bowls, a form with distinctive rim and base carinations; and (3) other bowls, a catch-all category including all open vessels which were neither lamps nor shallow bowls. Each of these three groups was coded separately and a variety of attributes was recorded on each.

The restricted vessels were subdivided on the basis of rim morphology, rather than overall vessel morphology. Three general rim form classes were defined: (1) round rim, (2) straight rim, and (3) flange rim restricted vessels. These forms are distinguished by the shape of the rim exterior. Within these rim classes, finer subdivisions were made on the basis of variations in lip orientation and thickness and the point of maximal rim thickness (as illustrated in Figure 4.5). In many respects, these initial divisions were heuristic, and provided a way of putting some initial order into the mounds of sherds that were being examined. Subsequent analyses, using statistical methods and computer manipulation, were conducted to verify and, where necessary, redefine these initial typological divisions.

A variety of metric attributes were recorded on each vessel class. These are illustrated in Figures 4.2 through 4.5. All measures that could be accurately made were taken on each rim sherd. Sherds were measured using a standard rim diametre chart (to the nearest cm., for diametres), a vernier calipers (to the nearest .01. cm., for thicknesses and heights), and a goniometer (to the nearest 5^0, for angles). Sherds were measured only if at least three cm. of the rim was preserved, enough for an accurate measure of rim diametre. Restricted vessels were measured only if neck diametre and neck height were measurable. Certain variables were added in subsequent seasons which had not been recorded in 1983. The addition of other variables, such as rim and body angle, renders the 1983 sample from NMQ1 and NMQ2 largely incomparable with samples measured later, but provides a much better assessment of vessel variability. As a result, samples from NMQ1 and NMQ2 will be largely excluded from subsequent analyses.

Definitions of most measured variables can be assessed from the illustrations (Figure 4.2-4.5). A few, however, should be defined more explicitly. Rim angle was defined as the orientation of the vessel from the interior neck carination to the interior rim top. Lip angle was defined as the orientation of the rim interior at the lip. Body angle was the angle from the horizontal of the vessel wall below the neck carination, and was measured only if the vessel wall was preserved for at least two centimetres below the neck. Angle measures are illustrated in Figure 4.5. Body thickness was measured two cm. below the neck inflection point on restricted vessels, and base thickness was measured two cm. below the base carination on all vessels, to assure comparability between measures.

While the recording techniques used and measurements taken on the Vijayanagara ceramics were at the level of the attribute, the ultimate goal of the analysis is to go beyond the attribute level to the behaviorally significant dimensions of vessel shape, size, and rim morphology. The attributes recorded are at best only partial measures of these dimensions. The best way to assess such dimensions as vessel shape or size is, of course, through an analysis of whole or nearly whole vessels, an opportunity rarely afforded to archaeologists, and seldom possible in this analysis. The dimensions of shape and size in this study are therefore rather crudely assessed through the statistical analysis of the multi- and univariate relationships which provide the most accurate measure of them. While not an ideal, or even a terribly adequate approach, it is the best available, and avoids discounting completely the very important dimension of vessel shape, which typically is the characteristic of a vessel observed most readily and assigned the greatest importance by vessel users and producers (Arnold 1985:5).

The end result of this stage of the analysis is the definition of a number of classes of vessels, grouped on the basis of formal similarities in shape, size, and rim form. I will elaborate on the particular methods used in the construction of the classfication in the discussion of specific classes below, but a few general statements about the overall approach are in order here.

I have attempted throughout the analysis to consider general vessel shape, vessel size, and rim form as three separate (though partially interrelated) dimensions of variability which, if taken together, characterise vessel form. Vessel classes were divided into smaller groups on the basis of patterned and easily definable categorical differences or, more usually, on the basis of modal distributions of single variables, variable ratios, or multi-variate measures such as principal component scores. The variables or scores selected were those which best measured the dimension under examination and which exhibited the clearest modality in the distribution of values. As discussed above, in many cases the dimension under study could not be accurately assessed given the partial nature of the sample. In such cases the classes defined should be constructed as a best approximation and not as a fully accurate or completely satisfactory assessment of formal variability in the Vijayanagara ceramic inventory. It is hoped that larger samples of complete vessels will, in the future, aid in the refinement of some aspects of the classification presented here.

WARE CATEGORIES

The categorical attributes of surface colour and surface treatment, as well as information on vessel wall thickness, provided the basis for defining ceramic ware categories. Three ware classes were defined. These are: Plain Ware, Burnished Ware, and Coarse Ware. The vast majority of the vessels were Plain Ware, in black, brown, or, infrequently, red (Table 4.2). These sherds are characterised by smoothed or lightly polished surfaces and wall thicknesses ranging from .5 to .8 cm. The Burnished Ware group is characterised by a highly lustrous red or black surface finish, often on extremely thin-walled vessels (less than .5 cm.), brown Burnished Ware sherds are seldom found, and red Burnished sherds are the most common. The Coarse Ware vessels range from one to three centimetres in wall thickness, and have a distinctive red or light brown paste with high percentages of coarse sand and organic inclusions, and roughly finished surfaces. Coarse Ware vessels include such forms as earthenware ovens and ring well linings.

Macro-examinations of the sherds using hand-lenses and thin section-analyses (Rautman, in press) do not reveal dramatic variability in raw material selection and paste preparation by vessel form or across the site. Many of the vessels appear to have had some sort of colouring agent or slip applied to them prior to firing. However, with the exception of the Red Burnished Ware vessels, these slips are not easily identifiable.

As will be discussed below, there is a definite relation between some of the ware classes and certain vessel forms, though for no form is this an absolute relation. Thus, while most of the small lamps are of red or light brown Plain Ware, black Plain Ware lamps are also found. In contemporary Kamalapuram, variation in ware colour is dependent upon vessel function and season of production and use, because red wares are believed to be particularly efficacious in cooling liquids. Red vessels are therefore in greatest demand during the hot season (March-April through September) and are sold for twice the price of equivalent black vessels which are produced in the workshop year-round (Sinopoli and Blurton 1986). It is not yet possible to extend this practice back to Vijayanagara times with any certainty, though it must be noted that Vijayanagara red Burnished Ware vessels are frequently forms that are best interpreted as liquid storage and serving vessels and occur in relatively low frequencies in the Vijayanagara ceramic inventory.

A small number of painted sherds were recovered from Vijayanagara. These sherds, which number less than two dozen, were either covered with a white slip (or thin plaster?) after they were fired and painted with red and black pigments in simple linear designs (Figure 4.6), or were painted with white paint directly on the vessel body. The painted vessels were most likely painted by their users after they were purchased from potters, perhaps, as known from ethnographic contexts, for use in religious ceremonies. A painted vessel recovered from ASI excavations near the Mahanavami Diba, for example, was decorated with a number of Shaivite symbols including the linga, crescent moon, and swastika.

MORPHOLOGICAL CATEGORIES

In the remainder of this chapter, I will focus on the definition of morphological vessel classes for the Vijayanagara ceramics. For the sake of brevity, all of the analytical steps taken for each class will not be elaborated in detail. Rather, certain analytical stages and processes will be presented in considerable detail, while others will be summarised. The classification of the unrestricted vessel classes will be presented first, followed by a discussion of the restricted vessels classification.

Unrestricted Vessel Forms

Vijayanagara unrestricted vessels include shallow saucers or lamps, shallow carinated bowls, and other bowls. The unrestricted vessels comprise a relatively small percentage of the Vijayanagara ceramic inventory, with a total of 171 lamps, 923 shallow bowls, and 470 other bowls measured. The low frequencies of unrestricted forms is probably partially due to the limited range of functions permitted to such forms by Hindu dietary rules and practices; in particular, to sanctions against the use of earthenware in food consumption activities. The scarcity of lamps is somewhat more suprising as these are vessels which might be expected to have been used frequently and in large numbers at Vijayanagara, though perhaps only during restricted times of year or in limited spatial settings. I will consider each of the unrestricted vessel forms, and divisions within them, separately.

Unrestricted Vessels: Lamps. Although I hesitate to ascribe definite functions to most Vijayanagara vessel forms, I have little hesitation in ascribing a function to these small saucer-shaped vessels. This can be done on the basis of ethnographic analogy and traces of use on the archaeological samples. Contemporary vessels virtually identical in form to the archaeological samples are used today in Kamalapuram and throughout India as oil lamps (dipa) primarily used in temple worship. The religious context of use and their simple functional requirements have probably contributed to the great continuity in vessel form. Approximately one-sixth of the 171 lamp sherds analysed from Vijayanagara exhibit some evidence of burning around the rim or on the vessel interiors.

Dipas manufactured in Kamalapuram today are entirely handmade, using pinch-building techniques. The Vijayanagara inventory, however, includes both handmade and wheel-built forms. The wheel-built vessels, only three of which were recovered, have string-cut bases and circular wheel traces on their interior surfaces. Given the small number of wheel-formed lamps, it is likely that this was not a regular manufacturing practice, but took place during throwing when only small amounts of usable clay remained on the wheel, assuming that the modern practice of throwing off the hump existed in the past. Among the hand-built lamps, techniques varied from crude pinching, resulting in uneven wall thicknesses and visible finger impressions, to more finely formed vessels, possibly slab-built, with flattened or rounded bases. No lamps appear to have been mould-made, though there is some indication that they were pressed against a hard surface (probably the ground) while being formed. Evidences for this are the many vessels with flattened bases and impressions of sand, chaff, and small pebbles on the exterior basal surface.

The Vijayanagara lamps are atypical of the rest of the Vijayanagara ceramic inventory in vessel colour and paste inclusions. While organic inclusions are present in only a very small percentage of Vijayanagara vessels overall (3%), they are present in 22% of the lamps. Where present, organic inclusions comprise no more than 5% of total paste and, as in all vessel forms, sand is the most common inclusion. Whether the occurrence of organic inclusions in the lamps is deliberate or is an unintended consequence of manufacturing techniques is unclear. Lamp surface colour (on the interior surface) also differs from the majority of Vijayanagara vessel forms in that a large number of lamps are brown-light brown (n=65) or reddish-brown (n=31) in colour. Most Vijayanagara vessel classes are largely composed of black vessels, produced in reducing atmospheres. In contrast, only 42% of the lamps (n=71) are black. This variation probably results from the positioning of these small vessels at the top of the kiln or oven during firing, resulting in more complete oxidation of organic materials in the clay and, consequently, lighter colouring.

Four lamp shape classes were defined on the basis of categorical attributes rather than by statistical analyses of metric attributes. The defining attributes were rim form and base form. Each of these has two formal variants: rounded rims and angular rims; and rounded bases and flat bases. The intersection of these attribute states defined four morphological classes, L1-L4. Variant L1 has a rounded rim and base (n=11), variant L2 has a rounded rim and flat base (n=11), variant L3 has a flat rim and rounded base (n=29), and variant L4 has a flat rim and base (n=58) (Figure 4.7) Of these, variant L1 is smallest in size, with a mean rim diametre of 7.90 cm, and a mean base height of 1.74 cm. Significant differences exist between these four forms in rim diametre, rim thickness, and rim height. L1-L4 do not vary in temper percentages, but do vary in the presence of organic inclusions. Such inclusions are present in half of the sherds of L4 and over one-third of the L3 sherds (both flat rim), but are found in only 2 of the 18 round rim forms. Summary statistics on the Vijayanagara lamp forms are presented in Table 4.3 below.

Unrestricted Vessels: Shallow Bowls. The second, and most common, of the unrestricted vessel forms are round-based bowls with vertical or everted walls and thickened rims which I have called 'shallow bowls'. These vessels typically have pronounced exterior base carinations and are found in low frequencies in all areas sampled. Shallow bowls occur with significantly greater frequency than the lamps, and a total of 923 diagnostic shallow bowls were coded from Vijayanagara.

The vessels range in rim diametre from 8 to 39 cm. with a mean of 18.03 cm. Rim size exhibits a bimodal distribution with peaks at 16 cm. and 24 cm. (Figure 4.8a). The bowls may have served a number of functions: (1) they may have been used in cooking, particularly as griddles for breads, etc.; (2) they may have been used as plates or *thalis* in food serving; or (3) they may have served as lids for other earthenware vessel forms. The relatively small diametre of most of the vessels makes the first interpretation unlikely, with the possible exception of the 153 vessels which are greater than 23 cm. in rim diametre (see below). Few of the shallow bowls have any evidence of patterned burning, i.e., on their exterior surfaces, that would support the cooking vessel interpretation. It must be acknowledged, however, that the burning of the Noblemen's Quarter structures at the time of their abandonment may have resulted in considerable charring of vessels located therein, possibly obscuring the patterns that did exist. The long exposure and greater fragmentation of the East Valley samples results in small rims with little preservation of evidence of base of body treatment and use.

The second possible function proposed for these vessels, that of use as food serving implements, seems unlikely for the majority of them due to their rounded bases, relatively low frequencies in the Vijayanagara ceramic sample, and the ethnographic and historic documentation on Hindu food-serving practices. If the vessels had been regularly used in serving activities, I would expect them to be present in higher frequencies, as such portable and frequently used and cleaned vessels would have most likely had a high breakage rate.

The third possible function proposed for the shallow bowls is their use as lids, at least for the smaller, and most common size mode. No other good candidates for lids are present in the Vijayanagara ceramic inventory, though wood, cloth, banana leaves, or other organic materials may have served this purpose. Alternately, the various round-based storage vessels may have been stacked one atop another, as is a common practice today, with each vessel serving as a lid for the one below it. Nonetheless, the interpretation that many of these vessels were used as lids, with the larger variants of the form used as cooking implements, appears the most reasonable at this time, though it is certainly possible that a single form, such as these bowls, might have served different functions in different contexts.

Many of the shallow bowls appear to have been constructed using mould-building and hand-building techniques. The use of a mould is indicated by the very thin base thicknesses and pronounced, often flanged, base carinations. The moulds used may have been the broken bases of other vessels. Joints where vessel walls and rims were added on to the base are occasionally visible and this joint is the most common breakage point of the vessels. Finger and paddle impressions are visible in a small number of vessels, providing further evidence of construction techniques. Most of the vessels have smoothed (n=600) or polished (n=214) interior surfaces, and a small number are slipped (n=35), or slipped and burnished (n=40). Vessel rims are generally finely formed and regular, but no traces of wheel manufacture are evident.

Attributes measured on shallow bowls are illustrated in Figure 4.2. Although a number of categorical rim forms were defined in the field, these did not prove to be useful in later analyses and will not be considered here. The large majority of rims (n=781) have small lip thicknesses relative to rim thickness, and the point of maximal rim thickness is near the base of the rim. These were designated as "normal rims". One rim form which though small in number, is quite distinctive in form, is characterised by low sharply everted rims ("everted rim", n=36; Figure 4.9 a-f). The remainder of the shallow bowl rims were sufficiently distinctive in form and occurred either as unique examples or in very low frequencies. These were designated as "other rim" forms.

Vijayanagara shallow bowls were divided into two size classes—those less than or equal to 22 cm. in rim diametre and those greater than 22 cm. in rim diametre (Figure 4.8a). A third mode, of vessels greater than 29 cm. may also exist, but given the small sample size at this size range, I chose to group all the large vessels into a single group. As noted above, these size ranges may relate to functional differences within the shallow bowl group.

The most pronounced formal variation among the shallow bowls is in rim orientation, as measured by the variable rim angle (measured to the nearest 5^0). This variable exhibits a clear and pronounced modality (Figure 4.8b) with modes at 75^0 and 95^0, and a possible mode at 30^0. The vessels are thus divisible into very shallow open vessels with rim angles of 45^0 or less (n=394), and vessels with vertical or constricting walls with rim angles between 90° and 130^0 (n=491). These variations in rim orientation and the degree of restriction in the vessels may relate to vessel function, as they affect the ease of placing materials in and removing them from the bowls (if the vessels were used in cooking or serving). Workshop variability may also be reflected in this patterning. Mean attribute values of shallow bowl rim angle classes by size class (designated as B1-B6) are presented in Table 4.4 and rim profiles are illustrated in Figure 4.9.

Rim form varies considerably among the Vijayanagara shallow bowls. All of the vessels in the lowest rim angle class belong to the everted rim class, with rim height, lip thickness, and rim thickness roughly equal. The remainder of the rims, classed within the "normal rim" category, vary from elongated forms which are thin relative to their height, to forms which are as thick or thicker than they are high, resulting in a squat triangular or blocky rim. Variations in rim form are continuous and it is not possible to delineate clear-cut divisions within them.

The variation evident in shallow bowl rim form does not seem to be functionally related, nor is it related to vessel size or wall orientation (with the exception of the shallow angle vessels). It is possible that chronological variation accounts for these differences. Or, rim form variants may have been produced synchronically through conscious or unconscious workshop distinctions, resulting from differences in production steps or motions, different formal 'templates', or responses to consumer desires. Alternatively, these variations may be stochastic, resulting from day to day random variations in vessel production. Given the apparently continuous nature of rim form variations, only the initially defined distinctions between everted, normal, and other rims will be maintained at present.

Ware and colour of the shallow bowls exhibit no consistent patterning. Over half of the vessels are black Plain Ware (n=503), while a third are brown Plain Ware (n=277), and the remainder are of red Plain and Burnished Wares (n=82 and 31, respectively). The percentage of inclusions ranges between trace and 30, with most vessels containing between 5 and 15% inclusions of fine and medium grained sand. Only 4% of the sherds have organic inclusions, while 10% (n=95) contain red grit, and 4% (n=37) contain white grit or calcite inclusions. Neither inclusion type or colour exhibit any correlation with the shape or size classes defined above.

Unrestricted Vessels: Other Bowls. The remainder of the Vijayanagara unrestricted vessels have been grouped into the category 'other bowls'. This category includes a variety of distinctive vessel forms, each of which occurs in low frequencies in the sample, as well as a number of unique vessels. A total of 470 other bowls were coded.

The other bowl forms were divided into two broad morphological groups, each of which exhibits considerable internal variablity. These are (1) rounded and (2) carinated forms. The rounded bowls are characterised by hemispherical or rounded profiles with no clearly defined bases. The carinated forms have pronounced basal carinations. Not all bowls could be classed into these general shape categories, because of sherd size and changes in coding procedures between 1983 and 1986. Of the 299 bowls for which this attribution could be securely made, 152 are rounded and 147 are carinated in form. Finer formal variants were defined for the bowls on the basis of rim form or general vessel morphology. These are illustrated in Figures 4.10a and 4.10b.

Five groups were defined for the rounded forms: (1) normal rims, or simple rims with flat or rounded lips (n=25; Figures 4.10: a-c); (2) flanged bowls, which have a thick horizontal flange at the rim base (n=9; Figure 4.10: d-g). One of these bowls had a perforated base, and was probably used as a strainer; (3) bowls with flat-topped rims that thickened on the interior and exterior of the vessels (n=31; Figure 4.10: h-k); (4) inturning bowls with simple rims and with rounded lips, that turn in sharply at the rim (n=50; Figure 4.10: l-o); and (5) out-turning bowls with open profiles and folded rims which thicken on the vessel exterior (n=16, Figure 4.10: p-s).

Three formal variants were defined for the carinated bowls: (1) normal rims, with simple rounded or flattened lips (n=75; Figure 11: a-d); (2) bowls with high grooved rims, often with decorative impressions on the rim exterior (n=37; Figure 11: e-i); and (3) forms with flattened rims that thicken on the interior and exterior of the vessel (n=25; Figure 11: j-m). Sherds which did not fit into these categories were coded as 'other rim' forms.

Each of the other bowl forms exhibits considerable variability in size and shape and most certainly in function. Many of the bowls of all forms were quite large, with an overall sample mean rim diametre of 23 cm. The larger of these vessels may have been used as cooking vessels (e.g., griddles, a small number did have some evidence of exterior charring) or food preparation or serving vessels. The other bowls may alternatively been used as lids. None of the vessels appeared to have flat bases, even the carinated forms had slightly rounded bases. Given the relatively small sample sizes of each group, patterned variations within them are at best suggestive of formal classes, and no finer divisions were made. Summary descriptions of the forms and possible divisions within them are presented in Table 4.5. The 'other bowl' group is an interesting group in the Vijayanagara ceramic sample, since, though few in number, they exhibit tremendous diversity in form, and presumably, in the uses to which they were put.

Restricted Vessel Forms

Vijayanagara restricted vessels include all vessels with a neck (an inflection point below the rim at which the orientation of the vessel changes from inturning to out-turning). Included among the restricted vessels are a variety of vessel shape forms, ranging from shallow relatively open vessels to tall, long-necked vessels with small openings. The restricted vessels comprise the vast majority of measured vessels (n=13,025) and include a range of functional types. The diagnostic rims were divided into three groups on the basis of general rim form: 1) round rim, 2) flange rim, and 3) straight rim forms. These groups were distinguished on the basis of the shape of the exterior, visible surface of the rim. The round rim vessels have a curved or rounded exterior surface, the flange rims curve in below the lip and then sharply out to form an exterior ledge or flange, and the straight rim forms have a flat rim exterior. This classification was in part heuristic and a small percentage of the rims fitted somewhere between the three form classes. The classification was, however, quite useful in the initial sorting of the vessels and encodes consistent and regular variation in Vijayanagara restricted vessel rim form.

Although there are some definite relations between rim form and general vessel form in the Vijayanagara restricted vessels, there is, particularly among the flange and straight rim vessels, considerable overlap between the two. A single rim form can occur on a number of distinct vessel shape forms, and a single shape form may occur with a number of distinct rim forms. Because of this overlap, the flange and straight rim forms were treated as a single group (n=12,196) in the initial stages of the analysis. They were then subdivided into smaller more internally consistent classes on the basis of vessel shape, rim form, and vessel size. The round rim vessels (n=829) were treated separately because they were more limited in form and appeared to group into a small number of easily definable morphological types (some of which are paralleled by straight rim forms). I will first present the classification of the round rim forms and then turn to the remainder of the restricted vessels.

The vast majority of restricted vessels were constructed using a combination of paddle and anvil and wheel-making techniques, analogous to modern pottery making practices in the region (see Saraswati and Behura 1966; Sinopoli and Blurton 1986). Where sufficient portions of the vessel body are preserved, anvil impressions are readily visible on the vessel interior, though subsequent surface treatment, such as smoothing or polishing, has removed traces of paddle impressions on the exterior surfaces of the vessels. Ware categories and decorative treatment of restricted vessels will be discussed separately, below.

Round rim restricted vessels. A total of 829 round rim restricted vessel sherds were coded during the 1983 through 1986 seasons. Four initial categorical rim classes were defined for these jars (see Figure 4.5). It should be noted at the outset of this discussion that these 829 vessels have been grouped together solely on the basis of rim shape characteristics and do not comprise a meaningful formal or functional class. In fact, two major morphological groups can be defined for these vessels: 1) large broad-necked jars and 2) small narrow shallow vessels. These vessels undoubtedly differed considerably in function. The larger broad-necked jars appear most suited for storage purposes, while the smaller vessels may have been used in serving. These interpretations will be elaborated upon below.

Round rim storage jars. These are large vessels with thick out-turned rims (possibly folded), low necks, and sloping shoulders (round rim form 1 in Figure 4.5). No complete vessels of this form were found, so absolute size or volume cannot be computed, though it appears from rim diametre, rim height and thickness, and wall curvature, that they were quite large. Vessel rim diametres range from 18 to 43 cm., with a mean of 23.5 cm. Vessel walls are steep, with a high mean body angle, and the vessels appear to have been fairly tall. A total of 235 of these vessels were recovered from all areas of the site.

Interpretations of the use of these vessels are somewhat hampered by the absence of complete vessels. The broad low necks of the vessels (mean neck diametre equals 22.7 cm., not even one cm. less than mean rim diametre) makes it unlikely that they were used in water or other transport activities, as spillage would have been high. In addition, their large size would have made them quite heavy when full, and it is unlikely that they would have been moved very much. As a result, it seems likely they were used as immobile storage vessels with their contents removed by use of a scoop of some sort. Ceramic lids could have rested on the vessel rims or cloth covers could have been tied down at the rim base. Many of the rims exhibit some wear along the rim top, indicating that ceramic lids, or lids of other abrasive materials, were placed on them.

These large jars occur in low frequencies in the Vijayanagara ceramic inventory. Several factors may account for this: functionally equivalent forms with different rim shapes and vessel profiles may have existed, or the vessels may have functioned to store seldom or irregularly used materials. Breakage rates as a result of the context of vessel use may also affect the frequencies at which these vessels appear in the archaeological record; if they were non-mobile storage vessels placed in store-rooms or corners, breakage rates and consequent replacement rates would have been low. The existence of functionally equivalent flange or straight rim vessels will be considered below.

The round rim storage jars may be grouped into two formal classes on the basis of rim orientation and rim form. Rim orientation, measured by the attribute rim angle, exhibits a marked bimodal distribution (Figure 4.12). In the first group (RSI, n=115) the rim slopes in, with a mean rim angle of 99^0. The second round rim storage jar vessel form (RS2, n=120) is characterised by an everted rim with a mean rim angle of 67^0. Differences in other measured variables between the two forms were evaluated using the student-t statistical test. The student-t test permits a statistical comparison of sample means from each class, to assess whether or not they could have come from a single population. A 95% probability that vessels are not from the same population was used as the cut-off for retaining the defined classes (for a discussion of this and other statistical tests employed in this analysis, see Runyon and Haber 1972, or other introductory statistics texts). These tests provide a means of assessing the statistical basis of the divisions made along the variable rim angle, and also test what impact rim angle differences have on other aspect of vessel or rim form.

The two round rim storage jar forms differ significantly in rim shape, with the inturning forms having greater mean lip thickness, rim height, and neck height than the everted forms. The latter have significantly larger mean values of the two ratio variables, rim thickness/rim height and rim height/neck height (called relative rim thickness and relative rim height, respectively). The two vessel form variants do not differ significantly in mean rim diametre measures, though do differ in neck diametre, as a result of their differing neck-rim orientation, and in body angle. Summary data for these forms are presented in Table 4.6 and vessel profiles are illustrated in Figure 4.13.

Round rim serving or cooking vessels. The remaining 590 round rim vessels were analysed as single group. The vessels were divided into four categorical rim groups in the field. These groups, illustrated in Figure 4.5, are: (1) normal rims (n=52)—smaller variants of the storage jar rims, with thin lips and rims that thicken on the vessel exterior; (2) everted rims (n=391)—simple forms with rounded lips and no pronounced thickening at the rim; (3) rims which thicken on both the interior and exterior of vessels (n=107) producing a slight directional change at the interior rim top; and (4) ledge rims (n=32)—vessels with vertical necks and rims that turn out sharply to form a horizontal ledge. The remaining eight round rim vessels were unique in form and were classified as 'other' round rim forms.

Like all of the restricted vessel forms, these round rim vessels were produced using wheel-throwing and paddle and anvil techniques. The majority of the vessels were of Plain Ware (n=514). Of these, 323 were black, 154 brown, and 35 red in surface colour. Of the 74 Burnished Ware sherds, 61 were red, 10 black, and 3 brown. Most of the vessels in this group are small in size. A histogram of rim diametre revealed a trimodal distribution (Figure 4.12) and the vessels were accordingly divided into three size groups. The first, containing 490 members (83.1%) includes vessels from 4-16 cm. in diametre, with a mean of 11.5 cm. The second size group, with 75 members, ranges from 17-21 cm. in rim diametre, with a mean of 18.6 cm. Vessels in the third size group (n=29) range from 22-46 cm. in rim diametre, with a mean of 26.7 cm.

The small round rim vessels include all four of the rim forms described above — normal (46), everted (346), both inverted and everted (65), and ledge rims (24), along with several 'other' round rim forms. These small vessels, ranging from 4-16 cm. in rim diametre, were for the most part, too small to have been used in cooking. Some of them may have been used as storage vessels, the smallest of them perhaps used for storing rare spices or other items used in small quantity, while the larger of these vessels may have held condiments or ghee. Overall though, these forms can best be interpreted as serving vessels of some sort, used either as drinking cups or in serving foodstuffs. It is also possible that some of these vessels were used as ritual vessels. A large number of small jars were recovered in excavations of a rock-cut well located near the Mahanavami Diba and appear to have been deposited in ritual contexts (Sinopoli n.d.b); others of the vessels are found in a household shrine area identified in NMQ12 (see Chapter V).

The small round rim vessels vary considerably in rim angle and neck height. The former ranges from 20-90°, with a mean of 64°, and neck height ranges from 44-4.06 cm. with a mean of 1.69 cm. The everted and both inverted and everted vessels were grouped into two groups defined by the distribution of the neck height variable—those with necks less than 2.0 cm. in height (n=346) and those with necks greater than 2.01 cm. (n=42). Finer divisions were suggested by variable distributions but the resultant groups would have had so few few members that these were not made.

The final division of the small round rim vessels by rim form and neck height resulted in the definition of six groups. The most numerous are the low-necked everted rim vessels (RRs1, n=296), followed by low-necked both inverted and everted rim vessels (RRs3, n=50), small normal rim restricted vessels (RRs5, n=52), high-necked everted rim vessels (RRs2, n=32), ledge rim restricted vessels (RRs6, n=24), and high necked both inverted and everted rim jars (RRs4, n=10). Mean attribute values for the six groups are presented in Table 4.7.

An examination of the profiles illustrated in Figures 4.14 and 4.15 reveals that considerable variability exists within the defined groups, particularly among the everted rim vessels (RRs1). Variation within and between the groups does not have any apparent links to vessel function and all of the small round rim vessels may be considered as a single broad functional class (although, as discussed above, the vessels may have been used in a variety of activities). Variation within this class may result from workshop variability, chronological change, or selection by the vessels' users. The small round rim forms have functional and morphological equivalents among the straight and flanged rim vessels (Forms 1-6; see below). The round vs. straight and flange rim classification should not be viewed as hierarchically prior to overall vessel morphology, but, as was noted earlier, was a heuristic device for sorting the rims in the field and for preliminary data summaries.

The remaining 104 round rim vessels are larger in size, ranging from 17 to 46 cm. in rim diametre. The large normal rim vessels have been considered separately above (RS1 and 2). Forty-two of the large vessels have both inverted and everted rims, 45 have everted rims, and 8 have ledge rims. The remainder are 'other' round rims. As noted above, these vessels have been grouped into two size groups—17-21 cm. (n=69) and 22-46 cm. (n=25). These vessels, which also have flange and straight rim counterparts, may have served a variety of functions, as cooking or storage vessels (Figure 4.13b). Mean attribute values by rim form and size classes are presented in Table 4.8 for groups with more than 10 members (RRl1-3). Given the small sizes of these groups no finer divisions were attempted.

Flange and Straight Rim Restricted Vessels. The flange and straight rim vessels are the most numerous and most morphologically diverse of the Vijayanagara vessel forms. Flange rim forms are the most common of the two, with 7885 flange rim sherds measured, as compared to 4296 straight rim diagnostic sherds. Both varieties are found in all areas of the site. As discussed above, the initial division of these vessels into two rim form groups and into finer subgroups was largely a pragmatic decision, providing a framework for sorting the material in the field. The functional or behavioral significance of these morphological rim groups did not influence these decisions.

The classification of the flange and straight rim vessels proceeded in three stages. In the first, I attempted to develop some assessment of vessel shape, independent of rim form and absolute vessel size. As will be discussed in greater detail below, the comparatively small sample of complete or nearly complete vessels and the broad and seemingly continuous range of variability in the limited measures of form available in this data set made this a difficult goal to meet. The shape classes defined below are thus incomplete impositions on the continuous range of variability present in these data. Nonetheless, these classes do provide a useful framework from which to view the data, and do define and highlight significant variability in general vessel shape.

The second stage of the analysis of Vijayanagara restricted vessels was an examination of rim form independent of vessel shape and size. These analyses were oriented towards evaluating the adequacy of the categorical rim form groups defined in the field, and towards attempting to define subdivisions within these groups.

A large number of vessel classes or 'types' were defined for the flange and straight rim vessels, permitting discussion and analysis of spatial distributions of these classes within the Noblemen's Quarter at a number of levels. Distributions to be examined include: the analysis of the distribution of shape classes alone in order to identify activity specific areas; the distribution of the rim shape groups alone; or at the finest level, the distribution of the shape-rim-size groups. In the following discussion, I will first present the vessel shape classification, followed by a description of rim form variants, and the final divisions by shape, rim form, and size.

Vessel shape. The reconstruction of vessel shape is an important, though often extremely difficult, step in the construction of a classification of archaeological ceramics. In ethnographic studies among potters and pottery users, vessel shape is the most frequently cited dimension along which traditional classifications are constructed (Arnold 1985:5). One of the main impediments to an accurate analysis of vessel shape for the Vijayanagara restricted vessels was the paucity of diagnostic sherds which preserved any significant portion of the vessel below the rim and neck. The variable body angle, for example, was measurable for only 978 of the 9353 measured diagnostic flange or straight rim sherds. Variables such as vessel height, maximum diametre, and height to maximum diametre were measurable on even smaller numbers of sherds. No whole or nearly whole restricted vessels were recovered in the East Valley surface collection. Fortunately, a number of reconstructable vessels have been recovered from the Noblemen's Quarter Excavations, particularly in the excavations of the rock-cut well located to the south of NMQ7. Approximately 50 vessels from this and other areas in NMQ have been reconstructed by the DAM.

Although an adequate assessment of vessel shape was not possible given the available data, enough information was available to attempt a crude characterisation of this dimension. While the results of this classification are neither comprehensive nor completely satisfactory, they do provide a useful and meaningful way to group the vessels without ignoring this important dimension entirely. The restricted vessels include shallow open forms with low everted necks and more or less vertical walls. Also found are vessels with high vertical necks, with vessel walls that slope out sharply below the neck. These latter vessels were generally large, with much greater volumes and total vessel height (though smaller rim diametres) than the shallow forms. It is likely that the open shallow vessels were used primarily as cooking or serving vessels or for short term storage of dry foods, while the tall restricted vessels were used primarily for the transport and storage of liquids. Between these two extremes are a variety of other vessel forms.

Each of the shape classes described below exhibits considerable variability in rim form. Consequently, a consideration of rim form alone, which is the most accessible information for this data set, is not adequate to characterise vessel form or function, as might be possible in other, less complex, ceramic inventories.

A number of analyses were undertaken to attempt to define vessels shape classes for the Vijayanagara flange and straight rim vessels, working with the most complete vessels and with randomly selected subsamples of the total sample. Analysis focused on three attributes and one attribute ratio believed relevant to assessing vessel shape, i.e., on attributes that were partial expressions of the dimensions shape. These were: (1) the orientation of the vessel from neck to rim (measured by the attribute 'rim angle', measured on the vessel interior to the nearest 5°); (2) neck height; (3) body angle; and (4) a ratio of rim and neck diametres computed by the equation:

$$\frac{\text{rim diametre-neck diametre}}{2(\text{rim diametre})}$$

This ratio was computed to measure the difference between the two diametres independent of absolute vessel size. Standardised neck height was similarly used to factor out the impact of absolute vessel size on neck height.

The first subsample analysed was the group of 978 diagnostic flange (n=634) and straight (n=344) rim sherds for which body angle was measurable. The distribution of the body angle measure was strongly bimodal with peaks at 40° and 70°. Rim angle was also weakly bimodal, with peaks at 50° and 70°. The other variables were approximately normally distributed. In order to consider the four variables simultaneously, an average linkage-cluster analysis, with Euclidean distances, was conducted on this sample.

Cluster analysis is a technique which groups objects or cases on the basis of similarity coefficients (see Orton 1980: 47-55; Hodder and Orton 1975:173-186; Kintigh and Ammerman 1982). Cases which are most similar are grouped closest together, while those which are most distinctive are far apart. Cluster analyses can proceed in two ways. In some methods, such as single linkage and average linkage cluster analysis, each case begins as a unique cluster and is successively linked into larger clusters on the basis of the degree of similarity between cases, until in the last step of this sequential analysis, all cases are combined into one large cluster. The graphic representation of such analyses is called a dendrogram or tree graph. The second approach, characteristic of k-means cluster analysis, begins with all cases grouped into a single cluster, and subsequently divides them into smaller, and more cohesive groups. These approaches differ also, in the coefficient which is used to measure similarity, and in the precise way in which they group cases. In all methods, a large number of variables can be incorporated into the analysis.

Cluster analysis results do not provide a direct measure of the significance of the clusters defined. Clusters are *always* produced by the analysis, and it is up to the researcher to decide (1) what the different groupings or clusterings of the data mean, and (2) what level of clustering to accept as the final or "best" solution.

For example, a cluster analysis of 100 cases with four variables measured for each, will yield solutions which range from each case forming an individual cluster, to all cases being combined into a single cluster, with a range in between. It is from this intermediate range, of two, four, ten, etc. clusters, that the researcher must choose the solution which best accounts for the data. Ideally, one would wish a solution in which each cluster is meaningfully distinctive from each other cluster, but internally coherent. Choosing the 'right' number of clusters, and the right approach to use is largely a matter of judgement. The coherence of each cluster can be assessed through an 'error of fit' (Sum Squared Error, or SSE) statistic, which is computed as the average distance of each object from the centre of its respective cluster, and expressed as a percentage of the average distance from the centre of the whole group of objects, when treated as a single cluster. The error of fit value is equal to 100% when there is one cluster, and declines as the number of clusters increases. Pronounced changes in the error of fit value between clustering levels indicate that the clustering solution is creating groups that are coherent (Orton 1980:53-54).

In the analysis of the 978 Vijayanagara sherds with body angle measures, the nine cluster solution was selected as best accounting for the data on the basis of change in Sum Squared Error (SSE) values and a visual assessment of vessel profiles by cluster, and motivated by a desire to end up with a limited number of clusters that appeared to vary meaningfully (Figure 4.16). Clusters 5,7,8, and 9 each contained less than five members, and will not be considered in any detail here. Mean attribute values for clusters 1-4, and 6 are presented in Table 4.9.

The statistical significance of inter-cluster differences over all variables was assessed using analysis of variance tests when assumptions of equal variance and normal distributions were met. Otherwise Kruskal-Wallis non-parametric analysis of variance tests were used. Cluster means differed significantly for all attributes but body diametre, for which samples sizes were too small. A discriminant analysis of the clusters revealed that the attributes body angle and rim angle were most important in distinguishing between them (F-statistic=454.34 and 343.57, respectively). The rim-neck diametre ratio was also significant in the discrimination of the nine clusters (F=5.229, signif=.0004), but the neck height variable was not significant. Vessel forms included in each cluster are illustrated in Figure 4.17.

Clusters 1-3 are characterised by relatively steep body angles, though they differ considerably in rim and neck orientation. These vessels lack pronounced outsloping shoulders below the neck and present a broad, more or less open, profile. Cluster 1 contains 318 members and is characterised by low, outsloping necks and vertical walls. These vessels tend to be relatively open and shallow in form, with a mean rim angle of 42^0 and a mean body angle of 74^0. Cluster 2 contains 247 members. These vessels have a somewhat steeper rim angle, with a mean of 60^0, and a more acute body angle of 62^0. The cluster 2 vessels, then, have higher and steeper necks, than cluster 1 vessels. They also tend to be relatively shallow forms, though are somewhat deeper than cluster 1 vessels, and have a more angular profile. In addition, given the relatively small area of the body preserved on many of these vessels, it is likely that some of the vessels may have been quite large overall, reminiscent of the shape of the round rim storage vessels. Cluster 3 contains only 15 members. These are characterised by relatively vertical necks (mean rim angle = 79°), and slightly outsloping body angles (mean = 69°).

Clusters 4 and 6 are characterised by much lower body angles than clusters 1-3 vessels. The vessels slope outward dramatically below the neck, and have globular profiles. Cluster 4 contains 27 members, and is characterised by relatively low, out turning necks (mean rim angle = 36°) and out-sloping shoulders (mean body angle=44^0). Cluster 6 is the largest single cluster, with 363 members. These vessels have steep, vertical necks, with a mean rim angle of 73^0, and sloping shoulders (mean body angle =43^0). Each of the clusters contains vessels which vary considerably in rim diametre, indicating that these 'shape' categories are valid over a wide range of vessel sizes.

The different shape groups defined by the cluster analysis undoubtedly reflect different functional groups of Vijayanagara vessels. The shallow, open necked vessels in cluster 1, seem unlikely to have been used for transport or storage. Their open profile, with rim diametre approximately equal to maximum vessel diametre, would have led to high spillage, and their shallow form would result in relatively small volume. Vessels similar in form to those in clusters 1 and 3, are used today in the region as cooking vessels. Vessels in cluster 2, while also open, are relatively steeper necked and taller than cluster 1 or 3 vessels. As with the latter vessels, it seems unlikely that these vessels would have been efficacious in activities such as water transport or water storage, because of their relatively small volumes, and high spillage and evaporation rates from their broad mouths. Cluster 2 vessels may also have been used in cooking, and could have been used in the storage of dry foodstuffs.

The vessels in cluster 6, with their steep necks and globular bodies, also exhibit considerable range in rim diametre, from ca. 10-36 cm. These vessels appear to have been relatively tall, and of much greater volume than the cluster 1-3 vessels, and would have had maximum diametres two or more times greater than their rim or neck diametres. Such forms would be well suited to storing or transporting water or other liquids. In addition, the larger of these vessels had necks broad enough to be reached into with a hand or scoop, and could have been used in storing dry foodstuffs, such as rice or grains. Cluster 4 vessels had similarly globular bodies, with low and outsloping necks. Given the rarity of these forms in the sample (n=27), they may represent variants of the cluster 6 shape class. Each of the clusters described above includes both flange rim and straight rim forms, and each exhibits a considerable range of variability within the general forms described.

The difficulties of extending the classification of this sample of Vijayanagara restricted vessels to the total sample are threefold. The first problem is the representativeness of this sample and the resultant classification; whether these sherds, which are mostly from excavations in the Noblemen's Quarter, can in any sense be considered as representative of the total range of vessel forms, and what impact other factors, such as vessel size and breakage patterns may have had on this sample. The second, and perhaps more important difficulty with the extension of this classification to all Vijayanagara vessels, is that the most important variable in constructing the groupings—body angle—was not measurable on the remainder of the sample. The other three variables—rim angle, neck height, and the diametre ratio—were measurable. Finally, the adequacy of the classification in accounting for Vijayanagara vessel shape must also be considered. Important variables, such as vessel height, maximum diametre, height to maximum diametre, and so on, could not be measured for the vast majority of vessels in this sample. Certainly, a sample of whole vessels would produce a much more refined classification, and considerably more variability is present in the data than this classification suggests. But the groups defined in this analysis are legitimate as far as they go. Larger samples of whole vessels would only serve to subdivide them further into more refined groups and would not negate the results of this analysis.

Average-linkage cluster analyses of the three variables, rim angle, standardised neck height, and rim-neck diametre ratio, were conducted on the sample of sherds with body angle measures and on four random samples of 400 rims from NMQ3 alone, and from the total NMQ3, NMQ4, and the East Valley samples. In each of the cluster analyses, rim angle was the most important in distinguishing between the clusters, with the other variables playing lesser, though still significant roles. In each case, mean standardised neck height and mean rim-neck diametre ratio variables differed significantly between clusters.

Although rim angle was of primary importance in all five of the three-variable cluster analyses, the breaks at which clusters were defined were not identical in each case. Figure 4.18 illustrates the range of rim angle values in each cluster for each analysis. As a result, in defining classes for the total sample I chose to make the division at a broader level than selected for the cluster analyses. Rim angle was clearly the major variable defining the clusters in all of the analyses, with standardised neck height second in importance, and rim-neck diametre ratio playing a less important, but still significant role. In a discriminant analysis, conducted to evaluate the impact of each variable on the clusters defined by the Random Sample #3 cluster analysis, the F-statistic for rim angle discrimination was 926.09 (signif.=0.00), while that for standardised neck height was 3.37 (signif.=.0030), and for rim-neck diametre ratio was 2.61 (signif.=.0170).

Because of the major impact of rim angle in these analyses I chose to divide the total sample on the basis of that variable alone. The five 'rim angle classes', which will very loosely be referred to as 'shape classes', defined were: (1) less than or equal to 20°, (2) 25 to 35°, (3) 40 to 60° (4) 65 to 90°, and (5) greater than or equal to 95°. These cut-off points were selected by choosing the most frequently defined points in the various cluster analyses. Somewhat different cut-off points could undoubtedly have been selected with satisfactory results and to that extent this classification is arbitary, but still, I feel, yields useful results and is a better solution than ignoring vessel shape entirely, or placing it subsidiary to rim form. These classes certainly do not adequately account for the full range of vessel shape variation among the Vijayanagara restricted vessels, but do provide a partial account of that dimension.

A comparison of the results of the 4-variable cluster analyses with the groups defined by these rim angle cuts on the sample of 978 sherds with body angle measures, may help to evaluate the adequacy and the limitations of this latter approach (Table 4.10). Although there is not complete concordance between the two classifications, most of the clusters do fit primarily into one of the rim angle classes, with a small number of cases placed in an adjacent class. Seventy-eight percent of cluster 1 members belong in the 40.60° degree rim angle class. Cluster 2 is the most problematic, as its members are roughly evenly divided between the 40.60° and 65.90° rim angle classes, with sixty percent of the cases in the 40.60° class and the remainder in the 65.90° class.

Cluster 2 contains, as described above, vessels which on the average, have relatively steep rim angles and slightly outloping body angles. It is likely that these vessels served a number of purposes, and their grouping into two rim angle classes, which as will be discussed below, are interpreted to relate to vessel use, may, to some extent, be representative of the functional variation within the cluster. The three most numerous rim angle classes (25.35°, 40.60°, 65.90°) contain members from two or more of the clusters. This obscures some of the variability represented in the more complete cluster analysis, but still maintains the significant, though not absolute, distinctions between the orientation of the vessels above the neck and their orientation (and presumably, maximum height and diametre) below the neck.

The final classification of Vijayanagara flange and straight rim restricted vessels into rim angle classes has the following frequency distribution (Figure 4.19): 57 vessels (.8%) are in the less than 20° class; 188 vessels (1.9%) are in the 25-35° class; 4590 vessels (47.2%) are in the 40-60° class, 4320 vessels (44.5%) are in the 65-90° class, and 11 (.01%) vessels are in the greater than 90° class.

As with the 4-variable cluster analysis discussed above, tentative functional assignations may be made for the rim angle classes. The 25.35° and 40.60° classes primarily include open necked vessels with large rim and neck diametres relative to maximum diametre. Most of these vessels are fairly shallow, with rounded bases, and would be suited for use as cooking or dry storage vessels. In form, they closely resemble cooking vessels (*gadigeh*) manufactured in the region today. In addition, a number of vessels of this general shape are charred on their base exterior, and less frequently, on the interior, a further support of the cooking vessel interpretation. The 65.90° class with steep near-vertical necks largely includes vessels with out-sloping shoulders and globular bodies. These vessels are generally taller than they are wide, and resemble in form a number of modern water serving, transport, or storage vessels.

Clearly the rim angle classification groups a large number and range of vessels into an overly small number of classes. As will be discussed below, these classes can be refined somewhat by incorporating imformation on vessel size. Given the nature of the sample, however, a number of attributes of major importance to assessing vessel shape cannot be considered. These include such attributes as vessel height, maximum diametre, height to the point of maximum diametre, presence/absence of a base carination, base form (i.e., the 'roundedness' of the base), and so on. Such attributes are measurable on only a handful of the more than 12,000 diagnostic restricted vessel sherds examined from Vijayanagara. As a result, a totally accurate and concise summary of vessel shape is not possible for Vijayanagara ceramics at present.

The limitations of the analysis of vessel shape will necessarily impose major limitations on the effectiveness of analyses of ceramic distribution patterns. Many of the aspects of vessel variability which we would expect to be important in workshop differentiation, social differentiation, and the intended function of a vessel, simply cannot be fully assessed with the available data. Nonetheless, a partial assessment will be attempted in the hope of defining and interpreting spatial patterning in the Vijayanagara ceramics across the site, and in setting guidelines for future research.

Rim shape classification. Along with the measurements made on each of the flange and straight rim diagnostic sherds, the vessels were divided into a number of categorical rim shape groups. These groups, fourteen in all, were defined on the basis of lip thickness and orientation and the point of maximum rim thickness. The rim forms and their designations are illustrated in Figure 4.5. While a few of these forms proved difficult to distinguish from one another in subsequent analyses (particularly some sherds coded as form 2 (inverted lip) and form 4 (both inverted and everted lip) of both flange and straight rim forms) and were consequently reassigned to other groups, these categorical forms for the most part defined consistent and regular rim shape groups. Rims which did not fit into any of the defined groups were coded as 'other'. A variety of attributes were measured on the rims, including lip angle, rim top angle, lip thickness, rim thickness, and rim height. The definitions of these attributes differed slightly between rim forms. The measurements made on each of the rim forms are illustrated in Figures 4.4 and 4.5.

The analysis of these data had two goals. The first was to quantify and evaluate the differences between the predefined rim groups. The second goal was to look for significant morphological divisions within those broadly defined rim groups in order to subdivide the rims into more internally consistent rim shape groups. Given the scale of Vijayanagara and of pottery production at the site, as well as the large numbers of ceramics analysed and the tremendous variability within them, the decision of how finely to subdivide the vessels took on considerable importance. I wanted neither to obscure significant variability in the data by defining too few groups, nor to create a classification so fine-grained that it would become totally impossible to work with or to abstract meaningful patterning from. I therefore chose to compromise between these two extremes in accordance with the primary aims of this research, that is, to define rim shape groups that are visibly distinctive and might easily have been identifiable by pottery users.

Because of the fragmentary nature of our data, archaeologists are often limited to studying and classifying pottery through its rims. A quantitative study of rim shape presents a number of hazards for archaeologists, in part because we see the rims from a very different perspective than the vessels' users. That is, we typically look at sherds in cross-section while the users of whole vessels would have observed rims from the outside and/or above. The analysis of cross-sectional form does provide useful information on construction techniques, vessel function (e.g., if and how a lid could have been set on the vessels, whether materials could have been poured from the vessel, and so on) and on chronological changes in rim morphology. Rim shape is however, probably far less important to the construction of indigenous classifications of vessels than are other dimensions, such as general vessel shape and proportion and vessel size and, as a result, must be carefully evaluated when the analysis is oriented toward reconstructing such 'meaningful' systems.

In all cases the analysis of rim form variants followed a similar procedure. First, a descriptive summary of the data was generated by the computer (using the MIDAS statistical program at the University of Michigan; other statistical programs such as SPSS or SAS are also available for main frame and personal computers). Descriptive statistics and distributions which were examined include variable means and standard deviations; histograms of attribute distributions were produced, and the general rim form groups were compared. Second, scatter plots and histograms were produced to examine inter-variable relations for all pairs of variables, and correlation coefficients were calculated. In some cases, individual sherds were reassigned to different rim groups if it was determined at this stage that they had been coded incorrectly in the field or in entering the data into the computer. The distributions of a number of ratio variables were similarly examined. The ratio variables included: (1) lip thickness/rim thickness ('relative rim thickness'); (2) rim height/neck height ('relative rim height'); (3) rim thickness/rim height; (4) lip thickness/rim height; (5) rim angle/lip angle; and (6) lip angle x rim height.

Where clear modes were evident in the distribution of a variable or variable ratio, these were used to subdivide the data into smaller groups which were examined in a manner similar to that outlined above, and were compared to each other using various tests of significance, such as analysis of variance or appropriate non-parametric tests. If no clear patterns were evident in single or bivariate distributions, multivariate approaches such as principal components analysis were applied in order to look for patterning manifest only through more complex variable interrelations. The distribution of principal component scores were plotted and examined to look for multimodal distributions. If these approaches yielded no clear divisions along which rims could be sorted, the original cases were left as coded.

In all stages of the analysis I made extensive use of rim profile drawings to get a visual assessment of the groups being defined quantitatively. All sherds remained at the site of Vijayanagara after measurement, so remeasurement or reevaluation of the ceramics themselves was not possible. Through examining drawings, some statistically valid groups were rejected because they did not appear to yield visibly satisfactory divisions. Approximately one-tenth of the ca. 16,000 diagnostic sherds measured were drawn, although not all of the drawings appear in this volume. Decisions based on examinations of profiles are clearly based on judgement, and other researchers might not have made the same decisions that I did. Rechecking statistical results against drawings of the vessels themselves provides an important complement to, and test of, the statistical approaches which convert the actual artefacts under study to an abstract numerical quantity.

No single variable or variable ratio proved to be the one which characterised or subdivided all of the rims. Each form was treated independently and subdivided on the basis of the variable or variables which 'worked' best. Detailed information on the approaches and the results of this classification of Vijayanagara rim forms will not be presented here. Table 4.11 summarises information on the approaches used for each rim class, the basis of the typological divisions, and the forms defined. In this section, I will describe in summary form the flange and straight rim variants.

A total of 20 rim form groups were defined for the flange and straight rim restricted vessels, incorporating 10,688 sherds. This number is less than the total sample of 12,181 because the defining attributes for individuals forms were not always measurable. For example, in cases where lip angle measures were used to subdivide the rims, only rims measured after 1983 could be used. The rim groups are designated by two letters and a number (Table 4.12). The first letter, 'S' or 'F', indicates whether they are straight or flange rims. The second letter denotes the categorical designation for the rim form (N—normal, I—inverted, E—everted B—both inverted and everted, T—thickened, L—ledge, G—bulging). The number designates the variant of the larger category, if more than one variant was defined. Summary information on the number of rims per group, the methods and/or variables used to classify them, and the defining characteristics of the groups are presented in Table 4.11. Profile drawings of rims in each of the groups are illustrated in Figures 4.20 and 21.

The rim groups are widely disparate in size. Group SN, for example, contains 2179 members, while FT2 contains only 77. In this case, the large size of SN results from the fact that variability in this rim form is in large part dependent upon variation in vessel shape and neck orientation and is thus accounted for by the vessel shape classification. Since no clear modalities were apparent among the normal straight rims in any other attributes, no finer divisions could be securely made. Divisions within categorical groups were made on the basis of bimodal or polymodal distributions of variable ratios or principal component scores, and the resulting bounds between forms are seldom neat or absolute. The forms defined may be perceived as centering on but varying more or less widely around a mean.

Final classification: Vessel shape, rim form, and vessel size. The next stage of the classification of Vijayanagara flange and straight rim vessel forms was the addition of vessel size divisions to the shape and rim classifications disscussed above. Vessel size is most effectively measured by total volume, a measure not calculable for the vast majority of vessels in this sample. A second approach to calculating vessel size is to control for shape as much as possible and examine the distribution of various diametre and height attributes. For the Vijayanagara sample, the most accessible measure of size within the shape or 'rim angle classes' is the attribute rim diametre. Rim diametre, which was measured on the rim exterior to the nearest centimetre, is, however, affected by rim form; a rim which thickens on the exterior or slopes outwards, will have a somewhat greater diametre than a rim which does not thicken, even if the orifice opening and overall vessel size of the two vessels are the same. I therefore chose to examine size distribution by rim group within shape classes. The rim groups used were the 11 large categorical groups from which rim variants are defined, rather than the individual variants themselves. Histograms of rim diametre were examined for each of these 11 broad rim groups by rim angle class. Several histograms were produced for each group, with varying interval widths and midpoints. Interval width was always 2 cm, or greater to minimise the effect of measuring biases and sherd irregularities on variable distributions. Where clear modalities were evident, these were used to to define size classes. For some of the rim groups, such as the bulging flange rims, which clearly represented a coherent morphological group, size was plotted for the total sample without dividing by rim angle class.

Size groups defined on the basis of these distributions are presented in Table 4.13. As with all of the Vijayanagara ceramic analyses, size modes were not as clear or as easily definable as I would have liked and this is not a neat classification. In some cases, size distributions were normally distributed with a small number of cases at the extremes of the distribution. These extremes were noted as outliers and were classed separately. The groups with strongly bimodal or polymodal distributions are indicated by an 's' in the last column of Table 4.13, while those with weaker or more tenuous size divisions are indicated by a 'w'.

The simple intersection of the size, shape, and rim form classes results in the definition of more than 100 categories. That classification is both unwieldy to work with, and so fine-grained that many of the categories contain fewer than 30 members. The final stage in this analysis was, therefore, to create a manageable set of categories which were sufficiently numerous and which differed significantly and meaningfully. This involved grouping some small classes which were basically similar in form and, presumably, in function, such as the small diameter straight everted rim forms. In addition, groups with less than 20 members were discarded from the analysis.

The resulting classification contains 47 flange and straight rim vessel forms, differentiated on the basis of vessel shape, rim form, and vessel size. Information on each of these groups is summarised in Tables 4.14 and 4.15, which organise the vessels into six general morphological, or 'vessel-use', groups. I expect that overall vessel shape is largely determined by the intended function of the vessel, and thus encodes information on that aspect of ceramic use. Vessels of the same basic shape may vary in size and consequently in use, from individual serving vessels to large cooking pots, for example. Rim form has some impact on vessel function, as has been noted earlier, but is primarily a characteristic that is not functionally constrained.

Each of the dimensions considered in this analysis—shape, size and rim form—is limited by some broad constraints, imposed by a vessel's function. Within these constraints, a broad range of variation is to be expected. Although it cannot be considered in this analysis, it should be remembered that the 'intended function' of a vessel, or that function for which it is best suited, is not necessarily the one for which a vessel is used in all contexts. In more familiar terms, an aluminum pot can easily and effectively serve as a pot for cooking various foods, a pot placed under a leaky roof, a storage vessel, or a wide variety of other purposes, and may be put to a number of other uses once it rusts or cracks or otherwise can no longer serve its original purpose. Similar flexibility is readily observed at water pumps throughout rural India, where a large variety of vessels, some well suited to the purpose and some not, are brought to be filled with household water. Such patterns must certainly have obtained in the past as well. In the Vijayanagara ceramics traces of plaster on sherds indicate their use as architectural fragments and as containers for building materials. For the most part, however, the varying uses to which vessels may have been put cannot be determined from this sample. I merely bring it up to stress that the functional inferences presented below are not intended to be a complete catalogue of the full range of uses of these vessels.

With that caveat aside, the 47 restricted vessel forms described in Tables 4.14 and 4.15 can be grouped into six basic vessel-use classes. In the first group (classes 1-6, n = 363), designated as RV1, are small relatively shallow vessels which could have been used in serving individual portions of food or drink or in some other limited function, such as holding condiments or spices (Figure 4.22). The second group, RV2, (classes 7-19) consists of open, relatively shallow vessels of medium size (ca. 16-26 cm. in diameter). Note that since size classes were defined separately for each rim-shape group there is some overlap between the size groups among different rim forms, and my use of the words 'small, medium, or large' is primarily for ease of presentation. These vessels have low out-turning necks and steep body angles, and are typically as wide or wider than they are high (Figures 4.22 and 4.23). They are associated with a variety of rim forms, and, with 4052 sherds, are the most common class in the Vijayanagara ceramic sample. Such vessels would be best suited for use as cooking vessels, with secondary uses in food preparation and the short-term storage of dry foods. The third group, RV3, (classes 20-25, n=370) are larger variants of group 2, and were probably similarly used for cooking or storage. They range from 23-45 cm. in diametre, and are shallow, relatively open vessels (Figure 4.24).

The fourth vessel group (classes 26-30, n=625), RV4, contains small vessels (rim diametre equals 7-18 cm.) with more or less vertical necks and globular bodies. These vessels were probably used as serving vessels or for water transport, as the small orifice would minimise spillage (Figure 4.25). The fifth group, RV5, (classes 31-42) is the second most numerous of the functional classes with 2799 members, and contains larger vertical necked vessels ranging from 14-26 cm. in diametre. These vessels were probably used for the storage of water and/or other comestibles. The smaller vessels in the group may have been used for transport as well, though it is expected that most of them would have had a quite large overall volume (Figures 4.25-27). The sixth group of vessels, RV6, (classes 43-47, n = 351) contain larger vertical-necked vessels ranging from 21-33 cm. in rim diametre (Figure 4.27). These vessels were probably used for storage.

The 47 groups defined above contain a total of 8650 rims from the Noblemen's Quartern (compounds NMQ3-NMQ12), the East Valley, and the Islamic Quarter (1984-1986 samples). The remaining rims from those areas were grouped into shape-rim-size categories which contained fewer than 30 members. They were not considered useful for much of the subsequent analyses and in many cases appeared to represent extremes on one end or another of a distribution rather than a legitimate vessel class. These rims are incorporated into the analysis of ceramic distribution at the level of vessel shape and rim form, while vessels from NMQ1 and NMQ2 are primarily incorporated at the level of rim form.

OTHER VESSEL FORMS

A variety of other Vijayanagara vessel forms were also identified, including Coarse Ware trays and well linings, and water pipes, pedestal bases, and nosed lamps. Many of these forms occurred in very low frequencies and will be only briefly described. Other forms which occurred as unique examples will not be considered here.

Coarse ware vessels. A total of 1434 Coarse Ware sherds were recovered from Vijayanagara. The vast majority of these were body sherds or small unmeasurable rim fragments. Coarse Ware vessels have wall thicknesses of greater than 1.0 cm. and a distinctive paste with high percentages of organic and coarse sand inclusions. Three major Coarse Ware vessel types are identifiable: (1) ring well linings, (2) cooking stoves, and (3) large open trays or vats (Figure 4.28). Coarse Ware forms may also have been used as decorative architectural fittings of some sort, but more complete or in situ specimens are needed to evaluate this. All of the Coarse Ware artifacts were hand-built. Most are red or light brown in color, sometimes with dark inner cores, indicating that they were fired in oxygen-rich environments, possibly in open firings or on the outer edge of a large oven firing.

The ring well linings are large open cylinders, ranging to 60 + cm. in diameter and between 15-20 cm. in height. These pieces thicken at the top and bottom and have flat horizontal lips, and were stacked one atop the other to line wells and drains. A large number of ring well sherds were found to the north of NMQ3 (Unit NQ3.7). A well was later identified in that area. A similar well was observed in profile in the administrative center of the city, southwest of the Mahanavami Diba. The well was a large rubble-lined feature with an interior earthen-ware lining. The ring well pieces rested pieces rested one on top of another and extended a depth of at least two meters below the ground surface. Small numbers of ring well fragments were recovered from the Noblemen's Quarter and East Valley.

The second Coarse Ware vessel form identified is a three-sided cooking stove. This form is most readily identifiable by the characteristic triangular knobs located along the rim top on which cooking vessels were set. Two nearly complete stoves were recovered in excavations in front of NMQ1. They stood ca. 20 cm. high and were horseshoe shaped with two to three knobs along the rim. Lit coals would have been placed inside on the base of the vessel and a cooking pot placed above it. Several of the cooking stove sherds exhibited traces of burning on the interior. The Vijayanagara stoves differ considerably in form from their modern counterparts produced in Kamalapuram, which are square in form and much larger than the archaeological examples.

A small number of rims from very large Coarse Ware vessels were recovered. These vessels included large trays and holemouth jars or vats. The trays range in diametre from 40-60 cm. These vessels may have been used in a variety of household or industrial task—such as for long-term storage of large amounts of foodstuffs or other goods, as large mixing bowls, as troughs or drinking vessels for animals (perhaps similar to the modern 'cow pots'; see Junker 1985), and so on. Other unidentifiable Coarse Ware sherds were recovered; some with incised decorations. Some of these pieces may have served as the upper portion of ring wells which extended above the ground surface, or as some other sort of architectural fittings

Water pipes. Earthenware water pipes were found in small numbers in all sample areas except for the Islamic Quarter. A total of 110 water pipe sherds were identified, with 88 of these from NMQ4. They are long cylindrical vessels with high thin flanged rims (Figure 4.29). Before the discovery of some large sherds of this form a number of water pipe rims were mistakely coded as flange rim restricted vessels. Those that were illustrated were removed from that sample, though undoubtedly a few were incorrectly included in the restricted vessel sample. The Vijayanagara earthenware water pipes, like their contemporary counterparts *(haranagiley* in Kannada) were used to drain water from the flat-roofed structures during the brief summer monsoon. Only two water pipe sherds were recovered in the East Valley, indicating that the predominant architectural forms in the area were not the substantial flat-roofed structures known from the Noblemen's Quarter area.

Pedestalled Base Vessels (Incense Burners). These vessels, typically constructed in two sections, have high cylindrical bases, with a cup-shaped opening above them. They take a variety of more or less ornate forms, some of which are illustrated in Figure 4.30. It is likely that these vessels were used as incense burners, or perhaps, as lamps. Some 60 pedestalled vessels were examined.

Nosed Lamps. Eight nosed lamps sherds were recovered at Vijayanagara (Figure 4.31). These are low vessels with diametres of 8-10 cm., and elaborate appliqué and incised decorations on the exterior. One of the vessels appeared to have had a handle.

Gaming Pieces. Probable earthenware gaming pieces at Vijayanagara take two forms. The first are simple worked sherds with rough or rounded edges. These are 2-3 cm. in diametre and are found in low frequencies in all areas of the site. The worked sherds may have been used as tools or abraders of some sort, but did not appear to be associated with any other materials or activity areas. The second type of earthenware gaming pieces are small conical pieces with flat bases (Figure 4.31). These pieces stand two to three cm. high. Most of the conical gaming pieces I observed were recovered in excavations in the king's palace area.

Spouts. Approximately 60 spouts were recovered from all sample areas. These are typically on red Burnished Ware vessels, and were located on the vessel body (see Figure 4.31). Holes were cut into the vessel wall and the spouts were attached, after the completed vessels had dried slightly, but before firing. It is expected that the spouts were most common on the bulging flange rim vessels (form 30), which have been interpreted as water serving vessels.

CONCLUSIONS

The classification of Vijayanagara ceramics presented in this chapter is certainly open to questioning and refinement. As archaeologists we hope that our subjects divided their material world into neat typological compartments which we can readily assess and replicate. The potters of Vijayanagara were not so compliant; or, possibly, they were over-compliant, and produced large numbers of slightly variable categories, not easily identifiable archaeologically. The vessel categories that I have defined are neither neat nor, I fear, easily replicable. I have, however, tried to be explicit and logical in their definition and presentation, in order that these groups might encompass meaningful variability in Vijayanagara ceramic forms. The fragmentary nature of the sample necessarily imposes some profound limitations on the analysis. This chapter, therefore, is not intended to present the final classification of Vijayanagara ceramics, but, rather, is a 'working classification', which will be refined with larger samples of more complete vessels, improved chronological control, and an assessment of its usefulness in further analyses. A partial assessment is presented in Chapters V and VI below.

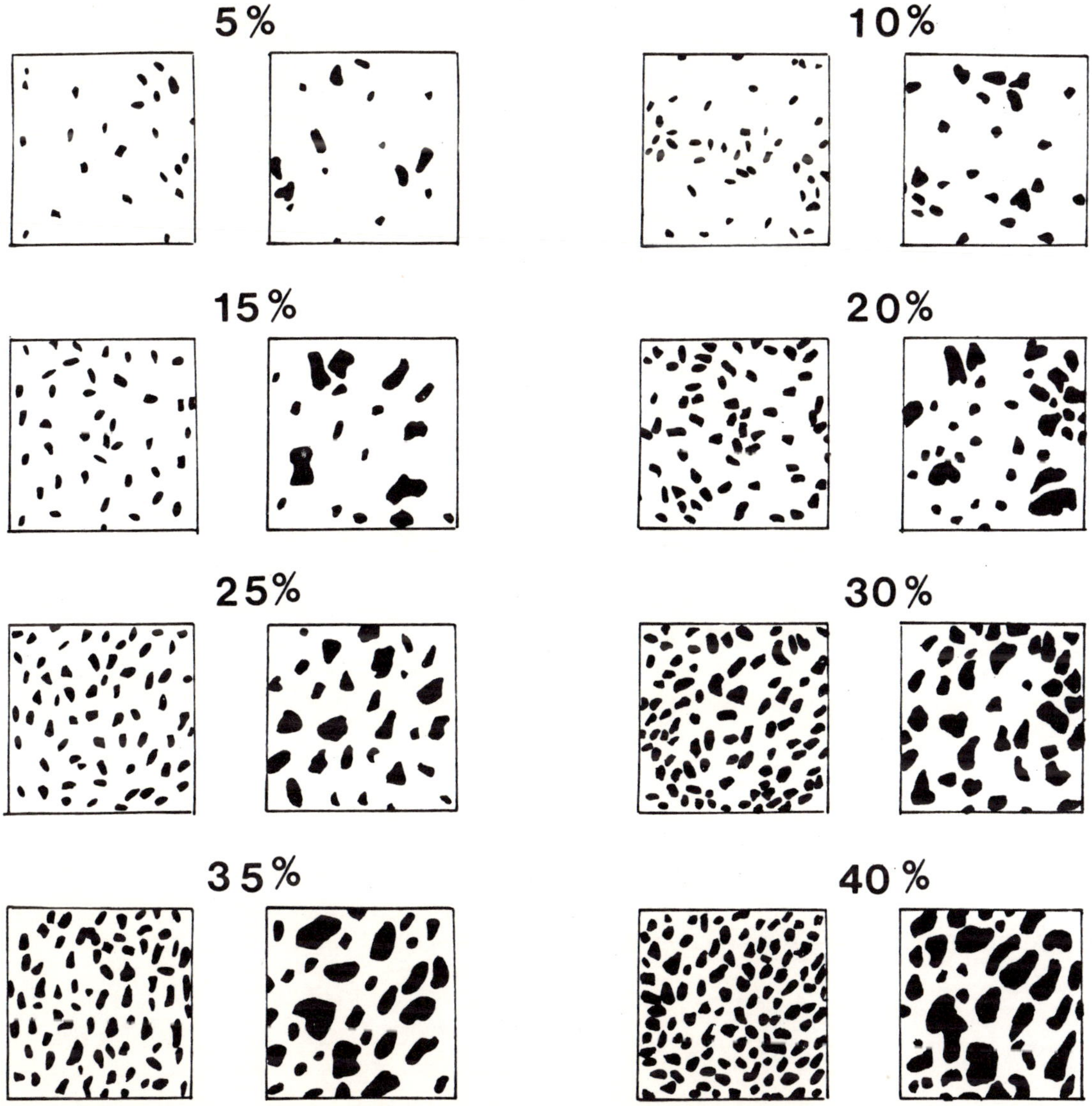

Figure 4.1 Graph of Geological Densities

LAMPS

A. Flat Rim, Flat Base

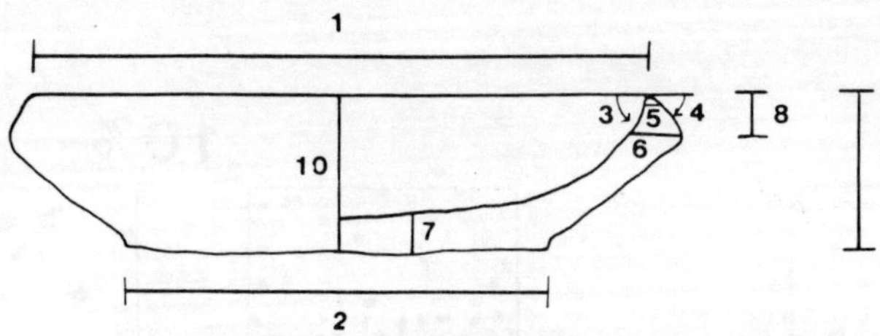

1. Rim diameter
2. Base diameter
3. Rim angle
4. Base angle
5. Lip thickness
6. Rim thickness
7. Base thickness
8. Rim height
9. Base height
10. Vessel height

B. Round Rim, Round Base

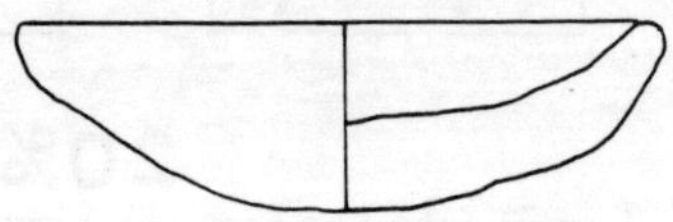

SHALLOW BOWLS

A. Normal Rim

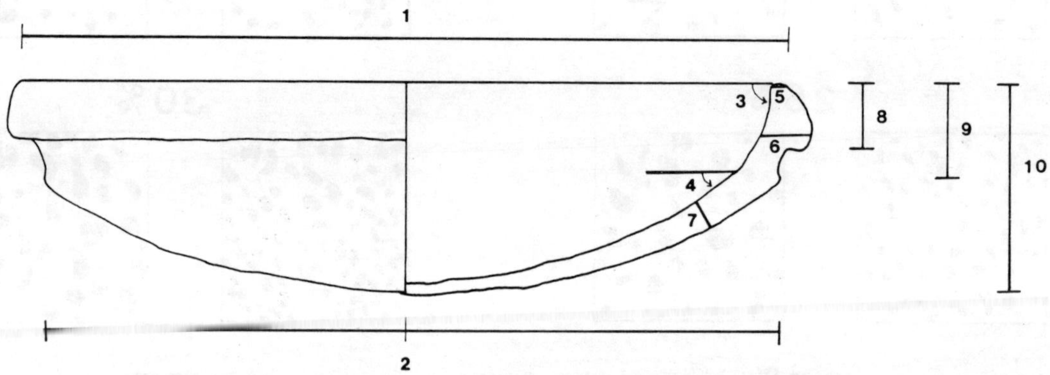

B. Everted Rim

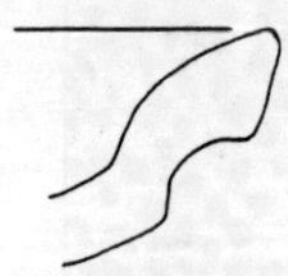

1. Rim diameter
2. Base diameter
3. Rim angle
4. Base angle
5. Lip thickness
6. Rim thickness
7. Base thickness
8. Rim height
9. Base height
10. Vessel height

(all measurements in cm., angle measures to the nearest 5°)

Figure 4.2 Variables Recorded Lamps and Shallow Bowls

OTHER BOWLS

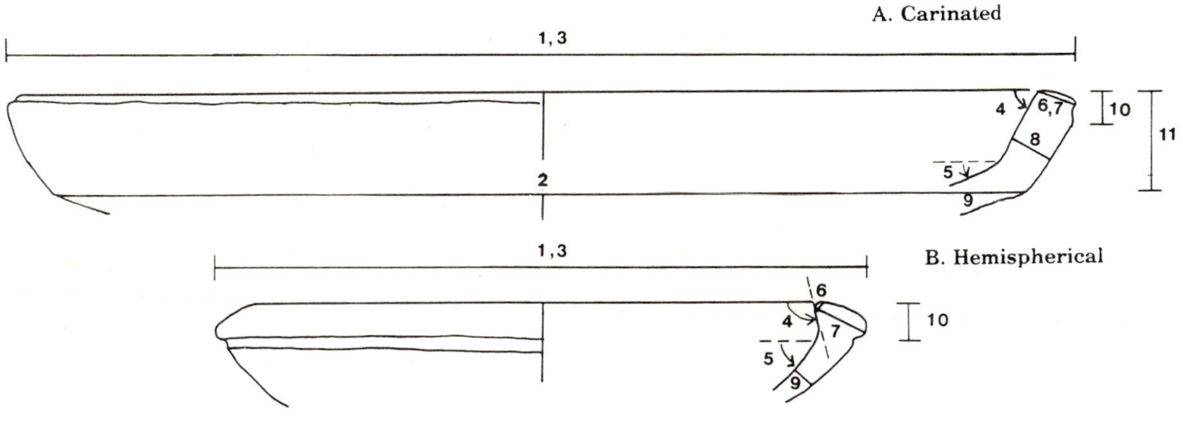

1. Rim diameter
2. Base diameter
3. Maximum diameter
4. Rim angle
5. Base angle
6. Lip thickness
7. Rim thickness
8. Side thickness
9. Base thickness
10. Rim height
11. Base height
12. Vessel height (not shown)

ROUND RIM RESTRICTED VESSELS

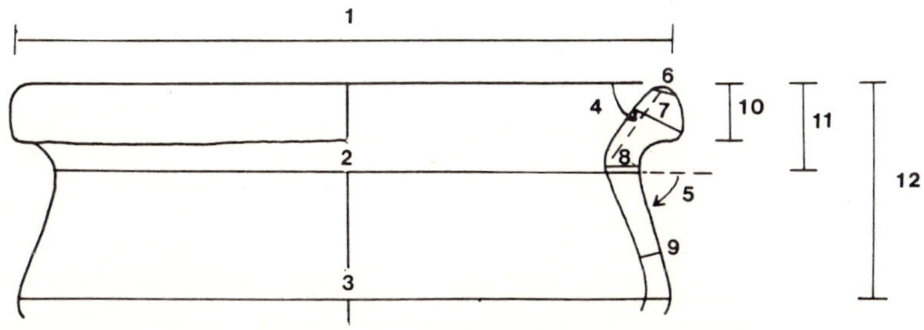

1. Rim diameter
2. Neck diameter
3. Maximum diameter
4. Rim angle
5. Body angle
6. Lip thickness
7. Rim thickness
8. Neck thickness
9. Body thickness
10. Rim height
11. Neck height
12. Maximum body height

Figure 4.3 Variables Recorded on Other Bowls and Round Rim Restricted Vessels

STRAIGHT RIM RESTRICTED VESSELS

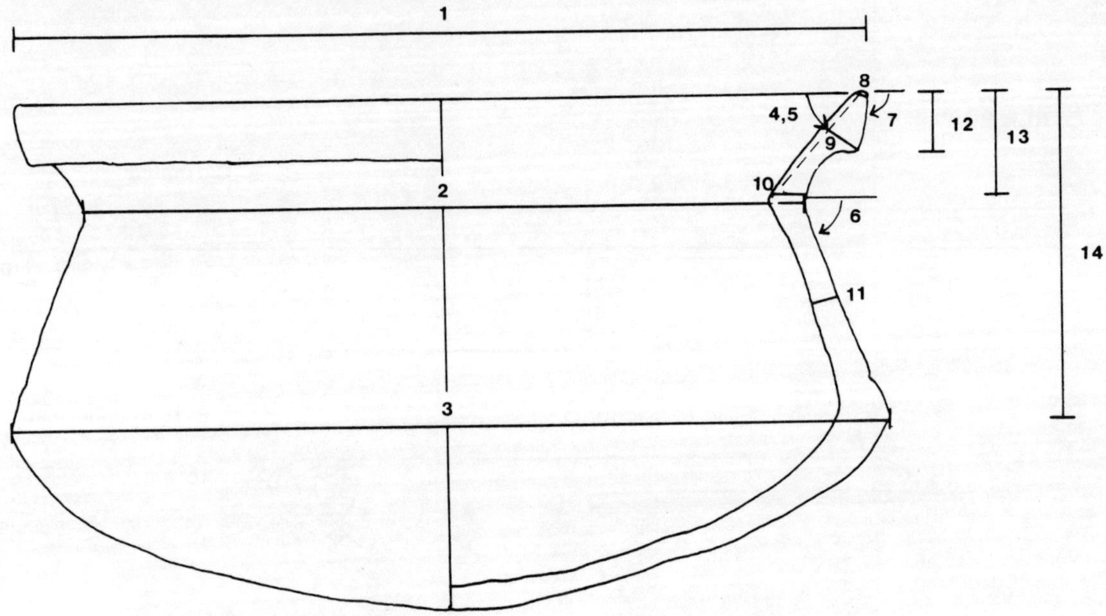

FLANGE RIM RESTRICTED VESSELS

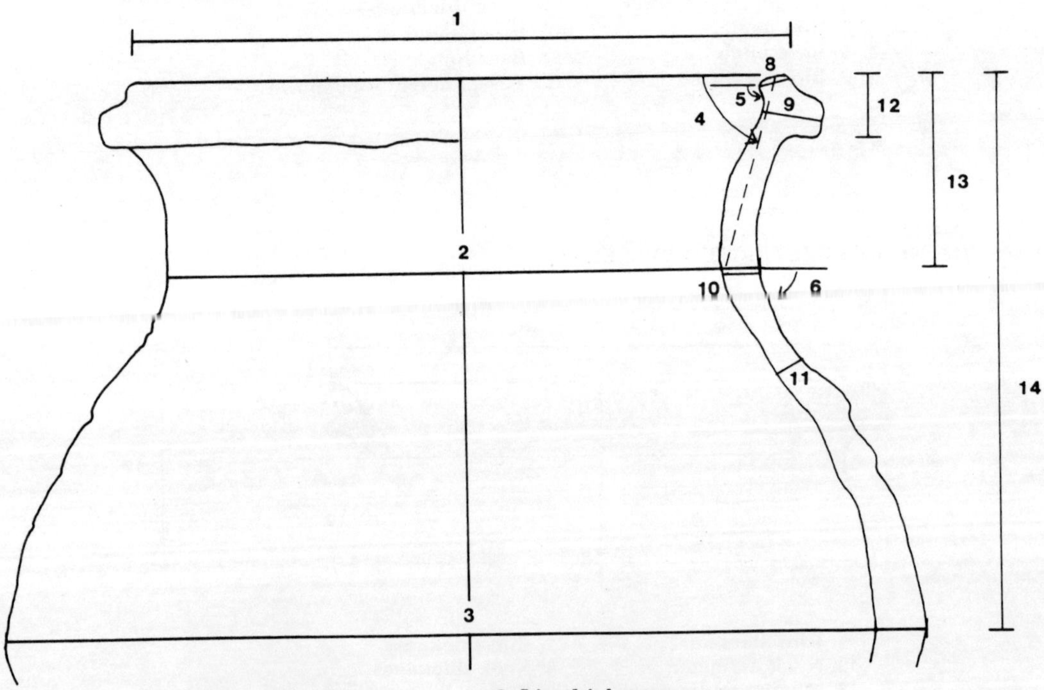

1. Rim diameter
2. Neck diameter
3. Maximum diameter
4. Rim angle
5. Lip angle
6. Body angle
7. Rim top angle (straight rim only)
8. Lip thickness
9. Rim thickness
10. Neck thickness
11. Body thickness
12. Rim height
13. Neck height
14. Maximum body height

Figure 4.4 Variables Recorded on Flange and Straight Rim Restricted Vessels

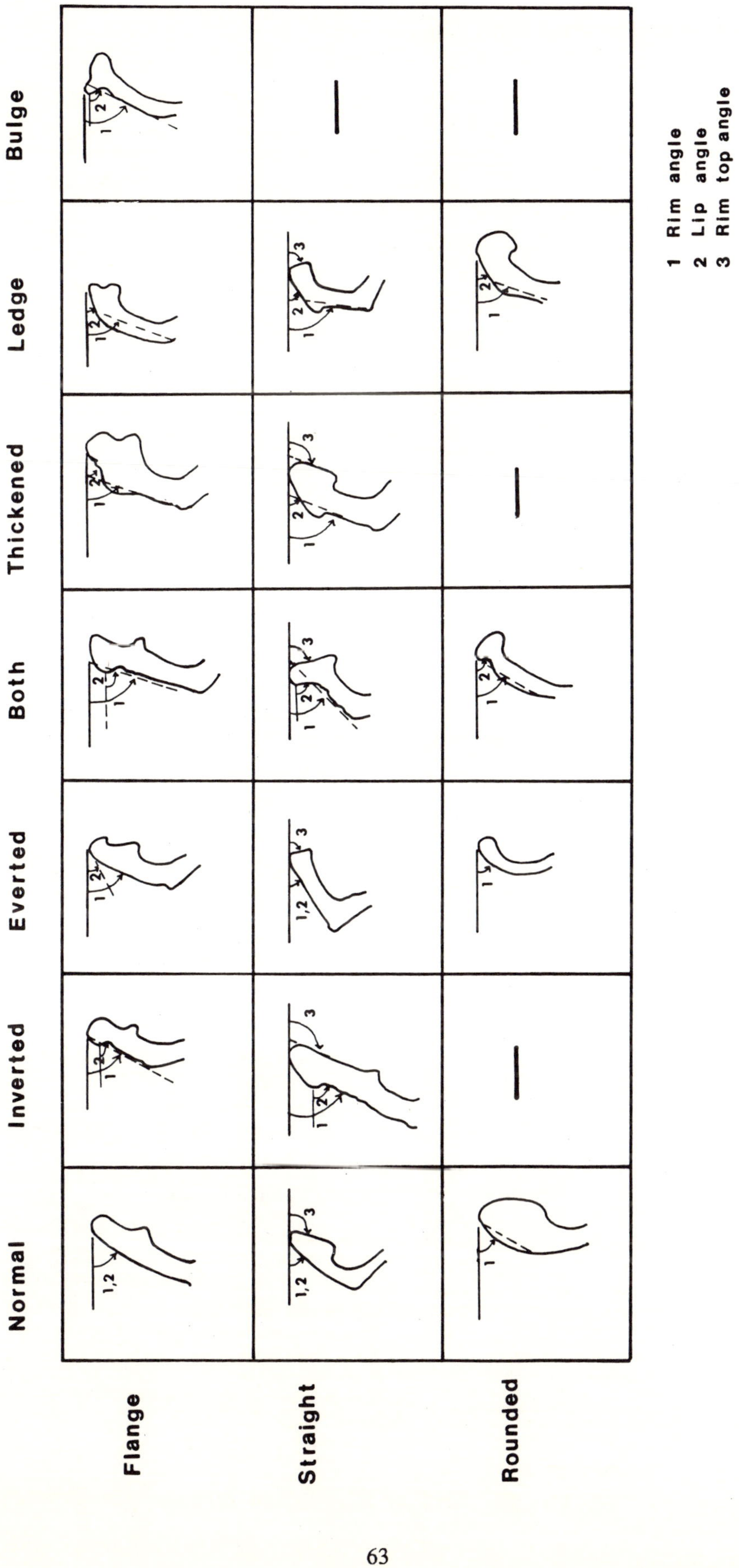

Figure 4.5 Variables Recorded on Restricted Vessel Rim Forms

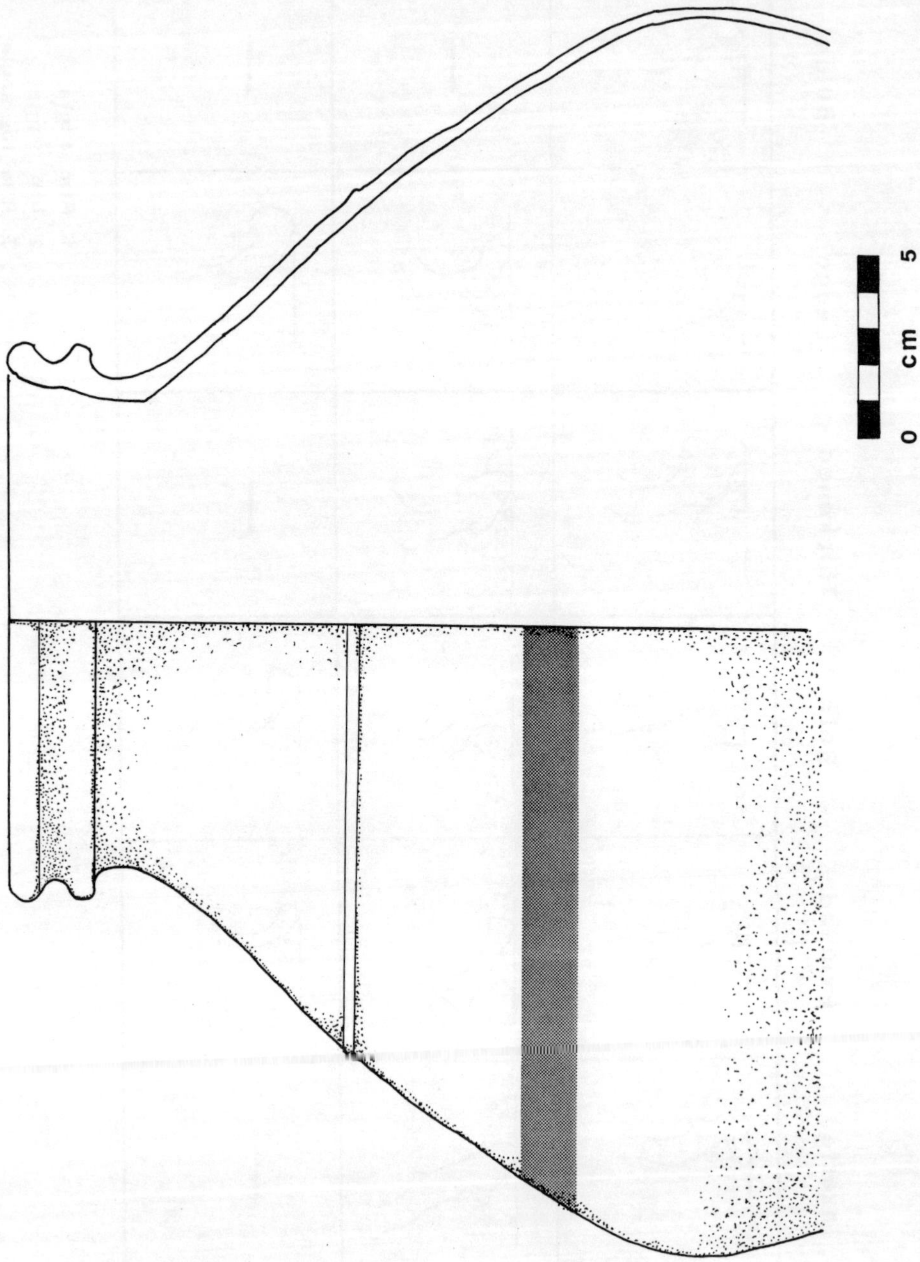

Figure 4.6 Vijayanagara Painted Vessel

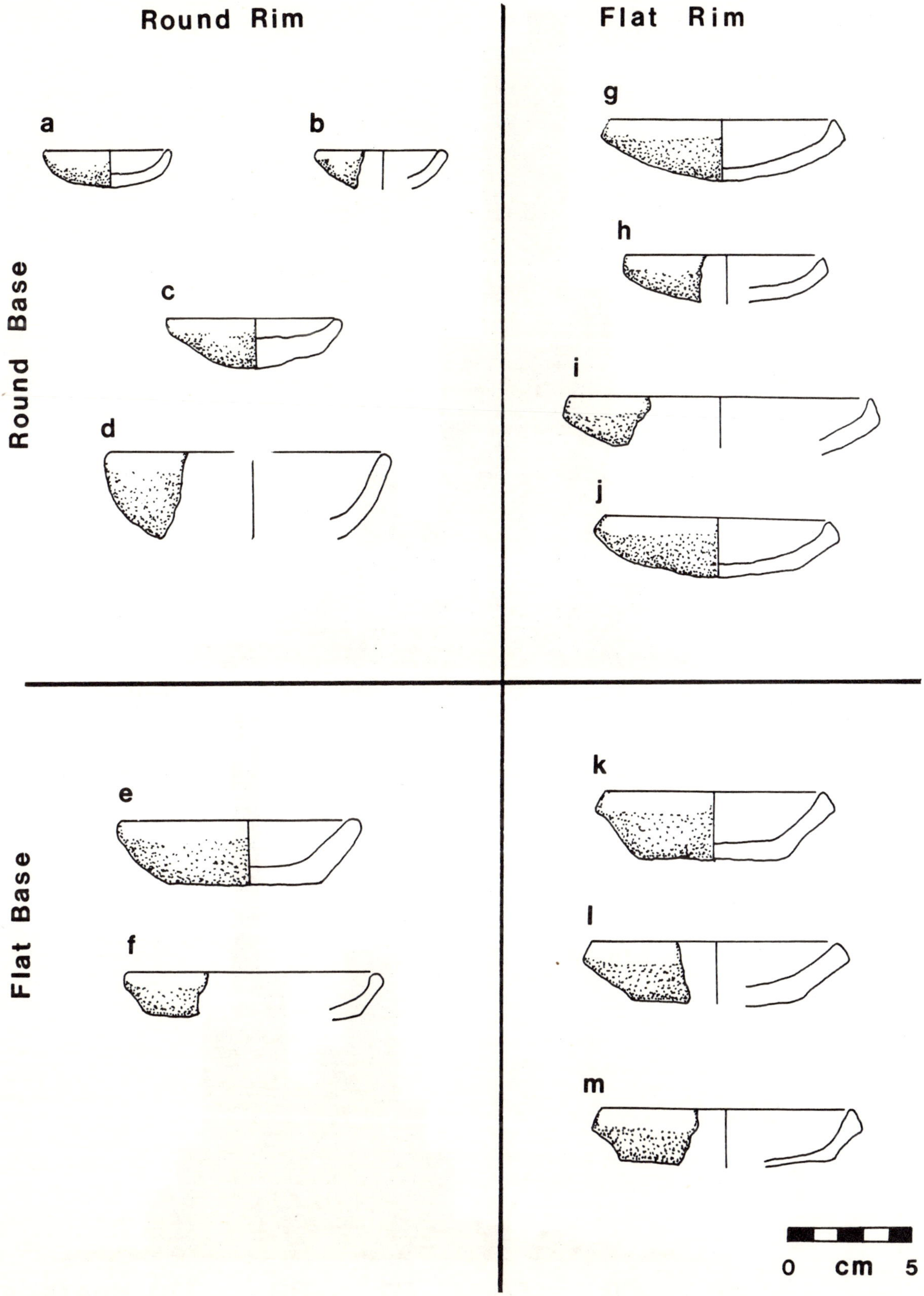

Figure 4.7 Vijayanagara Lamp Forms

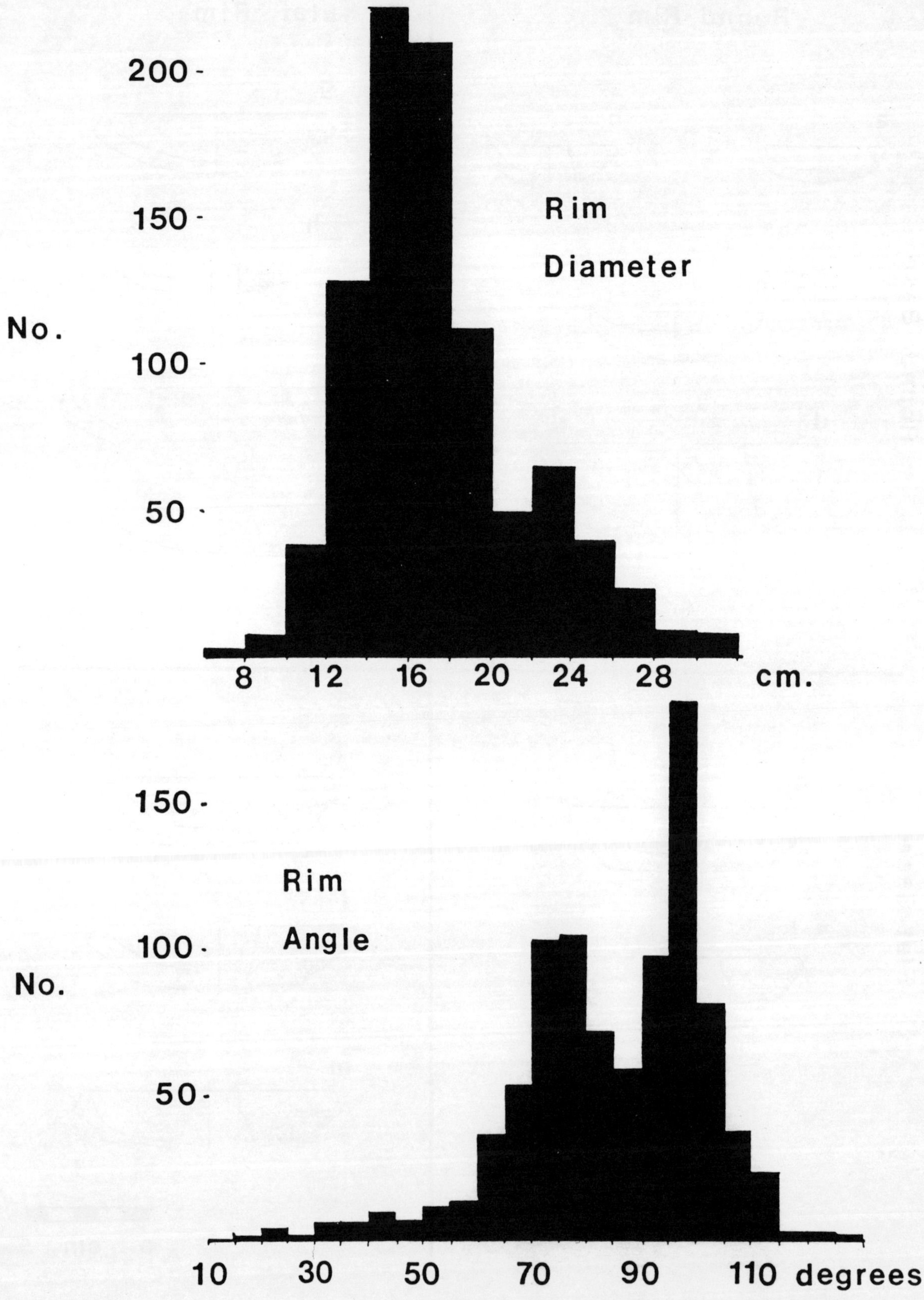

Figure 4.8 Vijayanagara Shallow Bowl Histograms: a. Rim Diametre b. Rim Angle

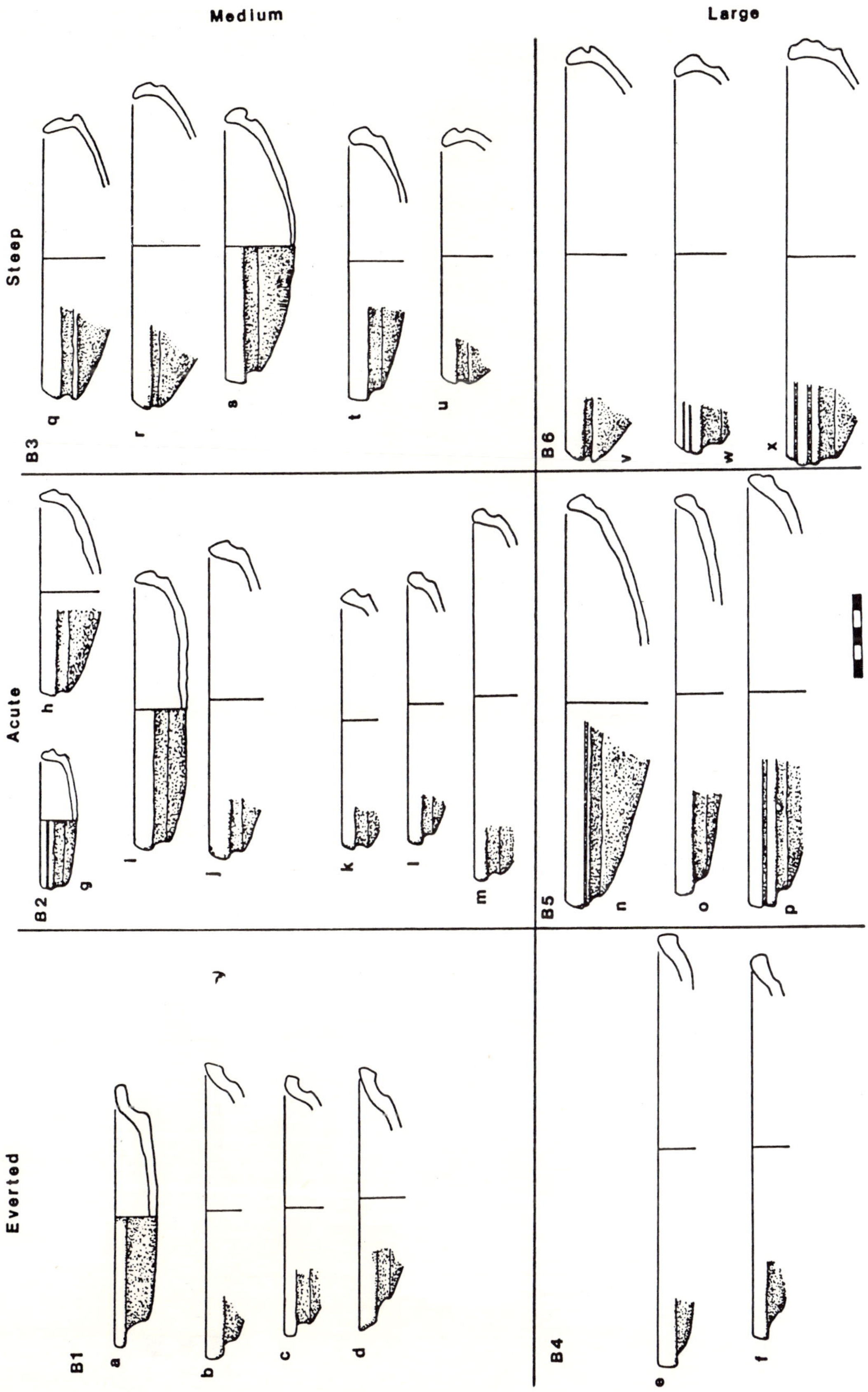

Figure 4.9 Vijayanagara Shallow Bowl Forms

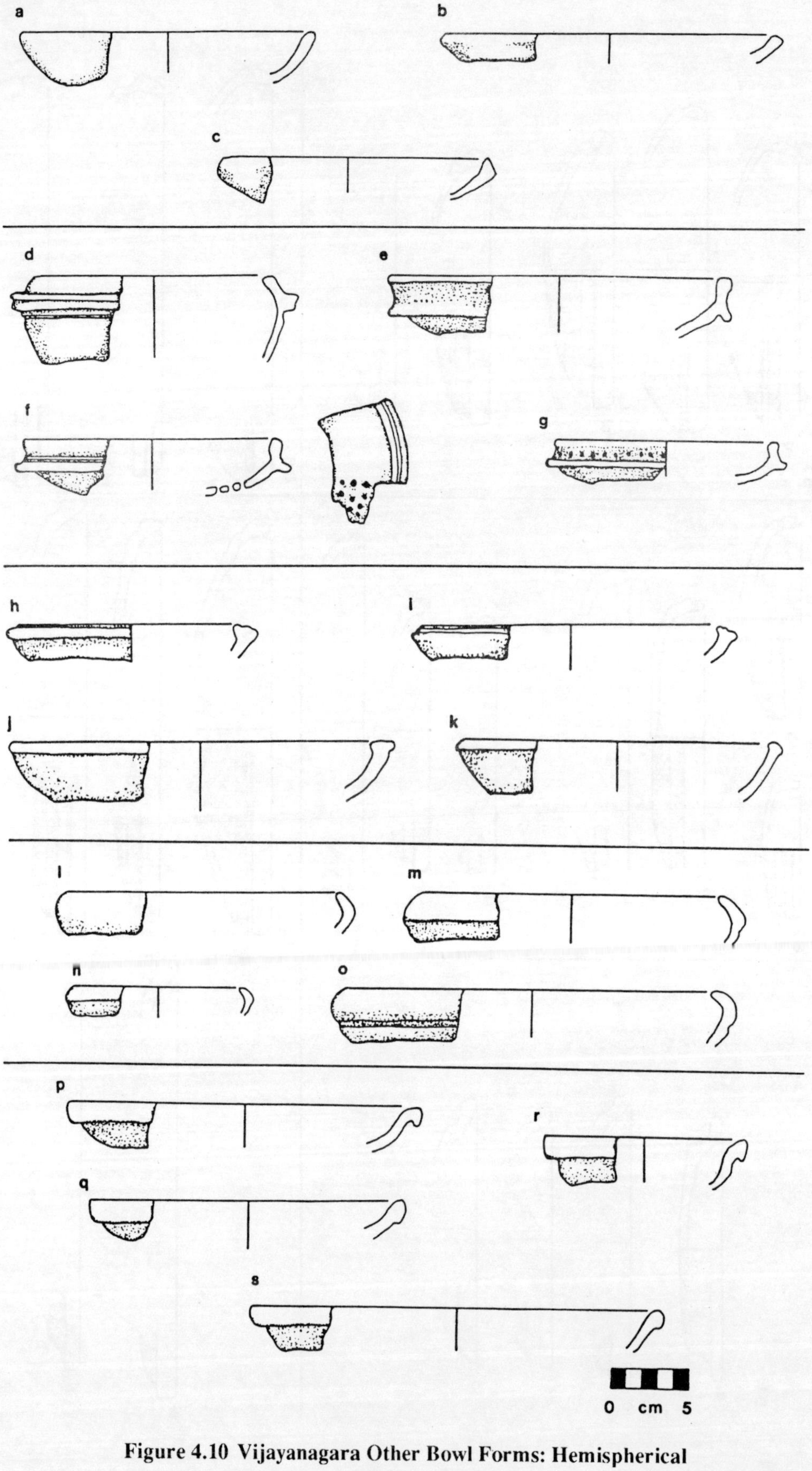

Figure 4.10 Vijayanagara Other Bowl Forms: Hemispherical

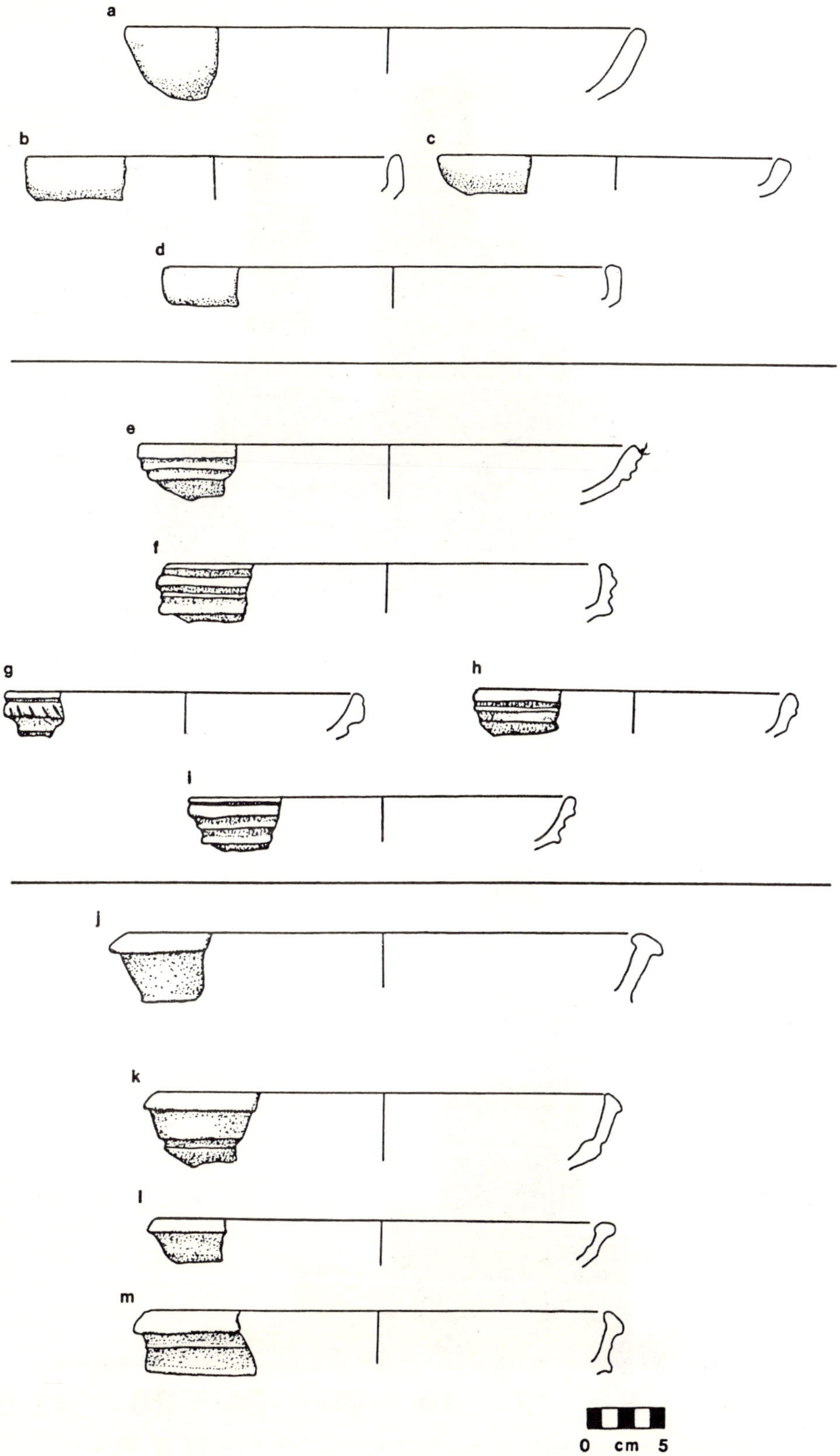

Figure 4.11 Vijayanagara Other Bowl Forms: Carinated

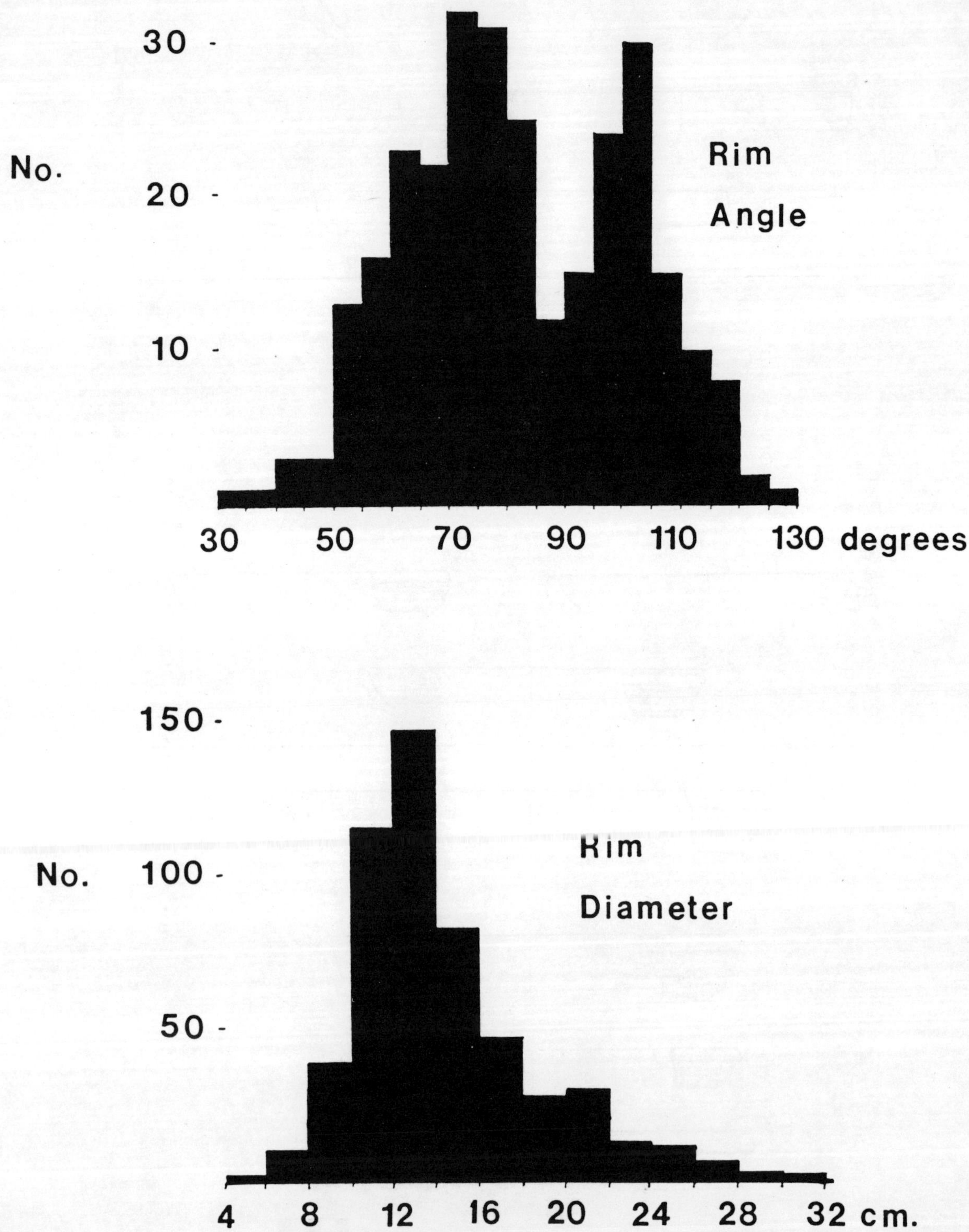

Figure 4.12 Vijayanagara Round Rime Storage Jars: Histograms of Rim Angle and Rim Diametre

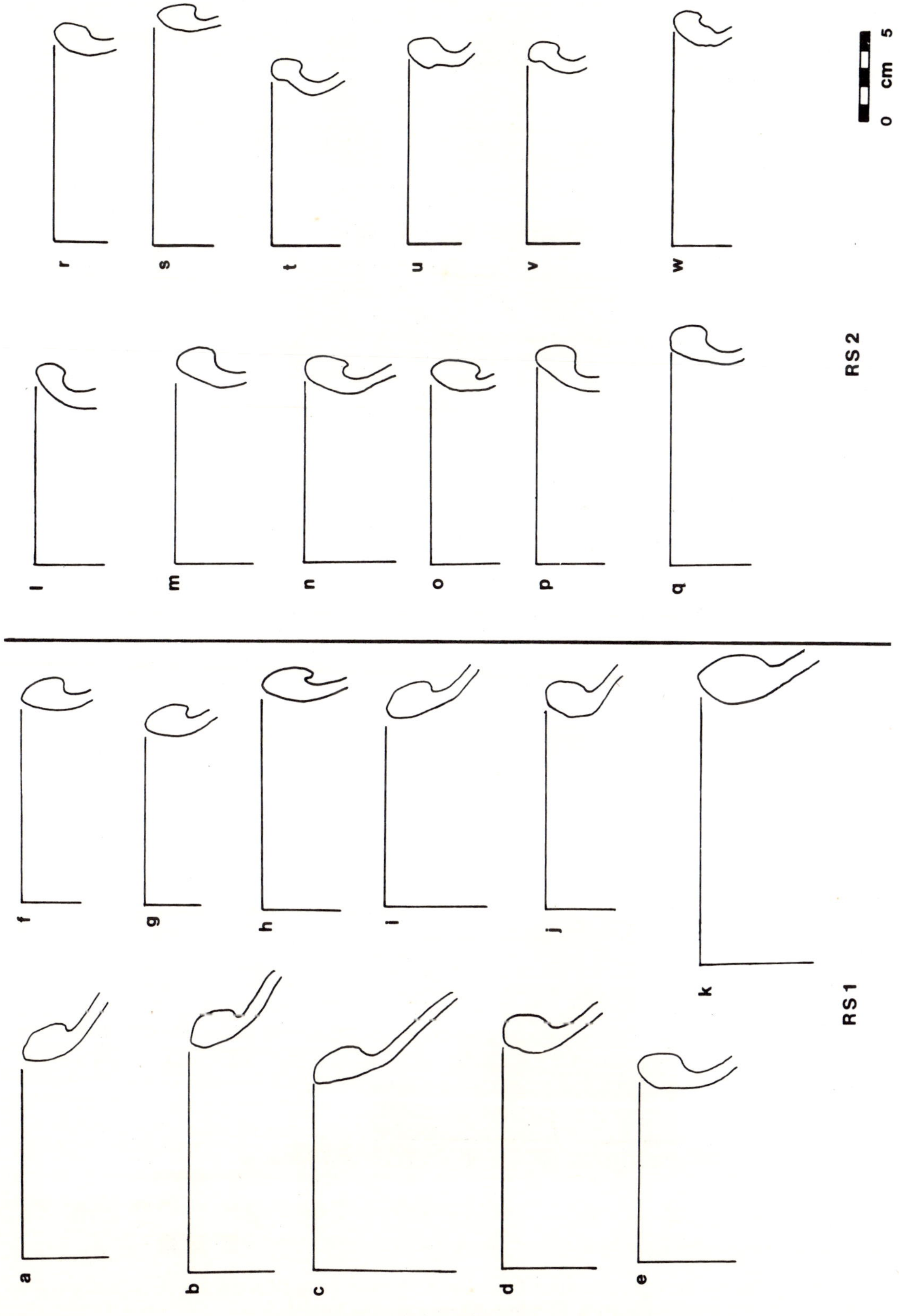

Figure 4.13 Vijayanagara Round Rim Storage Jars

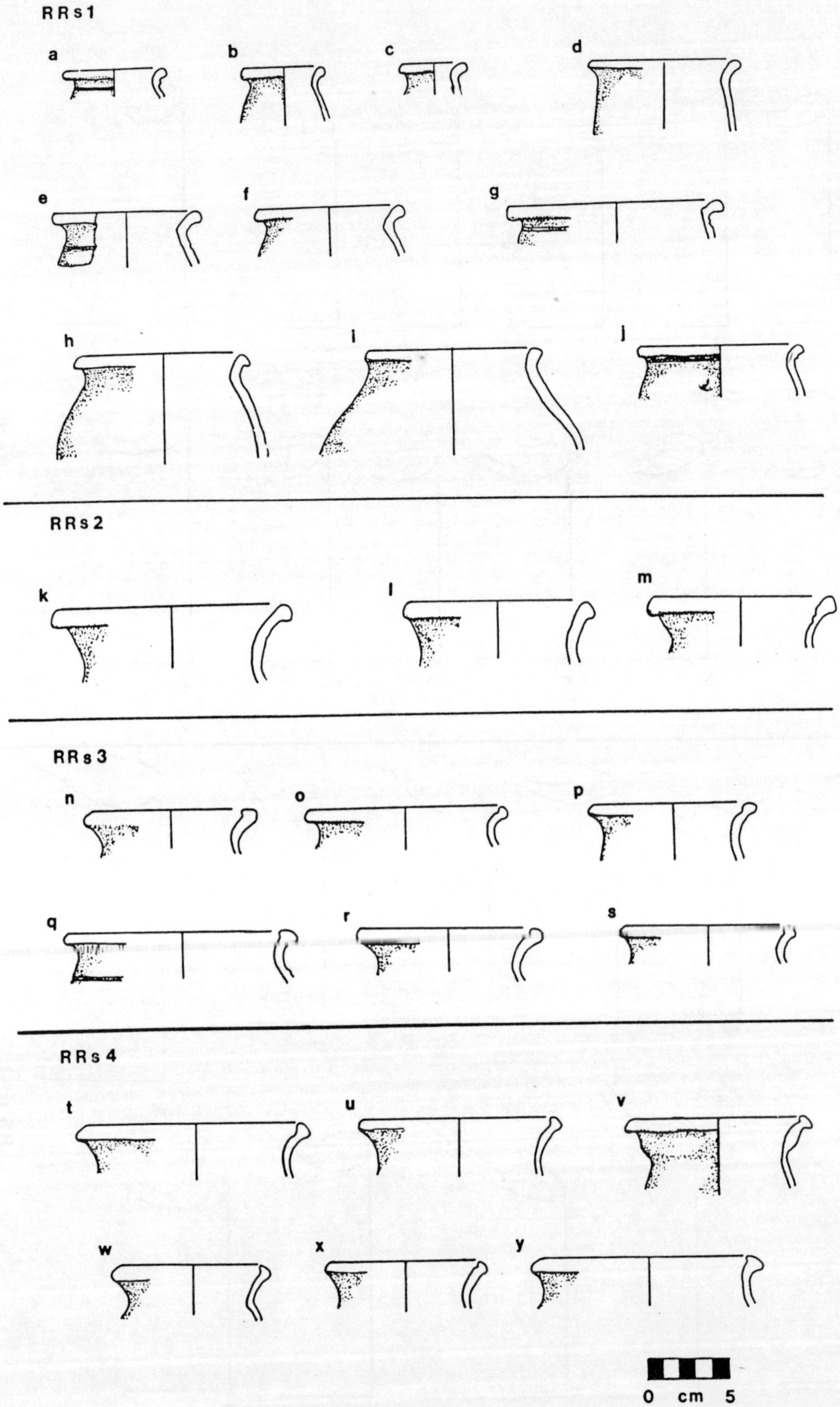

Figure 4.14 Vijayanagara Round Rim Jars

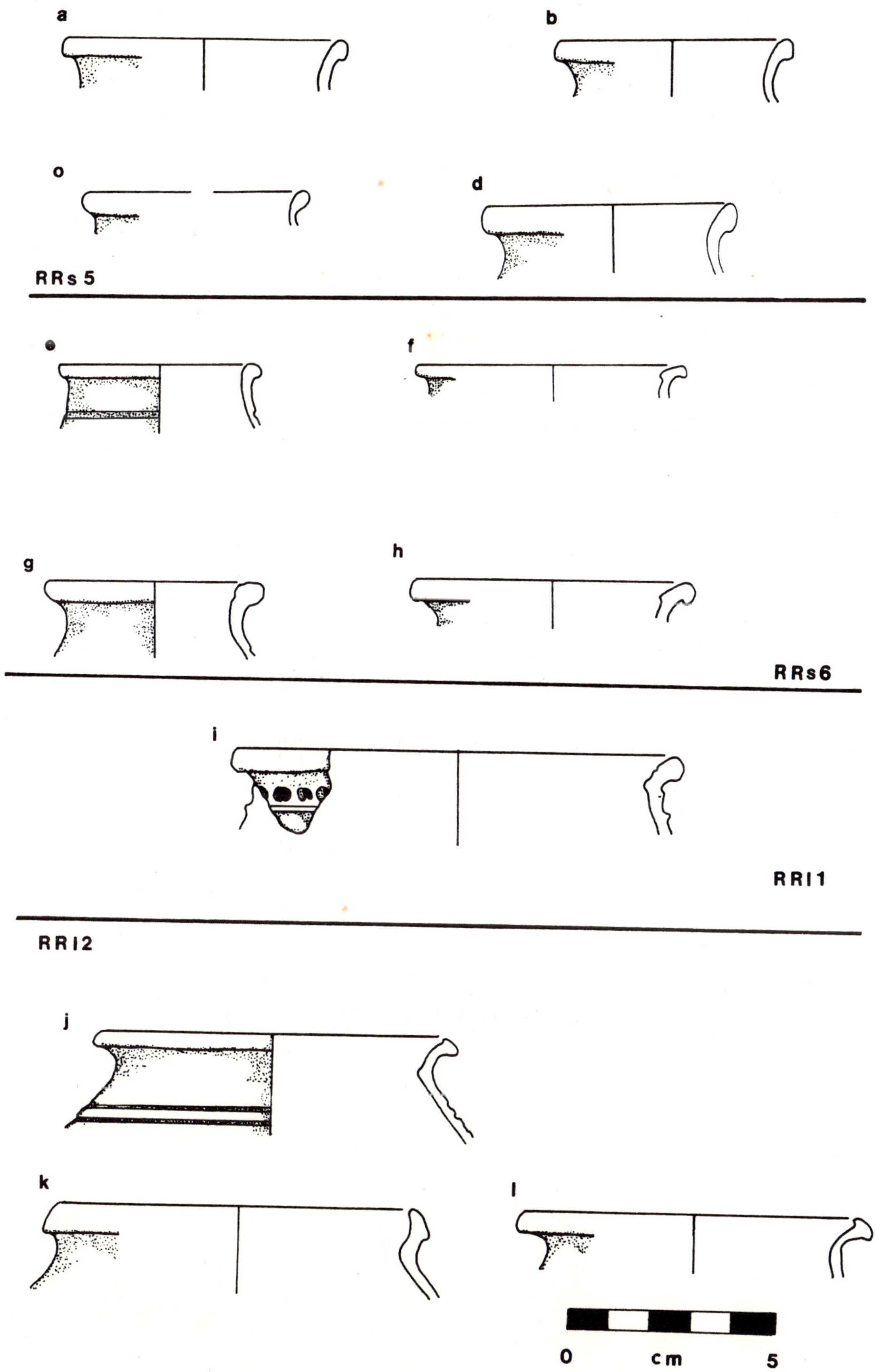

Figure 4.15 Vijayanagara Round Rim Jars

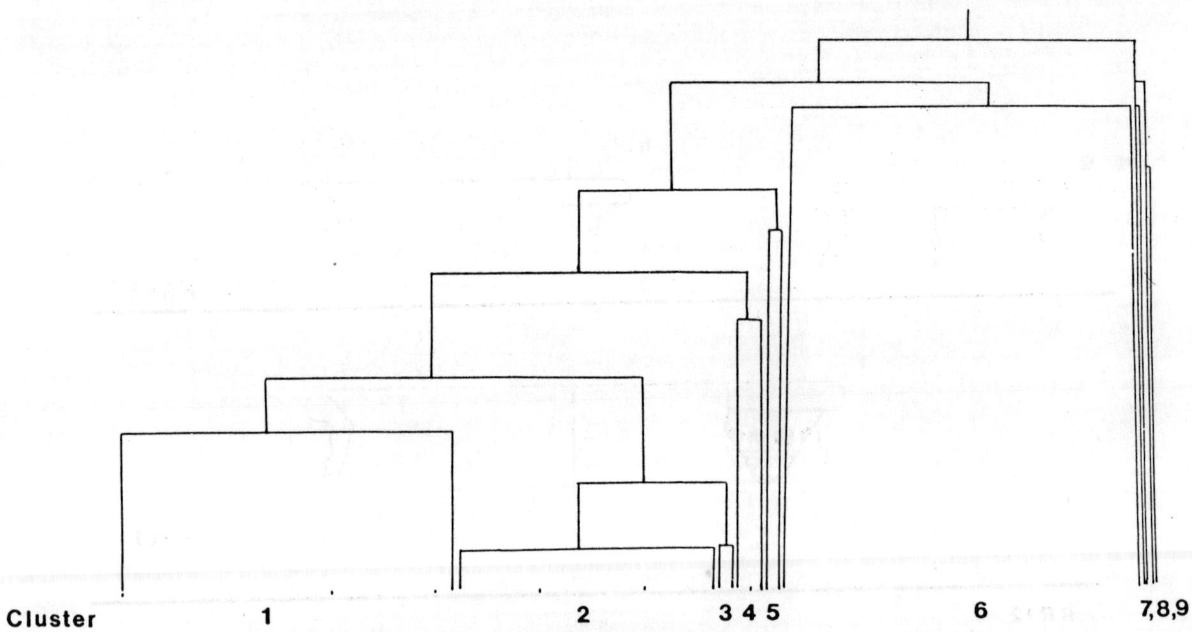

Figure 4.16 Dendrogram of Cluster Analysis of Flange and Straight Rim Vessels with Body Angle Measures

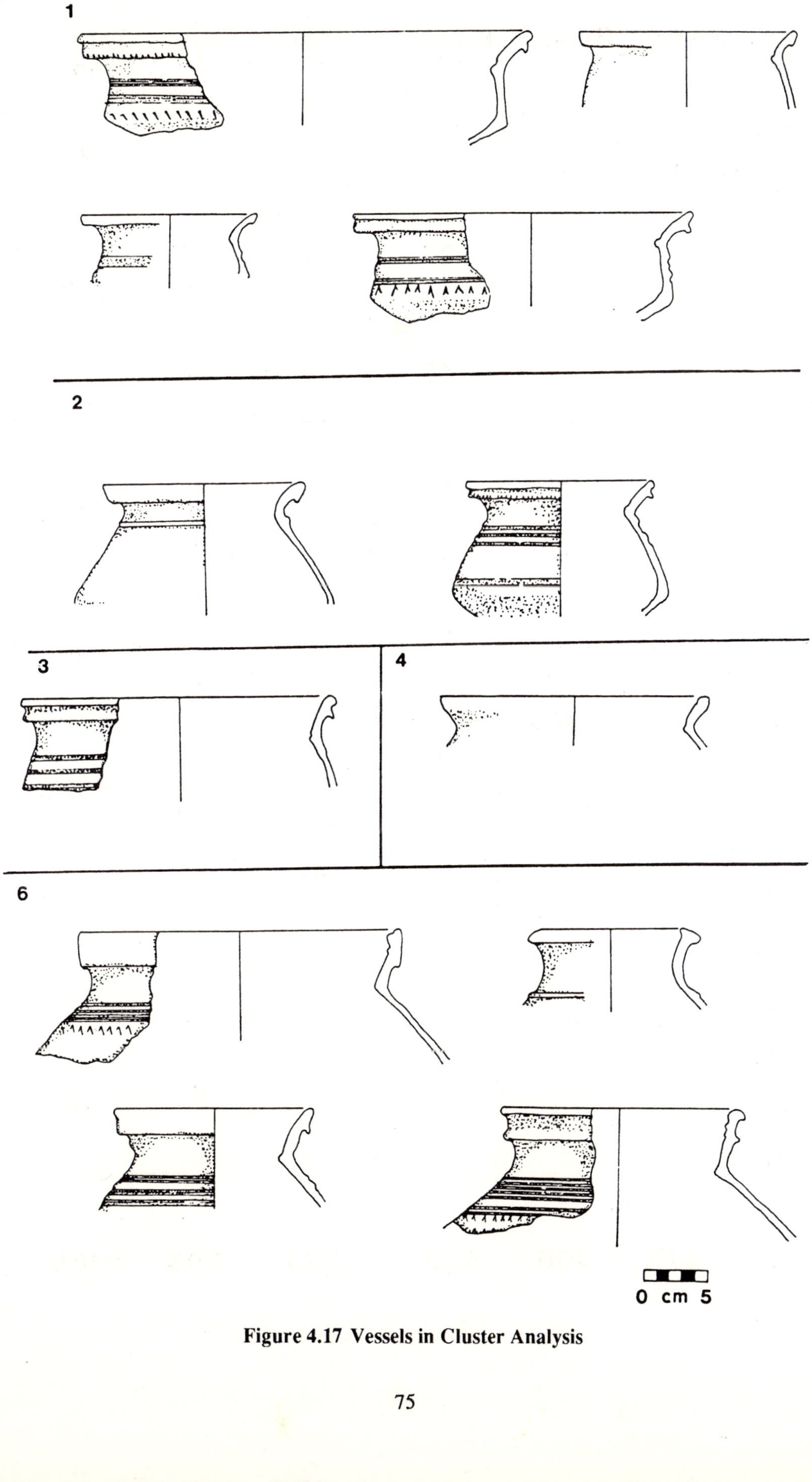

Figure 4.17 Vessels in Cluster Analysis

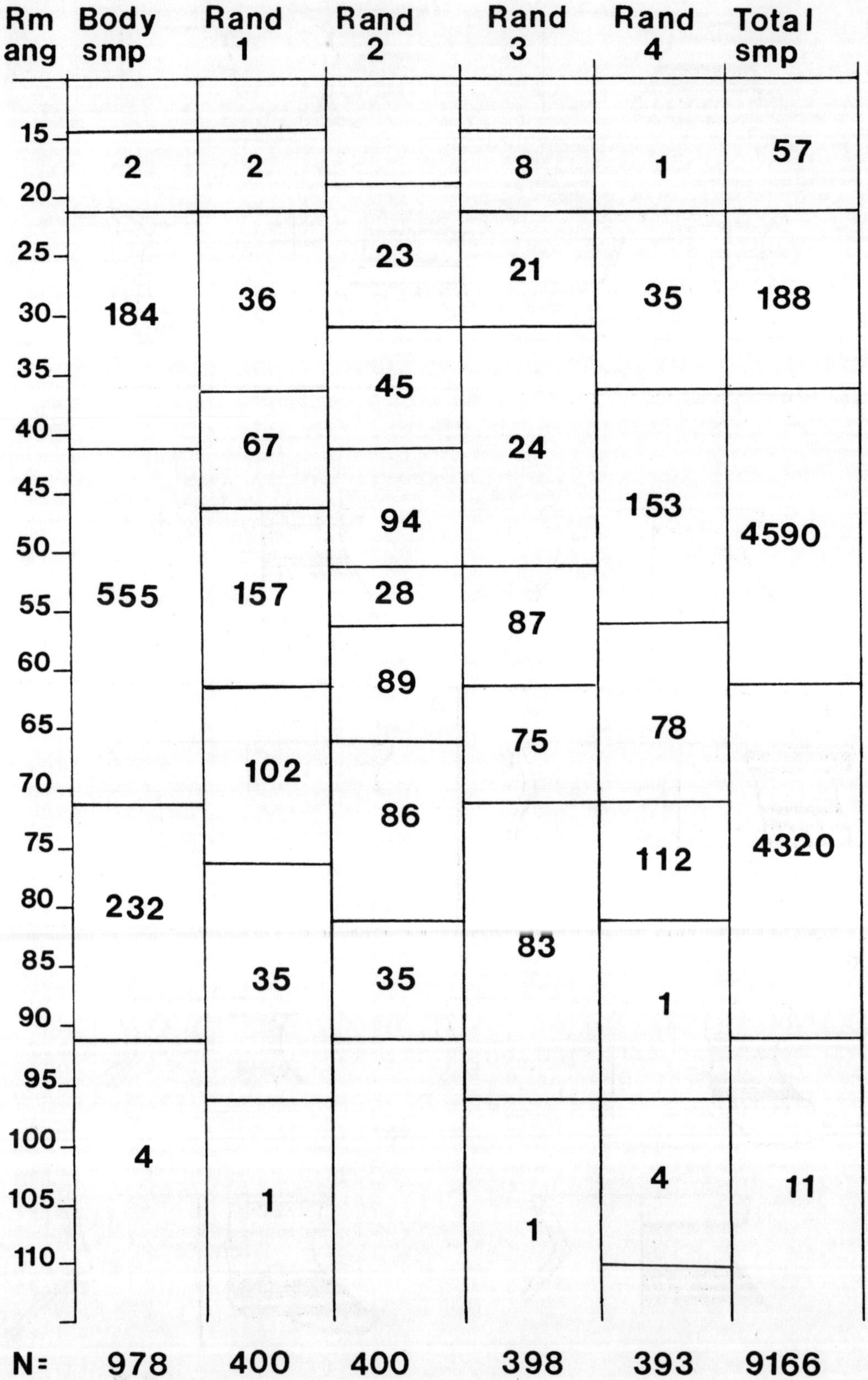

Figure 4.18 Rim Angle Values by Analysis

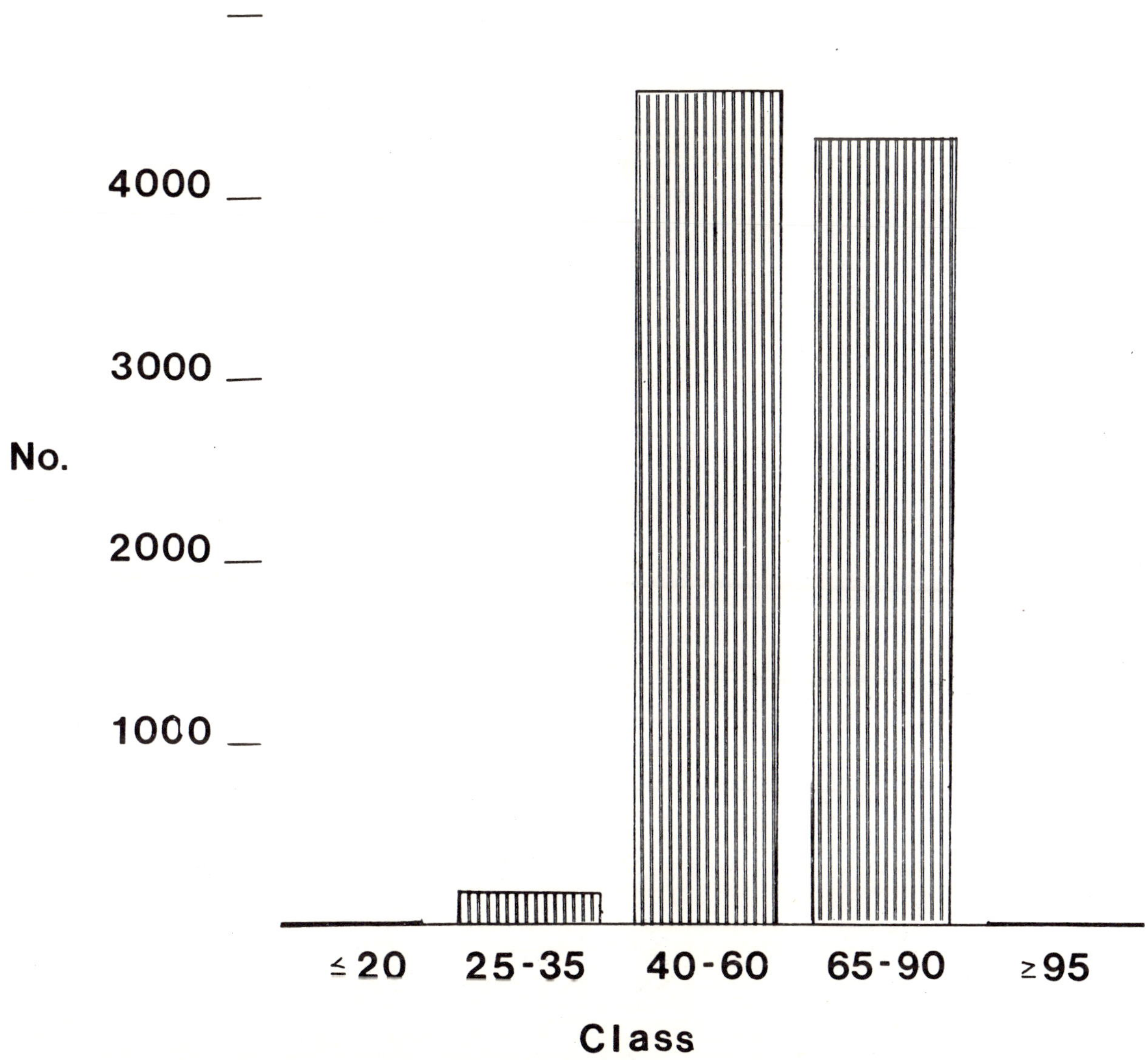

Figure 4.19 Frequency Distribution of Rim Angle Classes

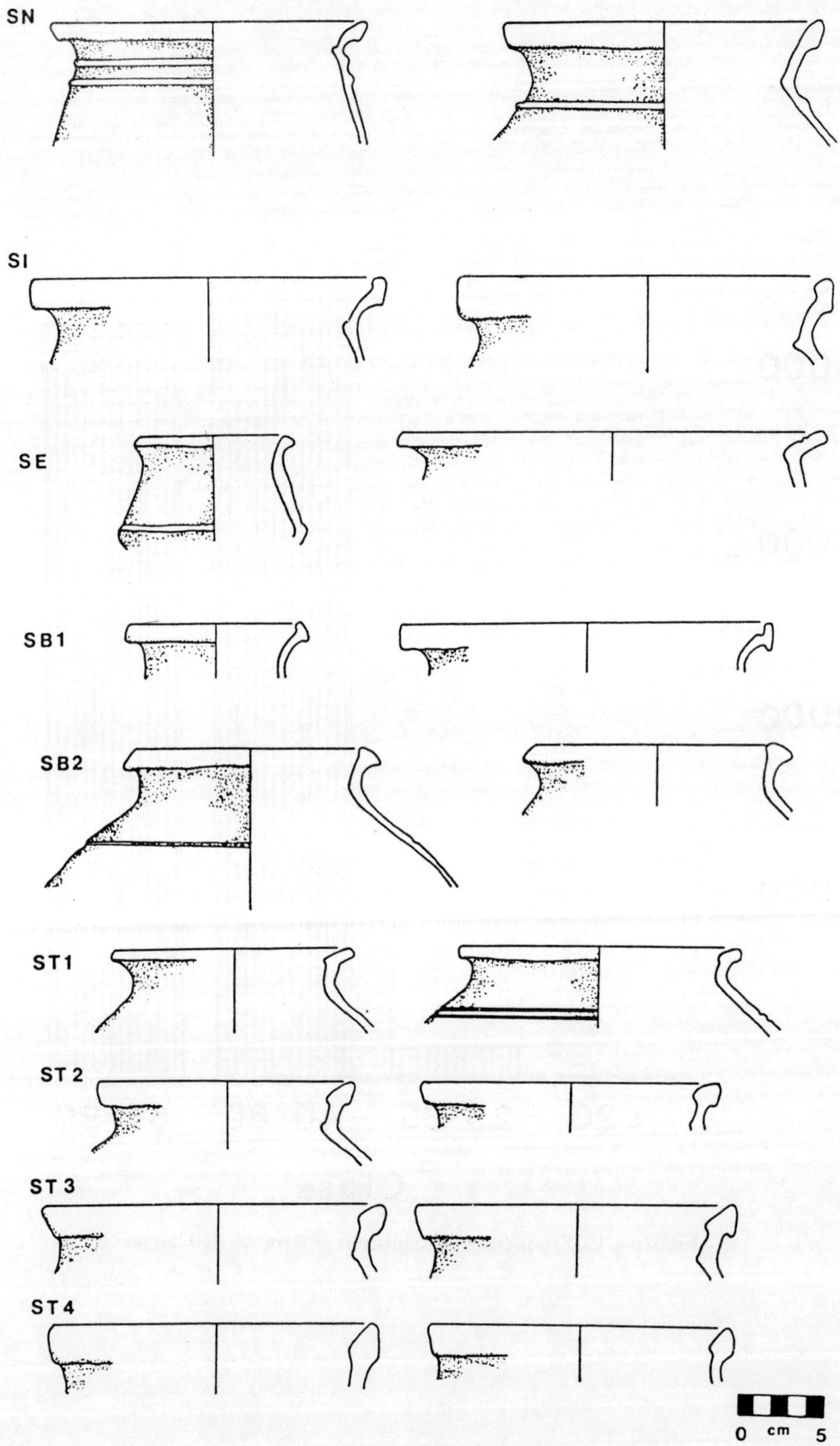

Figure 4.20 Vijayanagara Straight Rim Vessel Rim Classes

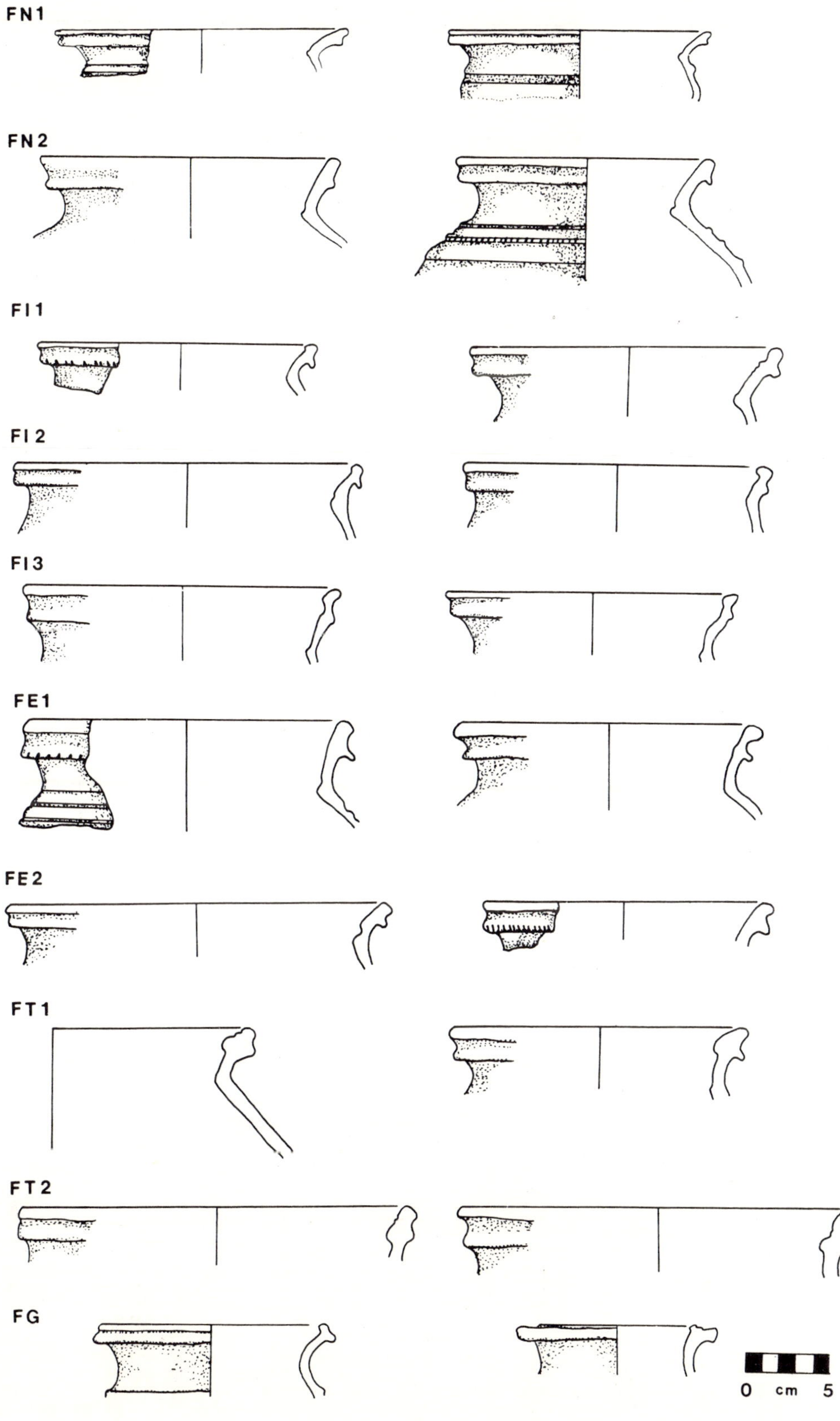

Figure 4.21 Vijayanagara Flange Rim Vessel Rim Classes

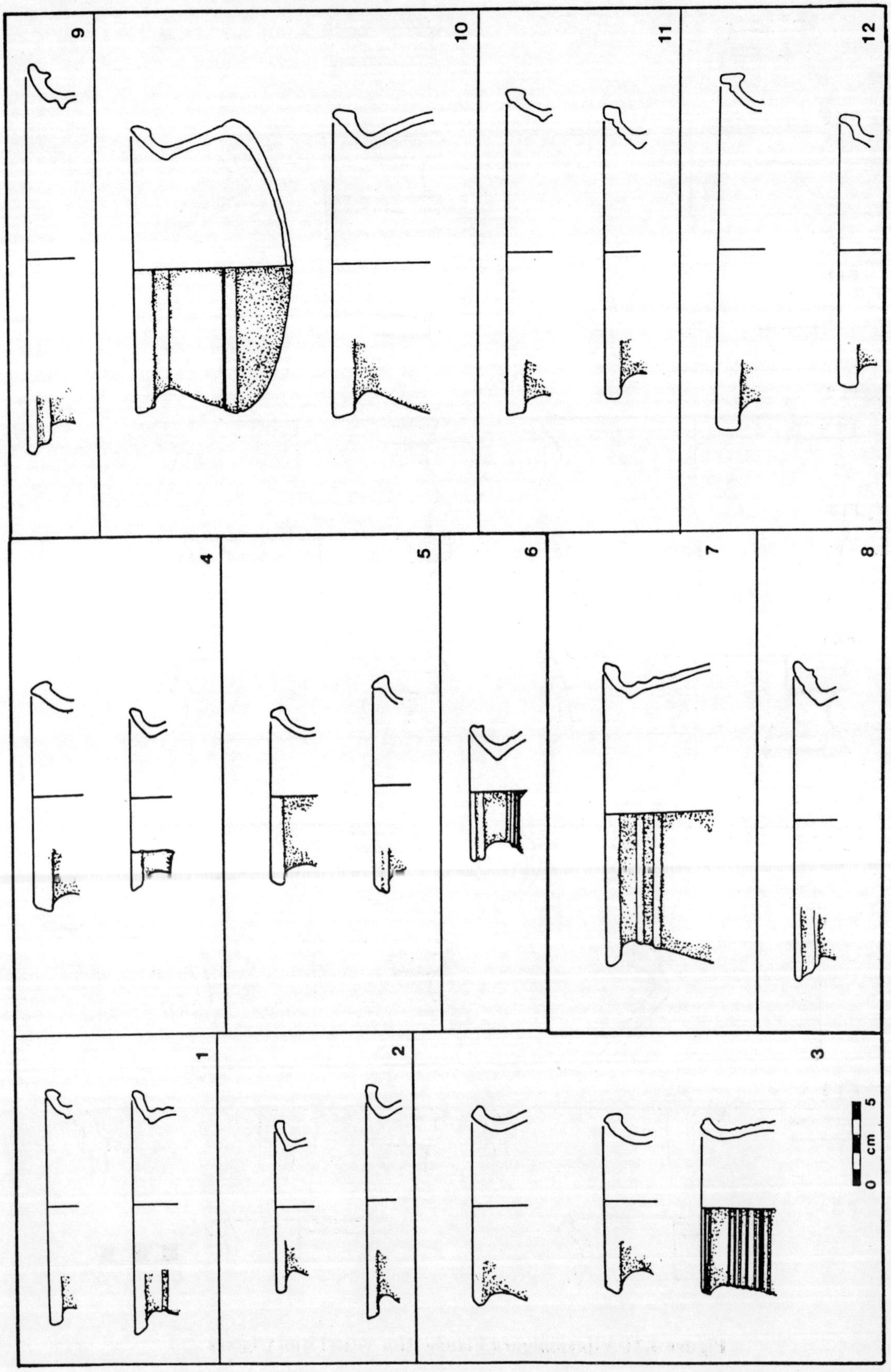

Figure 4.22 Vijayanagaaa Flange and Straight Rim Vessels Final Classification: RV1, RV2

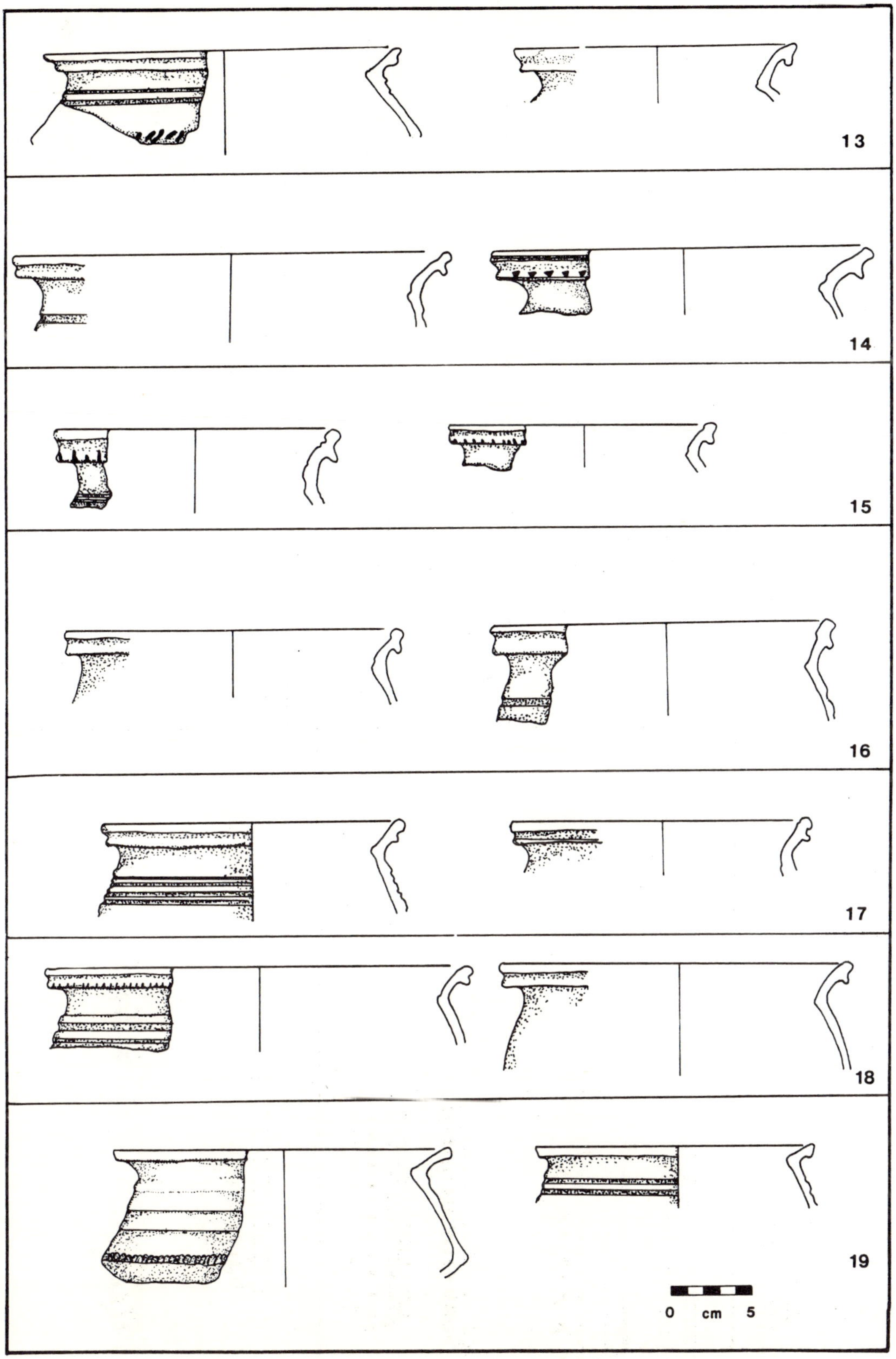

Figure 4.23 Vijayanagara Flange and Straight Rim Vessels Final Classification: RV2

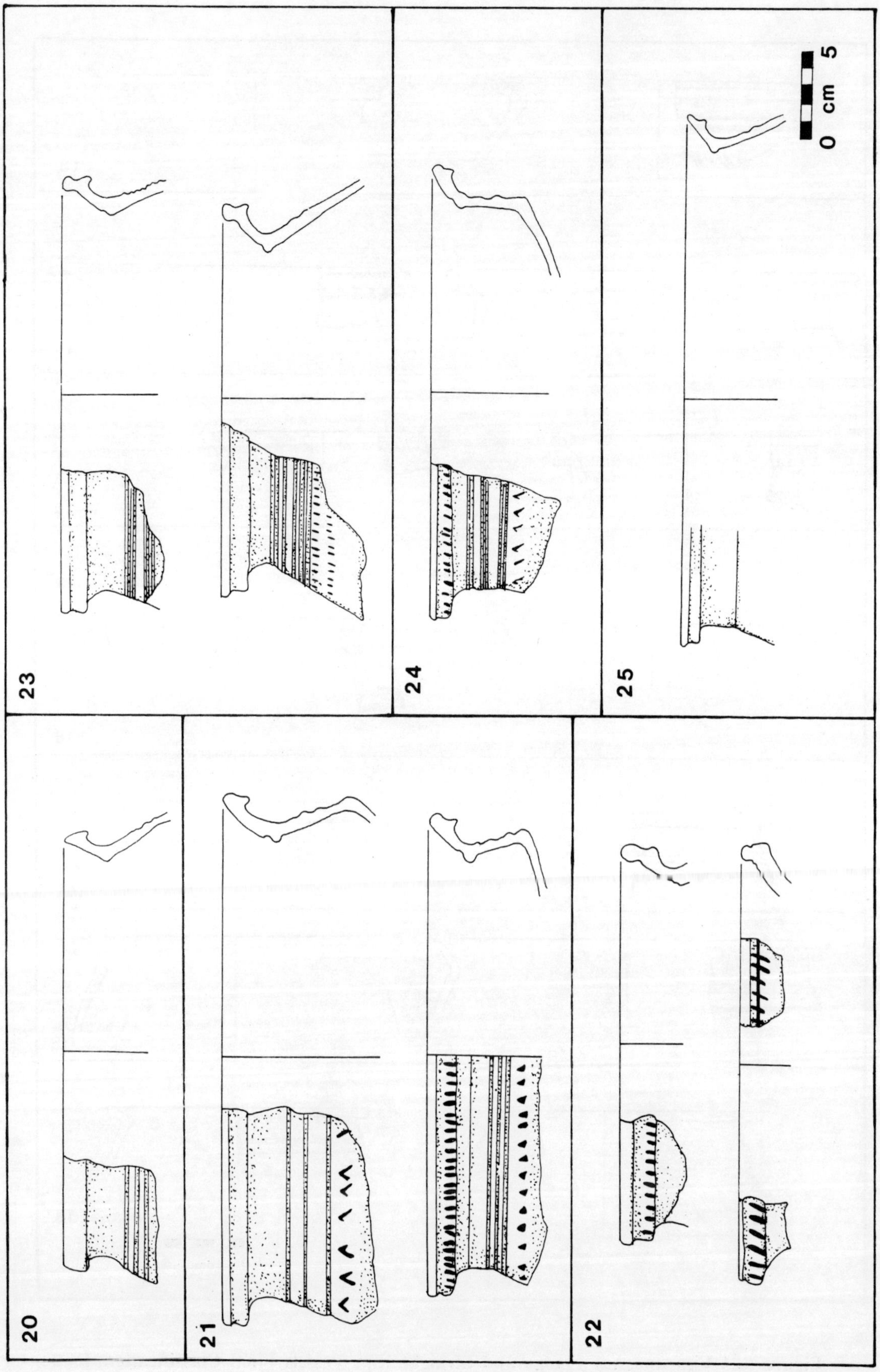

Figure 4.24 Vijayanagara Flange and Straight Rim Vessels Final Classification: RV3

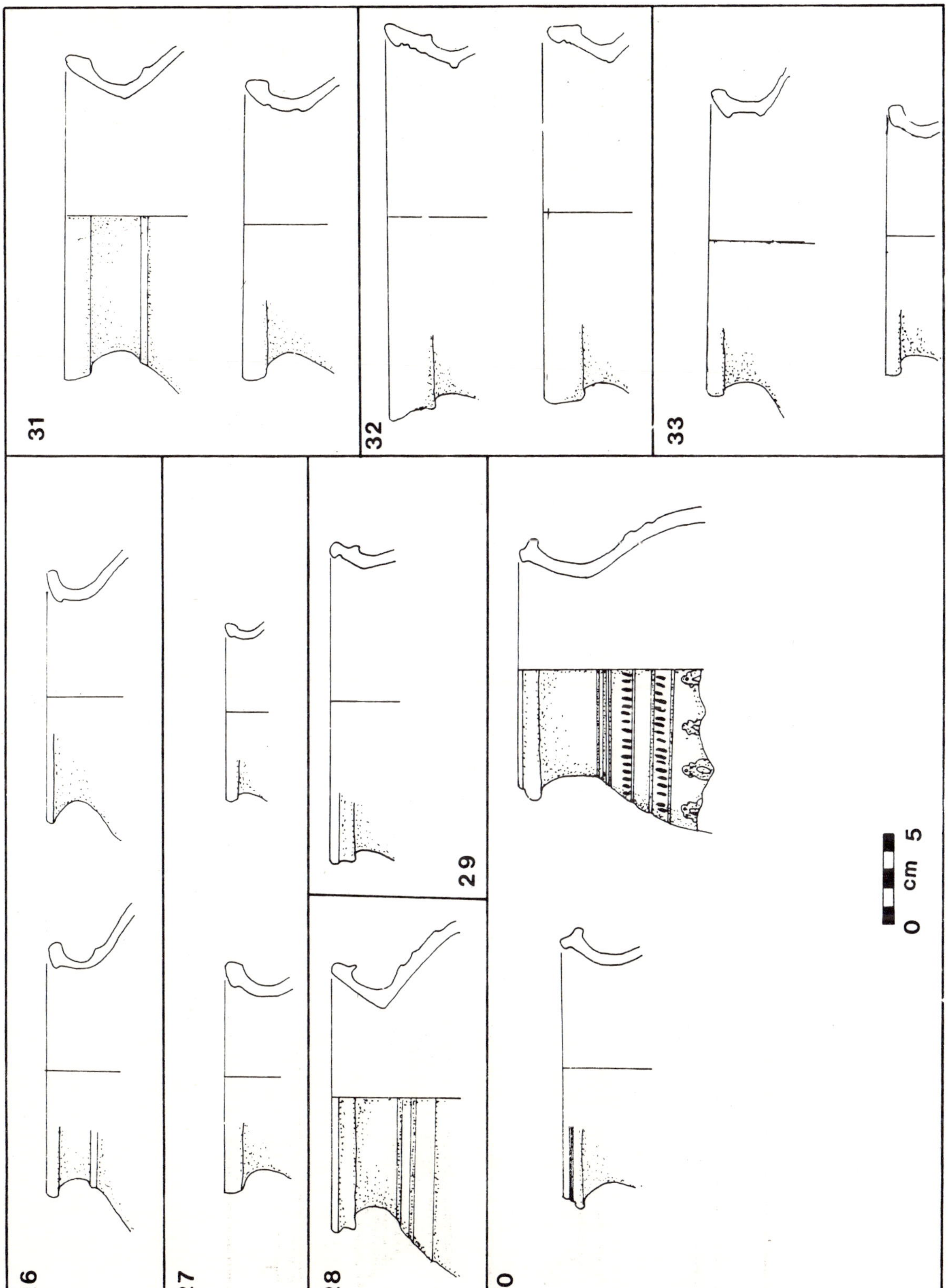

Figure 4.25 Vijayanagara Flange and Straight Rim Vessels Final Classification: RV4, RV5

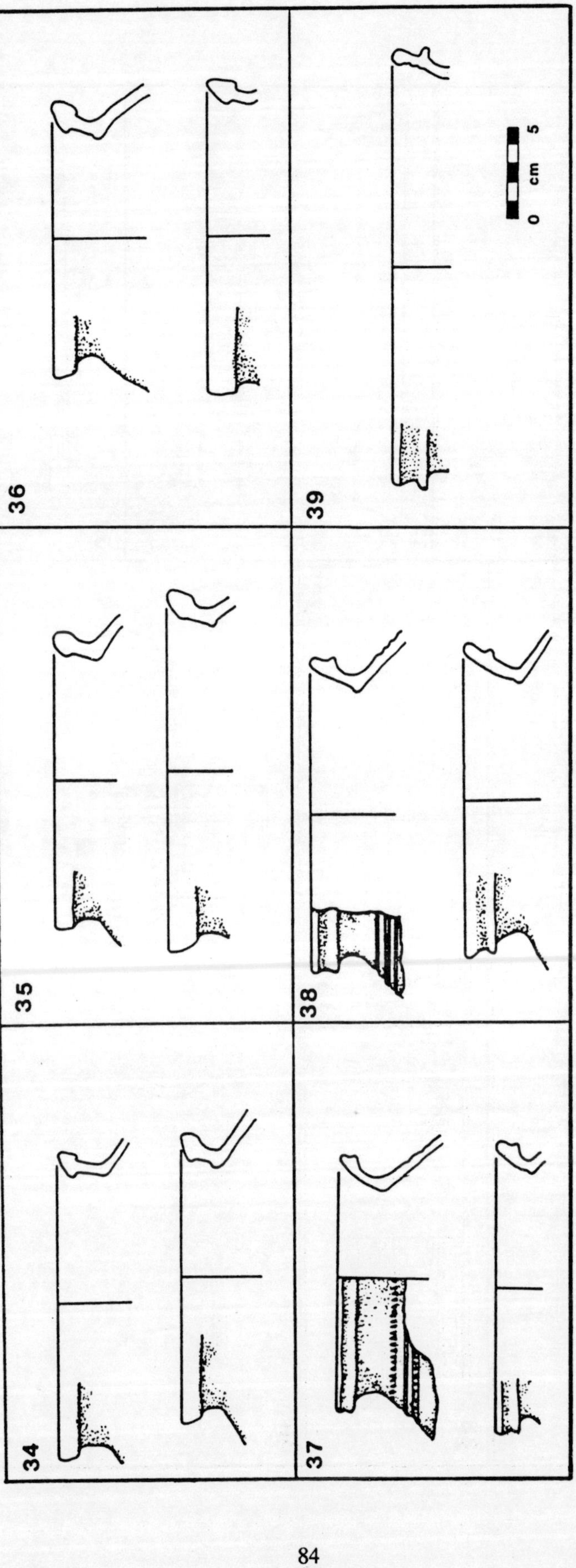

Figure 4.26 Vijayanagara Flange and Straight Rim Vessels Final Classification: RV5

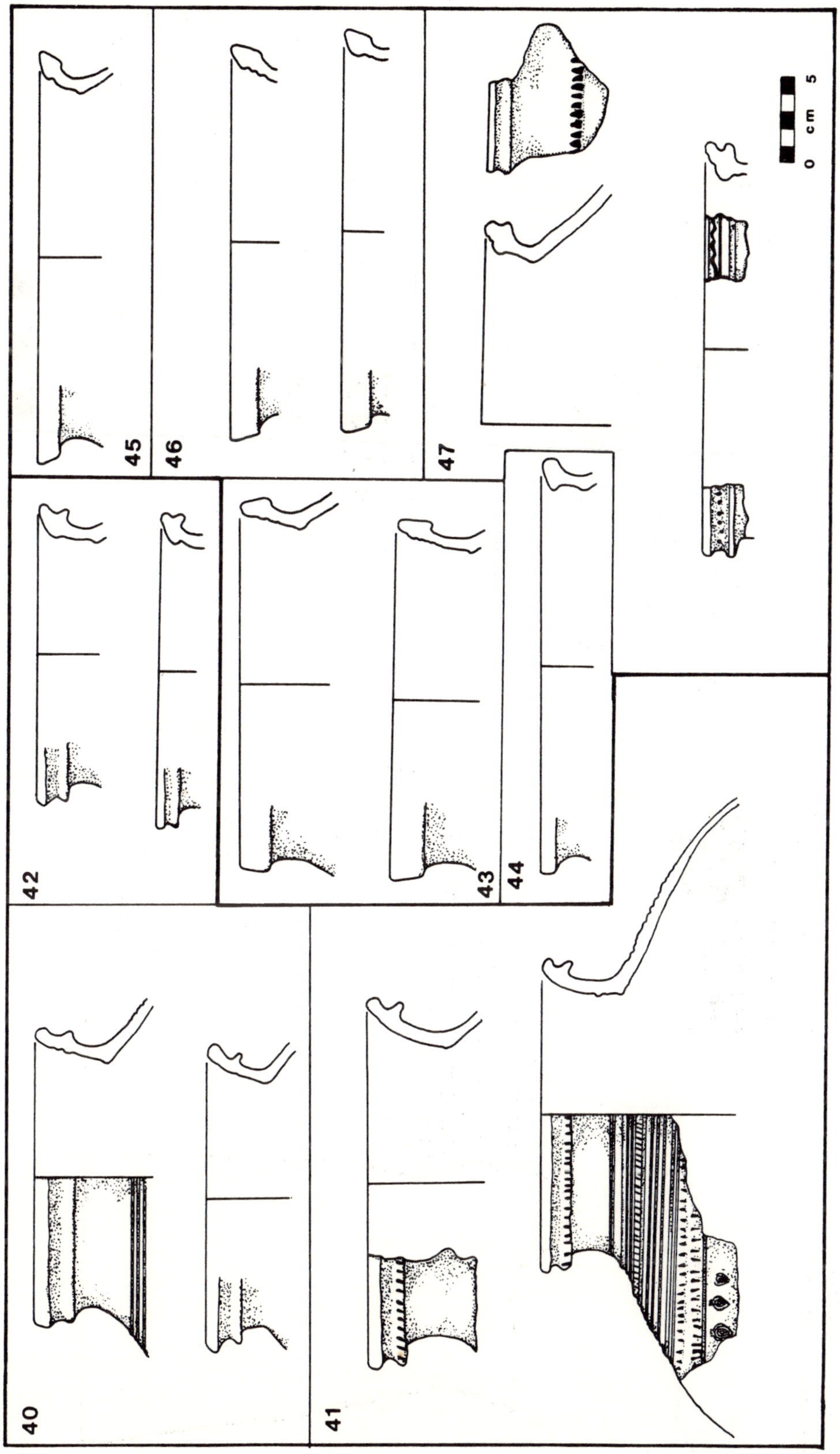

Figure 4.27 Vijayanagara Flange and Straight Rim Vessels Final Classification: RV5, RV6

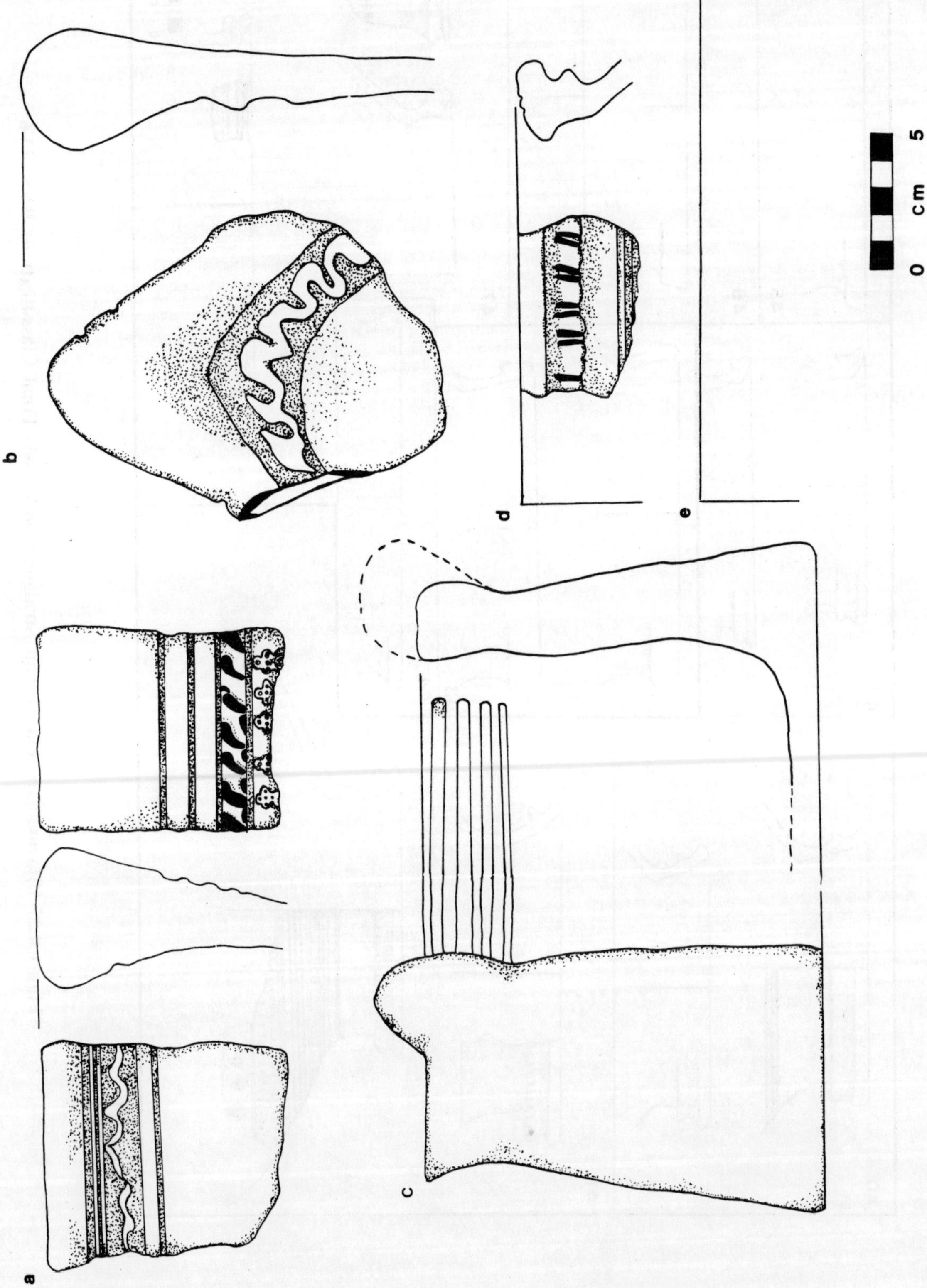

Figure 4.28 Vijayanagara Coarse Ware Vessels

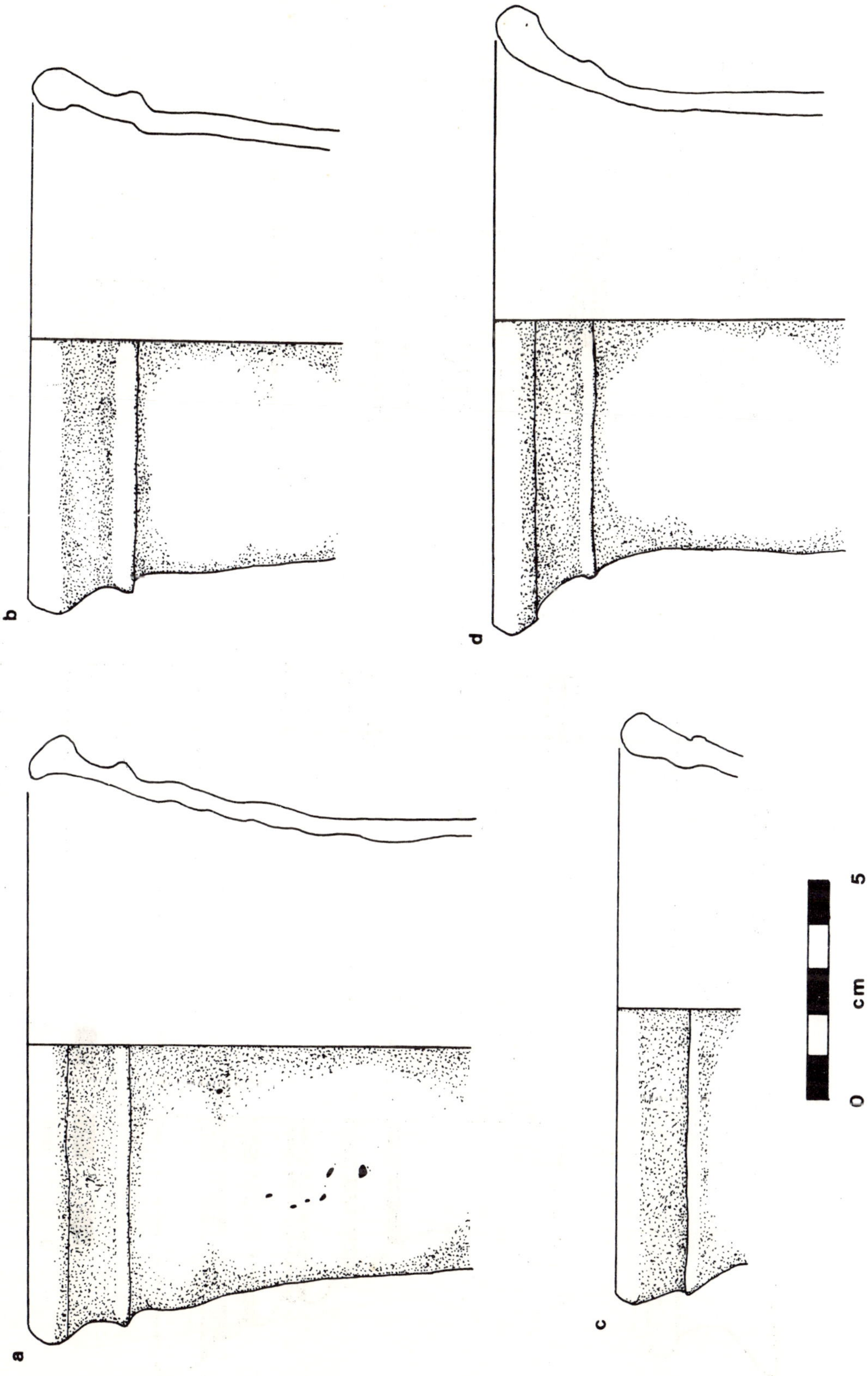

Figure 4.29 Vijayanagara Water Pipes

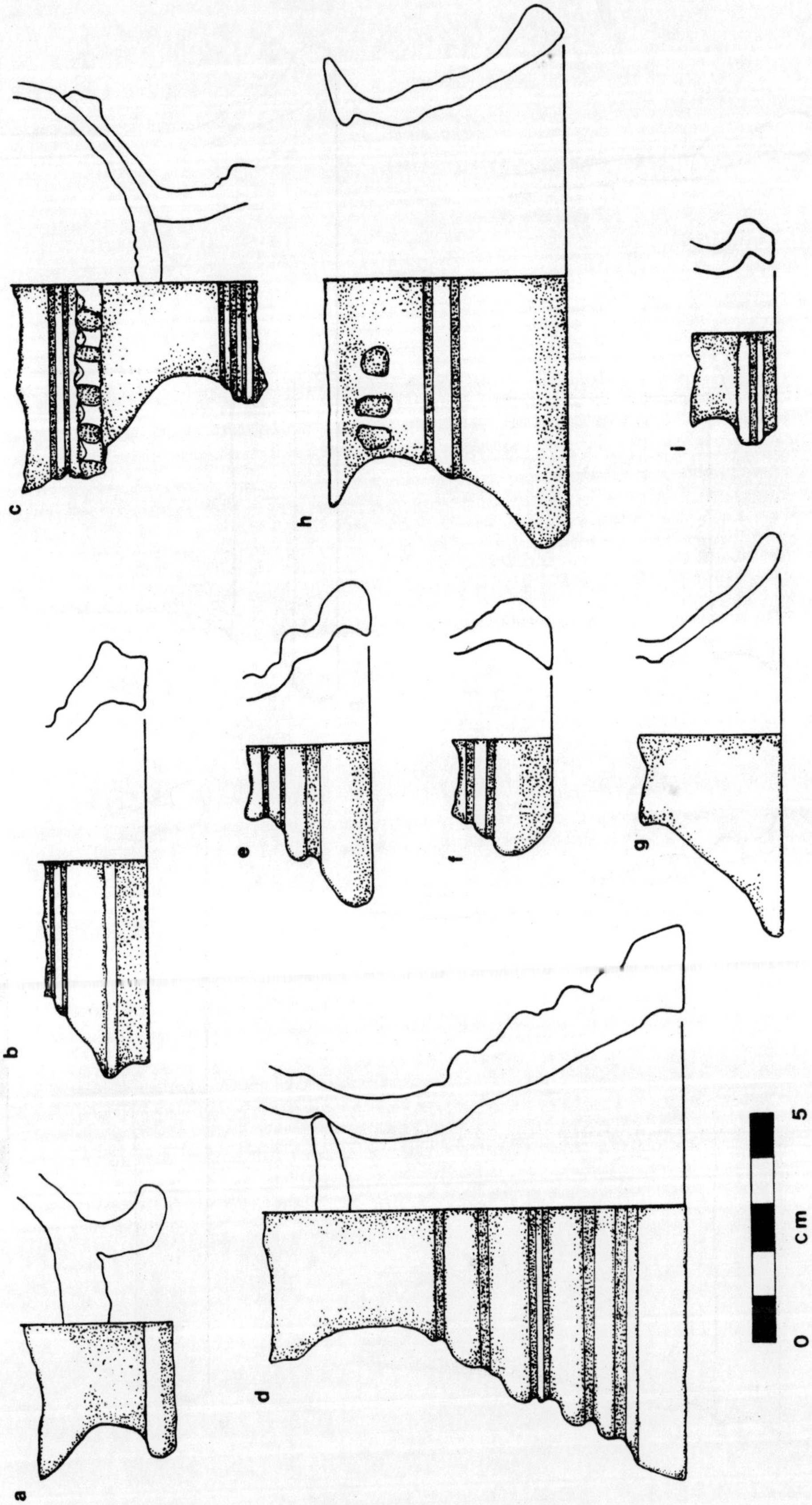

Figure 4.30 Vijayanagara Pedestalled Vessels

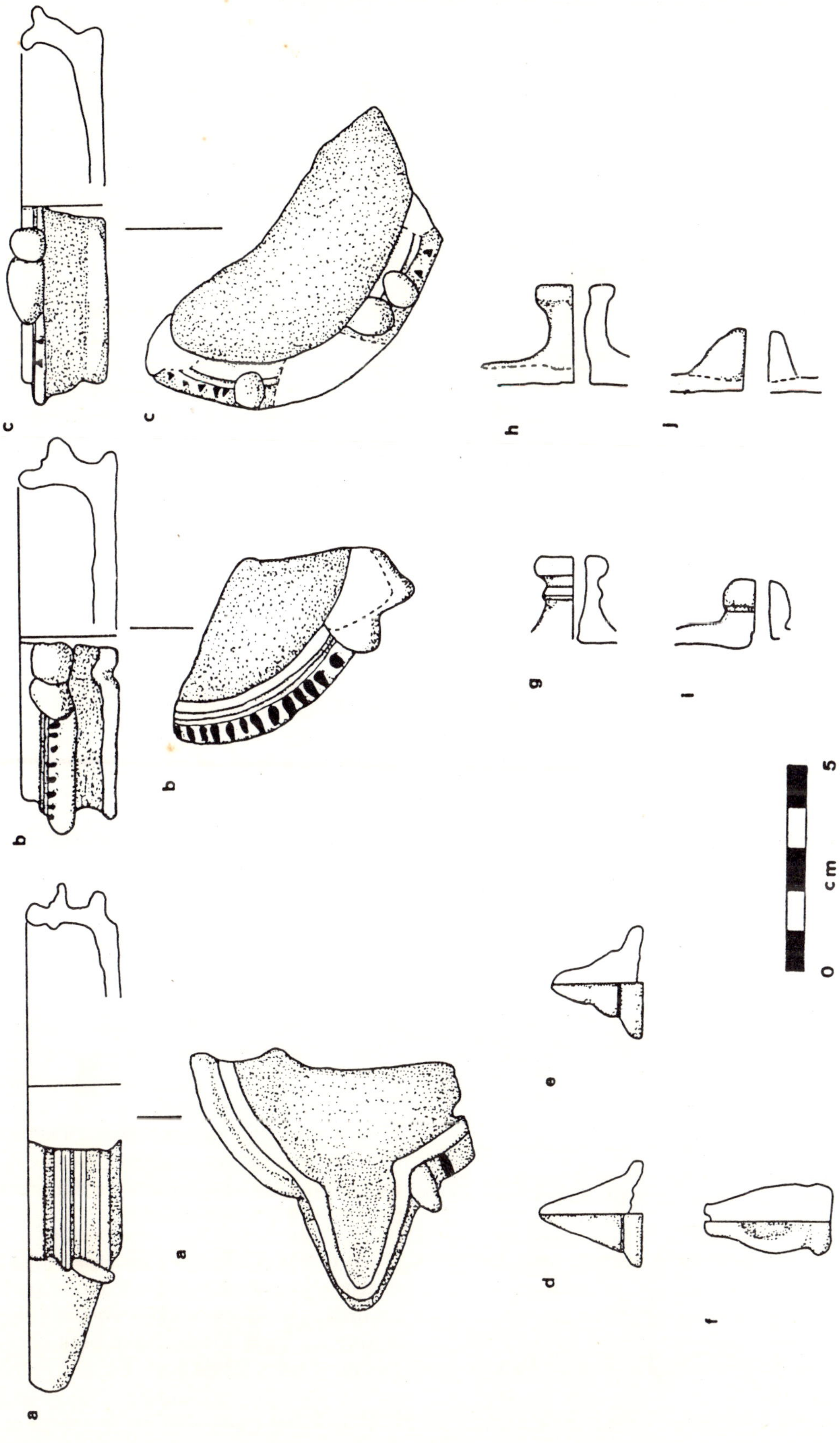

Figure 4.31 Vijayanagara Nosed Lamps, Gaming Pieces, and Spouts

V. Ceramic Distributions in the Noblemen's Quarter

The study of the spatial distributions of archaeological ceramics recovered in excavations and surface collections may provide a great deal of information on site structure and on past behaviors. Where recovery contexts are well-controlled, and where we can assume that materials were deposited near to their area of use, the distribution of ceramic classes can permit us to examine many of the questions discussed in Chapter I, above. These include the range of activities which occurred across a site, social organization, the location and nature of economic activities involving ceramics, be it ceramic production, or other activities in which ceramic vessels are employed, as well as status differences as indicated by differential access to material items within a settlement and between sites. The examination of all of these questions requires that the ceramic sample to be examined is representative of the full range of ceramics present in the area being studied. If only certain classes of ceramics are saved, or only certain areas sampled, we will be unable to accurately assess their relative importance across a site or make adequate comparisons between sites in a region.

Collection procedures for Noblemen's Quarter ceramics were summarised in Chapter III, as were the goals for the analysis of Noblemen's Quarter ceramics. To restate these goals briefly: analysis of the Noblemen's Quarter ceramics can permit us to examine the distribution of activities within and between palaces, and allow us to develop a better understanding of the uses and nature of Vijayanagara palace structures. This is particularly the case for the compounds which exhibit evidence of burning (Compound 1, 2, 3, 4, 5, 6, 10, and 12), since floor level deposits appear to be in situ, and vessels can therefore be assumed to be found near their area of use. Materials from the other, less well-preserved compounds, believed to be chronologically early, may contribute to the development of a ceramic chronology for the Noblemen's Quarter and for Vijayanagara ceramics as a whole. In addition, the Noblemen's Quarter ceramics can be compared to the ceramics from other broad regions of the site where collections have been made, the East Valley and Islamic Quarter, in order to examine broader social or economic differences between these areas and to attempt to examine patterns of settlement and community organisation in this large imperial city.

The analysis of the distribution of ceramics within and between Noblemen's Quarter compounds will be conducted at a number of levels. Variations in overall ceramic densities, ware frequencies, frequencies of vessel-use classes, and of rim forms, will all be examined in order to consider differences in the uses to which compounds were put, and the range and location of activities which occurred within them.

Throughout the analyses the relative frequencies of the various classes to be examined are computed as a ratio of total counts from each spatial unit. Frequency values are then plotted directly onto maps or compared further using various cluster analysis or other techniques, in order to define groups of clusters of similar units. The distributions of the various classes and clusters are then assessed with respect to the architectural features of each area. Before proceeding to the specifics of these analyses, a few general comments on ceramic distributions are in order.

As noted above, this analysis made extensive use of relative frequencies of vessel classes. These frequencies were computed so that total sample sizes of the units could be factored out, and comparisons could be made across units of widely disparate sample sizes. Units with fewer than 10 or 20 sherds, depending on the analysis, were not considered, or were merged with nearby units to form larger samples. The effects of sample size on the occurrence of various classes will be considered below. The factors which contribute to the frequencies of particular ceramic classes found in a sample include both the overall percentages of the vessels actually used in an area and the differential breakage and discard rates of the vessel classes.

The rate at which vessels are broken and discarded depend on the form of the vessels, the activities they are used in, and their frequency of use. Ethnographic studies of vessel *use-life* have been conducted by Foster (1960), David and Hennig (1972), David (1972), DeBoer and Lathrap (1979) and Longacre (1985) among traditional pottery users in Mexico,

Africa, South America and the Philippines. Using the available ethnographic literature, DeBoer (1985) has attempted to develop a general model for ceramic use-life, employing three inter-related variables: vessel size, frequency of use, and vessel value (computed as manufacturing cost plus procurement cost). Vessel size affects the ease and frequency of movement of vessels; very large vessels are seldom moved and therefore would be dropped less frequently than smaller vessels. High frequency of use provides more opportunities for breakage. Value is incorporated into this model with the assumption that valued vessels would be treated with more care than more easily replaceable post. To these variables might be added the nature and context of use. Cooking vessels are subjected to repeated heating and cooling, and thermal stress leads to physical weakening of the vessels. Vessels carried daily to wells to collect water may be dropped along the way. The proximity of children and domestic animals to vessels has also been shown to contribute to increased breakage rates (Longacre 1985: 341).

Despite our ability to define the relevant variables affecting ceramic breakage rates, it is still not easily possible to develop a quantitative model of breakage rates for particular contexts. The importance of these considerations to the present study lies in the need to recognize that the relative frequencies of vessel classes from the Vijayanagara provenience units are not simply a reflection of the frequencies with which these vessels were used in those areas.

Comparisons of vessel frequencies between areas demand the simplifying assumption that similar vessels were used in a similar manner across the site, and that breakage rates are more or less constant for any given functional class of vessels. This assumption, while necessary at this stage of our understanding, is problematical. The ethnographic work of Junker (1985) in South India, indicates that vessels of a single form might be used differently in different contexts (for example, the *maggi,* a form used as a ritual vessel in weddings and as a drinking vessel in domestic contexts; see also Miller 1985). If this simplifying assumption is accepted, however, variation in relative frequencies of particular ceramic classes can be taken to reflect significant and actual variation between areas, although the *precise* importance of specific vessel classes, or the activities in which they were used, can not be calculated. The samples from floor levels in the Noblemen's Quarter might, however, reflect more accurately the frequency of use of vessels, if, as discussed above, the buildings were abruptly abandoned in 1565 when the Vijayanagara army was defeated.

CERAMIC DENSITIES

The densities of ceramics, measured in terms of the quantities of sherds recovered in each provenience unit in the NMQ sample can provide information on the nature of the deposit (e.g., trash midden vs. floor deposit) and on the intensity and nature of use of an area. The size of the sherds recovered in each area also has some bearing on these questions. For example, areas where sherds are generally small and heavily broken up may include paths which were frequently trod upon or other areas of heavy activity. Areas containing large sherds from a large number of vessels might include trash deposits or other depositional contexts, such as inside of or around wells where, over time, a certain number of vessels can be expected to be lost or broken. Areas containing large sherds from a small number of vessels may include storerooms with vessels deposited in situ.

The consideration of ceramic densities in the NMQ sample will focus primarily on sherd counts per unit. Unlike the East Valley sample, total weights of each sample were not recorded due to the lack of control I had over ceramic collection strategies and the consistency of collection. Analysis will focus primarily on sherd counts and relative frequencies of the various ceramic classes. The sizes of individual provenience units within each NMQ compound are highly variable, since spatially contiguous units were grouped together. In order to control for the effect of unit size on overall ceramic counts I computed both the spatial area (square metres) and volume (cubic metres) of each unit. The calculation of unit volume was hampered by the inconsistency of information recording initial and final excavation depths. The calculated volumes must therefore be viewed as best approximations, rather than as absolute assessments. Unit area and volume are presented in Table 5.1.

For compounds NMQ2-4, information is presented both on diagnostic sherd counts and body sherd counts from each provenience unit. Body sherds were not counted from units in NMQ5-10 and NMQ12, because of changes in ceramic collection practices between 1984 and 1986. The collection of ceramics from architectural compounds of medieval sites in India, and Vijayanagara in particular, is a relatively recent pratice, and has yet to be fully or adequately systematised in the NMQ area. Labourers and excavators tended to focus their collecting on diagnostic sherds and large body sherds rather than the more desirable course of collecting all sherds within an excavation unit. While I am assuming that, over the course of any one season, collection procedures were comparable between compounds and units, it was clear that by 1985-1986 virtually no body sherds were being collected at all, thus rendering some of the approaches used in the analysis of materials excavated prior to 1985 invalid.

Information on the ratio of diagnostic to total sherd counts (diagnostics plus bodies) is presented for units from NMQ2-4. This ratio—"breakage ratio"—was computed in order to provide an assessment of sherd size and degree of breakage on the assumption that if vessels were broken into many small pieces the ratio of measurable diagnostics to total sample size would be low. Values for breakage ratio may range from 0.00 to 1.00; high values indicate little breakage and low values indicate high breakage rates. As noted earlier, the extent of breakage may provide information on the contexts of deposition and the use of areas. A second ratio is also presented in Table 5.1. This is the ratio of diagnostic sherds to unit volume, calculated in order to assess the relative density of sherds per cubic metre of deposit in each provenience unit.

Throughout the NMQ samples, densities of diagnostic sherds range from 3.5 sherds per cubic metre to 97.0 sherds per cubic metre, with a mean of 17.8 diagnostic sherds per cubic metre. Considerable variation exists between compounds in mean ceramic densities. Highest mean densities are found in MMQ3, with 32.3 diagnostic sherds per cubic metre, and NMQ5, with 25.9 diagnostic sherds per cubic metre. Lowest mean ceramic densities are found in NMQ10, with 8.4 diagnostic sherds per cubic metre, and NMQ8, with 10.0 diagnostics per cubic metre. Each compound, however, exhibits considerable internal variation in densities between provenience units.

An examination of the overall distribution of ceramics by provenience unit reveals some general patterns. While the units are highly variable in spatial extent and volume, the total ceramic sample from each unit is not highly correlated with unit size, and the number of sherds found per cubic metre is highly variable. The density figures presented in Table 5.1 reflect the overall mass of ceramics as well as the degree of breakage. In addition, ceramic densities also reflect, in part, the uses to which individual provenience units were put, and the importance of ceramic vessels in those activities.

In NMQ3, for example, Unit 3.7, with 229 diagnostic sherds, has a low breakage rate, with a ratio of diagnostics to total sherd counts of .571, but an overall density of only 19.7 diagnostic sherds per cubic metre. This unit, located to the north of the compound wall is near a well and the high number of ceramics here may relate to the accumulation of whole or nearly whole vessels around and in the well. A second area of NMQ3 with large quantities of ceramics is Unit 3.1. This unit contains the greatest total number of sherds of any NMQ3 unit, with 289 diagnostics, and 1093 total sherds. The density of diagnostic sherds per cubic metre in Unit 3.1 is 68.8, also a very high value. The ratio of diagnostics to total sherd count is .264, indicating higher breakage rates than in Unit 3.7. This walled area with a packed earth surface, located to the west of the main structure, contains a ground stone mortar, and may be interpreted as a food preparation area.

A third area in NMQ3 with high ceramic densities is unit 3.8 with 97.0 sherds per cubic metre, and a total of 337 diagnostic and body sherds in an excavation unit only 10 cm. in depth. This area is located outside of the northwest corner of the compound wall, and is tentatively interpreted as a refuse or dump area used by the occupants of the compound. Units within the main structure, Units 3.2 and 3.3, contain low numbers of diagnostic sherds and low breakage ratios (.151 and .204, respectively). Units 3.4. and 3.5 are located within the compound walls on the plaster surface to the north of the main structure. Despite their contiguity, they vary considerably in breakage ratios and overall ceramic density and, as will be discussed below, in the morphological or vessel-use classes found within them. These differences might result from a functional division of space within an architecturally undifferentiated area.

Similar patterns hold for each of the NMQ compounds. In general, ceramic densities tend to be low within the main structure of a compound, and higher in courtyard areas, subsidiary structures, or areas outside of the compound walls. The latter areas may have been used as refuse areas by the occupants/users of the compounds. No major refuse areas have yet been located at Vijayanagara, though it is certainly reasonable to expect that they existed. It is also possible, and from the density of materials seems likely, that certain quantities of materials were discarded nearby the occupation areas. Food waste and other organic materials would likely have been quickly consumed by domestic animals such as cows or dogs, leaving behind non-organic materials including ceramics.

Ceramic densities are relatively low in the poorly preserved compounds NMQ8 and NMQ10, though are considerably higher in NMQ7 and NMQ9. None of these compounds, however, exhibits the extremely high densities found in parts of NMQ2 and NMQ3, indicating perhaps, that these areas were not used as ceramic dumps following their abandonment. This has important implications for the identification of possible chronological variation in ceramic forms, for if the compounds had very high ceramic densities, and were in fact used as dumps by residents of later compounds, then considerable chronological mixing would be found in the ceramics from these areas. Given the comparatively low ceramic densities in these compounds, we may assume that such mixing was relatively minor.

Variation in overall ceramic densities between compounds may relate in part to the differing depositional histories of the compounds. But these variations probably also result from differences in the major activities associated with the compounds. As discussed in detail in Chapter II, the eleven compounds vary considerably in form, and undoubtedly in use. On the basis of architecture alone, NMQ3, NMQ5, and NMQ12 are the simplest and most domestic appearing of the compounds, with the clear food preparation area in NMQ3 and an absence of outlying structures. NMQ2, with its complex of outlying rooms, and NMQ4, with its elevated central chamber and broad lower platforms, and, possibly, NMQ10, were probably not primarily residential structures, though it is possible that people resided in them. Ceramics and other domestic materials may have been a somewhat less important facet of the material inventory of these compounds than they were in those compounds interpreted as residential compounds.

WARE DISTRIBUTIONS

Information on ware frequencies from the NMQ compounds was derived from diagnostic sherd counts of flange and straight rim jar forms. Black and brown Plain Wares predominate in all of the compounds. The significance of distinctions between these two wares is not clear; ware colours may largely be related to position in the kiln during firing rather than to deliberate decisions of the potter or pottery user. While I will maintain and consider these distinctions in the present discussion, variation in frequencies of these ware classes should be treated cautiously. A second note of caution should be applied to units with small sample sizes. These units may contain the remains of only a small number of vessels and if numerous sherds from a single vessel are recovered, ware counts may be significantly affected.

Variations in ware distributions may be linked to a number of factors. It is possible that wares are linked to workshop differences—if some potters produced primarily brown Plain Ware, some black Plain Ware, some Burnished Wares, and so on. If pronounced ware groups can be defined in various areas of the site these might then be tied to differences in distribution patterns of different workshops. Certain wares, such as the Coarse Ware vessels are functionally specific and their presence in various provenience units can provide information on activity areas. Other wares, such as the red Burnished Ware, may be linked to a particular time of year, and may also represent a somewhat greater labour investment than the Plain Wares, in production time and in fuel needed for firing. This would presumably be reflected in an increased cost/value of these vessels and their distributions at Vijayanagara may provide information on differences in access to such materials. Whether workshops specialised in particular wares cannot yet be evaluated. Some differences in ware distributions are identifiable between the NMQ compounds, if not yet easily interpretable.

An additional strategy is being taken to consider workshop and ware variability. This is the petrographic analysis of ceramic thin-sections conducted by Alison Rautman (Rautman and Sinopoli 1985; Rautman, in press). Preliminary analyses of 92 sherds from all sampled areas of Vijayanagara indicate that there are significant differences between the areas in percentages of the various mineral inclusions in the sherds, in the degree of roundedness of the materials, and in the fineness of the paste.

Overall ware distributions in the NMQ compounds are presented in Table 5.2. Since, as noted above, body sherds could not be counted for all NMQ compounds, the ware counts presented in this table are derived from the total flange and straight rim restricted vessels from each compound. These are the most numerous of the vessel classes, and with the exception of the relatively rare flange bulging rim form, are not typically associated with any individual ware category. In all compounds the most numerous category is black Plain Ware, followed in frequency by brown Plain Ware, and, usually, red Burnished Ware.

A chi-square test of significance indicates that the compounds do differ significantly in the relative frequencies of these different wares, although their quantitative ranking is consistent between compounds. NMQ1, NMQ2, and NMQ9 contain significantly more black Plain Ware sherds than would be expected if no relation existed between wares and compounds. Compounds NMQ3, NMQ4, and NMQ8 contain more brown Plain Ware sherds than expected, and compounds NMQ4, NMQ5, and NMQ12 contain more red Burnished Ware sherds than expected if no relation existed between ware categories and individual compounds. These patterns are difficult to interpret, first, because the differences, though statistically significant, do not indicate dramatic differences between compounds since, for example, black Plain Ware is the most common ware in each compound. Second, as discussed earlier, the significance or intentionality of variations between black and brown Plain Wares is difficult to assess, and may result from unintentional factors in vessel production, or from post-production factors (i.e., a number of vessels may have been been blackened in the fires which destroyed many of the NMQ compounds). More interesting factors such as variation in workshop production and relations between vessel-use categories and ware classes, may play a role in inter-compound ware differences, but this can not be determined at present.

Ware distributions within compounds do not exhibit a great deal of variation between provenience units. Considering compound NMQ3, for example, where body sherd counts are available, some variations can be noted. Overall, black Plain ware sherds account for 47% of the total NMQ3 sample, red Plain Ware for 4%, and brown Plain Ware for 30% of the sample. Burnished Wares are scarce, comprising only 2% of the total sample, with approximately equal numbers of red and black burnished sherds. Nine percent of the sherds are decorated and five percent are of Coarse Ware. Unit 3.7 contains 40% Coarse Ware sherds. This unit is located near a ring well and most of the 70 Coarse Ware sherds recovered are fragments of that well. Unit 3.7 also contains unusually high percentages of decorated sherds (27%), perhaps due to the breakage and deposition of decorated water transport vessels near the well. Units 3.4 and 3.8 contain somewhat higher percentages of black Plain Ware than the mean (57 and 56%, respectively). Unit 3.1, the 'food preparation' area, contains low percentages of decorated sherds (7%) and a relatively high percentage of Coarse Ware sherds (5%), mostly sherds from cooking stoves. Burnished Wares are scarce throughout the sample; they occur with greatest frequency in Units 3.4 and 3.2 (4 and 2%, respectively). As discussed in Chapter IV, red Burnished Ware is particularly associated with a variant of the small vertical-necked serving vessels. The comparatively high percentages of red Burnished and red Plain Wares inside the main palace, may indicate that serving and consumption activities were important in those areas.

Similar distribution patterns may be observed in the other compounds. These patterns seem to result, in large part, from variations in the distributions of vessel-use classes between compounds and will therefore be accounted for in subsequent analyses of these distribution of vessel-use classes.

MORPHOLOGICAL/VESSEL-USE CLASSES DISTRIBUTIONS

As discussed in Chapter IV, the Vijayanagara ceramics may be divided into a number of broad classes on the basis of overall vessel morphology. Interpretations of primary vessel use of these classes were made on the basis of overall vessel form and analogies to contemporary vessel forms. For the restricted vessels six broad morphological or use classes were defined (RV1-RV6) including: (1) small serving vessels (RV1), (2) medium food preparation or short-team storage vessels (RV2), (3) large food preparation or short-term, storage vessels (RV3), (4) small vertical-necked serving or transport vessels (RV4), (5) medium vertical-necked transport or storage vessels, and (6) large vertical-necked storage or transport vessels (RV6).

The unrestricted vessels-use classes include lamps, probable lids (most shallow bowls), and probable food preparation or serving vessels (most 'other bowls'). Given the small sample sizes of these last categories, in this discussion I will consider shallow bowls and other bowls as two independent classes and not attempt to subdivide them further. Other classes of earthenware vessels identified at Vijayanagara include drain pipes, ring well linings, and incense burners.

Two major approaches were taken in considering the distributions of these broad vessel classes in the Noblemen's Quarter Area. First, frequencies of the various classes were plotted by unit and variations in their distributions were visually assessed. Second, a k-means cluster analysis (Kintigh and Ammerman 1982) was run on the frequency data in order to look at relations between units and to define groups of units characterised by similar ceramic assemblages. K-means is a non-hierarchical divisive clustering technique. Cases are grouped into clusters by minimising variances within clusters and maximising variances between them. The program used, developed by Kintigh, also permits an assessment of the level of overall clustering in the data, by comparing the actual clusters to analyses run on randomised data (see Kintigh and Ammerman 1982: 39).

A number of k-means cluster analyses were conducted on the NMQ samples. In some, the nine major functional classes were used. In others, only the six restricted vessel classes, which comprise the vast majority of the Vijayanagara ceramic inventory were considered. In each of these analyses, the values used were the relative frequencies of each class as a ratio of the summed count of the nine functional classes. The nine variable k-means analyses did not reveal significant patterning in the data. The analysis using the six restricted vessel classes did exhibit significant patterning, when compared against five repetitions of the clustering procedure using randomised data. Only the restricted vessel k-means results will be considered here. Analyses were performed on samples from all NMQ compounds (67 units; excluding compounds NMQ1 and NMQ2 which, as discussed earlier, either lack good provenience data or were not included in much of the typological classification; units which contained fewer than 15 diagnostic sherds were also excluded from this analysis), the well-preserved 'burnt' compounds (51 units), and the poorly preserved 'early' compounds (16 units). This discussion will primarily focus on the the sample of well-preserved units.

Summary information on the counts and percentages of the nine morphological vessel classes is presented in Table 5.3. General similarities between the compounds in the overall frequencies of the vessel classes are apparent. Lamps occur in extremely low frequencies, as do the other unrestricted vessel forms. Of the restricted vessel classes, class RV2— the medium food preparation/short-term storage vessels — is most common in all compounds, and in most units within each compound. Overall, Class RV2 accounts for 36% percent of the NMQ vessels. Class RV5 vessels — the medium vertical-necked transport and storage vessels — are the second most common vessel class, accounting for 29% of the diagnostic sherds. The other restricted vessel classes occur in relatively low frequencies in the overall NMQ samples (from 3-7% of the total sample).

Histograms were plotted of the frequencies of each of the vessel classes at 2, 4, and 5% intervals. These histograms reveal the overall range of distributions of each variable and in some cases, multi-modal distribution patterns. Classes RV1, RV2, and RV5 have non-normal distribution patterns. Class RV1, the small serving vessels, occurs in low frequencies throughout the sample, though in three units account for 15-20% of the vessels. Class RV2 vessels, the medium food preparation/short-term storage vessels, exhibit the broadest range of variation of any vessels, class, ranging from 9 to 54%, though small sample sizes and the wide spread of this variable makes this pattern difficult to interpret. Class RV5, the medium vertical-necked transport or storage vessel also exhibits a poly-modal distribution with possible peaks at 22 and 35%.

Before considering the results of the cluster analyses which permit comparisons between compounds, I would first like to briefly discuss the distributions of individual vessel - use classes. Individual provenience units in the NMQ sample are characterised by somewhat different ceramic assemblages, and dominated by different vessel classes. These variations are interpreted as resulting primarily from differences in the major activities which took place within those areas, particularly in the burnt compounds. The discussion of individual vessel classes will be followed by a presentation of the k-means cluster analysis results. Then, using both individual class data and cluster results, ceramic distributions will be summarised by compound. Finally, the various NMQ compounds will be examined in a comparative perspective.

Individual Classes

In this section, each vessel-use class will be considered separately, and their general range and areas of high and low frequencies, by compound and provenience unit, will be discussed. Summary data on the counts and frequencies of the nine vessel-use classes per compound are presented in Table 5.3. Information by individual provenience unit is presented in Tables 5.4 and 5.5.

Lamps are scarce throughout the entire Vijayanagara ceramic sample, with a total of 49 coded from NMQ3-NMQ12. Lamp counts per compound range from 1 in NMQ10 to 12 in NMQ12. The low frequencies of lamps in the NMQ area, and in the other sampled areas, indicate that these vessels were not of major importance in providing light in any of those areas; metal lamps or torches may have been used instead. It is likely that these small vessels were used, as they are today, primarily in worship at temples or shrines and are therefore not common in residential areas (though see discussion of NMQ1 below). The frequency of lamps per provenience unit ranges from none in the vast majority of units, to 18.2% in Unit NMQ5.4. Other units with relatively high frequencies of lamps include NMQ8.1 (6.5%), NMQ12.3 (6.0%), NMQ12.5 (8.3%), and NMQ12.7 (5.9%). A large number of lamp sherds were also found in a single provenience unit in NMQ1 (n=26; location unknown). Lamps often occur in association with pedestalled vessels, interpreted as incense burners, and the co-occurrence of these two vessel-use classes probably indicates the presence of a household shrine or place of worship. The large number of lamps found in or around the central chamber of the NMQ12 palace structure indicates that this room was used as a shrine by the occupants of the household, though a variety of other activities probably occurred there as well.

Shallow bowls are more common than lamps, with 304 bowls coded from NMQ3-12 (7.5% of the total diagnostics). As dicussed in Chapter IV, these vessels may have been used as lids or as cooking vessels ('griddles'). Shallow bowl counts per compound range from 14 in NMQ6 to 65 in NMQ4. Shallow bowl frequencies per compound range from 6.1% of total diagnostics in NMQ9 to 6.8% in NMQ5 to 9.5% in NMQ4, and 9.7% in NMQ6. Within each compound, shallow bowl frequency varies considerably between provenience units, from none in a small number of units to 26.1% of diagnostic sherds in Unit NMQ10.5. High shallow bowl frequencies are often associated with relatively high frequencies of RV5 and RV6 transport/storage vessels. The association of these forms indicates that the bowls may indeed have been used as lids, and may be most common in areas where storage of water or foodstuffs was important.

A total of 144 **other bowl** forms were analysed from NMQ3-12 (3.6% of total diagnostic sherds). As discussed in Chapter IV, the vessels included in the other bowl category exhibit a great deal of variation in general vessel shape and in vessel size and, presumably, in how they were used. Mean other bowl frequency per compound ranges from 1.7% in NMQ9 to 5.3% in NMQ12. High frequencies of other bowls by provenience unit are found in Unit NMQ10.1 (11.8%), Units NMQ12.4, NMQ3.2, and NMQ5.4 (9.1%), and Units NMQ9.2 and NMQ4.13 (8.7 and 8.6%, respectively). Given the broad range of uses to which these vessels were probably put, the significance of other bowl distribution patterns is unclear.

Class RV1 of the restricted vessels are small narrow cup-like vessels which range from 6-16 cm. in rim diametre. For the most part too small to have been used in cooking, these vessels have been interpreted as serving vessels which could have been used as drinking vessels or for holding individual servings or foodstuffs, such as yogurt or dal. They are found in low frequencies in the Vijayanagara ceramic inventory of the Noblemen's Quarter (total=223, 5.5% of the total diagnostics). The relative scarcity of these vessels indicates that they were not of major importance as serving vessels; it is likely that metal vessels or banana leaves would have served that purpose. RV1 Class vessels may have been used with specific materials or foodstuffs, or in particular contexts of use (such as wedding or other rituals), or may have been used as storage vessels for small quantities of goods, such as spices.

The percentage of RV1 vessels found in the NMQ provenience units ranges from none to 18.2%, with a sample mean of 5.5%. Overall RV1 distributions are highest in NMQ3, with a mean of 7.9%, and NMQ4, with a mean of 6.9% of diagnostic vessels. Compounds with low overall frequencies of RV1 vessels include NMQ8, with 3.2%, and NMQ9 with 3.6%. Such differences may relate to the overall importance of serving activities in these compounds. Within compounds the frequencies range from 3.4% in NMQ3.7 to 18.2% in NMQ3.2. Unit NMQ3.7 is located to the north of the compound near a ring well and it is not surprising that serving vessels occur in low frequencies here. Unit NMQ3.2, on the other hand, is located inside of the main structure of NMQ3, an area where we might expect serving and consumption activities to be important. In NMQ4, RV1 frequencies range from 3.9% in NMQ4.2 to 11.9% in NMQ4.7. Similar patterns and ranges hold for most other NMQ compounds.

Class RV2 is the most common of the Vijayanagara vessel classes. These are relatively shallow vessels, with low everted necks and rounded bases, which have been interpreted as cooking vessels or vessels used in the short-term storage of dry foodstuffs. The high percentages of these vessels in the ceramic inventory likely results both from their frequency of use and from high breakage rates related to contexts and stresses of use. A total of 1430 RV2 vessels were coded from the nine NMQ compounds, comprising 35.3% of the total diagnostic sherds. Overall frequencies of RV2 vessels by compound range from 25.2% in NMQ10 to 42.1% in NMQ4. NMQ7 (27.9%) and NMQ12 (29.9%) are also characterised by relatively low frequencies of RV2 vessels, perhaps indicative that food preparation activity areas are not well-represented in the samples from those compounds. Even the compounds with proportionately few RV2 vessels, however, include some provenience units with very high frequencies of these vessels. In NMQ10, for example, Unit NMQ10.2 contains 41.4% RV2 vessels while in NMQ7, Unit UMQ7.1 contains 33.7% RV2 vessels, and in NMQ12, Unit NMQ12.6 contains 39.5% RV2 vessels. The highest frequency of RV2 vessels is found in Unit NMQ4.1, with 53.8% of the diagnostic sherds belonging to this class. This unit is located in the narrow corridor between the northwest edge of the main structure and the compound wall and may have been a dump area of some sort. In units NMQ3.3 and NMQ4.2, 52.9% of the diagnostic vessels are of the RV2 class of food preparation and dry storage vessels.

Class RV3 includes vessels similar in shape to those of Class RV2, but larger in size. They have also been interpreted as cooking or short-term storage vessels, and occur in much lower frequencies than RV2 vessels. Only 206 RV3 diagnostic sherds were coded from the nine NMQ compounds, 5.1% of the total sample. Compound NMQ7 contains the highest overall frequencies of these forms, with RV3 vessels accounting for 7.7% of the diagnostic sherds coded. Compound NMQ12 contains the smallest percentage of RV3 vessels, with only 3.7% of coded diagnostics falling in this class; while in compound NMQ4, 3.8% of the diagnostics belong to the class of large cooking and food storage vessels. Frequencies of these vessels per provenience unit range from none to 15.4% in Unit NMQ7.4. Two of the five units coded from NMQ7 contain more than 10% RV3 vessels (NMQ7.4, NMQ7.2), while 3 of the 8 units coded from NMQ9 contain more than 10% diagnostic RV3 vessels (NMQ9.3-9.5). The presence of these large cooking vessels may be indicative of activities involving preparation of large quantities of food, either for feasting activities in public places, or for large domestic units.

Class RV4 is comprised of small-vertical necked vessels, with rim diametres ranging from 7-18 cm. These vessels have globular bodies and have been interpreted as serving or transport vessels, probably used for water. A total of 231 RV4 vessels were coded from the nine NMQ compounds, representing 5.7% of the total diagnostic sample. Compound NMQ12 contains the highest frequency of these vessels with 33 of 432 diagnostics, or 7.0% of all diagnostic sherds belonging to this class. RV4 vessels also occur in comparatively high frequencies in compound NMQ5, where they account for 7.0% of all diagnostic sherds. RV4 vessels are comparatively scarce in compounds NMQ6 where they account for only 3.6% of all diagnostic sherds. Frequencies of RV4 vessels per provenience unit range from none to 18.2% in Unit NMQ9.6. Areas with high relative frequencies of RV4 vessels may include areas in which serving was important.

Restricted vessel **Class RV5** is the second most common Vijayanagara vessel form, with 1193 diagnostic sherds coded from NMQ compounds NMQ3-NMQ12, 29.4% of the diagnostic sample. These vessels range from 14-28 cm. in rim diametre and have high vertical necks and large globular bodies. I have interpreted these as storage or transport vessels, again probably used for water. Class RV5 vessels outnumber total RV2 cooking vessel class counts in compound NMQ6, NMQ7, NMQ8, NMQ9, NMQ10, and NMQ12. They occur with greatest relative frequency in compound NMQ10, where they account for 40.6% of the total diagnostic sherds. They are rarest in compound NMQ3, where they count for only 21.2% of all diagnostic sherds. Frequencies of RV5 vessels exhibit considerable variation between provenience units in individual compounds. In NMQ3, for example, they range in frequency from 5.9% of the diagnostics in NMQ3.3, located inside of the main structure, to 32.5% of diagnostics in NMQ3.8, a unit located outside of the compound wall and a possible dump area. In NMQ10, the frequencies of RV5 vessels per provenience unit range from 26.1% in Unit NMQ10.6, located within the compound to the east of the main structure, to 60.7% in Unit NMQ10.6, located immediately to the southwest of NMQ10.5 These dramatic differences between the two NMQ10 units point to some pronounced differences in the activities which occurred in these adjacent areas.

Restricted vessel **Class RV6** contains larger variants of Class RV5, as well as the large round rim restricted vessels with low insloping necks. These large tall vessels were probably not easily movable when full and have been interpreted as storage vessels. Only 268 RV6 diagnostic sherds were coded from the nine NMQ compounds, 6.6% of the total diagnostic sample. They vary in overall frequency per compound from 3.9% of the diagnostics in NMQ4 (27 of 686 diagnostic sherds) to 10.4% of the diagnostics from NMQ7 (46 of 444 diagnostic sherds). Three of the five NMQ7 sample units lie to the south of the compound walls, near a large well and the other two units lie near water facilities within the NMQ3-10 compound block. The presence of comparatively large quantities of RV6 vessels in this compound may result from the importance of water collection and provisioning in these areas. In NMQ7 the frequencies of RV6 vessels per provenience unit ranges from 4.7% in NMQ7.1 to 25.6% in NMQ7.5, with more than 10.0% RV6 vessels in the remaining three provenience units. These vessels also account for 25.0% of the diagnostics from NMQ9.8 and 18.4% of all diagnostics from NMQ9.5

Although this discussion has focused in large part on differences between compounds and individual provenience units in the relative frequencies of the nine vessel-use classes, what is most impressive about these patterns is the striking similarities between compounds in overall patterns of ceramic distribution. The classes of medium cooking and short-term storage vessels (RV2) and water transport and storage vessels (RV5) are the most common vessel classes in all compounds, though do offer somewhat in their relative importance. In no case does a class that is relatively rare in the overall sample assume a major importance in any individual compound, though it may be important in individual provenience units. The RV2 and RV5 classes are the major ceramic classes in the total Vijayanagara assemblage. They are interpreted as serving two major uses: cooking and water storage. Had ceramics been used as dining vessels, we would expect much larger quantities of shallow bowls and other bowls in the inventory. These are not found in the NMQ area. Had lamps been a major source of household lighting or had these compounds been used as primarily places of worship, these forms would also be common.

Means Cluster Results

The overall similarities in ceramic distributions between the nine sampled NMQ compounds point to some general similarities in the ways that these compounds were used. As will be discussed below, differences in ceramic distributions between compounds and provenience units allow us to consider behavioral and social variation between the architectural compounds of the Noblemen's Quarter area.

In the discussion of individual vessel classes and their distributions, presented above, I did not take into account contextual differences between compounds in the nature of their archaeological deposits. In particular, we may expect pronounced differences in the nature and significance of ceramic distributions between the burnt compounds, from which we have floor level deposits, and the poorly preserved compounds which consist today of foundations, from which we have fill deposits. In the subsequent discussion of the k-means cluster analysis performed on the relative frequencies of vessel-use classes, these contexts will be considered separately, with a primary focus on the well-preserved floor level deposits.

A number of k-means cluster analyses were conducted using a computer program developed by Kintigh (1982) at the University of Michigan computer facilities. Like all clustering techniques, k-means is a complex algorithm which involves considerable computation, and is too cumbersome to be done without the aid of the computer. The data used in the cluster analyses were the relative frequencies of the vessel-use classes from each provenience unit which contained more than 15 diagnostic sherds. Smaller units were discarded from the analysis because of the problem of sampling error. Analyses were conducted using all nine vessel-use classes, and using only the six restricted vessel-use classes.

As discussed in Chapter IV above, cluster analysis is a technique which groups cases on the basis of their overall similarity, according to some specific measure of similarity. A large number of variables can be incorporated into a cluster analysis, permitting the consideration of the importance of a variety of factors or variables in cluster determination rather than just the one or two variables incorporated into simpler statistical techniques.

K-means is a non-hierarchical divisive clustering technique. Divisive means that cases are divided into successively smaller groups at each stage of the analysis. At the initial stage, all cases are grouped into one large cluster, at the next stage they are divided into two clusters, next, three, and so on. Non-hierarchical refers to the ability of this technique to reassign cases between clusters at subsequent stages of analysis. That is, if cases 3 and 6 and cases 4 and 7 are grouped together at the two cluster level of analysis, they will not necessary be grouped in the same way at the 5 cluster level of analysis, in which for example, cases, 3, 4, and 6 may be classed in the same cluster, and case 7 in another cluster. This is very different from most clustering algorithms in which the groupings at one level of the analysis determine the groupings at subsequent levels.

In k-means analysis, cases are grouped into clusters by minimising variances within clusters and maximising variances between them. The program used also permits an assessment of the level of overall clustering in the data, by comparing the actual clusters to analyses run on randomised data and considering changes in the Sum of Squared Errors between actual and random data (see Kintigh and Ammerman 1982: 39). In the analysis of the nine vessel-use classes from the NMQ compounds, no significant patterning was evident in the data; therefore only the analyses of the six restricted vessel classes will be discussed.

The k-means analysis of units with secure provenences examined restricted vessel class frequencies from 51 NMQ provenience units—either floor and fill level deposits from burnt compounds, or floor level units from areas outside of the compound walls. The six cluster solution was selected on the basis of decreases in the Sum of Squared Errors (%SSE) as evaluated against two runs with randomised data and by an examination of mean vessel class frequencies by cluster. Information on each cluster mean is presented in Table 5.16, along with a list of the provenience units assigned to each cluster.

As evident in Table 5.16, each cluster is characterised by a very different ceramic assemblage or different 'ceramic signature'. These will be considered in some detail. Cluster 1, with 11 members, is characterised by a high frequency of transport and storage vessels, and by a low frequency of serving vessels. Food preparation vessels of classes RV2 and RV3 also occur with relatively low frequency in Cluster 1, where they comprise 31.4% of the total vessels, vs. 37.1% in the total sample. Cluster 2, with 18 members, on the other hand, contains a very high proportion of the RV2 food preparation vessels (44.3%) and relatively low frequencies of serving and transport or storage vessels. This cluster may be characterised as a 'cooking or dry storage' cluster. Cluster 3, with only 3 members, contains the highest overall proportion of serving vessels of any of the clusters, with a mean of 8.7% RV1 small serving vessels and 15.7% RV4 small water or other liquid serving vessels, with a combined mean of 24.4% serving vessels. Large cooking vessels are extremely rare in cluster 3 (.6%), and medium cooking vessels occur with somewhat lower frequency than in the overall sample. Water transport vessels of class RV5 occur in relatively large numbers in this cluster (32.6%).

Cluster 4 of the 6 cluster solution k-means cluster contains 4 members, and is characterised by high frequencies of RV1 small serving vessels (15.4%) and by high frequencies of RV2 cooking vessels (41.9%). Water serving, transport, and storage vessels occur in relatively low frequencies in this cluster. The dominant activities represented in Cluster 4, then, are food serving and preparation. Cluster 5, with 6 members, is characterised by high frequencies of RV5 water transport/storage vessels (12.5%) and high frequences of the large cooking/dry storage vessels of class RV3 (11.1%). The medium cooking/dry storage vessels are relatively rare in this cluster (RV2, only 21.9%), as are the large water storage vessels (RV6, 2.9%). Cluster 6 contains 6 members and is characterised by very high frequences of RV6 large water storage vessels (14.6%) and by low frequencies of food preparation vessels. Small water serving vessels of class RV4 occur in somewhat higher then expected frequencies in this cluster. Areas characterised by ceramics of this cluster may have been used as storage and distribution/serving areas for liquids, in particular, water.

The spatial distributions of the k-means clusters in the Noblemen's Quarter are illustrated in Figures 5.1 and 5.2 (see also, Table 5.6). A comprehensive discussion of their distribution will be presented in the subsequent section of this chapter, in the consideration of each compound individually. Some general comments can be made at this point, however.

Of the 13 provenience units which are located outside the compound walls of the NMQ3-10 block or of NMQ12, seven are grouped in cluster 1, four in cluster 2, one in cluster 3, and two in cluster 6. Both clusters 1 and 6 are associated with water transport and storage, and 9 of the 13 units located outside of the compound walls fall in this group. The three units to the south of compound NMQ7 (NMQ7.1-7.3), and the unit to the north of NMQ3 (NMQ3.7) are all associated with water facilities, a rock-cut well in the case of the NMQ7 units and a ring well at NMQ3. The high frequencies of water vessels in these areas likely relates to the proximity of these features; as procurement locations, and, perhaps, in the case of the NMQ7 units, as storage areas. Each of the NMQ7 units are also characterised by relatively high frequencies of shallow bowls, probably used as lids on storage jars. Of the four units located outside of the compound walls which contain ceramics assigned to cluster 2, three are located immediately adjacent to the cluster walls, in areas which may best be interpreted as dumps (see, in particular, Unit NMQ8.1). In these contexts, the cluster 2 ceramic assemblages may be seen as containing kitchen refuse. The other area, Unit NMQ6.1, which is characterised by cluster 2 ceramics, also contains a number of grinding stones and may, like Unit NMQ3.1 (see below) be interpreted as a food preparation area.

A number of compounds appear to be dominated by particular ceramic clusters. For example, in NMQ4, cluster 2 is dominant, with eight out of 13 provenience units classed in this cluster, which is dominated by food preparation vessels. In NMQ 10, four of the seven provenience units included in the analysis were assigned to cluster 1, which is dominated by serving and transport vessels. Overall differences between compounds will be considered below. Before considering general patterns of ceramic distributions within and among the NMQ compounds, I will briefly consider the distributions of the other, less common vessel classes.

OTHER VESSEL CLASSES

Included in the category of other vessel classes are: Coarse Ware vessels, including ovens and ring well linings, earthenware drain pipes and roof tiles, and pedestalled vessels or incense burners. Each of these classes is rare in the Vijayanagara ceramic assemblage, but given the functional specificity of each class, their distributions can lend important supporting evidence to the distributions of the more common unrestricted and restricted vessel classes. The counts of these other vessel classes by compound are presented in Table 5.7. It should be noted that the counts of some of these vessels undoubtedly represent an underestimate of the total numbers recovered in these areas. Ring wells, for example, were identified primarily by rim sherds, and in the area to the north of NMQ3, a large number of ring well body sherds were also found. In addition, small fine ceramic pieces, such as pedestals or gaming pieces were frequently treated separately by the excavators. These were bagged and removed from the general ceramic assemblages, and were therefore not included in these analyses. The same limitation also applies to small highly burnished jars (of class RV1) which were probably used in ritual contexts, and to earthenware figurines, which were extremely rare in the Vijayanagara ceramic assemblage, though not nonexistent.

Drain pipes and roof tiles are abundant in compound NMQ4, where 88 drain pipe sherds were examined. These were found primarily in two provenience units, located on opposite ends of the lower tier of the main palace structure. A flat roof likely overlay these chambers and the drain pipes served to drain off monsoon rains that accumulated on the roof. Other vessels placed on the roof of the structure may also be included in the sampled deposits. Unit 4.11 in NMQ4A also contained considerable numbers of drain pipe fragments (n=19), indicating that the single room rectangular structure in that area also had a flat roof. Eighteen drain pipes were identified from NMQ5, with most coming from Unit NMQ5.1, in the alley between NMQ3, 4, and 5. These pipes may have been used for draining water from the three NMQ compounds, or may provide evidence for roofed structures within the alley itself. A large number of drain pipes are also found in the units surrounding the main structure of NMQ10, and probably were originally associated with the flat roof of that structure.

Roof tiles were quite rare in the NMQ ceramic inventory, perhaps indicating that the roofs were indeed used as living surfaces, with plaster rather than tiled surfaces. A number of roof tiles were found in NMQ4A, with 20 in Unit 4.3 and 3 in Unit 4.12. This small 'gymnasium' and latrine compound, then, appears to have been fully roofed.

Coarse Ware sherds were found throughout the NMQ area, and include ring well sherds, small cooking ovens, and large storage vats or trays. Not surprisingly, the ring well sherds are most common in Unit NMQ3.7 located to the north of the NMQ3 compound wall, where a ring well has been identified. More than 40 ring well sherds were identified in this unit. A number of ring well sherds are also associated with the latrine complex in NMQ4. A number of Coarse Ware oven sherds were found in NMQ3 as well, these primarily associated with Unit NMQ3.1, which also contains a grinding stone.

Pedestalled bases are rare throughout the NMQ sample, and counts per compound range from none in the NMQ7 samples to 10 from NMQ12. NMQ12 contains twice as many pedestalled vessels as NMQ4, the compound with the next highest counts. In NMQ12, these vessels are found primarily in two units: NMQ12.7, the central room of the main structure, and NMQ12.6, a probable dump area which lies outside of the compound walls. The central areas of the structure are also characterised by a large number of lamps and small highly burnished jars, all indicative of a household shrine located in the core of the main structure.

THE DISTRIBUTION OF VESSEL—USE CLASSES IN THE NOBLEMEN'S QUARTER COMPOUNDS WITH GOOD PROVENIENCE: INTERPRETATION AND SUMMARY

The analysis of the distribution of morphological or vessel-use classes in the excavated Noblemen's Quarter compounds NMQ3-NMQ6, NMQ7, NMQ10, and NMQ12 which have floor-level deposits and good stratigraphic and vertical control has yielded some expected and some unexpected results. Before considering specific interpretations of the NMQ provenience units, a few general points should be made.

The interpretations of each unit are based on the statistical dominance of particular vessel classes in the units. In each provenience unit an array of vessel classes is found; no unit is clearly dominated by a single vessel class. Each of the units examined included some fill deposits, even those noted as solely floor level deposits by the excavators. Some mixing of materials from floors and fills must be assumed for each unit. It must also be acknowledged that some of these interpretations are based on small sampling sizes and sampling errors may result in the inaccurate representation of certain classes. Questions concerning archaeological processes also impact on our interpretations of these areas: the collapse of upper storeys could result in mixing of materials; the effects of soil accumulation and deflation after site abandonment have undoubtedly contributed to some movement of materials from their original depositional contexts. These issues cannot be adequately evaluated with the available data, but are acknowledged here as having played a role in the ultimate distribution of the ceramic materials analysed from the Noblemen's Quarter area.

The interpretations of functionally differentiated areas in the NMQ compounds ultimately rest upon the adequacy of interpretations of primary vessel uses as presented above and in Chapter IV. These interpretations, based on overall vessel morphology, analogies to contemporary South Indian forms, and the suitability of particular forms to particular uses, are not comprehensive. Certainly, earthenware vessels were used for many more purposes than those considered here. The interpretations of vessel uses have considerable room for improvement and elaboration. The association of particular vessel classes with architectural and archaeological features which can be independently evaluated can aid in this refinement. In turn, the patterned variability of the various ceramic classes can help in the clarification of our interpretations of the archaeological contexts.

Turning now specifically to ceramic distributions in individual compounds, the distributions of ceramic classes in Compound NMQ3 provide strong support for archaeological and architectural interpretations of compound use (Figure 5.3). Unit NMQ3.1, with a very high ceramic density, has, as expected, been shown to contain high percentages of Class RV2 food preparation and dry storage vessels along with high percentages of bowls (lids) and of large storage vessels. Serving vessels and medium water transport-storage vessels occur in low frequencies in this unit, which was classed in cluster 2 of the k-means analysis. A number of earthenware stove fragments were also recovered in Unit NMQ3.1. Ceramic distributions in this area thus support the interpretations developed from the archaeological context and facilities that this was a food preparation area.

Units NMQ3.2 and NMQ3.3 are located inside of the main structure of the compound, and contain both fill and floor deposits. Although somewhat different in ceramic composition, both of these units were classed in cluster 4 of the k-means analysis, and contain relatively high frequencies of RV1 small serving vessels. Unit NMQ3.2 contains much higher frequencies of water storage vessels than Unit NMQ3.3, in which RV2 and RV4 water serving vessels are more common. While most of the nine broad vessel classes are found in these units, serving vessels are unusually common, indicating that food and liquid consumption may have been of particular importance in these areas inside the main palace structure.

Unit NMQ 3.4 is located in the plaster-surfaced plaza to the north of the main structure, against the northern wall of the compound. This unit was assigned to cluster 3 and contains high percentages of small serving vessels and relatively low percentages of cooking or storage vessels. This finely-surfaced area may have served as a gathering place or living area during the hot weather. Unit NMQ3.5 is located to the southeast of Unit NMQ3.4 and contains a very different ceramic inventory. It is classed in cluster 6 of the k-means analysis, and contains high percentages of large storage vessels (RV6) and of shallow bowls. Also common in this unit are the small vertical-necked serving-transport vessels (RV4). As noted earlier, this unit is located near the probable compound entryway and near a well, and may have been a locus for storing water within the compound.

Unit NMQ3.6 is a fill level located in the corridor to the south of the main structure. It is classed in cluster 2 of the k-means analysis and contains high frequencies of classes RV2 and RV3 vessels. The precise depositional context of this deposit is difficult to interpret, though it seems unlikely that these vessels would have been in use or deposited as trash in the area in which they were recovered. Their location might result from the collapse of an upper storey or, possibly, their use in construction (perhaps in the compound walls?), or from other post-abandonment archaeological processes.

Units NMQ3.7 and NMQ3.8 are located outside of the NMQ3 compound walls. Unit NMQ3.7, located to the north of the compound not far from the well, contains floor and fill deposits found above a packed-earth surface. This area also contains a number of poorly preserved walls, with associated grinding stones, perhaps a residential area for serving groups associated with the NMQ compounds. A very large number of sherds were recovered from this unit, with a fairly low breakage rate. Serving vessels (RV1 and RV4) are scarce in this area, while RV5 and RV2 vessels are common. Unit NMQ3.8 also contains large numbers of sherds and an extremely high density of ceramic materials (337 sherds per cubic metre) in a fill deposit. This unit was classed in cluster 2 of the k-means analysis, containing high frequencies of water transport and storage vessels (RV5 and RV6). Unit NMQ3.8 may be interpreted as a dump area, used perhaps by the occupants of NMQ3 and/or by the users/residents of the adjacent compounds (NQ4-NMQ7), and by users of the well. Densities of ceramics are much lower in Unit NMQ3.7 (only 35 per cubic metre). This area, with its packed-earth surface, may have been along a path or public open area associated with the well, and the materials found here may be related to breakage of vessels filled or cleaned at the well.

Compound 4 in the Noblemen's Quarter is divisible into two major areas, designated as (central) NMQ4 and NMQ4A. These areas were linked by a doorway through the major east-west wall which encloses an open area to the east of the main structure of the central compound. Some traces of earlier architectural construction are evident in this open area. Ceramics were coded from seven units in NMQ4 (4.1-4.7) and from six units in NMQ4A (4.8-4.13). The NMQ4 compound is the largest of the excavated NMQ compounds, with the exception of NMQ1, and is architecturally complex. It appears to have been built relatively late in the NMQ sequence. Ceramic densities in NMQ4 are generally low, and several of the provenience units contained fewer than 25 diagnostic sherds. In this discussion, variation between individual provenience units in the distributions of vessel classes will first be considered, followed by a discussion of general differences between the central NMQ4 area and NMQ4A (Figure 5.4).

Units NMQ4.1-4.4 in the main compound of NMQ4 are all grouped into cluster 2 of the k-means analysis. This cluster is characterised by relatively high percentages of RV2 food preparation and dry storage vessels, and low frequencies of serving and transport vessels. This does not accord with expectations for the main structure of a palace complex where we would expect food preparation to be of negligible importance, and serving and possibly, storage of greater importance. Of these units, Unit NMQ4.3 has relatively high frequencies of RV4 serving vessels which accords with our expectations.

Striking variation in ceramic frequencies occurs between Units NMQ4.4 and NMQ4.7, located in close proximity in the northern chamber on the lower tier of the main structure. Unit NMQ4.4 is composed mostly of floor deposits and 4.7 of floor and fill deposits. These two contiguous units differ significantly in frequencies of RV2 vessels (48.1% vs. 23.8%), RV3 vessels (1.9% vs. 7.1%), RV4 vessels (17.3% vs. 31.0%), and RV6 vessels (5.8% vs. 2.4%). The units were grouped into different clusters in the k-means analysis. While the differences between these two samples may result from differences in the division of space within this chamber, this seems unlikely. Rather, problems of sampling error caused by relatively small sample sizes from these units (63 and 52 diagnostics) may have biased the samples, or the differences between the units may be reflecting differences between floor and fill deposits.

Unit NMQ4.5 is located outside of the structure, near its southern edge, and is composed entirely of fill deposits. This unit contained only 25 diagnostic sherds. Unit NMQ4.5 was classed in cluster 5 of the k-means analysis, characterised by high percentages of RV5 vessels. This fill deposit may include materials from the collapsed roof of the main palace structure, as well from areas surrounding the structure. Unit NMQ4.6 is located on the lower tier of the main structure and includes primarily floor deposits from the central and southern chamber. Unit NMQ4.6 was assigned to cluster 4 of the k-means analysis and contained high percentages of RV2 and RV3 vessels and of the small serving vessels of Class RV1.

The remainder of the NMQ4 samples come from the NMQ4A area. Four of the six units in this area were classed in cluster 2 of the k-means analysis, characterised by high percentages of cooking and dry storage vessels. Again, these distributions do not accord with our expectations for the gymnasium latrine area and may provide evidence of ceramic mixing.

Unit NMQ4.8 is located near the compound wall which separated NMQ4A from the main NMQ4 area, within a small complex of walls and drains. The sample of 47 diagnostic sherds comes from fill deposits. Sherds in this unit are highly fragmented, with a breakage ratio of .204, though it is not clear if this deposit contains deliberate fill or refuse deposition, or if it has been accumulated after the abandonment of the compound. Unit NMQ4.8 was classed in cluster 1 of the k-means analysis, containing high frequencies of class RV2 restricted vessels, and of shallow bowls and other bowls. Medium vertical-necked transport vessels (RV5) are relatively scarce in this sample.

Units 4.9-4.11 are located in the toilet area of NMQ4A, with Unit NMQ4.9 located near the toilet, unit NMQ4.10 near the entryway to that facility, and unit NMQ4.11 located in an area of drains behind the toilet area. Each of these units is composed of floor and fill deposits, with fairly high ceramic densities (64, 71, and 84 sherds per cubic metre). Ceramic samples from these units, gratifyingly, contained relatively high frequencies of water transport/storage vessels and of shallow bowls (lids?), and lower than average frequencies of RV2 and RV3 cooking short-term storage vessels. Units 4.9-4.11 also contained large numbers of Coarse Ware sherds interpreted as well or drain linings.

The two spatial divisions of NMQ4, central NMQ4 and NMQ4A, exhibit some general differences in overall ceramic distributions. The central NMQ4 area contains a higher percentage of class RV2 and RV3 vessels, which have been interpreted as associated with food preparation or short-term storage. Area NMQ4A contains higher frequencies of Class RV4 and RV5 vessels, which have been associated with water transport, storage, and serving. NMQ4A also contains somewhat higher percentages of shallow bowl forms, which have been interpreted as lids, as well as Coarse Ware drainage pipes. The distributions of ceramics in NMQ4A, while not as clear-cut as might be hoped, do exhibit patterns that would be expected in an area devoted to personal hygiene.

It is unfortunate that no samples could be analysed from areas outside of the main structure in the central NMQ4 compound. The open area to the east of the structure, with its enigmatic complex of wall stubs, contained very little deposition and negligible ceramic samples. The area behind the structure contains a possible grinding stone and a flagstone surface, and is perhaps equivalent to Unit NMQ3.1

Ceramic samples designated as coming from Compound NMQ5 included two distinctive areas. Units NMQ5.4-NMQ5.7 are located within the main structure and walled architectural compound, while units NMQ5.1-NMQ5.3, and NMQ5.8 are found in the alley which lies to the east of the compound. As might be expected these areas differ somewhat in the ceramics found within them. In particular, the alley contains higher frequencies of RV4 small water serving vessels and RV3 large food preparation or dry storage vessels than the main compound samples. The main compound, on the other hand, contains higher than expected frequencies of RV5 storage and transport vessels.

Units within the main compound were grouped into three k-means clusters, evident of a wide range of activities. Units NMQ5.4 and NMQ5.6 were assigned to cluster 1, characterised by high frequencies of water storage and transport vessels. Unit NMQ5.4, located to the north of the main structure near the northern boundary of the compound, also contains high frequencies of lamps and other bowl forms. This may have been a storage area, similar to Unit NMQ3.5 in compound 3 which is also located near the main entry of its compound. Unit NMQ5.6, located on the lowest tier of the main structure, contains high frequencies of shallow bowls and other bowls, and relatively high frequencies of RV6 large storage vessels.

Unit NMQ5.7, located on the uppermost tier of the main structure, was classed in cluster 5 of the k-means analysis, and also contains relatively large numbers of storage and transport vessels of class RV5. Small water serving vessels of class RV4 are also quite common here. The final unit within the main compound of NMQ5 is Unit NMQ5.5, which was classed in k-means cluster 1. A number of drain pipe sherds, and large Coarse Ware vessel fragments were also found in this unit. Unit NMQ5.5 likely includes both floor and fill deposits, and may have, in part, served as a kitchen area for the occupants of compound NMQ5.

Three k-means clusters are found in the alley area to the east of NMQ5. Units NMQ5.2 and NM5.3 are classed in cluster 2, characterised by relatively high frequencies of RV2 vessels. These units differ considerably in the frequencies of the less common vessel classes. In Unit NMQ5.2 are found high frequencies of RV3 large food preparation/dry storage vessels and RV4 small serving vessels, while Unit NMQ5.8 contains relatively high frequencies of other bowls, RV1 small serving vessels, and RV6 large storage vessels. Unit NMQ5.1 which lies between units NMQ5.2 and NMQ5.3 is characterised by a very different ceramic assemblage and was classed in k-means cluster 5, with high frequencies of transport and storage vessels, and large food preparation or dry-storage vessels. Large numbers of drain pipe fragments are also found in this area. The fourth unit from the alley is NMQ5.8, located on the southern edge of the alley. This unit, which belongs to k-means cluster 6, is also characterised by large numbers of RV5 and RV6 water storage and transport vessels, and of RV4 serving vessels. Like the main NMQ5 compound, the units from the alley include ceramics representative of a wide range of activities. Whether these represent in situ deposits, indicating that this area was actually used for preparation of foods, storage, and serving, or whether these are fill deposits of refuse from the main compounds, is, at present, difficult to ascertain.

Unfortunately, no units could be coded from inside of the NMQ6 compound, with its complicated architectural history. Ceramics were examined from three units located outside of the compound walls, immediately to the west of the NMQ6 compound. Traces of walls are found in the westernmost of these units, while in Unit NMQ6.3, located adjacent to the compound wall, no architecture is present. As noted earlier, these areas, with their less substantial architecture, may represent servants quarters or other service areas associated with the major Noblemen's Quarter compounds.

Ceramic samples from the NMQ6 units are relatively small, with no unit containing more than 61 diagnostic sherds. Units NMQ6.1 is classed in cluster 2 of the k-means cluster analysis, while Units NMQ6.2 and NMQ6.3 are classed in cluster 1. Cluster 1 is characterised by relatively high frequencies of RV5 and RV6 storage and transport vessels and by low frequencies of serving vessels. RV2 and RV3 food preparation and dry storage vessels are rare in Units NMQ6.2 and NMQ6.3. Shallow bowls are common in Unit NMQ6.3, and may have been used as lids on the large storage vessels. Unit NMQ6.1., on the other hand, contains very high proportions of cooking vessels. Unit NMQ6.1 may have been a residential area, while Units NMQ6.2 and NMQ6.3, located closer to the major compound wall, may have been less intensively occupied, used either as storage or dump areas.

Five sample units were examined from Compound NMQ7 (Figure 5.6), though only three of these will be considered in this discussion. Samples located inside of the main compound will not be examined, as this discussion is limited to deposits from above floor archaeological contexts. The three units to be considered NMQ7.1-NMQ7.3, like the NMQ6 units, lie outside of the compound walls, at a considerably greater distance than the NMQ6 units discussed above. Traces of small earth and stone walls are found in this area, and grinding stones are abundant. A large rock-cut well, which was apparently used for dumping waste products after it ceased serving its original use, is located near Unit NMQ7.2, and contained tremendously high densities of ceramics, including a large number of nearly complete vessels (Figure 5.7).

Unit NMQ7.1 was assigned to cluster 1 of the k-means analysis, while Units NMQ7.2 and NMQ7.3 belong to cluster 6. Each of these clusters is characterised by high percentages of transport and storage vessels of classes RV5 and RV6, with the latter being more common in cluster 6 (mean of 15.6%). Lamps are common in Unit NMQ7.1, perhaps evident of a residential use of this area, and shallow bowls and other bowls are common in all three units. Unit NMQ7.2 also contains relatively high frequencies of class RV3 large food preparation/dry storage vessels and of RV4 small serving vessels. The ratios of vessels found in the area of the rock-cut well, may, in part, reflect ceramic breakage ratios, as well as the nature of vessel use in this area of the site.

Ceramic samples from the main part of NMQ7, and NMQ8, and NMQ9 are not included in this discussion, as they are primarily derived from sub-floor levels in the compounds, and are therefore not relevant to considerations of vessel use and activity distribution. NMQ10 is in a considerably better state of preservation and will be considered in this analysis. Ceramics were examined from seven provenience units in Compound NMQ10 (Figure 5.6), three of which lie immediately outside of the compound walls. The other four units lie within the compound to the east and north of the main structure. No samples were examined from within the structure itself.

The units located outside of the compound walls fall into two k-means clusters — cluster 1 (NMQ10.1 and NMQ10.7) and 2 (NMQ10.2). Units within the compound were assigned to clusters 1 (Units NMQ10.3, NMQ10.4), 5(NMQ10.6) and 6

(NMQ10.5). Each of these three clusters contains relatively high frequencies of RV5 water transport and storage vessels, and cluster 6 contains a high frequency of large RV6 storage vessels. As with all NMQ provenience units, each of the NMQ10 units contains a variety of other vessel forms, though, in general, food preparation and short-term storage vessels occur in relatively low frequencies in this area.

The final NMQ compound from which floor-level ceramic samples are available is Compound NMQ12 (Figure 5.8). Ceramics were examined from eight provenience units: two outside of the compound wall, four in the main structure, and two outside but adjacent to the main NMQ12 structure. Five of the six k-means clusters are represented in this sample, indicating that a wide diversity of activities occurred within this compound. Units NMQ12.6 and NMQ12.8, located outside of the compound walls, were assigned to clusters 1 and 3, respectively. Units inside the main structure assigned to cluster 1 (NMQ12.7), cluster 2 (NMQ12.4, NMQ12.5), and cluster 6 (NMQ12.3), while units adjacent to the main structure were assigned to clusters 1 (NMQ12.1) and 5(NMQ12.2).

As noted earlier, a large number of oil lamps and pedestalled vessels were found in Units NMQ12.5 and NMQ12.7 on the uppermost tier of the structure, indicative of the presence of a household shrine (Figure 5.9). High frequencies of RV6 storage vessels are found in Unit NMQ12.3, a side chamber of the structure, perhaps used as a storeroom. Serving vessels are common in Unit NMQ12.1, located immediately behind the main structure, and food preparation vessels are common in Unit 12.4 on the lowest tier of the main structure. The ceramics of the NMQ12 compound indicate both the spatially discrete distribution of activities within the compound and the presence of a wide array of activities.

The ceramic distributions of the seven NMQ compounds discussed here aid in the consideration of the distributions of activities and the range of activities which occurred within each of these distinct, yet broadly similar architectural compounds. As will be discussed in the next section, some general differences between compounds can be shown to exist, in their ceramics inventories, and in the presumed uses to which they were put. The ceramic patterns discussed in this section, at the level of the individual compound and provenience unit, are complicated by the nature of our samples and the adequacy of the present classification. Nonetheless, the discussion presented here does, I hope, serve to demonstrate the usefulness of ceramic analysis for examining and interpreting the Noblemen's Quarter area of Vijayanagara.

NOBLEMEN'S QUARTER COMPOUNDS COMPARED

The analysis of the spatial distributions of the nine vessel-use classes in the Noblemen's Quarter points to some broad similarities and differences among the individual compounds (Figure 5.10). Ceramic distribution patterns in the Noblemen's Quarter, in turn, illustrate some general patterns characteristic of all Vijayanagara ceramics, particularly, the importance of various ceramic classes in the industry overall. These analyses also permit the identification of social and functional variations within this area of this site. Overall distributions of the nine ceramic classes are broadly similar in each of the NMQ compounds, though some, relatively minor but important, differences exist among the individual compounds. In all compounds, classes RV2 and RV5 are the most common, indicating the relative importance of ceramics in food preparation and storage, even in elite contexts. Other classes play a much less important role, and are found in much lower frequencies in the ceramic assemblage.

As noted earlier, each of the ceramic classes defined undoubtedly obscures considerably variability in vessel use. These variations most likely relate to variations within the broad vessel-use categories defined. Formal variants within the RV2 class interpreted as cooking vessels, for example, may incorporate vessels used for the preparation of different sorts of foods; i.e., rice vs. vegetable dishes vs. meat dishes. As discussed earlier, the nature of the ceramic sample, in particular, the absence of whole vessels in the sample, precludes the definition of finer morphological classes at this stage of analysis.

The NMQ area, as interpreted from archaeological and ceramic evidence, appears to be a very diverse and complex area, chronologically and socially. Unlike our traditional models of caste society, where members of different castes reside in discrete, isolated residential districts, it appears that both high and low status groups may have resided in close proximity in this area of Vijayanagara. The high status groups, who may themselves encompass a variety of social or caste groups, resided within some of the NMQ compounds, while lower status individuals and groups appear to have resided in less durable structures located near the compounds, traces of which are found to the north, south and east of the NMQ3-10 block.

Just who were the individuals or families that resided within the NMQ palace compounds is difficult to say. The location of these compounds within the city's royal centre and the proximity of the compounds to the royal residential area, points to the interpretation that the occupants or users of the Noblemen's Quarter area were important individuals or families. Although non-earthenware goods found in the NMQ area are not a subject of this study, it should be noted that compound NMQ1, the largest of the NMQ compounds, contained over 80 pieces of blue on white Chinese porcelain, including what appears to have been a set of small bowls. The presence of such large quantities of these exotic, and presumably, valued goods, again points to the high status of the occupants of this household, and perhaps, a special relationship with Chinese emissaries to the site, or directly with China. Among the interpretations proposed for the Noblemen's Quarter area is that the compounds were the houses of regional rulers or *nayakas,* who resided in them during those portions of the year, such as during the Mahanavami festival, when they visited the capital.

Despite the fact that all of the NMQ compounds may be classed as one coherent form of Vijayanagara architecture, considerable variation is evident between compounds, both in their plans, and in the ceramic assemblages found within them. Each compound varies considerably in size, layout, and complexity. In terms of the ceramic assemblages, certain of the compounds, such as NMQ3, NMQ5, and NMQ12, contain a wide range of vessel-use classes, and presumably, a wide range of activities involving ceramics, including food preparation, serving, storage, and worship, occurred within them. These compounds may best be interpreted as domestic or residential compounds and their comparatively simple architectural plan supports these interpretations. The NMQ1 compound may also have been a residential compound, though the size of the compound, and the numerous outlying structures would indicate that the residents, were at the very least, very important people in the city and state of Vijayanagara. NMQ3, NMQ5, and NMQ12 each cover less than half of the area of the NMQ1 compounds.

Others of the Noblemen's Quarter compounds, including NMQ4 and NMQ10, and probably NMQ2, are much more restricted in the frequencies and distributions of ceramic vessel-use classes found within them, and in the k-means clusters assigned to them. These compounds are interpreted as being primarily non-residential compounds, although some people may have resided in them. Again, the architectural plans of these compounds provide supporting evidence for these interpretations. Compound NMQ4, for example, includes a great deal of open, public space, when compared to other compounds, such as NMQ3. There is a very large open area to the east to the main structure, and the lowest tier of the structure is an extremely large open area. The structure's central chamber is unique among Vijayanagara palace structures in being a platform, rather than a room. Local leaders may have used this platform on ceremonial or other occasions to address individuals standing or seated on the lower levels of the structure, or in the open courtyard. Compound NMQ4 also includes a structure which has been convincingly interpreted as a gymnasium by its excavators (see Nagaraja Rao 1985b). The NMQ4 compound may, therefore, best be interpreted as a non-residential compound, perhaps a meeting hall, or other public gathering place. The ceramics found in the compound indicate that food preparation and serving were important facets of the whatever activities occurred within NMQ4.

Compound NMQ10 is much simpler in plan than NMQ4, though contains a number of poorly preserved platforms or structures to the east and north of the main structure. Compound NMQ10's palace structure is, in fact, a relatively minor portion of the total compound area. The ceramic assemblage of the NMQ10 area is dominated by storage and transport vessels; this compound has the lowest frequencies of RV2 cooking vessels of any of the analysed compounds. A limited array of activities involving ceramics seems to have occurred within this small compound, which may perhaps have been a public or administrative structure of some sorts (a similar interpretation has been made for compound NMQ2 by its excavators; Nagaraja Rao 1983b).

The limitations of the ceramic samples, which have been expounded upon in great detail above, in particular, the limited stratigraphic control and the impact of mixing of floor and fill deposits, undoubtedly have some effect on the ceramic distribution patterns observed in the Noblemen's Quarter compounds. Despite these and other limitations, however, some very clear patterns can be observed in the distributions of the vessel-use classes, patterns which both help to define expected and unexpected bounded spatial areas within individual compounds, and which help to characterise compounds as a whole.

NOBLEMEN'S QUARTER RESTRICTED VESSEL RIM CLASSES

An examination of the Noblemen's Quarter restricted vessel rim classes was conducted in order to examine possible chronological variation in rim forms between the different excavated NMQ compounds. Architectural evidence of chronological variation defined an independent dimension against which the frequencies of the flange and straight rim classes could be examined. Rim forms were selected for a number of reasons. First, rim shape does not, in general, appear to be tightly linked either with vessel form, or with the intended use of the vessel, and may therefore have a relatively free range of variation as compared to other more constrained aspects of vessel morphology. Second, it appeared on preliminary examination, that certain forms were more common in compounds that appeared to be architecturally early than in compounds that appeared to be later. Summary information on rim form frequencies by compound is presented in Table 5.8.

Overall distributions of each rim class were examined by compound and the chi-square statistic of significance was computed. The compounds do differ significantly in the occurrences of the 20 rim classes, but these differences do not seem to be directional. That is, there seems to be no relation between the architecturally derived chronology and rim class frequencies. Only one rim class, the FE1 class, seems to vary in a way that would be expected if there was chronological variation in rim classes. This class occurs in higher than expected frequencies in the 'earlier' compounds NMQ7, NMQ8, NMQ9, and NMQ10, and in lower than expected frequencies in the 'later' compounds NMQ3, NMQ4, NMQ5, and NMQ12. The ST1 and ST4 rim classes also exhibit weak patterning.

Other attempts were made to try identify chronological variation in rim form frequencies between compounds, including cluster analysis of relative frequencies of rim classes by provenience unit (using only well-controlled provenience units), and a computation of Brainerd-Robinson similarity coefficients for use in a seriation (using a program developed by S.A. Gregg, see Cowgill 1972). No consistent ordering with a logical relation to the architectural evidence could be identified in any of these analyses.

The failure to identify chronological variation in rim forms from the NMQ compounds may result from a variety of factors, involving both sampling problems (see above) and the nature of ceramic production and change at Vijayanagara. Potential mixing and problems of stratigraphic control in the NMQ samples have been discussed in detail above, and certainly may play an important role here in distorting any patterns that do exist. Nonetheless, it seems that if there were strong variation over time in rim form at Vijayanagara, this analysis should have been able to detect it, given the evident chronological range in Noblemen's Quarter architecture.

It may be the case, then, that the Vijayanagara ceramic inventory as a whole showed very little directional change over the 200 plus year occupation of the site. The conservatism of potters as a group and of social demands for pottery forms undoubtedly contributed to the long term continuities evident in historic South Indian pottery. It should be noted that it would be easily possible to lose many modern ceramic forms produced in the area in the Vijayanagara assemblage, indicating a very conservative ceramic tradition indeed.

This is not meant to imply that there were no changes in the Vijayanagara ceramics over time (and indeed there are also marked changes from Vijayanagara times to the present). Rather, the conservatism of pottery making traditions in the area may have limited those changes to fairly small ranges within accepted boundaries. In addition, the organisation of ceramic production at Vijayanagara was organised at a relatively small scale, primarily in nuclear or extended family workshops, much as production is organised today throughout Hindu India (see Sinopoli 1987, n.d.b.) Each workshop would have operated more or less independently, though regulated to some extent by caste and subcaste proscriptions concerning production. Forms would have been produced according to the generally accepted models of what vessels of particular types should look like. Some temporal changes would have undoubtedly occurred within individual workshops, as a result of differential skills of successive generations of producers, learning processes, and, possibly, change in materials and fuels used, as sources were exhausted over time. If the products of an individual workshop could be identified, and a long temporal sequence of vessels recovered, it might be possible to identify such changes.

There is no reason, however, to assume that different workshops would undergo similar small-scale changes in their products simultaneously. As one workshop began to produce rims with thicker lips, another might produce rims with thinner lips, and so on. The overall picture of Vijayanagara ceramics then, when examined from the perspective of samples from a number of workshops, such as is probably the case in the NMQ ceramics, would be of little or no change over time in ceramic forms. And this is indeed the case. While it may be possible in the future to identify and examine the products of individual workshops in order to test the validity of this argument, this is not possible at present, and the development of Vijayanagara ceramic chronology awaits further fieldwork.

DISCUSSION

The analysis of the Noblemen's Quarter ceramic distributions, presented in this chapter, has aided in the refinement of our understanding of the uses to which these compounds were put, and the range of diversity in use within this residential and public district of the city. It is apparent that the compounds served a variety of uses, and that they also represent a considerable time span in the development of the city of Vijayanagara. In the subsequent chapter the Noblemen's Quarter ceramics will be placed in the context of ceramics from other areas of the city, in order to place the Noblemen's Quarter in a broader perspective, as a distinctive area within a large urban centre.

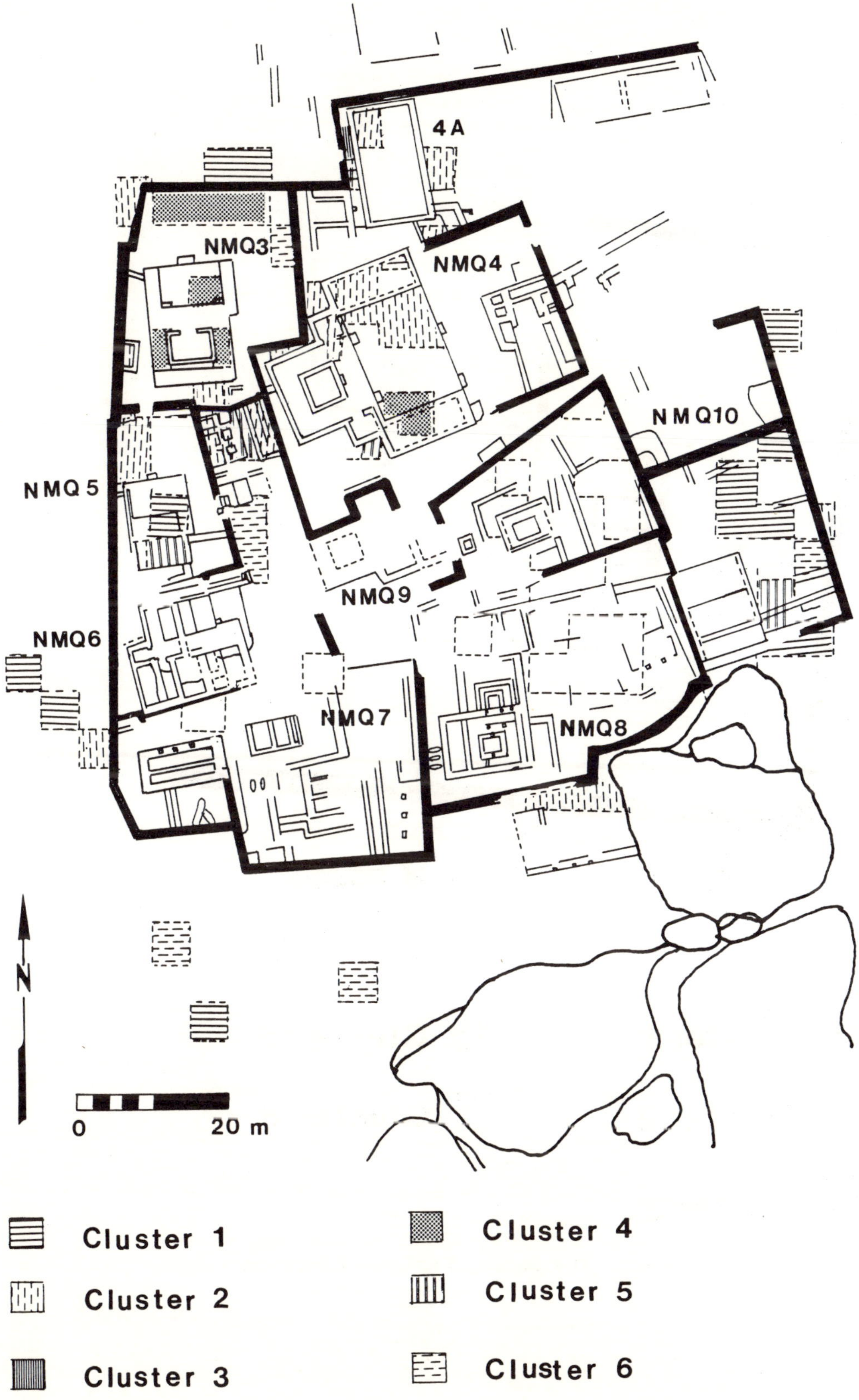

Figure 5.1 Distribution of K-Means Clusters in NMQ3-10

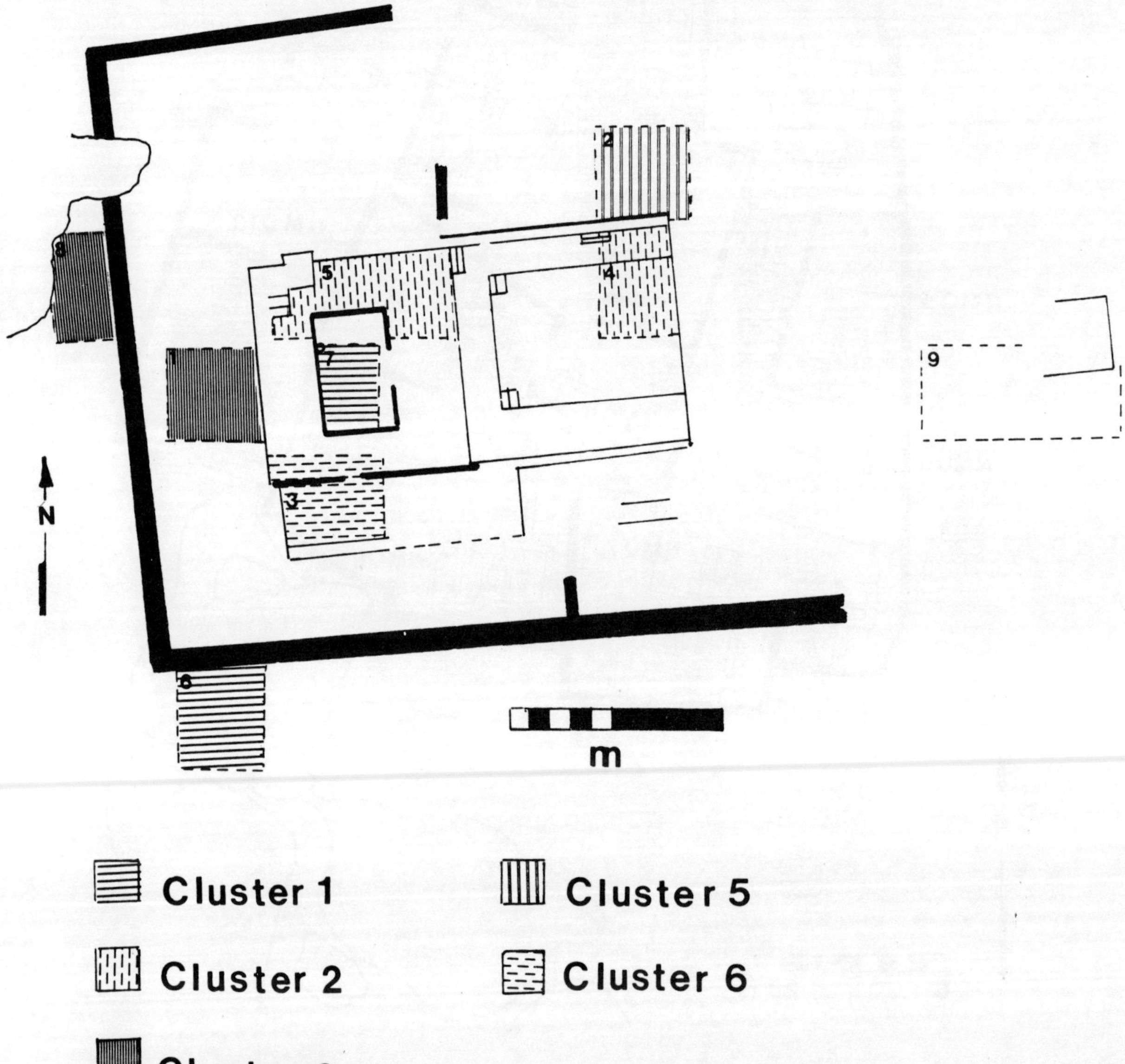

Figure 5.2 Distribution of K-Means Clusters in NMQ12

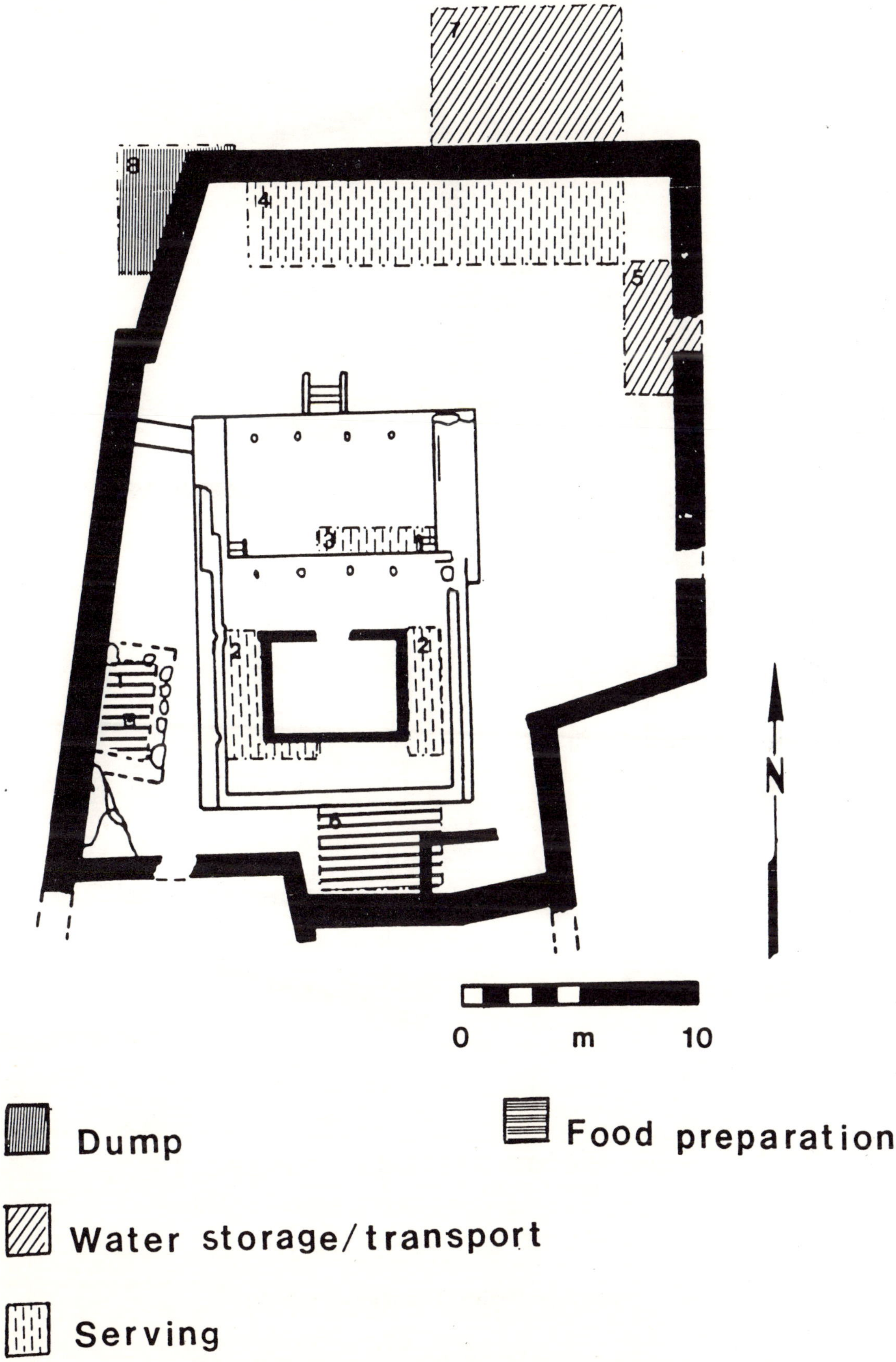

Figure 5.3 Activity Distributions in NMQ3

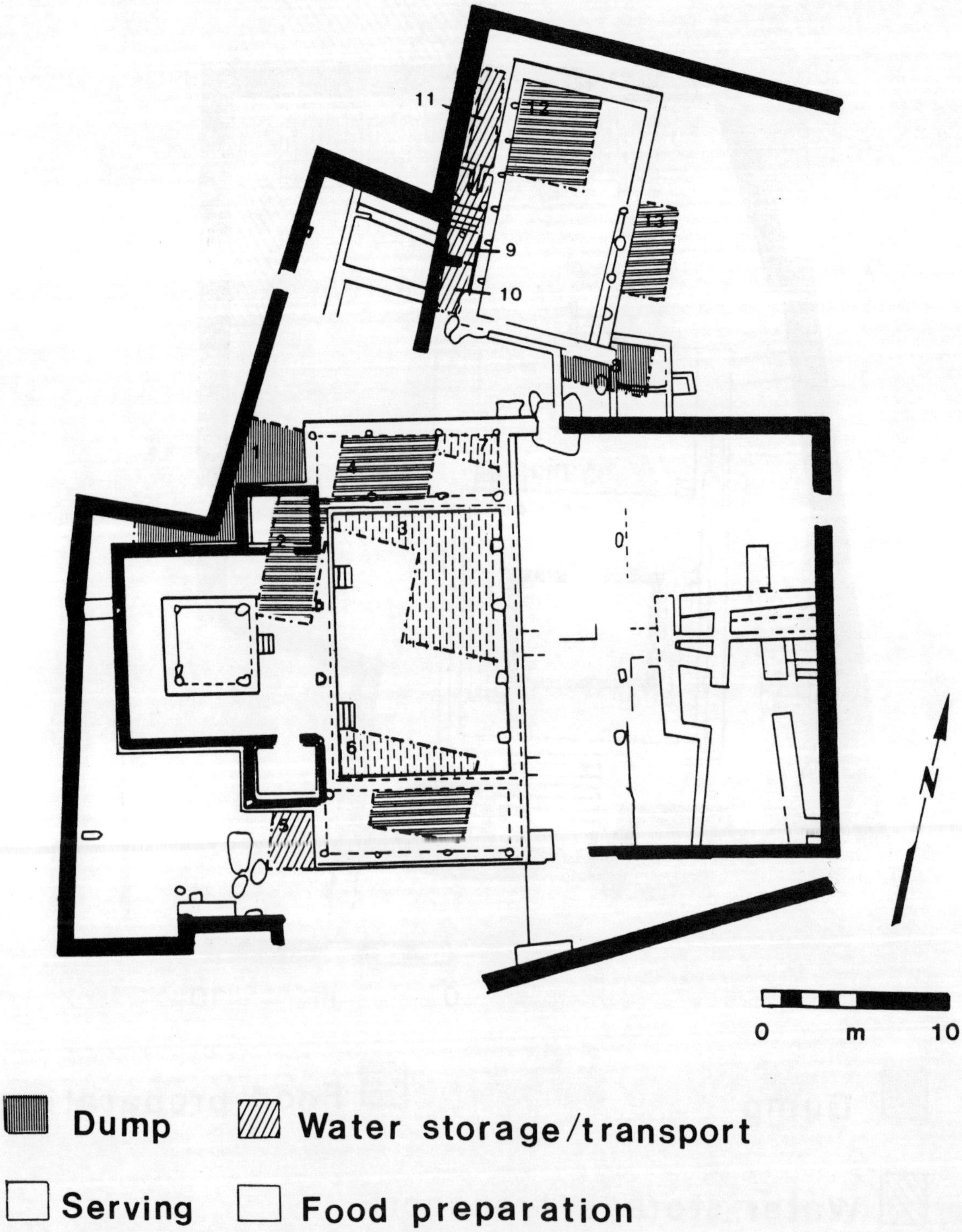

Figure 5.4 Activity Distributions in NMQ4

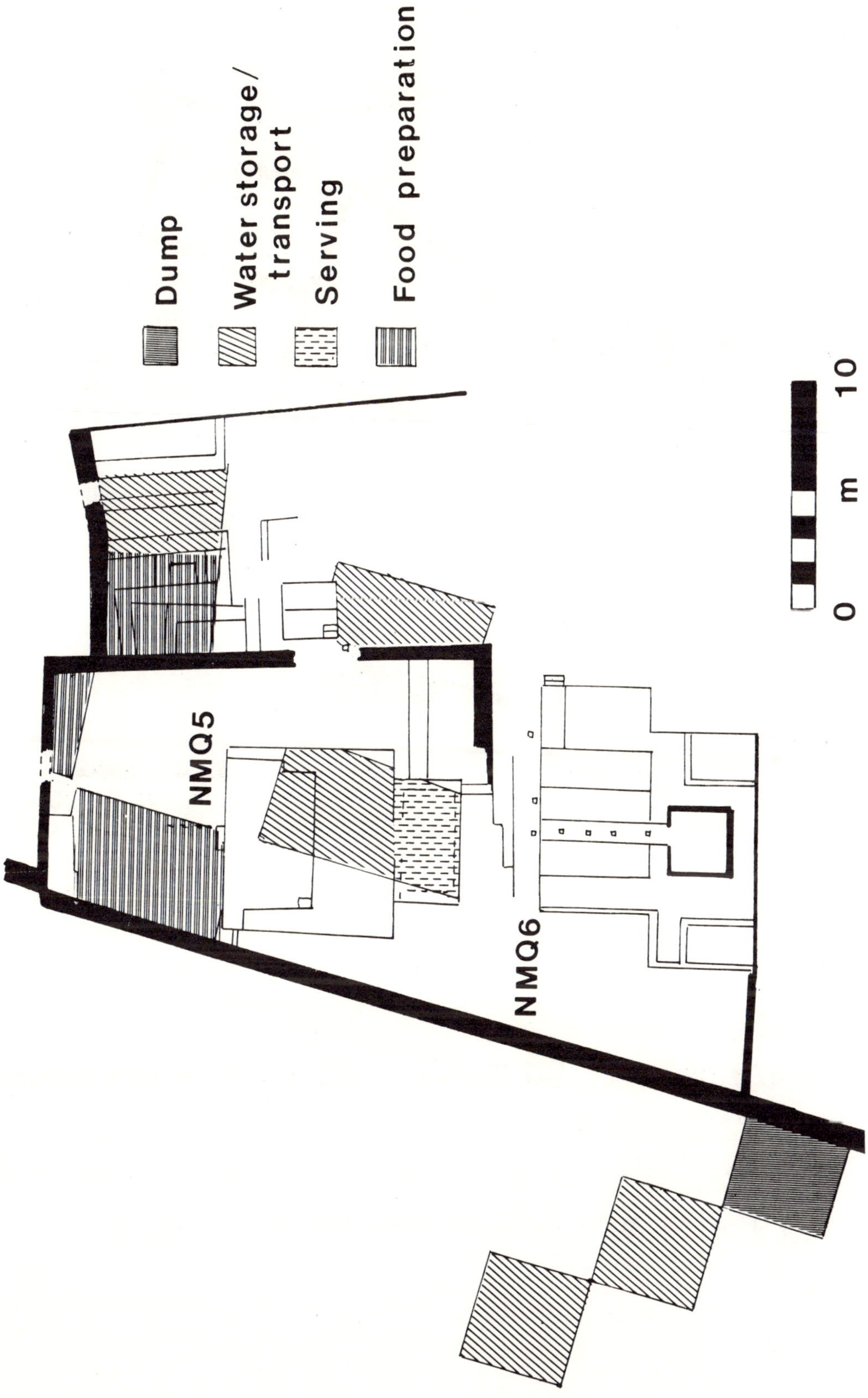

Figure 5.5 Activity Distributions in NMQ5 and NMQ6

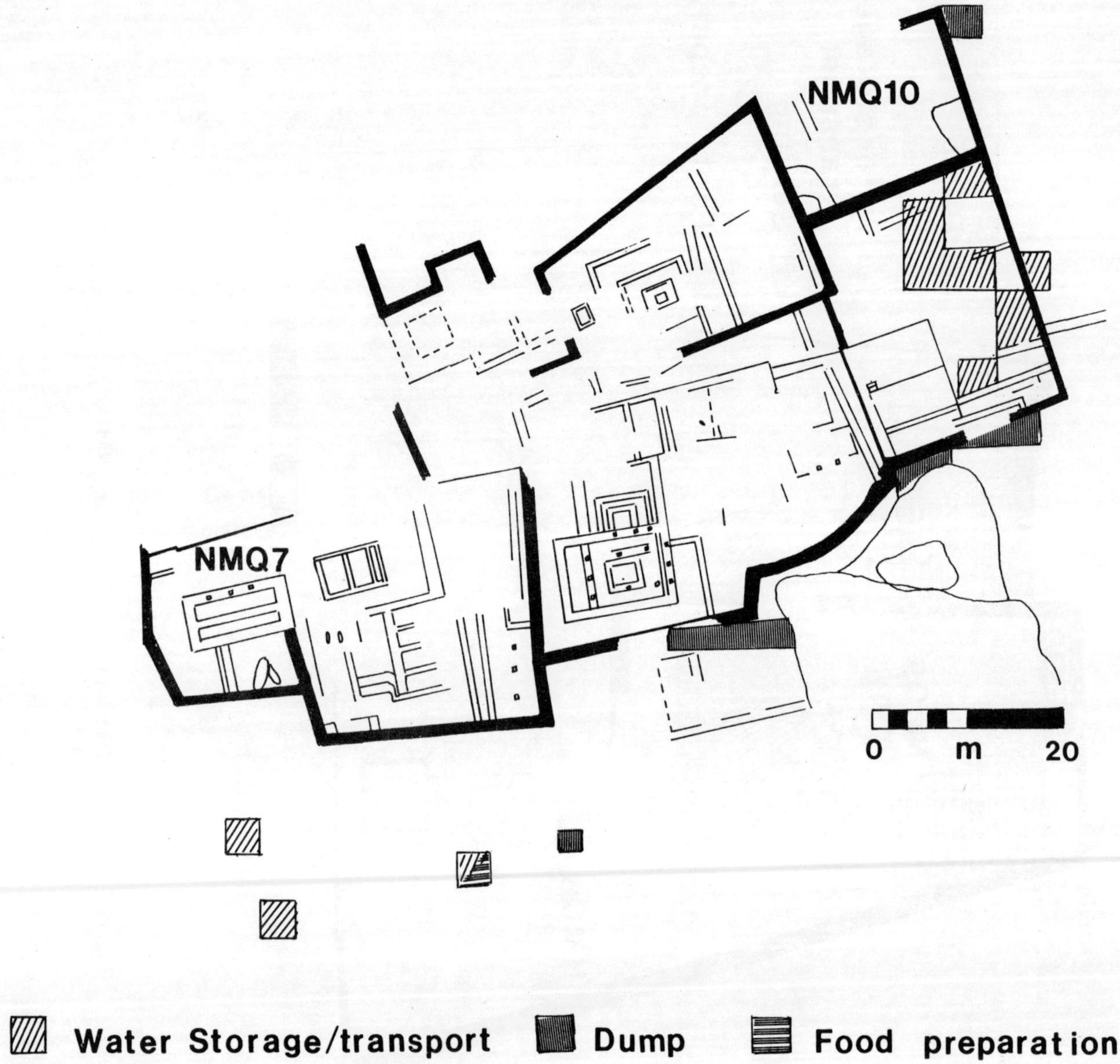

Figure 5.6 Activity Distributions in NMQ7-10

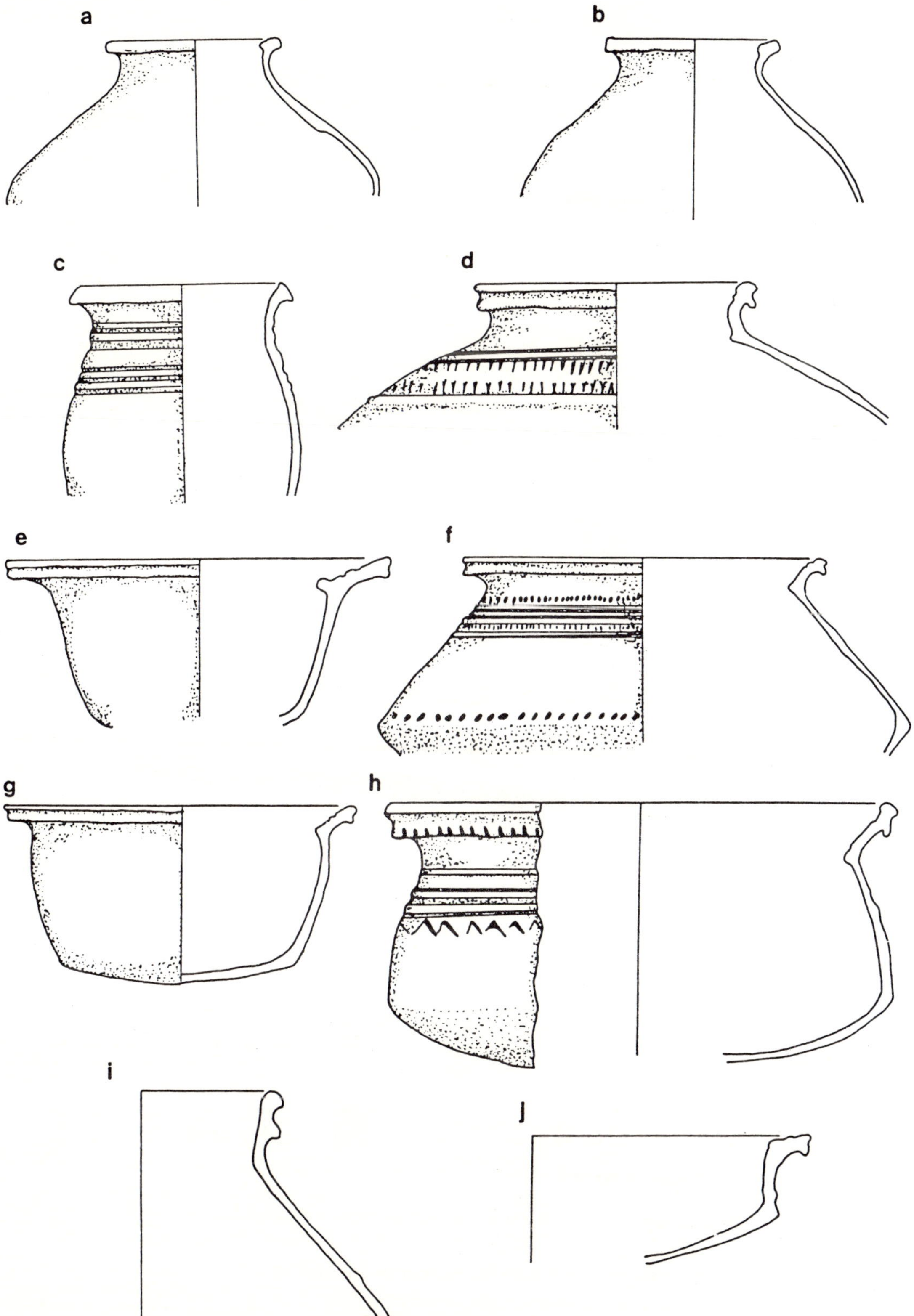

Figure 5.7 Vessels from the Rock-Cut Well South of NMQ7

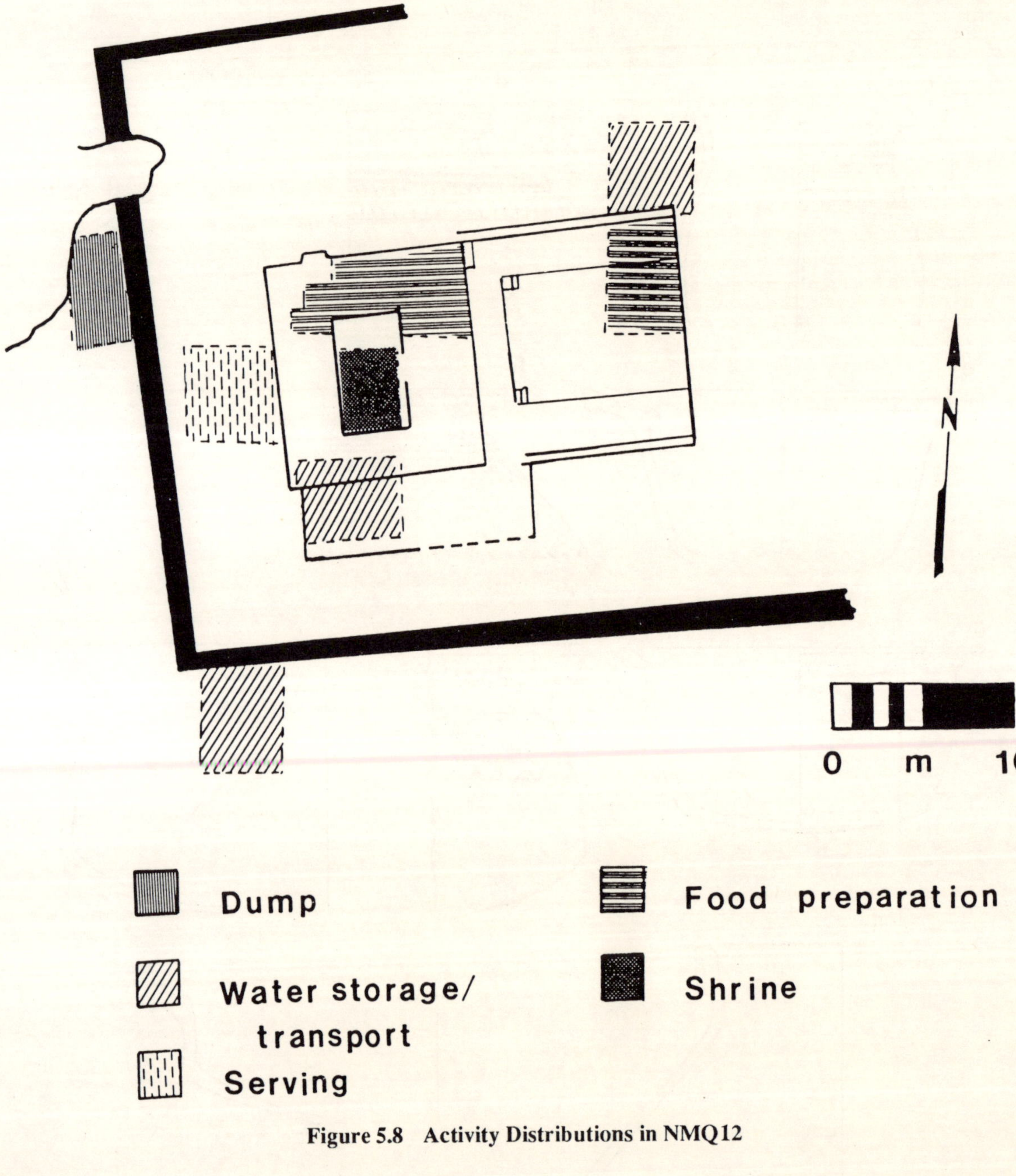

Figure 5.8 Activity Distributions in NMQ12

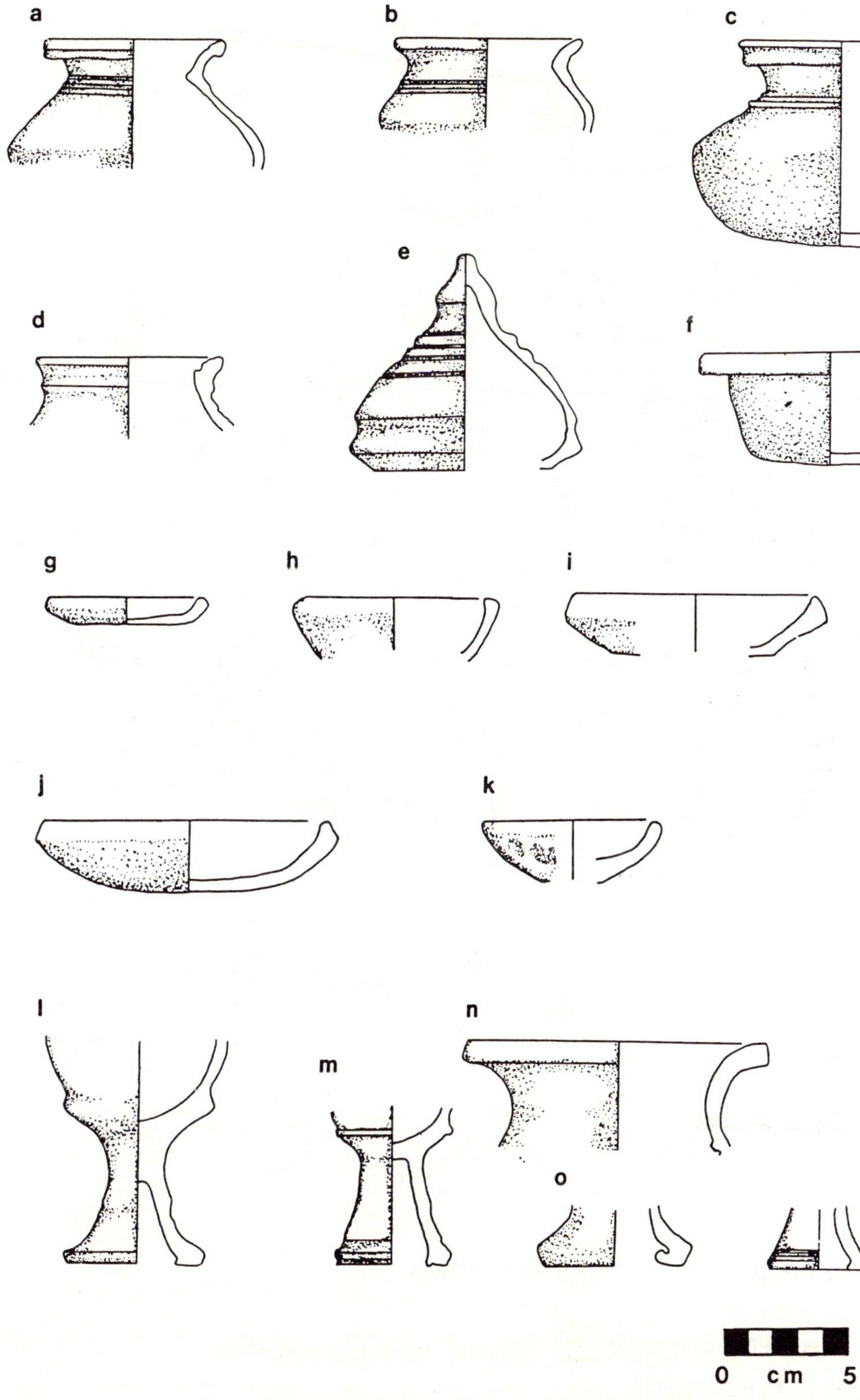

Figure 5.9 Vessels from the NMQ12 Shrine

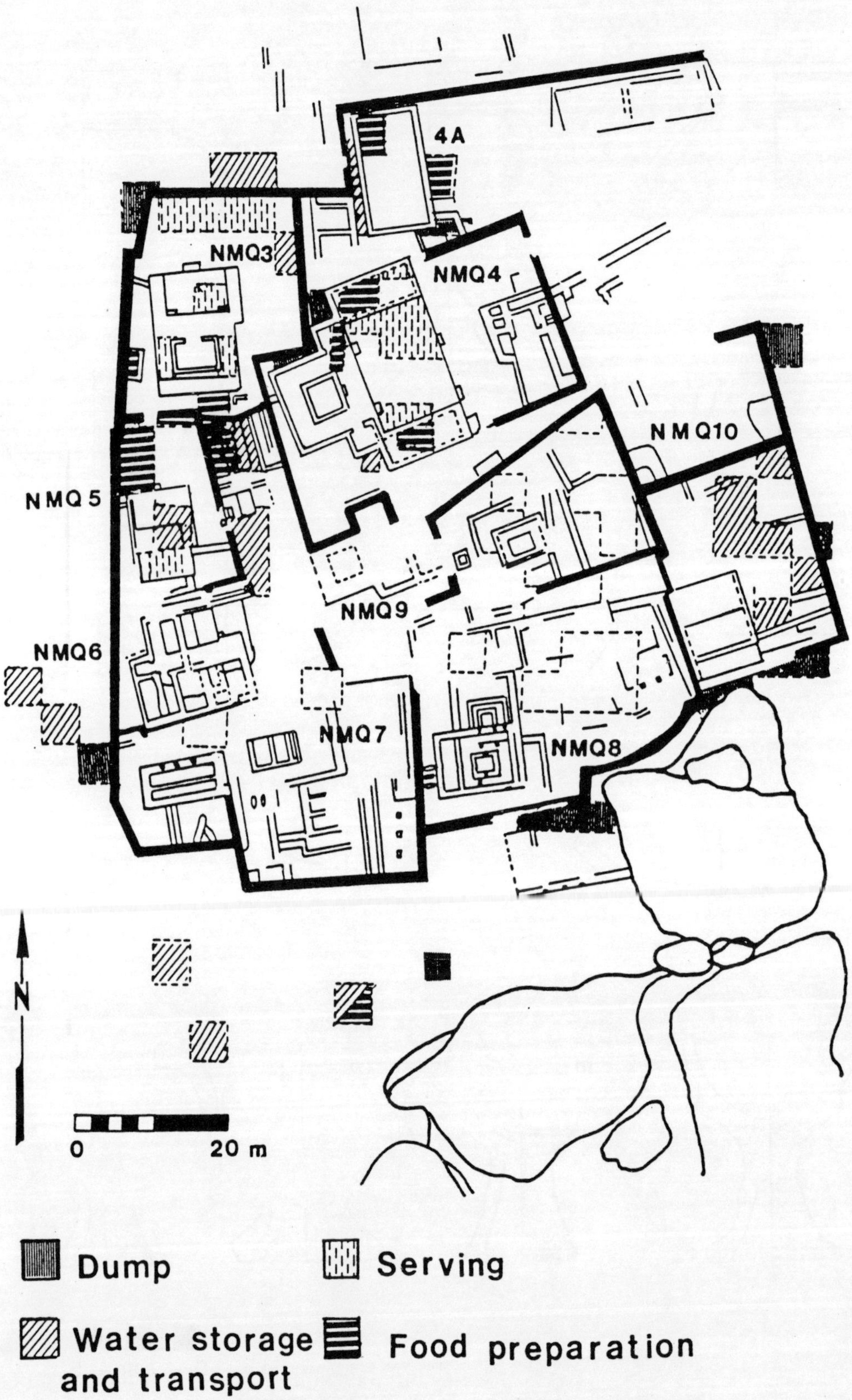

Figure 5.10 Activity Distributions in NMQ3-10

VI. Camparision of Noblemen's Quarter, East Valley and Islamic Quarter Ceramic

In Chapter V, I examined the distributions of ceramics within the Noblemen's Quarter, in order to consider variation within and among compounds in the activities that occurred within them, and the ceramics that were deposited as a result of these activities. In this chapter, I wish to consider the Noblemen's Quarter ceramics as a whole and compare them to ceramics from two other areas of Vijayanagara: the East Valley and the Islamic Quarter. These areas and the ceramic collections derived from them were discussed in Chapters II and III.

The three areas of Vijayanagara examined in this analysis — the Noblemen's Quarter, East Valley, and Islamic Quarter — each represent very different districts of the imperial capital. Though all are found within the city walls, they are separated from each other by distances of 1.5 to 3 km. They include elite and non-elite residential areas and a range of religious and social diversity. In this chapter, I will examine overall differences between these three broad areas of the site in ceramic distributions. The western and eastern halves of the East Valley will be considered separately, since these appear to be socially distinct. Detailed analyses of ceramic distributions within the East Valley have been carried out, and will be the subject of a future publication. For present purposes, my concern with these areas is at a much broader scale, to examine regional and community differences within the city of Vijayanagara.

The comparison of ceramics from these broad areas of the site may be useful in considering both cultural differences between them in the definitions of appropriate material forms in different communities within the city, as well as in a consideration of production and distribution networks. Some cultural differences within and between the sample areas can be observed from ceramic analysis. These include higher than expected frequencies of Burnished Wares in the eastern half of the East Valley, which may result from an increased importance of ceramics as status goods in the non-elite eastern half of the valley in contrast to the Royal Centre western half of the valley. Also evident are the relatively high frequencies of shallow and other bowls in the Islamic Quarter, when contrasted with predominantly Hindu areas of the site. This may be interpreted as resulting from differing proscriptions governing the use of earthenware in domestic activities. Other differences in various aspects of ceramic distributions may also be examined and interpreted in the context of our knowledge of the social and settlement structure of Vijayanagara.

Despite the many accomplishments of recent research at Vijayanagara, we have, at present, very limited knowledge of the community structure of Vijayanagara, that is, how or if individuals or groups distributed across the enormous city of Vijayanagara interacted with one another or defined themselves in contrast to other groups at the site. This has implications both for the significance of social variation in ceramic forms and for the understanding of ceramic production and distribution networks. If, for example, the residents of the Islamic Quarter and the Noblemen's Quarter, were fully isolated from each other, then we might expect relatively little focus on pronounced differentiation of material culture, since material culture need not be called upon to define or express active social oppositions. If, however, these groups did interact regularly, then material culture, such as clothing styles or diet, might serve to distinguish among them. The same patterns might apply across the site if different regions of the site had a pronounced community identity, derived from spatial proximity, or other factors, including place of origin, language differences, and so on.

The community organisation of Vijayanagara may also have had an impact on the organisation of production and distribution across the city, in particular for this study, on the production and distribution of earthenware vessels. If production took place within residential districts or neighbourhoods, we would expect that ceramic workshops would have been dispersed across the city and that occupants of those neighbourhoods acquired ceramics produced near to them. We might then expect localised differences in ceramic pastes, wares, and possibly vessel forms, which would reflect these neighbourhood workshops. If, on the other hand, ceramic workshops were located away from the main residential core of the city, and potters distributed their products in a number of markets throughout the site, we might expect greater homogeneity in many ceramic characteristics across the site. As discussed earlier, no ceramic workshops have yet been identified within the urban core or royal centre of Vijayanagara, and it appears that workshops were located outside of the core area of the city. As will be discussed below, it seems likely, however, that certain workships may have distributed their wares in relatively limited areas of the size.

The discussion of ceramic distributions among the three sampled areas will contrast and interpret ceramic frequencies of the different ceramic classes defined in the typological analysis presented in Chapter IV — wares, vessel-use classes, rim form classes, and shape-size-rim class variants.

WARE CLASSES

The Noblemen's Quarter, East Valley, and Islamic Quarter are each characterised by fairly similar ware distributions. All are dominated by black and brown Plain Wares, with significantly fewer red Plain Ware sherds and red or black Burnished Ware sherds. These similarities illustrate the consistency of Vijayanagara ceramic wares overall. Some differences do exist between the sampled areas in the relative proportions of the different ware classes. Sherd counts by ware class and area are illustrated in Table 6.1. The Noblemen's Quarter area is characterised by somewhat greater than expected frequencies of black Plain Wares and red Burnished Ware sherds. The western half of the East Valley contains higher than expected frequencies of black and brown Plain Wares and comparatively low frequencies of black or red Burnished Wares. The eastern half of the East Valley, on the other hand, had higher than expected frequencies of red Plain Wares and Burnished Wares. The Islamic Quarter is also characterised by higher than expected frequencies of red Plain Wares, as well as of black Plain Ware sherds.

The differences in ware frequencies between the sample areas are statistically significant. Such differences may result from a variety of factors, including cultural selection, workshop differences, and so on. Given the relatively limited nature of intra-area and inter-area variations in ware frequencies, it does not appear that either colour or surface treatment were particularly important in distinguishing among ceramic users or producers.

VESSEL—USE CLASSES

Differences in the distributions of the nine vessel-use classes between the three sample areas may occur as a result of a differing array of activities involving ceramics in each of the areas. Such activities can result in the use of ceramics as domestic vessels (possibly, in contrast to metal vessels used by some segments of the population), in manufacturing or industrial contexts, in markets, and so on. Differing conceptions of appropriate ceramic use may also produce regional variation in the occurrence of vessel-use classes, for example, the use of earthenware for dining in non-Hindu areas. In addition, similar forms could be used in different ways in different areas, though this cannot be examined in this study.

Although the overall ratios of the nine vessel-use classes are quite similar between the three sample areas, some significant differences exist in the relative frequencies of these classes (Table 6.12). In general, the two halves of the East valley are relatively similar in the frequencies of ceramic classes, and the Noblemen's Quarter and Islamic Quarter samples have some pronounced similarities to each other. The Noblemen's Quarter ceramics are characterised by higher than expected frequencies of RV3 large food preparation vessels, and RV4-RV6 water serving, transport, and storage vessels. The medium food preparation vessels of class RV2 and the small serving vessels of class RV1 occur in lower than expected frequencies in the Noblemen's Quarter samples. Overall then, the Noblemen's Quarter ceramics appear to indicate a higher emphasis on the preparation of large quantities of food, and the serving and storage of higher quantities of liquids than occurred in the East Valley area. This pattern might be expected of a high status area, in which public gatherings and/or private receptions were important.

The two halves of the East Valley have very similar ceramic assemblages of the nine-vessel use classes. With the exception of other bowl frequencies, each half exhibits similar patterns of greater or less than expected frequencies of individual vessel classes. Higher than expected frequencies of RV1 small serving vessels are found in both halves of the valley, as are higher than expected frequencies of RV2 food preparation vessels. Water serving, transport, and storage vessels are found in somewhat lower than expected frequencies in these areas. The East Valley ceramics appear to represent overall, a domestic assemblage involved with the preparation and serving of food, and water storage and transport, and less involved with large scale public disposition of comestibles than in the Noblemen's Quarter. As with each sample area, internal variability exists within the East Valley in the relative frequencies of the nine vessel-use classes.

The Islamic Quarter sample is small and exhibits considerable variation between collection units, particularly between the Dharmashala area and the surface collection units dispersed across the quarter. When taken as a whole though, the Islamic Quarter ceramics differ considerably from the other sample areas. Unrestricted vessels occur in very high frequencies in the Islamic Quarter, where they account for as much as one-third of the vessels in some areas. This may result from the use of shallow bowls and other bowls as dining vessels in this area of the city. Also occurring in higher than expected frequencies in the Islamic Quarter are vessels associated with water transport, serving, and storage, while food preparation vessels occur with somewhat lower than expected frequencies. Like the Noblemen's Quarter, it appears that food and water serving may have been of greater importance in the sampled areas of the Islamic Quarter than food preparation. Given the small sample sizes, these patterns might more reflect the activities of the Dharmashala area than be representative of the Islamic Quarter as a whole.

RESTRICTED VESSEL RIM CLASSES

The frequencies of restricted vessel rim form variants were also compared between the three areas. The significance of the various flange and straight rim forms to the makers and users of Vijayanagara pots is difficult to ascertain. Some of the forms are clearly associated with particular vessel form variants and vessel-use classes. It is possible that other forms may result from chronological variation in the Vijayanagara ceramics, though such variation was not identifiable in the Noblemen's Quarter area. In addition, rim form variation may also result from inter- and intra-workshop variation, or from differences in consumer demands, particularly, demands related to definitions of appropriate forms for use by different segments of Vijayanagara's population. Although at present it is difficult to say precisely what rim form differences between sample areas indicate, some statistically significant differences can be identified.

Flange rim forms account for 63.4% of the total sample of flange and straight rim forms, with straight rims accounting 37.6% of the rims. Although flange rim forms predominate in all sample areas, the areas differ significantly in overall frequencies of flange and straight rims (Table 6.3). Flange rim frequencies range from 69.3% of the rims in the Noblemen's Quarter sample to 58.3% of the rims in the eastern half of the East Valley. As with the vessel-use class and ware distributions, the two halves of the East Valley are more like each other than they are like other sample areas.

The three sample areas also exhibit statistically significant variation in the distributions of the finer rim form classes (Table 6.4). The Noblemen's Quarter contains significantly higher than expected frequencies of FI2, FI3, FE1, FE2, and ST4 rim forms, and significantly lower than expected frequencies of FN1, FI1, SN, ST1, and ST2 rim forms. The western half of the East Valley contains significantly higher than expected frequencies of FN2, FT1, SN, ST1, and ST2 forms, and lower than expected frequencies of FE1, FE2, and SI rim forms. The eastern half of the East Valley contains signficantly higher than expected frequencies of FN1, FI1, SN, SI, and ST2 rim forms, and lower than expected frequencies of FN2, FI2, FI3, FE1, FT2, FG, and ST4 forms. It should be noted that the two halves of the valley differ considerably at this level of ceramic differentiation. The Islamic Quarter is characterised by significantly higher than expected frequencies of FI2, FI3, FG, AND ST4 forms, and lower than expected frequencies of FN2, FI1, SN, and ST1 forms.

As discussed earlier, the behavioral implications of the observed differences in rim form frequencies between the sample areas are, at present, difficult to ascertain, since we cannot adequately assess the significance of rim form — as a chronological indicator, social indicator, or in distinguishing between workshops. It is likely that rim form variation is the product of a combination of these and other factors, and it is clear that the sampled areas do exhibit significant, though far from absolute, variation in the distribution of these forms.

VESSEL FORM VARIANTS

At the finest level of the ceramic classification, a large number of vessel form variants were identified, distinguished on the basis of rim form, vessel size, and vessel shape dimensions. These forms, subgroups of the vessel-use classes, ideally reflect, at least in part, a finer level of ceramic differentiation recognised by members of Vijayanagara society. As discussed in Chapter IV, this level of classification is highly constrained by limitations of the data set, particularly the absence of whole vessels, and must therefore be treated cautiously. Because of the small numbers of diagnostic sherds from the Islamic Quarter, when divided over 75 ceramic classes, statistical comparisons of vessel form variant frequencies can only utilise samples from the East Valley and Noblemen's Quarter areas.

Only 109 *lamps* were classed into the four shape categories L1-L4. Given the small sample sizes, it is not possible to conduct statistical comparisons of the occurrence of lamp form variants across the site (Table 6.5). In terms of overall frequencies, the vast majority of lamps were found in the Noblemen's Quarter area, although even there lamps occur in very low frequencies compared to other vessel forms. The relatively high density of lamps in the NMQ area probably results from a somewhat differing array of activities in this area, possibly a greater emphasis on worship in households or shrines.

Shallow bowl variants SB1, SB3-SB6 exhibit significant variation in their frequency of occurrence in the sample areas (Table 6.6; class SB2 is not considered because of its rarity in the Vijayanagara ceramic sample). Distributions in the two halves of the East Valley, although different, are more like each other than either half is like the Noblemen's Quarter area. Because of their scarcity and wide variability, other bowl distributions will not be considered in this discussion.

Each of the restricted vessel classes, *RV1-RV6,* exhibits significant variation in the occurrence of vessel form variants between the Noblemen's Quarter, the west half of the East Valley, and the east half of the East Valley (see Tables 6.7.-5.12). For most of these forms the two halves of the East Valley differ dramatically in the frequencies of these forms, perhaps indicative that these relatively minor variations among functionally similar vessel forms did indeed play a role in the expression and definition of social identity within this area of Vijayanagara.

DISCUSSION

Significant differences in ceramic distributions were identified at all levels of ceramic variation. At some levels, such as the distribution of ware classes, the East Valley appeared as a relatively homogenous area, with differences between the two halves of the valley far less pronounced than differences between the East Valley and the Noblemen's and Islamic Quarters. This may indicate that it is indeed valid to think of the East Valley as a more or less discrete region or community within Vijayanagara, at least from the perspective of ceramic acquisition. That is, the occupants of the East Valley appear to have, for the most part, acquired their ceramic vessels from a limited set of workshops (although with considerable overlap) which produced wares that were technologically similar. In this sense, the Noblemen's Quarter and the Islamic Quarter may also be seen as discrete areas or communities within Vijayanagara. Ceramic workshops, wherever they were located, appear to have focused their distribution activities in limited areas of the city, perhaps in localised markets such as the Monday market in the East Valley, or through other distribution mechanisms.

At finer levels of ceramic variation, vessel-use classes, flange and straight rim form classes, and the finest level of variants defined within the vessel-use classes, the variation identified also indicates pronounced differences between the East Valley, Islamic Quarter, and Noblemen's Quarter. Vessel-use class distributions are similar throughout the East Valley, which again differs significantly from the Noblemen's Quarter and Islamic Quarter areas. Vessels-use class distributions are believed to relate to the array of activities involving ceramics in each area. The Noblemen's Quarter appears to be characterised by a greater emphasis on the serving of food and water than the other areas. In the Islamic Quarter, differences in vessel-use classes appear to result from differing constraints on vessel use, in particular on the absence of ritual restrictions on dining off of earthenware.

Rim form variants and vessel-form variants also differ significantly between the sample areas. In both of these cases, significant differences exist between the east and west halves of the East Valley, perhaps indicative that variation in these classes was important at an intra-community level within Vijayanagara. This may include chronological variations, as all three areas appear to have been occupied throughout much of the history of the city, or social variations at the level of relatively fine-scale variations within ceramic forms.

It should be noted that despite the statistically significant variation between the sample areas, the Vijayanagara ceramic inventory is, overall, distributed fairly homogeneously across the site. That is, no vessel class defined at any level of the ceramic analysis is exclusive to any one area of the site; all forms are found in all sample areas and dispersed throughout each of the sample areas. Ceramics clearly did not serve as major or primary markers of community, caste, or individual identity at Vijayanagara, though they appear to have played all of these roles to a limited extent in the medieval capital.

VII. Summary and Conclusions

This volume has set out to provide a detailed analysis of the ceramics of the imperial city of Vijayanagara, with a particular focus on the ceramics of the city's Noblemen's Quarter. This work was conceived and conducted from an anthropological perspective, with a concern towards using ceramics to enhance our understanding of a number of facets of Vijayanagara society. In the first chapter of this work, a range of questions which can be approached using ceramic data were presented. This broad overview was followed by a specific application, in the study of the archaeological ceramics of the Noblemen's Quarter of Vijayanagara. In this chapter I would like to briefly consider again the relevance and importance of ceramic analysis to an anthropologically oriented archaeology, and the success of the Vijayanagara ceramic analysis in answering specific research questions about the Noblemen's Quarter, and about the state and society of medieval Vijayanagara.

Anthropologically oriented archaeology is interested in many of the same questions as cultural anthropology—the organisation and disposition of social groups, economic systems, religion and ritual, political systems and ideology, and inter-societal social, political, and economic relations, among others. In examining these and other questions, archaeology has the advantage of an extremely long time frame; we need not look at cultures and their institutions from a 'snapshot' perspective, but rather can examine their origins, development, transmutations, and decline over centuries or millennia. What archaeology gains in time frame however, is often lost in the richness of the information available to us. Our objects of study are past cultures; our materials for studying them are the fragmentary traces which remain—the broken pots and other artifacts, the residues of foods produced and consumed, house plans, and the disposition of sites upon the landscape. In order to examine our true object of study we must recover, analyse, and interpret these fragmentary remains and extrapolate from them to the society in which they were produced.

This study has been concerned with one class of remains—ceramics. Ceramics are, as has been stressed throughout this work, one of the most ubiquitous classes of goods found in the archaeological record of post-Neolithic societies. Ceramics are extremely durable and were in common use worldwide prior to the modern period, when metal and plastic have largely overshadowed them. Ethnographic work on ceramic production has revealed some general regularities in both the social organisation and scale of ceramic production, and in the physical properties of ceramic vessels. These regularities may be applied and examined in the context of past societies. Within each society, present and past, ceramics are produced, distributed, and used in particular contexts which are affected and governed by varying social, political, economic, and ideological conditions. The embeddedness of ceramics, and of all material products of human labour, in the cultural setting in which they are found means that the analysis of archaeological ceramics can provide us considerable information about the culture that produced them.

Such studies of archaeological materials must be approached with great care, considering: first, the questions we wish to seek answers to concerning a past culture; second, what class(es) of available archaeological materials is most appropriate to examining those questions; third, how the techniques we apply to the study of archaeological remains contribute to our ability to evaluate the research questions, with a particular focus on the limitations of our data and of our analytical techniques; and, fourth, our criteria for deciding among alternate solutions to the questions we are asking. In Chapter I, some of the range of questions towards which ceramic analysis may be directed were examined. These include questions dealing with chronology, production and distribution systems, including long-distance trade, social group identity, and political organisation and change.

Given the nature of our data, and of the analytical process in general, archaeological studies rarely, if ever, provide conclusive solutions to the problems they address. Additional data may negate the results of an analysis; new measurement techniques may refine or dramatically alter prior interpretations. In this sense, the conclusions of any study may best be seen as hypothess or models to be tested rather than the final word on any topic. In addition, a successful study will often have unforeseen implications which permit old data to be seen from a new perspective, and cause new questions to arise which must be approached through further research. An analysis which does not succeed in answering fully the questions it sets out to examine, or which comes up with unexpected solutions, should not therefore, be viewed as a failed analysis, but rather, as a step in an ongoing and continually more refined process.

THE VIJAYANAGARA CERAMIC ANALYSIS

Chapter II-VI of this work have been concerned with the analysis of archaeological ceramics from the medieval Hindu empire of Vijayanagara. In Chapter II, detailed descriptions of the excavated compounds of the Noblemen's Quarter were presented; less comprehensive descriptions of the two other sources of ceramics discussed in this volume were also considered. Preliminary interpretations of these areas — the Noblemen's Quarter, the East Valley, and the main Islamic Quarter of the city—were derived from the architectural remains found within them and their general location within the capital. Much of the subsequent ceramic analysis was oriented towards evaluating and refining these interpretations.

The abundant historical information on the city and empire of Vijayanagara, the plentiful ethnographic information on Hindu social organisation, and the rich architectural and archaeological record at the site, provide a rich framework in which to view the archaeological ceramics of Vijayanagara. Unlike many prehistoric studies, this analysis starts out with many categories of information well-controlled . We know, for example, when the site was occupied and abandoned, its place in the local settlement hierarchy, its political import, and some information about the diverse religious, social, linguistic, and ethnic groups which resided within it. There are, of course, many unanswered questions about Vijayanagara. These include: questions about the lives of the non-elite segments of Vijayanagara society — the peasants and crafts people who in large part provided the economic base of the empire; questions concerning the organisation and integration of the capital—how or if this city, composed of a wide diversity of linguistic, religious, regional, and caste groups, functioned as an integrated whole; and questions about the economic functioning of the city — how food products and material goods were produced, distributed, and consumed. Answers to some of these questions may be sought through the analysis of archaeological remains.

The four primary goals of the Vijayanagara ceramic analysis were presented in Chapter III. These are: (1) to construct a classification system for the archaeological ceramics of Vijayanagara, (2) to examine the distribution of activities and divisions of functional space within the Noblemen's Quarter, (3) to examine the relations between ceramics and social forms and the distribution of social groups within the Noblemen's Quarter and across the three sample areas, and (4) to attempt to develop a ceramic chronology for the Noblemen's Quarter sample. It remains now to examine how well thse goals were fulfilled in the susbsequent analyses.

The Ceramic Classification

As was discussed in Chapter I, the first step of any ceramic analysis is to organise the materials under study into a systematic framework in which similar materials are grouped together and the materials are classed into coherent groups. Many different approaches may be used to construct such a framework. The approach taken in the Vijayanagara analysis was to construct a quantitative typology, using detailed metric and qualitative information recorded on large nombers of sherds, and statistical and computer-assisted analytical techniques. Since the study of medieval ceramics from South India is in its infancy, a fairly comprehensive classification was sought, which could encode a great deal of information on the vessels. A number of dimensions of ceramic variability were considered in this analysis. Wares, vessel shape, rim form, and vessel size were examined independently and together in order to develop a classification which could be utilised at varying levels of specificity in subsequent analyses.

A large number of categorical and quantitative variables were recorded on each diagnostic sherd and employed in the typological analysis. The procedures used in the ceramic classification have been presented in great detail in Chapter IV. They included simple descriptive statistical methods, such as histograms, scatterplots and correlation coefficients, as well as inferential parametric and non-parametric tests of significance. Where necessary, more complex multivariate statistical techniques were utilised to examine the interrelations of several measured variables in determining ceramic form. The end result of the classification was the definition of: three ware classes (Plain, Burnished and Coarse Wares) which were subdivided on the basis of colour; nine broad shape and size classes — which were interpreted as primarily being linked to vessel use on the basis of their overall form, use traces, and ethnographic analogies to modern forms; 20 flange and straight rim vessel rim forms; and some 75 vessel form variants, defined by the dimensions shape, size, and rim form.

The classification presented in Chapter IV should be seen as a working classification, subject to considerable refinement and reevaluation. The scarcity of complete vessels has certainly contributed to an underestimation of the variety of vessel shape classes present during Vijayanagara times. The nine classes defined in the analysis seem to represent significant divisions of the data, though it is likely that the users of the vessels would have recognised more than these. Cooking vessels, for example, would have undoubtedly been subdivided into classes geared towards different cooking activities—milk vs. vegetables vs. meat, for example—and each of these classes most likely looked somewhat different. Nonetheless, the nine shape classes defined do represent meaningful and significant variation in the data and proved very useful in subsequent analyses of ceramic distributions.

Other classes defined in the analysis may be overly fine. For example, ethnographic work on contemporary ceramic production in Malwa (Miller 1985) and Kamalapuram, Karnataka (Junker 1985) demonstrates that the dimension rim shape varies widely, even in the work of a single potter over the course of the a single day. This variation may result from unintentional and uncontrolled factors—the amount of clay available to work with, the mental state of the potter, i.e., how tired he is and how much attention he is paying to his work, the speed of the wheel as he forms the rim, and so on. Minor variations in rim form, such as were identified in the Vijayanagara ceramic classification, while legitimate, may actually not be the product of behaviorally or chronologically significant factors, but may rather, reflect uncontrolled and unconscious variation. Future analyses of Vijayanagara ceramics may therefore demonstrate that the rim classes defined do not aid in resolving broader research questions, and the categories may be condensed into a smaller number of classes.

An unintentional result of the ceramic classification procedure was the recognition that Vijayanagara ceramics are highly variable in form, far more variable than many other historic and prehistoric ceramic inventories. This variation occurs within a fairly limited range of ware and decorative classes, as the vast majority of the vessels are of black or brown Plain Ware. But virtually all of the quantitative variables measured exhibit an extremely wide range of variation within broad vessel classes. This range of variation frequently makes it difficult to identify modes or clearly defined subgroups within each class. Rather, what we see is a continous variation in the dimensions under study, with only relatively weak divisions identifiable within them.

In trying to understand why the Vijayanagara ceramic inventory is so varied in detail, while appearing so homogenous in terms of ware, decorative treatment, and gross vessel form, we can consider a number of factors. First, it may be that the Vijayanagara ceramic inventory is in fact not unusual, and that the techniques used in this analysis are merely more sensitive to recording and observing variation than most traditional ceramic classifications. That is, many classifications group vessels on the basis of their overall apparent similarity and do not examine, through quantitative measurement, the range of variation within the classes they define. This may be true in part, but even a more traditional classification of Vijayanagara ceramics would, I feel, record that there is much variation in many aspects of these materials.

A more plausible explanation of this variation may lie in the organisation and regulation of ceramic production at Vijaynagara. This argument has been presented in detail elsewhere (Sinopoli n.d.b.) and will only be summarised here. I believe that one reason that the Vijayanagara ceramics are so difficult to sort into fine types lies in the fact that ceramics were produced in a very large number of small familial workshops, rather than in large scale highly regulated workshops as are known from other complex societies. Modern workshops in the area of Vijayanagara can produce between 200 and 500 vessels every 10 days, or between 6000 and 7500 vessels in a year of 300 workdays (excluding rainy season, festivals, and so on; this may be a considerable overestimate). As discussed earlier, there is some evidence for believing that Vijayanagara period workshops were organised much like modern ones. If we assume that Vijayanagara had a mean population of ca. 250,000 individuals, or some 50,000 families, and that each family required some 20-30 ceramic vessels per year for domestic and ritual use, we can calculate that some 130 to 250 ceramic producing workshops would have been needed to meet these requirements. The values used in generating this estimate are clearly highly speculative since we do not have as yet estimates of Vijayanagara's population or of vessel requirements. Nonetheless, it seems clear that a large number of ceramic workshops would have been necessary to meet the needs of the city's population.

With so many workshops producing ceramics, we would expect just the sort of range of ceramic variation within general form classes that we in fact see in the Vijayanagara ceramics. Inter-workshop differences in materials, equipment, and fuels used, in learning, and in execution, could be expected to lead to considerable variability among vessels, even among potters who are attempting to produce broadly similar forms. This may be especially true among low status goods, such as earthenware vessels, where there is limited impetus to regulate production above the level of individual workshop or potter subcaste.

An additional reason for the broad but relatively subtle variation in Vijayanagara ceramics may relate to the complexity of Vijayanagara society itself. If, as has been proposed, some linkage can be made between social group identity and material culture, then the diversity of ceramics may be correlated in some manner with the diversity of social groups which resided at Vijayanagara. This need not be a direct or absolute correlation, since it is expected that social variation in material culture is meaningful at the level of interacting groups within a social system, rather than at a city- or society-wide level.

The goal of constructing a Vijayanagara ceramic typology has been successful in terms of producing a useful working typology, which can be utilised in examining various aspects of Vijayanagara society and culture. In the construction of this typology, I have attempted to be explicit in variable definition and measurement, and in the statistical techniques applied to the raw data. It is hoped that future studes at Vijayanagara and other South Indian sites can build on and refine the groundwork laid here to contribute to a better understanding of the abundant ceramic remains found in the region.

Activity Distributions in Noblemen's Quarter

The second goal of this study was to examine the distribution of activities involving ceramic use within the architectural compounds of the Noblemen's Quarter and, at a more general level, across the site of Vijayanagara. Such an examination can aid in supporting and refining interpretations of vessel-use derived on the basis of vessel morphology alone, and can permit consideration of the use of space and economic divisions within and between areas.

The eleven excavated compounds of the Noblemen's Quarter yielded abundant ceramic remains from well-controlled proveniences. The architectural plans of the compounds permitted independent interpretations of the uses to which each may have been put. The analysis of the distribution of the nine vessel-use classes throughout the Noblemen's Quarter served for the most part to corroborate these architectural interpretations. For example, Unit NMQ3.1 located to the west of the main NMQ3 structure, was interpreted on the basis of architectural evidence as a probable food preparation area. It contained a large stone mortar within a small chamber. The ceramics of that unit also served to support this interpretation. Large quantities of vessels interpreted as food preparation vessels and large storage vessels were found in this unit.

The association of particular ceramic vessel-use classes with particular provenience units in the Noblemen's Quarter was often not as pronounced as expected. The diversity of ceramic classes found in each unit results from a number of factors, including post-abandonment mixing and deposit formation and excavation techniques. Nonetheless, in compounds from which relatively well-controlled floor-level samples could be examined, it was possible, on the basis of ceramic analyses, to identify areas in which certain activities appeared to predominate. These areas could often also be recognised architecturally or by the presence of other artifacts. This provides considerable support for the vessel-use classes defined — that they were in fact used in the activities that I have proposed for them. In some units, interpretations of ceramic distributions provided a means for subdividing and interpreting areas that could not be distinguished on the basis of ceramics alone, for example, storage vs. serving areas within courtyards.

The excavated compounds of the Noblemen's Quarter differ considerably in scale and layout, and presumably in the uses to which they were put. Information on the layout of each compound was presented in Chapter II, with a consideration of the amount of area devoted to public vs. private space, the number of internal chambers, the occurrence of subsidiary buildings within each compound, and so on. Along with this architectural evidence, the overall distribution of vessel-use classes within each compound can contribute to interpretations of the nature of the dominant activities (involving ceramics) which occurred within them, and the primary uses to which they were put. Some compounds, such as NMQ3, and NMQ12, were on this basis interpreted as primarily domestic or residential compounds, while other compounds, including NMQ2, NMQ4, and NMQ10, were interpreted as having had more public functions, as 'offices', meeting halls, and so on. Compounds NMQ7, NMQ8, and NMQ9 were in a poor state of preservation, consisting primarily of foundation walls, and interpretations of their use were therefore not attempted.

Along with the compounds of the Noblemen's Quarter, a number of subsidiary structures located outside of the compound walls were identified. Many of these structures appear to have been the quarters of low status individuals, who probably served the residents of the elite compounds. Architecturally, these structures were poorly constructed, often single-roomed structures. Large numbers of grinding stones were found within them. The ceramics contained within three such units included high frequencies of large transport and storage vessels to the west of NMQ6. The presence of these presumably low status residences in such close proximity to the extremely high status NMQ compounds indicates that rather than being spatially isolated, as traditional Hindu ideology requires, members of high and low status castes may have lived in very close proximity in this area. The pronounced social distances separating them, reflected in house style and probably many other ways, may have been far more important than any spatial differentiation in distinguishing between the social groups resident in the Noblemen's Quarter.

In addition to examining vessel-use class distributions within the Noblemen's Quarter, their distribution was compared between the three sample areas. Overall distributions of vessel-use classes between the Noblemen's Quarter, the west and east halves of the East Valley, and the Islamic Quarter provided evidence of general differences in the importance of different activities within them. Although all vessel-use classes were found in all areas, the East Valley assemblages from both halves of the valley contained higher frequencies of small food preparation vessels than the other areas, and appeared to be more generalised domestic assemblages than either the Noblemen's Quarter or the Islamic Quarter ceramics. These latter two areas contained high frequencies of storage and transport vessels, water serving vessels, and large food preparation vessels and may have been overall, devoted more to non-domestic activities than the East Valley. In addition, the significantly higher than expected frequencies of unrestricted vessel forms in the Islamic Quarter have been interpreted as resulting from the use of these vessels as dining vessels, thereby providing evidence of differing cultural and religious proscriptions governing ceramic use between different subgroups of Vijayanagara's population.

The goal of examining the distribution of activities and the definition of functional space with the sample areas has, for the most part, been successfully achieved. Although the patterns observed in the ceramic distributions were rarely neat or absolute, they were statistically significant and, I believe, behaviorally significant. The examination of the spatial distribution of vessel-use classes within architectural compounds, between compounds, and across the site, does contribute significantly to our knowledge of the uses and definition of space at Vijayanagara, and to a lesser extent, to the cultural factors underlying these divisions.

Ceramic Forms and Social Identity at Vijayanagara

The third goal of this study was to examine the relations between ceramic forms and social groups as they were distributed across space at Vijayanagara. This analysis was predicated on the premises: (1) that social groups and in particular, castes, were spatially segregated at Vijayanagara, and (2) that ideologically important differences between these groups in food preparation and consumption and in ritual activities would contribute to the importance of ceramic vessels in distinguishing among such groups and expressing social group identity. I proposed that at this level of social differentiation, significant aspects of ceramic variability would be found within broad vessel-use categories, that is, at the level of variations within different classes of cooking vessels, serving vessels, and so on. The sorts of ceramic variation considered relevant to this study, then, potentially included variation in vessel proportions, rim form, wares, decoration, and so on, within generally similar forms.

The successful achievement of this analytical goal is limited by a number of factors. The first concerns the validity of the premises governing the research. As noted in the previous section, the assumption that social groups are spatially segregated in the Hindu city does not seen to hold in the Noblemen's Quarter area, or better, these groups are spatially segregated in close proximity to each other. If this is the case elsewhere at Vijayanagara, we might expect a mosaic distribution of social groups across the site, rather than the relatively neat broad residential areas we might otherwise expect. The fact that no pottery producing workshops have been found within the city walls, indicates that certain groups, such as potters, may have been spatially segregated. It appears though, that like the caste system itself, residential patterns within the Hindu city of Vijayanagara may have been far more flexible than Hindu ideology and the shastras would have us believe. Serving groups may have lived near their masters, while other groups who performed polluting work (literally and figuratively) such as potters, may have lived and worked at greater distances from the city core. At present, we cannot fully assess the heterogeneity or homogeneity or scale of residential communities within Vijayanagara.

The second premise concerning the existence of meaningful ceramic variation at the level of interacting social groups at Vijayanagara is as much an hypothesis to be tested as a basic belief underlying this study. That significant spatial variation in the distribution of ceramic form variants could be identified at Vijayanagara lends some support to this belief. It is not claimed however, that ceramics are necessarily the major or best medium by which social group identity was expressed at Vijayanagara. This is undoubtedly not the case. Ceramics are merely the most abundant class of materials currently available with which we can approach these questions. Nor is it claimed that the ceramic classification presented adequately summarises the relevant dimensions of variation in the Vijayanagara ceramics. Vessel shape, for example, is believed to be most important in expressing and communicating social information. This dimension of ceramic variation could not be adequately assessed for the Vijayanagara ceramics because of the absence of complete vessels in the sample.

Despite these limitations, some patterning of ceramic forms which apparently is associated with the distribution of social groups across the site could be observed. Differences between the three sample areas were pronounced at all levels of the ceramic classification, including the distribution of rim forms and vessel form variants. As elsewhere in the analysis, these differences, though statistically significant, were in frequency and not in kind, and all classes were found in all areas. The broad regional differences in ceramic distributions most likely are not the result of conscious choices distinguishing individuals or groups of the different areas. Rather, they appear to result in part: from differences in the workshops from which the occupants of each area acquired their vessels; overall differences between areas in the activities that occurred within them; and perhaps, social, religious, and economic differences in the composition of each area.

The analysis was successful in assessing and defining differences between the three sample areas — the Noblemen's Quarter, East Valley, and Islamic Quarter — in the ceramics found within them. Again, it is difficult to fully interpret these differences, though it seems that workshop distribution patterns, and social and cultural factors played a role. Chronological variation may also be important here though this cannot be assessed at present.

Ceramic Chronology

The attempt to define a ceramic chronology for Vijayanagara has, to date, been unsuccessful. It was hoped that the chronological variation evident in the Noblemen's Quarter architecture might be similarly evident in the ceramics recovered from the various excavated compounds. This did not prove to be the case, perhaps because of the limited context of recovery of the ceramics and chronological mixing of deposits, or perhaps a result of the presumed small-scale organization of ceramic production at Vijayanagara and the resultant wide range of variability of ceramic forms. The development of a successful ceramic chronology for Vijayanagara, if possible, awaits the excavation of a well-controlled stratigraphic sequence.

DICUSSION

This study of Vijayanagara ceramics, then, was largely succesful in answering the questions it set out to examine, and, as a result, we know somewhat more about the Noblemen's Quarter, and the city as a whole, than we did before the analysis. A ceramic classification was developed for Vijayanagara, which has relevance to and may be applied in the study of medieval sites from throughout South India. The use of space and functional divisions of space within and between architectural compounds of the Noblemen's Quarter was assessed, contributing to our understanding of this elite residential area of the site.

By examining Vijayanagara ceramics in the context of other knowledge about the site, we now understand a bit more about the imperial capital of Vijayanagara than we could before this analysis. The heuristic division of the site into discrete zones on the basis of architectural and topographic features is supported by the ceramic analysis. The East Valley is different from the Noblemen's Quarter is different from the Islamic Quarter —in the sorts of activities which occurred there, in economic relations with craft producers, and in other behavioral and cultural features. While these areas can certainly not be seen as closed communities, they may be seen as legitimate divisions within the larger city of Vijayanagara.

In addition, through this analysis, we were able to examine areas which could not be examined except through ceramic data. These areas, such as the East Valley, contain only limited architectural evidence on the ground surface, and could not otherwise be examined without extensive and time-consuming excavation projects. Given the scale of Vijayanagara, such excavations are clearly implausible and the analysis of surface distributions, including architectural traces, ceramics, and other artifacts, provide the only means for incorporating these areas into our understanding of the city and of the lives of all who lived there, rulers and ruled. It is hoped that this study represents a step along the way to a greater understanding of the history and culture of the imperial capital of Vijayanagara.

References Cited

Appadurai, Arjun, editor
1986 *The Social Life of Things*. Cambridge University Press, New York.

Arnold, D.E.
1976 Ecological variables and ceramic production: Toward a general model. In, *Primitive Art and Technology*. Ed. by J.S. Raymond, B. Loveseth, C. Arnold and G. Reardon, pp. 92-108. University of Calgary, Calgary Canada.
1985 *Ceramic Theory and Cultural Process*. Cambridge University Press, Cambridge.

Balfet, H.
1981 Production and distribution of pottery in the Maghreb. In, *Production and Distribution: A Ceramic Viewpoint*. Ed. by H. Howard and E.L. Morris, pp. 257-269, BAR International Series, 120.

Behura, N.K.
1978 *Peasant Potters of Orissa: A Sociological Study*. Sterling, New Delhi.

Binford, Lewis R.
1976 Forty-seven trips: A case study in the character of some formation processes in the archaeological record. In, *Contributions to Anthropology: The Interior Peoples of Northern Alaska*. Ed. by Edwin S. Hall. Ottawa National Museum of Man Mercury Series, 49.

Binford, L.R., S.R. Binford, R. Whallon, and M.A. Hardin
1970 *Archaeology at Hatchery West*. Society for American Archaeology, Memoir 35.

Birmingham, J.
1975 Traditional potters of the Kathmandu Valley: An ethnoarchaeological study. *Man*(n.s.) 10:370-386.

Boone, James L.
1987 Defining and measuring midden catchment. *American Antiquity* 52: 336-345.

Braun, David
1983 Pots as tools. In, *Archaeological Hammers and Theories*. Ed. by A.S. Keene and J.A. Moore, pp. 107-134. Academic Press, New York.

Cowgill, George L.
1972 Models, methods, and techniques for seriation. In, *Models in Archaeology*. Ed. by D.L. Clarke, pp. 381-424. Methuen, London.

Dallapiccola, A.L., ed.
1985 *Vijayanagara: City and Empire*. South Asian Institute, University of Heidelberg, Heidelberg.

David, Nicholas
1972 On the life span of pottery, type frequencies, and archaeological inference. *American Antiquity* 37: 141-142.

David, N. and H. Henning
1972 *The Ethnography of Pottery: A Fulani Case Seen in Archaeological Perspective*. McCaleb Modules in Anthropology, No. 21. Addison-Wesley, Reading, Mass.

DeBoer, Warren R.
1985 Pots and pans do not speak, nor do they lie: The case for occasional reductionism. In, *Decoding Prehistoric Ceramics.* Ed. by Ben A. Nelson, pp. 347-357. Southern Illinois University Press, Carbondale.

DeBoer, W.R. and D. Lathrap
1979 The making and breaking of Shipibo-Conibo ceramics. In, *Ethnoarchaeology; Implications of Ethnography for Archaeology.* Ed. by Carol Kramer, pp. 102-138. Columbia University Press, New York.

Deetz, James
1965 *The Dynamics of Stylistic Change in Arikara Ceramics.* University of Illinois Press, Chicago.

Doran, J.E. and F.R. Hodson
1975 *Mathematics and Computers in Archaeology,* Harvard University Press, Cambridge, Mass.

Douglas, Mary
1974 Deciphering a meal. In, *Myth, Symbol, and Culture.* Ed. Clifford Geertz, pp. 61-82. W.W. Norton and Company, New York.

Douglas, Mary and B. Isherwood
1980 *The World of Goods.* Penguim, Middlesex.

Ellen, Roy F. and Ian C. Glover
1974 Pottery manufacture and trade in central Moluccas, Indonesia: The modern situation and historical implication. *Man* (n.s.) 9:353-379.

Foster, George M.
1960 Life expectancy of utilitarian pottery in Tzintzuntzun Michoacan, Mexico. *American Antiquity* 25:606-609.
1965 The sociology of pottery: Questions and hypotheses arising from contemporary Mexican work. *Ceramics and Man.* Ed. by F.R. Matson, pp. 43-61. Viking Fund Publications in Anthropology, No. 41, New York.

Friedrich, Margaret Hardin
1970 Design structure and social interaction. *American Antiquity* 35:332-343.

Fritz, John M.
1983 The roads of Vijayanagara: A preliminary study. In, *Vijayanagara: Progress of Research 1979-1893.* Ed. by M.S. Nagaraja Rao, pp. 51-60. Vijayanagara Research Centre Series 1. Department of Archaeology and Museums, Mysore.

Fritz, John M. and George A. Michell
1984 The Vijayanagara documentation and research project: A progress report. In, *South Asian Archaeology 1981.* Ed. by B. Allchin, pp. 295-305. Cambridge University Press, Cambridge.
1985 Map series on cultural remains of Vijayanagara. In, *Vijayanagara, Progress of Research 1983-84.* Ed. by M.S. Nagaraja Rao, pp. 164-197. Vijayanagara Research Centre Series 2. Directorate of Archaeology and Museums, Mysore.

Fritz, John M., George A. Michell, and M.S. Nagaraja Rao
1985 *The Royal Centre of Vijayanagara: Preliminary Report.* University of Arizona Press, Tucson.

Goody, J.
1982 *Cooking, Cuisine and Class.* Cambridge University Press, Cambridge.

Hardin, Margaret Ann

1979 The cognitive basis of productivity in a decorative art style: Implications of an ethnographic study for archaeologists' taxonomies. In, *Ethnoarchaeology*. Ed. by Carol Kramer, pp. 750-100. Columbia University Press, New York.

1984 Models of decoration. In, *The Many Dimensions of Pottery: Ceramics in Archaeology and Authropology*. Ed. by S.E. van der Leeuw and A.C. Prichard, pp. 573-607. University of Amsterdam, Amsterdam.

Henrikson, E. and M. McDonald

1983 Ceramic form and function: An ethnographic search and archaeological application. *American Anthropologist* 85-630-643.

Hill, James N.

1970 *Broken K Pueblo: Prehistoric Social Organization in the American Southwest,* University of Arizona Anthropological Papers, 18, Tucson.

Hill, James N. and R.K. Evans

1972 A model for classification and typology. In, *Models in Archaeology*. Ed. by D.L. Clarke, pp. 231-274. Metheun, London.

Hole, Bonnie L.

1980 Sampling in archaeology: A critique. *Annual Review of Anthropology* 9:217-234.

Junker, Laura L.

1985 Morphology, function and style in traditional ceramics: A study of contemporary pottery from Bellary District, Karnataka. In, *Vijayanagara: Progress of Research, 1983-1985*. Ed by M.S. Nagaraja Rao. Vijayanagara Research Centre Series 2, Department of Archaeology and Museums, Mysore.

Karve, Irawati

1953 *Kinship Organization in India*. Deccan College Post-Graduate and Research Institute, Poona.

Kintigh, Keith W.

1982 K-Means cluster analysis on MTS. Manuscript on file, University of Michigan, Museum of Anthropology, Ann Arbor.

1985 Social structure, the structure of style and stylistic patterns in Cibola pottery. In, *Decoding Prehistoric Ceramics*. Ed. by Ben A. Nelson, pp. 35-74. Southern Illinois Press, Carbondale.

Kintigh, K.W. and A.J. Ammerman

1982 Heuristic approaches to spatial analysis in archaeology. *American Antiquity* 47:31-63.

Kramer, Carol

1985 Ceramic ethnoarchaeology. *Annual Review of Anthropology* 14:77-120.

Longacre, W.A.

1968 Some aspects of prehistoric society in East-Central Arizona. In, *New Perspectives in Archaeology*. Ed. by Lewis R. and Sally Binford. Aldine, Chicago.

1985 Pottery use-life among the Kalinga, Northern Luzon, The Philippines. In, *Decoding Prehistoric Ceramics*. Ed. by Ben A. Nelson pp. 334-346. Southern Illinois University Press, Carbondale.

Mahalingam, T.V.

1985 *Administration and Social Life Under Vijayanagara. Part II: Social Life* (Second Edition). University of Madras Press, Madras.

Mate, M.S.
1985 Daulatabad. In, *Recent Advances in Indian Archaeology*. Ed. by S.B. Deo and K. Paddaya. Deccan College Post-Graduate Research Institute, Poona.

Mehta, R.N.
1979 *Medieval Archaeology*. Ajanta Publications, Delhi.

Michell, George
1985a A never forgotten city. In, *Vijayanagara: City and Empire*. Ed. by A. Dallapiccola, pp. 196-207. South Asian Institute, University of Heidelberg, Heidelberg.
1985b Architectural traditions at Vijayanagara. I. Temple styles. In, *Vijayanagara: City and Empire*. Ed. by A. Dallapiccola, pp. 274-281. South Asian Institute, University of Heidelberg, Heidelberg.
1985c Architectural traditions at Vijayanagara. II. Islamic styles. In, *Vijayanagara: City and Empire*. Ed. by A.L. Dallapiccola, pp. 282-286. South Asian Institute, University of Heidelberg, Heidelberg.
1985d Architecture of the Muslim Quarters of Vijayanagara. In, *Vijayanagara Progress of Research 1983-84*. Ed. by M.S. Nagaraja Rao, pp. 101-118. Vijayanagara Research Centre Series 2. Directorate of Archaeology and Museums, Mysore.

Miller, Daniel
1982 Structures and strategies: An aspect of the relationship between social hierarchy and cultural change. In, *Symbolic and Structural Archaeology*. Ed. by I. Hodder pp. 89-98. Cambridge University Press, Cambridge.
1985 *Artifacts as Categories*. Cambridge University Press, Cambridge and New York.

Nagaraja Rao, M.S.
1983a Ahmadkhan's Dharmasala. In, *Vijayanagara Progress of Research 1979—1983*. Ed. by M.S. Nagaraja Rao, pp. 64-67. Vijayanagara Research Centre Series 1. Directorate of Archaeology and Museums, Mysore.
1983b Excavations. In, *Vijayanagara Progress of Research 1979-1983*. Ed. by M.S. Nagaraja Rao, pp. 9-29. Vijayanagara Research Centre Series 1. Directorate of Archaeology and Museums, Mysore.
1985a Research at Vijayanagara 1979 to 1983. In, *Vijayanagara: City and Empire*. Ed. by A.L. Dallapiccola. South Asian Institute, University of Heidelberg, Heidelberg.
1985b Excavations. In, *Vijayanagara Progress of Research 1983-84*. Ed. by M.S. Nagaraja Rao, pp. 5-17. Vijayanagara Research Centre Series 2, Directorate of Archaeology and Museums, Mysore.

Nagaraja Rao, M.S. editor
1983 *Vijayanagara: Progress of Research 1979-1983*. Vijayanagara Research Centre Series 1. Directorate of Archaeology and Museums, Mysore.
1985 *Vijayanagara: Progress of Research 1983-1984*. Vijayanagara Research Centre Series 2. Directorate of Archaeology and Museums, Mysore.

Nagaraja Rao, M.S. and C.S. Patil
1985b Epigraphical inscriptions to city gates and watchtoowers of Vijayanagara. In. *Vijayanagara Progress of Research 1983-84*. Ed. by M.S. Nagaraja Rao, pp. 96-100. Vijayanagara Research Centre Series 2, Directorate of Archaeology and Museums, Mysore.

Nicklin K.
1971 Stability and innovation in pottery manufacture. *World Archaeology* 3:13-48.

Orton, C.
1980 *Mathematics in Archaeology.* Cambridge University Press, Cambridge.

Patil. C.S.
1985a Palace architecture at Vijayanagara: The new excavations. In, *Vijayanagara City and Empire.* Ed. by A.L. Dallapiccola, pp. 229-239. South Asian Institute, University of Heidelberg, Heidelberg.
1985b Palace architecture at Vijayanagara. In, *Vijayanagara Progress of Research 1983-84.* Ed. by M.S. Nagaraja Rao, pp. 119-132. Vijayanagara Research Centre Series 2, Directorate of Archaeology and Museums, Mysore.

Plog, S.
1980 *Stylistic Variation in Prehistoric Ceramics.* Cambridge University Press, New York.

Pollock, Susan M.
1983a Style and information: An analysis of Susiana ceramics. *Journal of Anthropological Archaeology* 2:354-390.
1983b *The Symbolism of Prestige: An Archaeological Example from the Royal Cemetery of Ur.* Ph.D. Dissertation, Department of Anthropology, University of Michigan. University Microfilms, Ann Arbor.

Rappaport, R.A.
1971 Ritual, sanctity, and cybernetics. *American Anthropologist* 73: 59-76.

Rautman, Alison E.
in press Report on the petrographic analysis of ceramic shreds from Vijayanagara India. To appear in, *Vijayanagara Progress of Research 1985-1987.* Ed. by A. Sundara. Vijayanagara Research Centre Series: Mysore.

Redman, C.L.
1973 Multistage fieldwork and analytical techniques. *American Antiquary* 38:61-79.

Rice, P.M.
1981 Evolution of specialized pottery production: A trial model. *Current Anthropology* 22:219-240.

Rouse, Irving
1967 Seriation in archaeology. In, *American Historical Anthropology: Essays in Honor of Leslie Spier.* Ed. by C.L. Riley and W.W. Taylor, pp. 153-195. Southern Illinois University Press, Carbondale.

Runyon, P.P. and A. Haber
1972 *Fundamentals of Behavioral Statistics.* Addison-Wesley, Reading, Mass.

Rye, Owen S.
1981 *Pottery Technology: Principles and Reconstruction.* Taraxacum Inc., Washington D.C.

Saraswati, B.
1978 *Pottery Making Cultures and Indian Civilization.* Abhinav Publications, New Delhi.

Saraswati, B. and N.K. Behura
1966 *Pottery Techniques in Peasant India.* Memoirs of the Anthropological Survey of India, 13. Calcutta.

Schiffer, Michael B.
1976 *Behavioral Archaeology.* Academic Press, New York.

Sewell, Robert
1900 *A Forgotten Empire (Vijayanagara): A Contribution to the History of India.* Swann Sonnenscheir and Co. Ltd., London.

Sinopoli, Carla M.
1986 *Material Patterning and Social Organization: A Study of Ceramics from Vijayanagara, South India.* Ph.D. dissertation, Department of Anthropology, University of Michigan. University Microfilms, Ann Arbor,
n.d.a. *Approaches to Ceramics Studies in Archaeology.* Manuscript in possession of the author.
n.d.b. Standardization and specialization: Ceramic production at Vijayanagra, South India. To appear in, *Old Probelms-New Perspectives in the Archaeology of South Asia.* Edited by J. Mark Kenoyer. University of Wisconsin Archaeological Series, Madison.
n.d.c. The earthenware pottery of the Royal Enclosures of Vijayanagara. Manuscript submitted to the Archaeological Survey of India, New Delhi.

Sinopoli, C.M. and T.R. Blurton
1986 Modern pottery production in rural Karnataka. In, *Dimensions of Indian Art: Pupul Jayakar Seventy.* Ed. by L. Chandra and J. Jain, pp. 439-456. Agam Kala Prakashan, New Delhi.

Stanislawski, Michael B.
1969 What good is a broken pot? An experiment in Hopi-Tewa ethnoarchaeology. *Southwestern Lore* 35:11-18.
1973 Review of "Archaeology as Anthropology: A Case Study". *American Antiquity* 38:117-122.

Stark, Barbara L.
1985 Archaeological identification of pottery-production locations: Ethnoarchaeological and archaeological data in Mesoameria. In, *Decoding Prehistoric Ceramics.* Ed. by Ben A. Nelson, pp. 158-194. Southern Illinois University, Carbondale.

Steponaitis, V.
1983 *Ceramics, Chronology, and Community Patterns: An Archaeological Study at Moundville.* Academic Press, New York.
1984 Technological studies of prehistoric pottery from Alabama: Physical properties and vessel function. In, *The Many Dimensions of Pottery: Ceramics in Archaeology and Anthropology.* Ed. by S.E. van der Leeuw and A.C. Pritchard, pp. 79-122. University of Amsterdam, Amsterdam.

Thapar, B.K.
1957 Maski. *Ancient India.* 13: 86-88.

van-der Leeuw, S.E.
1977 Towards a study of the economics of pottery making. In, *Ex Horreo.* Ed. by B.L. van Beek, R.W. Brandt, and w. Goeman-van Waatering, pp. 68-76. University of Amsterdam, Amsterdam.

Verghese, I.
1971 Weekly market in a Mysore town. *Journal of the Indian Antropological Society* 6:107-118.

Washburn, D.
1977 *A Symmetry Analysis of Upper Gila Area Ceramic Design.* Papers of the Peabody Museum, 68. Harvard University, Cambridge, Mass.

Whallon, R.J., Jr.
1972 A new approach to pottery typology. *American Antiquity* 37:13-33.

1983 Methods of surface collection in archaeological survey. In, *Archaeological Survey in the Mediterranean Area.* Ed. by Donald R. Keller and David W. Rupp. pp. 73-83. BAR International series, 155.

Whallon, R.J. and James A. Brown, editors.
1982 *Essays on Archaeological Typology.* Center for American Archaeology Press, Evanston, Illinois.

Wheat, J., J. Gifford, and W. Wasley
1958 Ceramic variety, type cluster, and ceramic system in Southwestern pottery analysis. *American Antiquity* 24: 34-47.

Wheeler, R.E.M.
1946 Arikamedu: An Indo-Roman Trading Station. *Ancient India* 2:17-124.

Williams, D.F.
1981 The Roman amphorae trade with late Iron Age Britain. In, *Production and Distribution: A Ceramic Viewpoint.* Ed. by H. Howard and E. Morris, pp. 123-132. BAR International Series, No. 120.

Yellen, John
1977 *Archaeological Approaches to the Present.* Academic Press, New York.

APPENDIXES

Table 4.1

Categorical Attributes Recorded on All Vijayanagara Diagnostic Sherds

Attribute	Attribute States
Percentage of inclusions	none, trace, 5%, 10%,15%,...
Inclusion type	
Sand	absent, fine grain(<1mm.), medium grain(1-3 mm.), coarse grain(>3mm.)
Organic	absent, present
Red grit (hematite)	absent, present
White grit (calcite)	absent, present
Other[a]	absent, present
Body color	Munsell value(1983) black, red, brown, red-sandwiched (red-black-red), brown-sandwiched, gray-sandwiched, white, other
Surface color	Munsell value (1983) black, red, brown, white, other
Surface treatment	
Interior and exterior	smoothed, polished, burnished, partially burnished, slipped and burnished, paddle and anvil impressions, coarsely finished (e.g. sand, chaff, pebble and other impressions), other
Rim interior (1984)	none, polished, burnished

[a] material recorded in comment section

Table 4.2

Vijayanagara Ware Classes

Ware	Number of Sherds
Plain	
Black	24,484
Red	2152
Brown	12,478
Burnished	
Black	1015
Red	1106
Brown	295
Coarse	1434
Total	42,964

Sherd counts include body sherds from the Islamic Quarter and East Valley and Noblemen's Quarter Diagnostics

Table 4.3

Vijayanagara Lamp Classes: Mean Attribute Values

Attributes	L1	L2	L3	L4	Total Sample
Rim Form	Round	Round	Flat	Flat	
Base Form	Round	Flat	Round	Flat	
#	11	11	29	58	170
Rim diam[a]	7.91	8.81	9.66	9.30	9.45
Base diam	7.00(3)[b]	5.71(7)	6.67(9)	6.12(39)	6.18(60)
Rim angle(°)	56	55	60	60	59
Rm top ang(°)	65(6)	64(9)	70(28)	67	69(158)
Lip thick	.30(10)	.29(10)	.26	.24	.26(163)
Rim thick	.52	.59	.66	.73	.68
Base thick	.56(7)	.46(10)	.52(23)	.50(54)	.51(94)
Rim height	.36	.50	.67	.73	.66
Base ht	1.74(6)	1.44(6)	2.09(15)	2.03(49)	1.97(76)
Vessel ht	1.49(1)	1.57(5)	1.78(6)	1.94(14)	1.79(28)
Surf color[c]	6/4/1	5/1/4	10/2/17	23/10/25	71/31/65
Surface treatment[d]	8/3	6/5	7/21	11/45	77/82
Chaff[e]	10/1	9/2	21/8	42/16	133/37

a All measures in cm unless otherwise specified
b Value in parentheses equals number of sherds measured when less than total
c black/red/brown
d Exterior surface; smooth/coarse
e absent/present

Table 4.4

Vijayanagara Shallow Bowls: Mean Attribute Values by Size and Rim Angle Class

	Size and Rim Angle Classes						
Attributes	SB1	SB2	SB3	SB4	SB5	SB6	Total sample
Size Cl.	medium	large	medium	large	medium	large	–
Angle Cl.	low	low	acute	acute	steep	steep	–
#	23	10	315	79	429	63	923
Rim dm[a]	16.96	26.30	16.87	26.20	16.12	25.40	18.02
Base dm	13.87(15)[b]	22.60	15.89(297)	23.36(61)	16.17(362)	25.10(60)	17.48(828)
Rim ang	33°	39°	71°	69°	96°	95°	83°
Base ang	26°(12)	23°(5)	31°(125)	31°(40)	36°(177)	39°(31)	33°(390)
Lip th	.44	.56	.38	.49	.41	.50	.41
Rim th	1.00	1.14	.91	1.16	.90	1.08	.94
Base th	.65(11)	.59(6)	.54(107)	.61(41)	.56(153)	.63(30)	.57(348)
Rim ht	1.14	1.36	1.22	1.63	1.19	1.68	1.27
Grv ht	.79(15)	.93(5)	.93(249)	1.26(45)	.95(275)	1.33(26)	.98(617)
Base ht	1.91(22)	2.33	1.87(297)	2.46(73)	1.88(363)	2.57(59)	1.98(827)
Rl rm[c]	.44	.47	.42	.44	.45	.46	.44

[a] all measures in cm unless otherwise specified
[b] value in parenthesis equals number of sherds measured, when less than column total
[c] relative rim thickness equals lip thickness/rim thickness

Table 4.5

Vijayanagara Other Bowl Forms

Form	Description
Rounded	
Normal	n=25, range in diam. from 10-39 cm, with most vessels between 16 and 24 cm in size, typically open out-sloping forms with mean rim angle of 65°, possibly used as lids, food preparation or serving vessels.
Flange	n=9, distinctive form, ranges in size from 10-27 cm, vessels vary in overall height with some with steep walls and others more shallow. One was used as a strainer. Others may have been lids or serving vessels.
Flat thickened rim	n=31, range from 10-38 cm rim diam. with bimodality, 10-19 cm, 25-30 cm, steep lip angles, and generally steep walls below the rim, rim varies in orientation, particularly rim top angle. May have been lids or food preparation or serving vessels.
Inturning	n=50, inturning vessels with simple rims, sometimes with slightly thickened rims, range from 11-31 cm in rim diam., with most vessels between 15-24 cm. May have been used as lids or serving vessels.
Out-turning	n=16, from 12-31 cm in diam. with pronounced modes at 15 and 26 cm (12-18 cm, n=6 and 21-30 cm, n=6). Only form associated with distinctive ware – eight are of Burnished Red Ware. Five of the 16 vessels come form the Islamic Quarter. Probably used as serving vessels.
Carinated	
Normal	n=75, range from 13-34 cm in diam., with bimodal size distribution (13-17 cm, 18-33 cm), often with vertical walls (mean rim angle=88°), though includes both out-sloping and in-sloping forms. Probably used as serving, food preparation or cooking (griddles?) vessels.
Grooved	n=37, range from 19-43 cm in diam., possibly several size modes with most vessels between 23-32 cm in diameter. Typically have vertical or out-sloping walls, often decorated on exterior with simple vertical tics. In form these are similar to the larger shallow bowl forms described above. Probably serving or food preparation vessels.
Flat thickened rim	n=25, range from 21-45 cm, with most vessels between 25-31 cm. Walls slope out slightly, rim thickens to the interior and exterior. Probably serving or food preparation vessels.

Table 4.6

Vijayanagara Round Rim Storage Jars: Mean Attribute Values

Attribute	Inturning Form (RS1)	Out-Turning Form (RS2)	Total Sample
#	115	120	235
Rim diam	23.52	23.05	23.28
Neck diam	23.59	20.90	22.22
Rim angle	99°	67°	83°
Lip angle	80°	54°	67°
Body angle	48°(20)[a]	57°(10)	51°(30)
Lip thick	.84(93)	.76(90)	.80(183)
Rim thick	1.74	1.61	1.67
Neck thick	.73	.76	.75
Body thick	.57(24)	.72(14)	.63(38)
Rim height	2.39	1.97	2.18
Neck height	2.88	2.53	2.69
Rm th/ht	.77	.85	.81
Rel rm ht[b]	.90	.85	.78

[a] Value in parentheses equals number of sherds measured when less than total
[b] Relative rim height equals rim height/neck height

Table 4.7

Vijayanagara Small Round Rim Restricted Vessels: Mean Attribute Values

Attribute	RRs1	RRs2	RRs3	RRs4	RRs5	RRs6	Total Sample
Rim form	evert	evert	both	both	normal	ledge	
Neck ht	low	high	low	high			
#	296	32	50	14	52	24	468
Rim diam	10.8	12.3	12.1	13.3	13.9	12.2	11.3
Neck diam	9.1	10.2	10.3	11.4	12.1	10.2	9.4
Rim ang	62°	70°	67°	70°	64°	75°	64°
Lip ang	55°	61°	89°	89°	57°	48°	59°
Body ang	70°(34)	56°(4)	56°(6)	57°(3)	50°(1)	47°(3)	645°(52)
Lip th			.50	.51	.58	.66	.52
Rim th	.84	1.00	.97	.99	1.12	1.33	.90
Neck th	.51	.55	.54	.53	.60	.52	.52
Rim ht	.75	.99	.86	1.02	1.17	.91	.82
Neck ht	1.50	2.63	1.68	2.30	2.01	1.78	1.64

[a] Value in parentheses equals number of sherds coded when less than total sample

Table 4.8

Vijayanagara Large Round Rim Restricted Vessels: Mean Attribute Values

Attribute	RRl1	RRl2	RRl3	Total Sample
Rim form	everted	both	both	
Size class	large	large	v. large	
#	31	25	16	94
Rim diam	18.4	19.3	26.6	20.8
Neck diam	15.8	17.3	24.1	18.5
Rim angle	53°	66°	60°	59°
Lip angle	48°	102°	88°	67°
Body angle		62°(3)[a]		62°(3)
Lip th		.58	.70	.70
Rim th	.93	1.38	1.47	1.21
Neck th	.63	.64	.73	.67
Rim ht	.88	1.17	1.39	1.09
Neck ht	1.50	2.18	2.40	1.88

[a] Value in parentheses equals number of sherds coded when less than total sample

Table 4.9

Restricted Vessel Cluster Analysis: Mean Variable Scores

Variable	Cluster				
	1	2	3	4	6
#	318	247	15	27	363
Rim angle	42.48	59.92	79.33	36.48	73.17
Body angle	74.45	62.15	69.00	44.63	42.54
Rim-Neck Diam. Ratio	.081	.076	.056	.084	.065
Std. Neck Height	-.471	.023	.514	-.430	.635

Nine variable cluster solution; only the 6 largest clusters are presented

Table 4.10

Comparison of Four-Variable Cluster Analysis with Rim Angle Cuts

	Rim Angle Cuts			
Cluster	25.35	40.60	65.90	Total
1	69	246	0	315
Expect[b]	27	148	140	
2	0	157	105	262
Expect	22	123	117	
3	13	14	0	27
Expect	2	13	12	
5	0	37	326	363
Expect	31	170	162	
Total	82	454	431	967

[a] Only clusters 1-3, 5 are presented here.
[b] Expected values if there was no relation between the cluster analysis results and the rim angle classes.

Table 4.11

Vijayanagara Flange and Straight Rim Restricted Vessels: Rim Form Variants

Rim form	#	Basis of division	Formal variation
FN1	1209	principal comp.	low, nearly as thick as high
FN2	1125	(lip th,rim th,rm ht,nk ht)	large, high rim th/ht
FI1	382	lip an x rm th	rounded low lip, low rl rm th
FI2	417		rounded higher lip, higher rl rm th
FI3	178		angular high lip, high rl rm th
FE1	1045	rim th/rim ht	thick lip, high rims, rth/ht=.62
FE2	1244		thinner lips, low rims, rth/ht=.85
FT1	144	lip ang x rim ht	low lip angle, low rim ht
FT2	77		steep lip angle, high rims
FL	46	not divided	low lip angle, out-turned rim
FG	145	not divided	thickened rim base, steep lip angle
SN	2179	not divided	simple form, thin lips, low lip th/rm th ratio
SI	334	not divided	inturning thickened lip
SE	193	not divided	simple out-turning rim, lip th=rim th
SB1	87	principal comp.	acute rim tp angle, thick rims
SB2	178	(rmtp ang,rm th,rm ht)	finer, thin, steep rim top ang
ST1	418	lip th/rim ht	high rim th, low ht, narrow rect. ledges
ST2	384		blocky, low lip angle, mean rl rm th=.80
ST3	142		steep lip angle, med rim th, lip th
ST4	294		steep lip angle, large rim th, lip th, rm ht

Table 4.12

Vijayanagara Restricted Vessels: Size Divisions by Shape and Rim Form

Rim form	Shape class	Total sample	# of size groups	Size range rim dm (cm)	Mean diam	Sherds per group	Strength of div.[a]
FN	≤20	19	1	11–24	18.4		b
	25.35	255	4	10–14/15–22/23–28/29–35	12.8/18.5/24.4/31.7	25/191/51/7	w
	40.60	1345	2	10–26/27–45	18.3/30.8	1290/55	w
	65.90	555	3	10–14/15–26/27–33	13.1/18.4/28.5	64/478/12	w
FI	40.60	404	2	6–22/22–39	17.7/26.1	300/104	s
	65.90	170	3	10–18/19–24/25–36	16.2/21.0/27.7	78/70/22	s
FE	25.35	36	1	13–28	19.6		b
	40.60	492	3	8–15/16–25/26–37	13.8/19.3/28.0	88/3488/16	w
	65.90	548	3	10–13/14–23/24–37	12.2/17.7/26.1	25/504/19	w
FT	all	158	4	10–14/15–20/21–28/30–45	13.3/17.9/23.5/34.8	12/67/69/10	s
FL	all	22		11–29	16.5		
FG	all	97	3	9–15/16–21/22–28	12.0/17.4/23.6	68/20/3	w
SN	≤20	18	2	11–19/21–27	15.3/24.0	15/3	s
	25.35	188	3	8–13/14–22/23–28/29–40	12.9/17.7/23.4	37/132/7	w
	40.60	908	4	8–13/14–22/23–28/29–40	11.9/17.3/24.5/32.3	116/715/70/7	w
	65.90	299	3	11–13/14–20/21–30	12.4/17.0/23.1	25/208/66	w
SI	25.35	17	2	12–16/17–23	133.4/20/1	5/12	s
	40.60	107	3	13–16/17–23/24–30	14.4/19.8/26.1	19/72/16	w
	65.90	73	3	10–16/17–23/24–20	14.3/19.7/16.8	16/45/12	s
SE	≤20	11	2	6–16/24–27	11.9/25.0	8/3	s
	25.35	32	2	6–14/16–26	12.0/19.1	16/16	s
	40.60	45	2	7–15/16–25	11.9/18.6	26/19	s
	65.90	12	2	8–15/23	11.3/23.0	11/1	s
SB	25.35	17	2	11–16/18–27	13.7/22.4	7/10	s
	40.60	95	3	9–15/16–22/23–31	12.7/18.7/26.3	37/44/14	w
	65.90	33	3	7–14/15–17/18–27	11.8/16.0/23.0	23/4/6	s
ST	40.60	56	2	10–14/15–26	12.3/19.3	13/43	s
	65.90	798	3	7–14/15–21/22–33	12.9/17.4/24.3	209/464/116	
	≥95	7	1	7–24	14.29		

[a] 's' equals strong modality, 'w' equals weak modality
[b] These samples indicated some mulitmodality in size distributions but were not subdivided because of the small sample sizes

Table 4.13

Vijayanagara Restricted Vessels: Final Classification by Shape, Rim Form, and Size

	Shape class	Rim form	Size	# of sherds	Description	Funct. equiv.
					Small Serving Vessels (RV1, n=363)	
1.	25.35	S. normal	sm	41	8–14 cm in diameter, with simple rims and low everted necks, probably individual serving vessels	2,3–6 RRs1–5
2.	≤35	S. Everted	sm	27	6–16 cm in diameter, with simple rims and low everted necks, probably individual serving vessels	1,3–6 RRs1–5
3.	40.90	S. Everted	sm	48	7–15 cm in diameter,with simple rims and low relatively steep necks, probably individual serving or drinking vessels	1,2,4-6,RRs1–5
4.	40.60	S. Normal	sm	127	8–13 cm in diameter, low rims and necks, probably individual serving vessels	1–3, 5,6 RRs1–5
5.	40.60	S. Both	sm	38	9–15 cm, thin rims which turn in at lip, possibly limiting spillage, probably individual serving vessels	1–4,6 RRs1–5
6.	40.60	F. everted	sm	82	8–15 cm, small open vessels with low rims and necks, probably individual serving vessels	1–5 RRs1–5
					Medium Cooking or Storage Vessels (RV2, n=4052)	
7.	25.35	S. Normal	med	163	15–21 cm, open shallow vessels with low sharply everted necks, probably used for cooking or short-term storage	8,9
8.	25.35	F. Normal 1	med	168	15–21 cm, open shallow vessels with low sharply everted necks, probably used for cooking or short-term storage	7,9
9.	25.35	F. Normal 2	med	98	16–26 cm, open shallow vessels with low sharply everted necks, probably used for cooking or short-term storage	7,8
10.	40.60	S. Normal	med	865	15–21 cm, open relatively shallow form, probably used for cooking or short-term storage	11–19
11.	40.60	S. Inverted	med	80	17–23 cm, open relatively shallow form, probably used for cooking or short-term storage	8,11–19

Table 4.13 (continued)

	Shape class	Rim form	Size	# of sherds	Description	Funct. equiv.
Medium Cooking or Storage Vessels (RV2, n=4052)						
12.	40.60	S. Both 2	med	46	16–22 cm, open relatively shallow form with thin rims that turn in at the lip, probably used for cooking or short-term storage	10,11, 12–19
13.	40.60	F. Normal 1	med	705	10–26 cm, open relatively shallow form, probably used for cooking or short-term storage	10–12, 14–19
14.	40.60	F. Normal 2	med	961	10–26 cm, open relatively shallow form, probably used for cooking or short-term storage	10–13 ,15–19
15.	40.60	F. Inverted 1	med	199	6–22 cm, open relatively shallow form, with thickened inturning lip, probably used for cooking or short-term storage	10–14, 16–19
16.	40.60	F. Inverted 2	med	130	14–22 cm in diameter, open relatively shallow form; with thickened inturning lip, probably used for cooking or short-term storage	10–15, 17–19
17.	40.60	F. Everted 1	med	110	16–25 cm, open relatively shallow form, probably used for cooking or short-term storage	10–16, 18,19
18.	40.60	F. Everted 2	med	479	16–25 cm, open relatively shallow form, probably used for cooking or short-term storage	10–17,19
19.	20.60	S. Everted	med	48	16–27 cm, open relatively shallow form, probably used for cooking or short-term storage	7–18
Large Cooking or Storage Vessels (RV3, n=370)						
20.	40.60	S. Normal	lge	95	23–28 cm, open relatively shallow form, probably used for cooking or short-term storage	21–25
21.	40.60	F. Normal 1	lge	55	27–45 cm, open relatively shallow form, probably used for cooking or short-term storage	21,22–25
22.	40.60	F. Inverted 1	lge	47	23–32 cm, open relatively shallow form with thickened inturning lip, probably used for cooking or short-term storage	20,21,23–25
23.	40.60	F. Inverted 2	lge	71	23–39 cm, open relatively shallow form with thickened inturning lip, probably used for cooking or short-term storage	20–22,24,25
24.	40.60	F. Everted 2	lge	47	26–40 cm.,open, relatively shallow form with thickened out-turning lip, probably used for cooking or short-term storage	20–23,25

Table 4.13 (continued)

	Shape class	Rim form	Size	# of sherds	Description	Funct. equiv.
					Large Cooking or Storage Vessels (RV3, n = 370)	
25.	40.60	F. normal 2	lge	55	27–45 cm., open, relatively shalllow form with normal lip, probably used for cooking or short-term storage	20–24
					Small Vertical-Necked Serving or Transport Vessels (RV4, n = 625)	
26.	65.90	S. Thick 1	sm	148	7–14 cm, restricted high-necked vessels with acute body angles (prob. globular bodies), probably used in water transport, possibly serving	25–27, 28(?)
27	65.90	S. Thick 2	sm	79	7–14 cm, restricted high-necked vessels, probably used in water transport, possibly serving	24,26, 27,28(?)
28.	65.90	F. Normal 2	sm	59	11–14 cm, restricted high-necked vessels, probably used in water transport, possibly serving	24,25, 27,28(?)
29.	65.90	F. Inverted 2	sm	159	13–18 cm, restricted high-necked vessels, probably used for water transport or storage	24–26, 28(?)
30.	40.90	F. Bulge	sm	180	9–15 cm, restricted high-necked vessels, some with spouts on body, probably used as serving vessels, often on Burnished Red wares	24–28? RRs6
					Medium Vertical-Necked Transport or Storage Vessels (n = 2799)	
31.	65.90	S. Normal	med	310	14–20 cm, high-necked vessels, with globular bodies, probably used in water transport or water/liquid storage	32–42
32.	65.90	S. Inverted	med	101	17–23 cm, high-necked vessels, with rims that thicken on interior limiting spillage, probably used for water transport or storage	31,33–42
33.	65.90	S. Thick 1	med	182	15–21 cm, high-necked vessels with rims that thicken slightly at interior and turn sharply out so that lids might easily be fastened on, probably used in water transport or storage	31,32 34–42
34.	65.90	S. Thick 2	med	192	15–21 cm, high-necked vessels with rims that thicken on interior and exterior limiting spillage and easily covered, probably used as water transport or storage vessels	31–33, 35–42

Table 4.13 (continued)

	Shape class	Rim form	Size	# of sherds	Description	Funct. equiv.
					Medium Vertical-Necked Transport or Storage Vessels (n=2799)	
35.	65.90	S. Thick 3	med	65	15–21 cm, high-necked vessels with rims that thicken on interior and exterior limiting spillage and easily covered, probably used for water transport or storage	31–34, 36–42
36.	65.90	S. Thick 4	med	144	15–21 cm, high-necked vessels with rims that thicken on interior and exterior limiting spillage and easily covered, probably used for water transport and storage	31–35,36–42
37.	65.90	F. Normal 1	med	113	15–25 cm, high-necked vessels with low flange rims, probably used for water transport or storage	31–36, 38–42
38.	65.90	F. Normal 2	med	528	15–26 cm, high-necked vessels with high flange rims, probably used for water transport and storage	31–37, 39–42
39.	65.90	F. Inverted 2	med	75	19–24 cm, high-necked vessels, with thick inturning lip, probably used for water transport or storage	31–38, 40–42
40.	65.90	F. Everted 1	med	669	14–23 cm, high-necked vessels with high rims with exterior thickened lips, probably used in water transport or storage	31–39, 41,42
41.	65.90	F. Everted 2	med	341	14–23 cm, high-necked vessels with low flange rims with exterior thickened lips, probably used in water transport or storage	31–40,42
42.	40.90	F. Thick 1	med	79	15–20 cm,high-necked vessels with rims that thicken on the interior and exterior limiting spillage, probably used in water transport and storage	31–41
					Large Vertical-Necked Storage Vessels (n=351)	
.43.	65.90	S. Normal	lge	116	21–30 cm, high-necked vessels with simple rims, probably used for long-term(water/liquid) storage	44–47 RS1,RS2
44.	65.90	S. Thick 1	lge	39	22–33 cm high-necked vessels, with thick out-turning rims which could be easily covered, probably used for long-term storage	42,45–47 RS1,RS2
45.	65.90	S. Thick 2	lge	53	22–32 cm, high-necked vessels with rims thickened on interior and exterior, could be easily covered, probably used for long-term storage	43,44,46 47,RS1,2
46.	65.90	S. Thick 4	lge	95	22–29 cm, high-necked vessels with rims thickened on interior and exterior, could be easily covered, probably used for long-term storage	43–45,47 RS1,2
47.	40.90	F. Thick 1	lge	48	21–28 cm, high-necked vessels with thick rims on interior and exterior, could be easily covered, probably used for long-term storage	43–46 RS1,2

Table 5.1

Noblemen's Quarter Excavation Units: Area, Volume, Ceramic Density

Unit	Floor	Fill	Area (m^2)	Volume (m^3)	Diags	Total sherds	Break.	Diags/ m^3
2.1	+	–	20.3	16.2*[1]	215	975	.222	13.7
2.2	–	+	8.1	2.4*	64	162	395	26.7
2.3	+	–	5.4	1.6*	21	57	.368	13.1
2.4	+	–	12.5	3.8*	24	38	.632	6.3
2.5	+	+	22.8	6.8*	70	185	.378	10.3
2.6	+	+	4.5	1.4*	14	24	.583	10.0
2.7	+	–	13.7	4.1*	20	56	.357	4.9
2.8	+	–	13.8	4.1*	112	298	.376	27.3
2.9	+	+	8.8	2.6*	20	33	.606	7.7
2.10	–	+	20.6	11.3	112	1168	.096	9.9
2.11	+	+	9.4	6.1*	92	323	.285	15.1
2.12	+	–	14.1	4.2*	13	55	.236	4.2
2.13	+	–	20.8	6.2*	46	174	.264	7.4
2.14	–	+	25.5	20.4	337	480	.702	16.5
2.15	+	+	27.7	11.1*	167	1200	.139	15.0
2.16	–	+	22.4	6.7	109	353	.309	16.3
3.1	+	+	7.6	4.2	289	1093	.264	68.8
3.2	+	+	14.0	4.0*	32	216	.148	8.0
3.3	+	–	4.8	1.2*	40	236	.169	33.3
3.4	+	–	53.3	10.7*	99	663	.149	9.3
3.5	+	–	9.8	3.4*	32	106	.302	9.4
3.6	–	+	15.5	6.2	79	359	.220	12.7
3.7	+	+	38.9	11.6	229	402	.570	19.7
3.8	–	+	9.8	1.0	97	337	.288	97.0
4.1	–	+	14.3	11.4*	129	376	.343	11.3
4.2	+	+	16.9	11.8*	89	221	.403	7.5
4.3	+	+	42.0	25.2*	118	516	.229	4.7
4.4	+	–	16.6	4.2*	63	212	.970	15.0
4.5	–	+	6.8	3.4*	26	84	.310	7.6
4.6	+	–	29.5	7.4*	43	164	.262	5.8
4.7	+	+	4.8	2.4	52	191	.272	21.7
4.8[2]	–	+	7.8	2.0	47	230	.204	23.5
4.9	+	+	2.6	1.8	53	115	.461	29.4
4.10	+	+	2.8	.7	27	50	.540	38.6
4.11	+	+	6.4	4.8*	120	402	.299	25.0
4.12	+	+	21.0	7.0*	37	88	.420	5.3
4.13	+	+	10.5	2.1	43	173	.249	20.5
5.1	+	+	20.0	9.0	80			8.9
5.2	–	+	9.5	1.0	115			121.1
5.3	+	+	13.6	5.4*	40			7.4
5.4	+	+	4.1	1.8	33			18.3
5.5	+	+	36.5	23.8	266			11.2
5.6	+	+	20.3	6.0	61			10.2
5.7	+	–	12.2	1.8	30			16.7
5.8	–	+	34.5	6.9*	90			13.0
6.1	–	+	19.5	5.9*	38			6.4
6.2	+	+	20.3	6.1*	83			13.6
6.3	+	+	19.5	5.9*	61			10.3
7.1	–	+	20.3	6.1*	205			33.6
7.2	–	+	20.3	6.1*	79			13.0
7.3	+	+	20.3	8.1	52			10.3
7.4	+	+	16.2	4.1	129			6.4
7.5	–	+	20.3	6.1*	48			7.9
8.1	–	+	32.5	9.7*	33			3.4
8.2	–	+	60.9	15.2	141			9.3
8.3	–	+	20.3	2.0*	51			25.5

Table 5.1 (continued)

Unit	Floor	Fill	Area (m^2)	Volume (m^3)	Diags	Total sherds	Break.	Diags/ m^3
8.4	–	+	20.3	6.1*	73			12.0
8.5	–	+	29.4	13.2	46			3.5
8.6	–	+	20.3	5.1	31			6.1
9.1	–	+	10.0	2.0*	103			51.5
9.2	–	+	9.1	1.8	26			14.4
9.3	–	+	60.0	21.0	99			4.7
9.4	–	+	12.2	4.3	43			10.0
9.5	–	+	8.1	3.6	45			12.5
9.6	–	+	18.0	5.4*	31			5.7
9.7	–	+	8.1	1.2	31			25.8
9.8	–	+	3.0	.9	34			37.4
10.1	–	+	18.3	5.5*	20			3.6
10.2	–	+	8.1	2.4*	27			11.3
10.3	+	+	34.5	12.1	47			3.9
10.4	+	+	40.6	6.1	50			8.2
10.5	+	+	17.3	5.2*	26			5.0
10.6	+	+	20.3	6.1*	67			11.0
10.7	+	+	34.5	17.3	148			8.6
10.8	–	+	5.1	1.3*	20			15.4
12.1	–	+	16.2	4.9*	71			14.5
12.2	–	+	20.0	6.0*	41			6.8
12.3	+	+	16.2	8.9*	53			6.0
12.4	+	+	13.2	2.6	71			27.3
12.5	+	–	25.4	3.8	68			17.9
12.6	–	+	10.0	3.3*	59			17.9
12.7	+	–	13.2	5.9	32			5.4
12.8	–	+	11.2	3.9*	31			7.9
12.9	–	+	40.6	6.1	86			14.1

[1] Volume measures marked with an '*' are estimates, exact depth measurements were not available.

[2] Units 4.1–4.7 are from the main NMQ4 compound, Units 4.8–4.13 are from NMQ4A.

Table 5.2

Ware Distributions in the Noblemen's Quarter Compounds[1]

Compound	Plain			Burnished			Totals
	Black	Red	Brown	Black	Red	Brown	
NMQ1	893	35	182	16	58	2	1186
(exp)[1]	(746)	(50)	(306)	(25)	(54)	(5)	
NMQ2	717	41	273	23	26	6	1086
(exp)	(683)	(46)	(280)	(23)	(50)	(5)	
NMQ3	332	28	302	14	28	2	706
(exp)	(443)	(30)	(182)	(15)	(32)	(3)	
NMQ4	305	17	262	21	38	5	648
(exp)	(407)	(27)	(167)	(15)	(20)	(3)	
NMQ5	415	32	162	5	48	6	668
(exp)	(420)	(28)	(172)	(14)	(31)	(3)	
NMQ6	98	9	27	3	11	0	148
(exp)	(93)	(6)	(38)	(3)	(7)	(1)	
NMQ7	251	26	69	24	14	1	385
(exp)	(242)	(16)	(99)	(8)	(18)	(2)	
NMQ8	169	16	88	4	5	0	282
(exp)	(177)	(12)	(73)	(6)	(13)	(1)	
NMQ9	256	11	68	6	18	2	361
(exp)	(227)	(15)	(93)	(8)	(17)	(2)	
NMQ10	208	20	84	7	12	0	331
(exp)	(208)	(14)	(85)	(7)	(15)	(1)	
NMQ12	257	26	84	8	27	2	404
(exp)	(254)	(17)	(104)	(9)	(19)	(2)	
Totals	3901	261	1601	131	285	26	6205[3]

[1] Counts included in this table are derived from flange and straight rim diagnostic sherd counts only

[2] Expected frequencies if no relation existed between compound and ware category are computed by the formula: Row total x Column total/6205

[3] Chi-square statistic = 417.77, df=50, signif=.025

Table 5.3

Noblemen's Quarter Vessel-Use Class Counts and Frequencies by Compound

Comp.	Lamp	Sh. Bowl	O. Bowl	RV1	RV2	RV3	RV4	RV5	RV6	Tots.
NMQ3	9	51	37	60	333	33	38	167	34	762
Freq	.009	.073	.043	.079	.410	.050	.053	.212	.046	
NMQ4	8	65	17	49	289	26	39	166	27	686
Freq	.010	.095	.025	.069	.421	.038	.057	.242	.039	
NMQ5	7	42	27	25	223	29	43	184	38	618
Freq	.011	.068	.044	.040	.361	.047	.070	.298	.061	
NMQ6	1	14	5	6	47	7	5	50	9	144
Freq	.007	.097	.035	.042	.326	.049	.035	.347	.063	
NMQ7	8	33	12	23	124	34	26	138	46	444
Freq	.018	.074	.027	.052	.028	.077	.059	.311	.104	
NMQ8	3	24	8	10	103	19	15	104	31	317
Freq	.009	.076	.025	.032	.325	.060	.047	.328	.098	
NMQ9	3	22	6	13	110	26	20	126	36	362
Freq	.008	.061	.017	.036	.304	.072	.055	.348	.099	
NMQ10	1	20	9	16	72	16	12	116	24	286
Freq	.003	.070	.031	.056	.252	.056	.042	.406	.084	
NMQ12	12	33	23	21	129	16	33	142	23	432
Freq	.028	.076	.053	.049	.299	.037	.076	.329	.053	
Tot.	49	304	144	223	1430	206	231	1193	268	4051
Freq	.012	.075	.036	.055	.353	.051	.057	.294	.066	

Table 5.4

Noblemen's Quarter Vessel-Use Classes by Provenience Unit

Unit	Lamp	Sh. bowl	Oth. bowl	RV1	RV2	RV3	RV4	RV5	RV6	Tot.
3.1	4	19	16	14	123	7	15	35	16	249
3.2	0	1	2	4	8	2	0	5	0	22
3.3	1	3	0	5	19	2	3	2	0	34
3.4	1	5	5	15	30	2	5	17	3	83
3.5	0	4	0	1	8	0	2	5	4	24
3.6	0	4	4	6	31	5	1	15	1	67
3.7	3	13	7	7	93	9	4	62	5	203
3.8	0	2	3	8	22	6	8	26	4	80
4.1	3	10	1	8	64	3	1	24	5	119
4.2	1	5	2	2	27	3	2	7	2	51
4.3	1	3	1	7	42	2	10	16	6	88
4.4	0	7	2	3	25	1	2	9	3	52
4.5	0	0	1	1	6	3	1	11	0	23
4.6	0	3	1	4	16	4	1	6	3	38
4.7	0	5	2	5	10	3	3	13	1	42
4.8	0	4	3	3	17	3	2	8	1	41
4.9	0	3	1	3	18	1	3	11	0	40
4.10	1	4	0	1	2	3	1	8	0	20
4.11	2	8	0	8	33	0	11	35	4	101
4.12	0	7	0	2	15	0	0	12	0	36
4.13	0	6	3	2	14	0	2	6	2	35
5.1	1	6	2	1	21	9	7	21	3	71
5.2	0	6	4	4	40	9	10	29	5	107
5.3	0	1	3	3	13	0	2	6	3	31
5.4	6	2	2	2	8	2	1	9	0	33
5.5	0	16	8	11	93	3	13	63	16	223
5.6	0	5	4	3	15	0	1	16	4	48
5.7	0	2	1	0	9	3	2	14	0	31
5.8	0	4	2	1	24	3	7	26	7	74
6.1	0	2	0	2	18	2	2	11	1	38
6.2	1	5	3	2	19	4	2	21	4	61
6.3	0	7	2	2	10	1	1	18	4	45
7.1	8	16	2	12	58	8	4	56	8	172
7.2	0	5	5	2	15	7	7	20	9	70
7.3	0	3	3	3	14	1	3	13	6	46
7.4	0	9	1	6	24	18	7	39	13	117
7.5	0	0	1	0	13	0	5	10	10	39
8.1	2	2	0	2	15	2	0	7	1	31
8.2	1	8	1	4	42	6	6	39	12	119
8.3	0	1	2	0	15	2	5	12	3	40
8.4	0	5	1	2	14	7	1	29	9	68
8.5	0	6	4	1	9	1	2	13	3	39
8.6	9	2	0	1	8	1	1	4	3	20
9.1	0	4	1	5	42	7	1	37	8	105
9.2	0	1	2	0	15	2	5	12	3	40
9.3	1	4	1	2	23	9	6	32	5	83
9.4	1	3	0	1	12	4	2	14	1	38
9.5	0	2	2	2	9	4	5	7	7	38
9.6	0	4	0	1	4	1	4	7	1	22
9.7	1	4	0	1	7	0	0	9	3	25
9.8	0	0	0	1	7	0	2	11	7	28
10.1	0	0	2	1	5	1	0	7	1	17
10.2	0	3	2	1	12	2	1	8	0	29
10.3	0	3	0	2	11	2	3	10	3	34
10.4	1	6	1	2	7	1	2	14	3	37

Table 5.4 (continued)

Unit	Lamp	Sh. bowl	Oth. bowl	RV1	RV2	RV3	RV4	RV5	RV6	Tot.
10.5	0	6	0	0	6	0	1	6	4	23
10.6	0	0	1	1	6	5	3	34	6	56
10.7	0	2	3	8	21	5	1	31	6	77
10.8	0	0	0	1	4	0	1	6	1	13
12.1	0	0	4	5	16	1	8	22	3	59
12.2	1	6	1	0	10	3	4	12	1	38
12.3	3	1	3	1	13	0	3	17	9	50
12.4	0	3	5	3	21	1	2	17	3	55
12.5	5	5	3	4	20	9	1	12	1	60
12.6	0	2	2	2	17	0	1	16	3	43
12.7	2	10	1	2	3	1	2	12	1	34
12.8	0	2	1	3	9	0	7	8	1	31
12.9	1	4	3	1	20	1	5	26	1	62

Note: counts presented in this figure differ from total diagnostic counts because diagnostic drain pipes, Coarse Ware vessels, pedestals, decorated sherds, etc. are not included.

Table 5.5

Noblemen's Quarter Vessel-Use Class Frequencies by Provenience Unit

Unit	Lamp	Sh. bowl	Oth. bowl	RV1	RV2	RV3	RV4	RV5	RV6
3.1	.016	.076	.064	.056	.494	.032	.060	.141	.064
3.2	.000	.045	.091	.182	.364	.091	.000	.227	.000
3.3	.029	.088	.000	.147	.529	.059	.088	.059	.000
3.4	.012	.060	.060	.181	.361	.024	.060	.205	.036
3.5	.000	.167	.000	.042	.333	.000	.083	.208	.167
3.6	.000	.060	.060	.090	.463	.075	.015	.224	.015
3.7	.015	.064	.034	.034	.458	.044	.020	.305	.025
3.8	.000	.025	.038	.100	.275	.075	.100	.325	.063
4.1	.025	.084	.008	.067	.538	.025	.008	.202	.042
4.2	.020	.098	.039	.039	.529	.075	.039	.137	.039
4.3	.011	.034	.011	.080	.477	.023	.114	.182	.068
4.4	.000	.135	.038	.058	.481	.019	.038	.173	.058
4.5	.000	.000	.043	.043	.261	.130	.043	.478	.000
4.6	.000	.079	.026	.105	.421	.105	.026	.158	.079
4.7	.000	.119	.048	.119	.238	.071	.071	.310	.024
4.8	.000	.098	.073	.073	.415	.073	.049	.195	.024
4.9	.000	.075	.025	.075	.450	.025	.075	.275	.000
4.10	.050	.200	.000	.050	.100	.150	.050	.400	.000
4.11	.020	.079	.000	.079	.327	.000	.109	.347	.040
4.12	.000	.194	.000	.056	.417	.000	.000	.333	.000
4.13	.000	.171	.086	.057	.400	.000	.057	.171	.057
5.1	.014	.085	.028	.014	.296	.123	.099	.296	.042
5.2	.000	.056	.037	.037	.374	.084	.093	.271	.047
5.3	.000	.032	.097	.097	.419	.000	.065	.194	.097
5.4	.182	.061	.091	.061	.242	.061	.030	.273	.000
5.5	.000	.072	.036	.049	.417	.013	.058	.283	.072
5.6	.000	.104	.083	.063	.313	.000	.021	.333	.083
5.7	.000	.065	.032	.000	.290	.097	.065	.452	.000
5.8	.000	.054	.027	.014	.324	.041	.095	.351	.095
6.1	.000	.053	.000	.053	.474	.053	.053	.289	.026
6.2	.016	.082	.049	.033	.311	.066	.033	.344	.066
6.3	.000	.156	.044	.044	.222	.022	.022	.400	.089
7.1	.047	.093	.012	.070	.337	.047	.023	.326	.047
7.2	.000	.071	.071	.029	.214	.100	.100	.286	.129
7.3	.000	.065	.065	.065	.304	.022	.065	.283	.130
7.4	.000	.077	.009	.051	.205	.154	.060	.333	.111
7.5	.000	.000	.026	.000	.333	.000	.128	.256	.256
8.1	.065	.065	.000	.065	.484	.065	.000	.226	.032
8.2	.008	.066	.008	.033	.344	.049	.049	.320	.098
8.3	.000	.025	.050	.000	.375	.050	.125	.300	.075
8.4	.000	.074	.015	.029	.206	.103	.015	.426	.132
8.5	.000	.154	.103	.026	.231	.026	.051	.333	.077
8.6	.000	.100	.000	.050	.400	.050	.050	.200	.150
9.1	.000	.038	.010	.048	.400	.067	.010	.352	.076
9.2	.000	.043	.087	.000	.261	.043	.000	.391	.174
9.3	.012	.048	.012	.024	.277	.108	.072	.386	.060
9.4	.026	.079	.000	.026	.316	.105	.053	.368	.060
9.5	.000	.053	.053	.053	.237	.105	.132	.184	.184
9.6	.000	.182	.000	.045	.182	.045	.182	.318	.045
9.7	.040	.160	.000	.040	.280	.000	.000	.360	.120
9.8	.000	.000	.000	.036	.250	.000	.071	.393	.250
10.1	.000	.000	.118	.059	.294	.059	.000	.412	.059
10.2	.000	.103	.069	.034	.414	.069	.034	.276	.000
10.3	.000	.088	.000	.059	.324	.059	.088	.294	.088
10.4	.027	.162	.027	.054	.189	.027	.054	.378	.081

Table 5.5 (continued)

Unit	Lamp	Sh. bowl	Oth. bowl	RV1	RV2	RV3	RV4	RV5	RV6
10.5	.000	.261	.000	.000	.261	.000	.043	.261	.174
10.6	.000	.000	.018	.018	.107	.089	.054	.607	.107
10.7	.000	.026	.039	.104	.273	.065	.043	.403	.078
12.1	.000	.000	.068	.085	.271	.017	.136	.373	.051
12.2	.026	.158	.026	.000	.263	.079	.105	.316	.026
12.3	.060	.020	.060	.020	.260	.000	.060	.340	.180
12.4	.000	.055	.091	.055	.382	.018	.036	.309	.055
12.5	.083	.083	.050	.067	.333	.015	.017	.200	.017
12.6	.000	.047	.047	.047	.395	.000	.024	.372	.070
12.7	.059	.294	.029	.059	.088	.029	.059	.353	.029
12.8	.000	.065	.032	.097	.290	.000	.226	.258	.036
12.9	.016	.065	.048	.016	.323	.016	.081	.410	.016

Table 5.6

Noblemen's Quarter Restricted Vessel Classes:
K-Means Cluster Results

Class (Freq)	Cluster[1]					
	1	2	3	4	5	6
#	13	19	3	4	6	6
RV1	.067	.060	.087	.154	.021	.028
RV2	.269	.443	.296	.419	.219	.283
RV3	.045	.037	.006	.070	.111	.027
RV4	.041	.044	.157	.043	.069	.074
RV5	.356	.231	.326	.162	.425	.288
RV6	.060	.039	.042	.029	.029	.146

[1] Particularly high class frequencies are underlined

Cluster	Units
1	NMQ3.8, NMQ4.7, NMQ5.4, NMQ5.6, NMQ6.2, NMQ6.3, NMQ7.1, NMQ10.1, NMQ10.3, NMQ10.4, NMQ10.7, NMQ12.6, NMQ12.7
2	NMQ3.1,NMQ3.6,NMQ3.7,NMQ4.1,NMQ4.2, NMQ4.3, NMQ4.4, NMQ4.8, NMQ4.9, NMQ4.12, NMQ4.13, NMQ5.2, NMQ5.3, NMQ5.5, NMQ6.1, NMQ8.1. NMQ10.2, NMQ12.4, NMQ12.5
3	NMQ4.11, NMQ12.1, NMQ12.8
4	NMQ3.2, NMQ3.3, NMQ3.4, NMQ4.6
5	NMQ4.5, NMQ4.10, NMQ5.1, NMQ5.7, NMQ10.6, NMQ12.2
6	NMQ3.5, NMQ5.8, NMQ7.2, NMQ7.3, NMQ10.5, NMQ12.3

Table 5.7

Noblemen's Quarter Other Vessel Classes by Compound

Comp.	Roof Tile	Oven	Ring-Well	Drain Pipes	Incense Burner	Other
NMQ3	0	12	40[1]	8	4	
NMQ4	23	2	15	88	5	
NMQ5	0	0	0	18	2	
NMQ6	0	0	0	0	1	
NMQ7	0	0	0	0	0	1 nosed lamp, 1 conical lid
NMQ8	0	0	0	0	2	
NMQ9	0	0	0	6	3	3 nosed lamps
NMQ10	0	0	0	15	1	1 gaming piece, 1 conical lid
NMQ12	0	0	0	1	10	1 conical lid, 5 small finely burnished jars

[1] Estimated count

Table 5.8

Flange and Straight Rim Restricted Vessel Rim Form Distributions by Compound

Comp.	FN1	FN2	FI1	FI2	FI3	FE1	FE2	FT1	FT2	FL	FG	SN	SI	SE	SB1	SB2	ST1	ST2	ST3	ST4	Tot.
NMQ3	55	153	23	45	12	50	91	7	13	1	5	135	16	14	4	10	36	20	8	12	710
exp	58	137	20	40	18	89	101	9	10	2	9	104	20	10	6	10	21	17	7	23	
NMQ4	52	159	20	38	13	55	65	10	3	2	7	119	18	16	5	7	25	15	3	13	645
exp	52	125	18	37	16	77	92	8	9	2	8	95	18	9	5	9	19	15	6	21	
NMQ5	51	99	20	33	19	67	89	8	7	3	13	70	12	4	8	11	19	13	6	21	573
exp	46	111	16	33	14	72	81	7	8	1	7	84	16	8	5	8	17	14	5	19	
NMQ6	17	23	2	4	6	26	20	1	2	1	2	15	6	2	0	3	2	2	1	7	142
exp	12	27	4	8	4	18	20	2	2	0	2	21	4	2	1	2	4	3	1	5	
NMQ7	17	65	16	19	7	59	90	2	3	1	5	50	12	7	3	2	7	14	4	18	401
exp	33	78	11	23	10	50	57	5	5	1	5	59	11	6	3	6	12	10	4	13	
NMQ8	21	67	6	11	9	42	54	7	6	0	3	36	10	1	4	4	8	3	6	8	306
exp	25	59	9	17	8	38	44	4	4	1	4	45	8	4	3	4	9	8	3	10	
NMQ9	32	59	7	22	8	54	55	7	3	0	1	57	11	0	3	8	6	7	3	17	364
exp	30	70	10	21	9	46	52	5	5	1	4	53	10	5	3	5	11	9	3	12	
NMQ10	22	54	6	19	11	96	33	5	9	0	4	26	10	4	0	5	2	8	0	18	332
exp	27	64	9	19	8	41	47	4	4	1	4	49	9	5	3	5	10	8	3	11	
NMQ12	44	70	10	29	12	37	54	3	6	2	7	60	12	6	5	4	12	10	5	13	401
exp	33	78	11	23	10	50	57	5	5	1	5	59	11	6	3	6	12	10	4	13	
Total	315	749	110	220	97	486	551	50	52	10	47	568	107	54	32	54	117	92	36	127	3874

Chi-Square = 369.013 df = 152 sig. = .05

Table 6.1

Ware Classes by Sample Area

Area	Plain			Burnished			Totals
	Black	Red	Brown	Black	Red	Brown	
NMQ[1]	3901	261	1601	131	285	26	6,205
exp	3658	322	1864	152	165	44	
EVW	8808	691	4566	137	347	43	14,592
exp	8603	756	4384	357	389	104	
EVE	11062	1124	6055	741	448	226	19,656
exp	11158	1019	5906	480	523	140	
IQ	713	76	256	6	26	0	1,077
exp	635	56	324	26	29	8	
Tot	24,484	2152	12,478	1015	1106	295	41,530

Chi-Square = 654.909, df = 15, sig. = .01

[1] NMQ ware counts derived from flange and straight rim diagnostic sample; counts in all other areas are body sherd counts

Table 6.2

Vessel-Use Class Distributions by Sample Area

Area	Lamp	Sh. Bowl	O. Bowl	RV1	RV2	RV3	RV4	RV5	RV6	Tots.
NMQ	52	304	144	223	1430	206	231	1193	268	4051
exp	42	293	151	284	1619	149	193	1100	221	
EVW	22	155	94	186	1000	66	102	601	109	2335
exp	24	169	87	164	933	86	111	634	127	
EVE	22	235	91	278	1510	88	124	838	149	3335
exp	34	241	124	234	1333	123	159	906	182	
IQ	8	38	48	24	109	13	25	120	26	411
exp	4	30	15	29	264	15	20	112	22	
Total	104	732	377	711	4049	373	482	2752	552	10,122

Chi-Square = 278.991, df = 24, sig. = .001

Table 6.3

Distribution of Flange and Straight Rims by Sample Area

Area	Flange	Straight	Totals
NMQ	2677	1187	3864
exp	2450	1414	
EVW	1325	873	2198
exp	1394	804	
EVE	1889	1350	3239
exp	2054	1185	
IQ	258	139	397
exp	252	145	
Totals	6149	3549	9698

Chi-Square = 103.430, df = 3, sig. = .001

Table 6.5

Distribution of Lamp Form Variants by Sample Area

Area	L1	L2	L3	L4	Total
NMQ	6	7	21	55	89
EVall	4	3	7	2	16
IQ	1	1	1	1	4
Totals	11	11	29	58	109

Table 6.4

Distribution of Flange and Straight Rim Restricted Vessel Rim Form Distributions by Sample Area

Comp.	FN1	FN2	FI1	FI2	FI3	FE1	FE2	FT1	FT2	FG	SN	SI	SE	SB1	SB2	ST1	ST2	ST3	ST4	Tot.
NMQ	315	749	110	220	97	486	551	50	52	47	568	107	54	32	54	117	92	36	127	3864
exp	426	727	152	168	69	347	424	59	33	44	710	111	51	27	58	157	138	50	112	
EVW	279	459	115	58	24	117	193	43	14	23	431	56	25	9	38	129	96	32	57	2198
exp	242	414	87	96	39	198	241	34	19	25	404	63	29	15	33	89	78	28	64	
EVE	435	569	150	117	23	233	274	49	13	26	715	105	45	23	47	141	143	55	76	3239
exp	357	610	128	141	58	291	355	50	28	37	595	93	43	23	49	131	116	42	94	
IQ	40	48	7	27	29	36	45	7	4	15	67	11	5	4	7	6	15	3	21	397
exp	48	75	16	17	7	36	44	6	3	5	73	11	5	3	6	16	14	5	12	
Tot.	1069	1825	382	422	173	872	1063	149	83	111	1781	279	129	68	146	393	346	126	281	9698

Chi-Square = 657, df = 54, sig. = .005

does not include rare flange ledge rim forms)

Table 6.6

Distribution of Shallow Bowl Form Variants by Sample Area

Area	SB1	SB3	SB4	SB5	SB6	Total
NMQ	10	122	48	263	43	486
exp	12	168	42	229	34	
EVW	7	70	14	57	8	156
exp	4	54	14	74	11	
EVE	5	118	12	91	8	234
exp	6	81	20	110	16	
IQ	1	5	5	18	4	33
exp	1	11	3	16	2	
Totals	23	315	79	429	63	909

Chi-Square = 67.336, df = 12, sig. = .001

Table 6.7

Distributions of RV1 Form Variants in the Noblemen's Quarter and East Valley

Area	Fl. and St. Rim Forms						Rnd Rim Forms		Total
	1	2	3	4	5	6	Rs1	Rs2	
NMQ	16	13	42	45	12	40	51	8	227
exp	15	11	22	47	15	33	74	11	
EVW	11	6	11	38	15	16	69	9	175
exp	12	8	17	36	11	26	57	9	
EVE	18	13	11	55	16	42	98	16	269
exp	18	13	26	55	17	39	87	13	
Totals	45	32	64	138	43	98	218	33	671

Chi-Square = 50.414, df = 14. sig. = .005

Table 6.8
Distribution of RV2 Form Variants in the Noblemen's Quarter and East Valley

Comp.	Class													Tot.
	7	8	9	10	11	12	13	14	15	16	17	18	19	
NMQ	50	55	30	277	21	31	233	395	38	62	31	272	19	1496
exp	60	63	37	321	29	15	261	353	73	49	39	179	18	
EVW	55	48	31	218	20	9	162	241	72	29	22	79	7	993
exp	38	39	23	200	18	10	163	220	45	30	24	112	11	
EVE	56	65	37	363	36	19	304	308	85	39	51	128	21	1512
exp	61	63	37	324	29	15	264	357	74	49	39	181	18	
Total	161	168	98	858	77	41	699	944	195	130	104	479	47	4001

Chi-Square = 175.847, df = 24, sig. = .001

Table 6.9
Distributions of RV3 Form Variants in the Noblemen's Quarter and East Valley

Area	Class				Total
	20	21	22	23	
NMQ	45	16	12	36	109[1]
exp	38	22	19	30	
EVE	24	14	17	11	66
exp	23	14	11	18	
EVW	23	24	16	24	87
exp	31	18	15	24	
Totals	92	54	45	71	262

Chi-Square = 14.939, df = 6. sig. = .05

[1] does not include 101 RV3 vessels (classes 24–25, defined for the 1986 sample only.

Table 6.10

Distributions of RV4 Form Variants in the Noblemen's Quarter and East Valley

Area	Class					Total
	26	27	28	29	30	
NMQ	52	22	25	92	41	232
exp	73	39	20	55	36	
EVW	47	21	18	3	14	103
exp	32	17	13	25	16	
EVE	46	34	15	15	17	127
exp	40	21	16	30	20	
Totals	145	77	58	110	72	462

Chi-Square = 86.752, df = 8. sig. = .0001

Table 6.11

Distribution of RV5 Form Variants in the Noblemen's Quarter and East Valley

Comp.	Class												Tot.
	31	32	33	34	35	36	37	38	39	40	41	42	
NMQ	123	61	46	47	20	48	27	208	45	412	177	25	1239
exp	132	45	83	87	29	62	49	236	32	300	149	34	
EVW	51	11	61	61	16	37	45	135	5	85	78	19	604
exp	65	22	40	42	14	30	24	115	16	146	73	17	
EVE	113	26	72	80	27	50	35	168	20	154	68	30	843
exp	90	31	56	59	20	42	34	160	22	204	101	23	
Total	287	98	179	188	63	135	107	511	70	651	323	74	2686

Chi-Square = 249.097, df = 22, sig. = .001

Table 6.12

Distributions of RVG Form Variants in the Noblemen's Quarter and East Valley

Area	Fl. and St. Rim Forms					Rnd Rm Forms		Total
	43	44	45	46	47	RS1	RS2	
NMQ	61	15	21	61	21	46	59	284
exp	60	19	25	46	28	46	61	
EVW	19	13	11	11	16	19	22	111
exp	23	7	10	18	11	18	24	
EVE	34	8	15	16	17	23	35	148
exp	30	7	10	18	11	18	24	
Totals	114	36	47	88	54	88	116	543

Chi-Square = 31.767, df = 12, sig. = .005

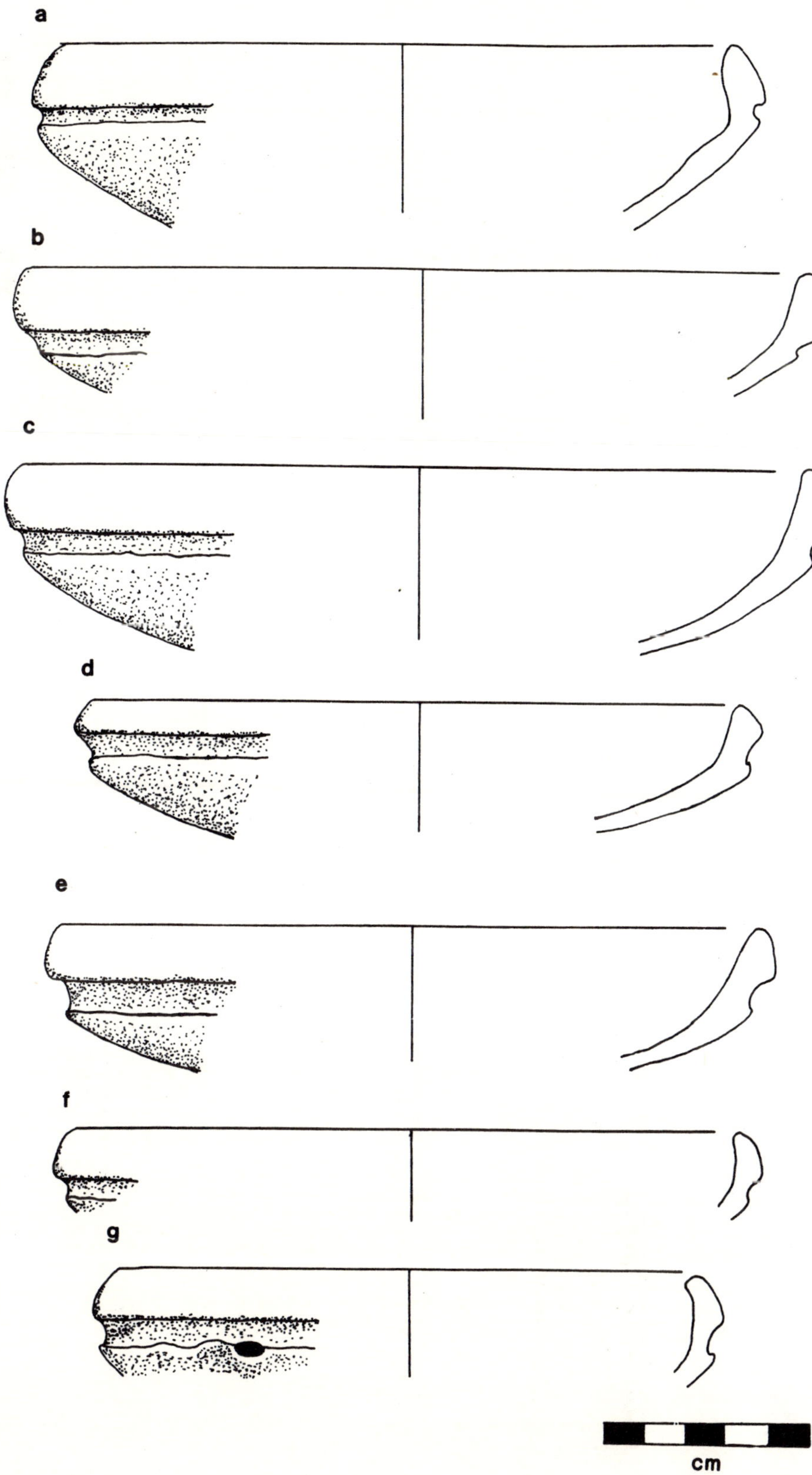

Figure A.1 NMQ1 Shallow Bowls

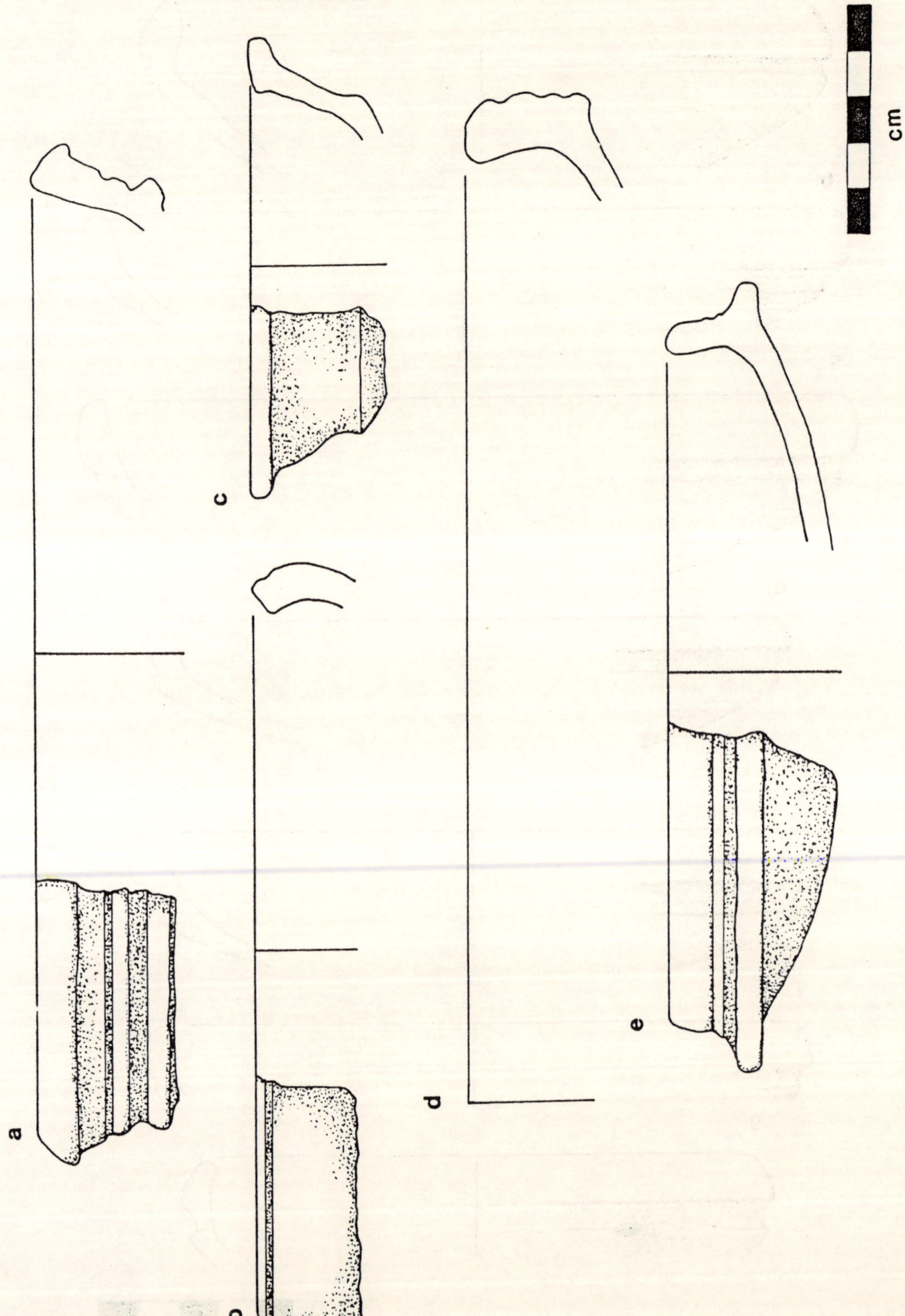

Figure A.2 NMQ1 Other Bowls

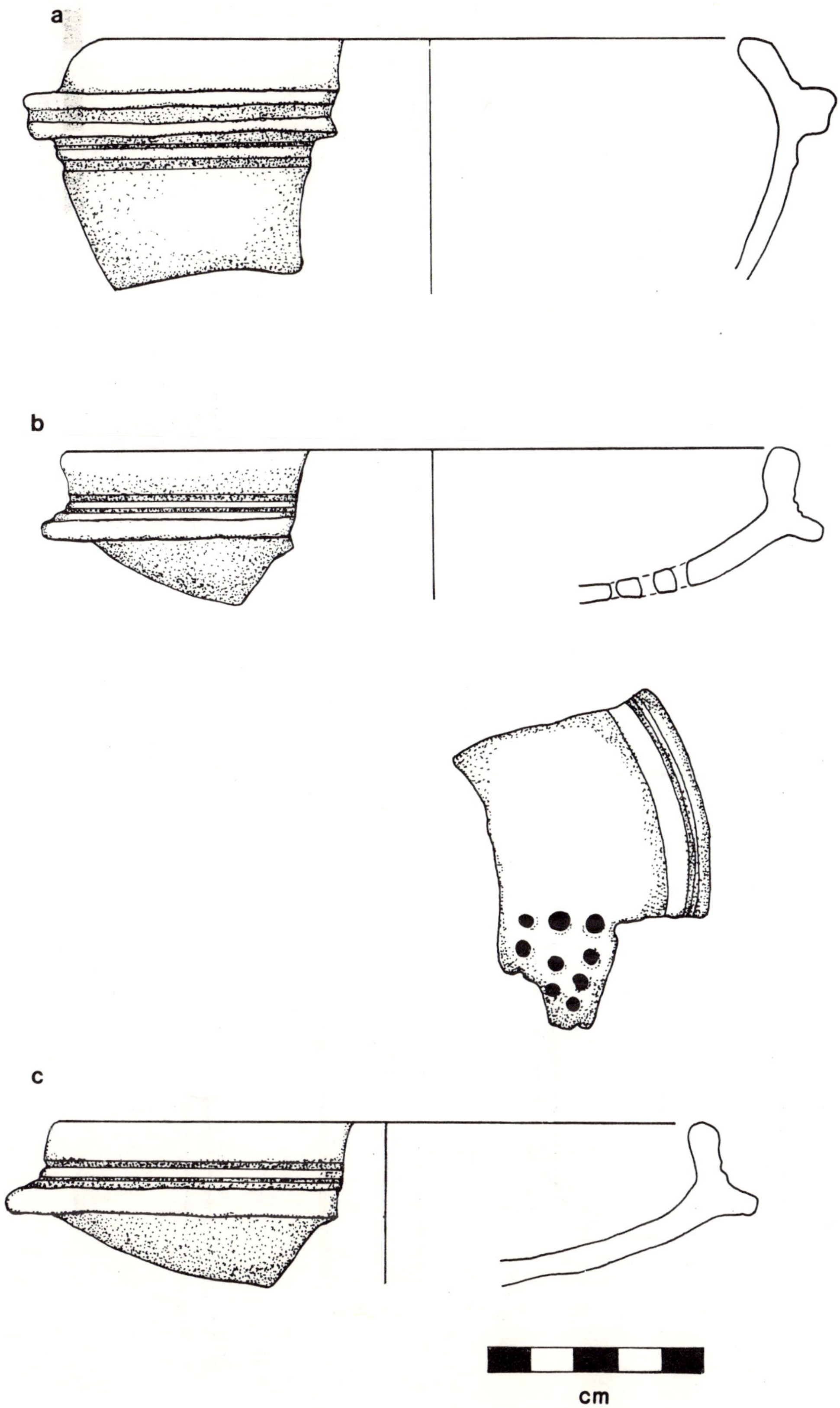

Figure A.3 NMQ1 Other Bowls

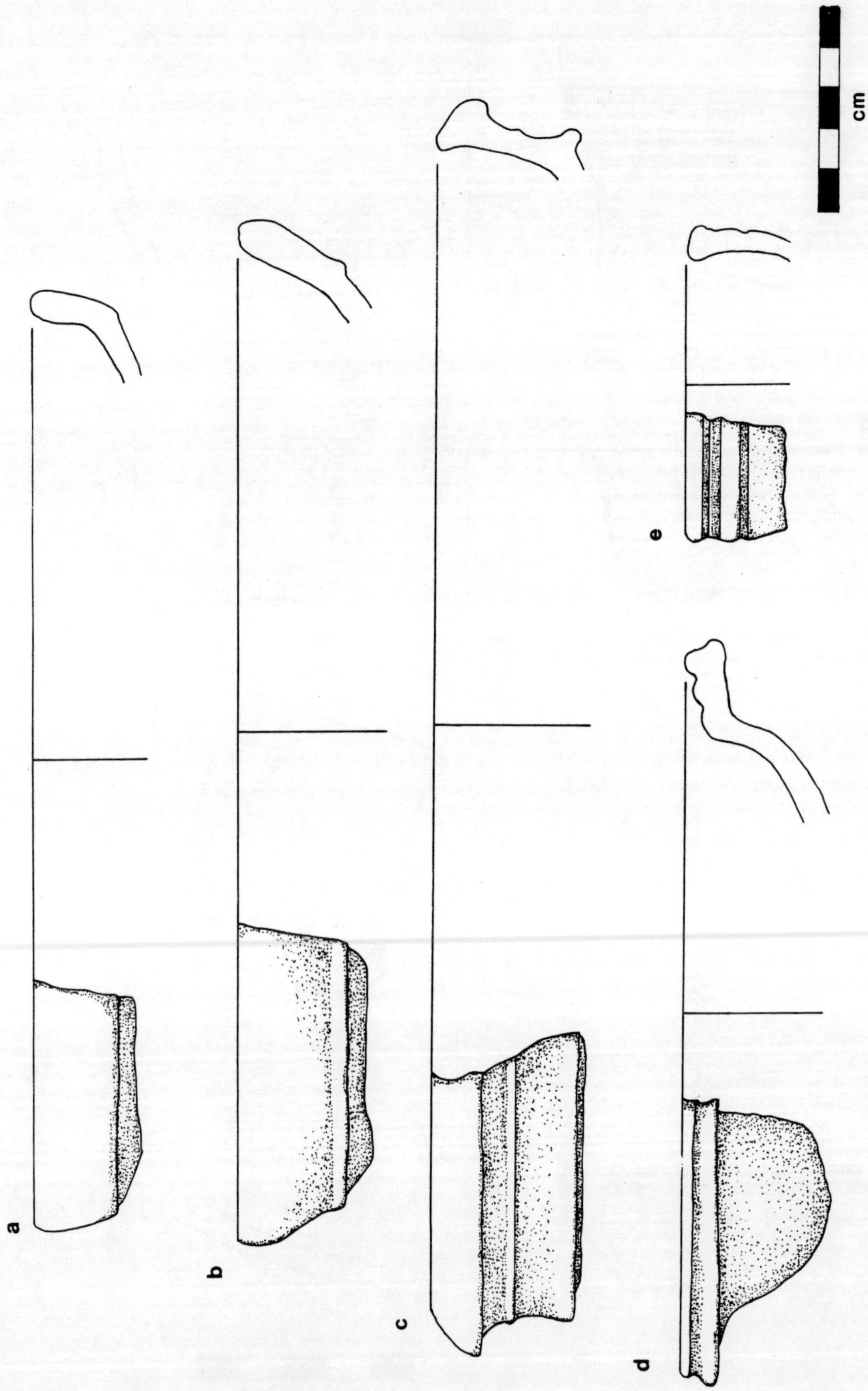

Figure A.4 NMQ1 Other Bowls

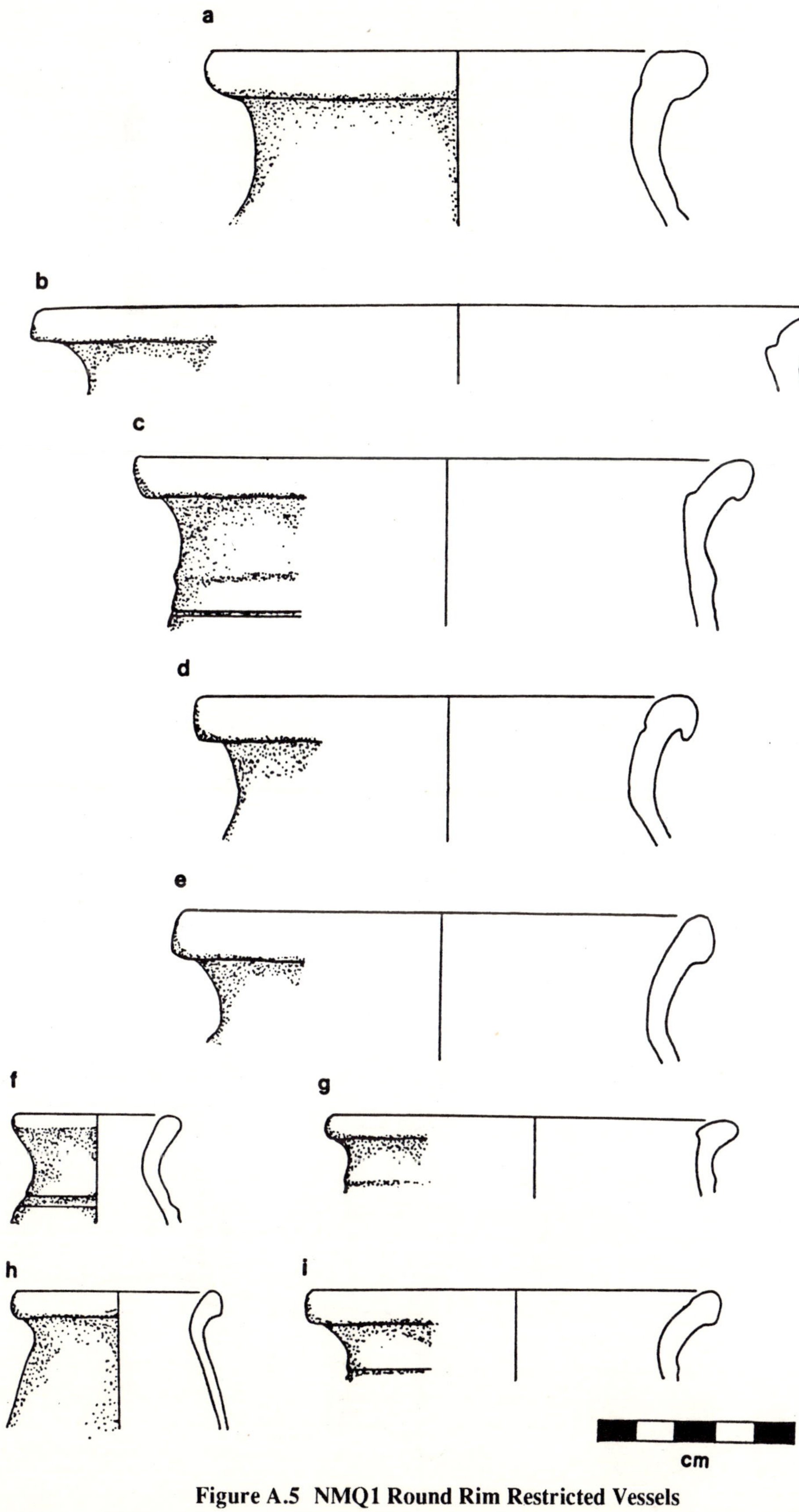

Figure A.5 NMQ1 Round Rim Restricted Vessels

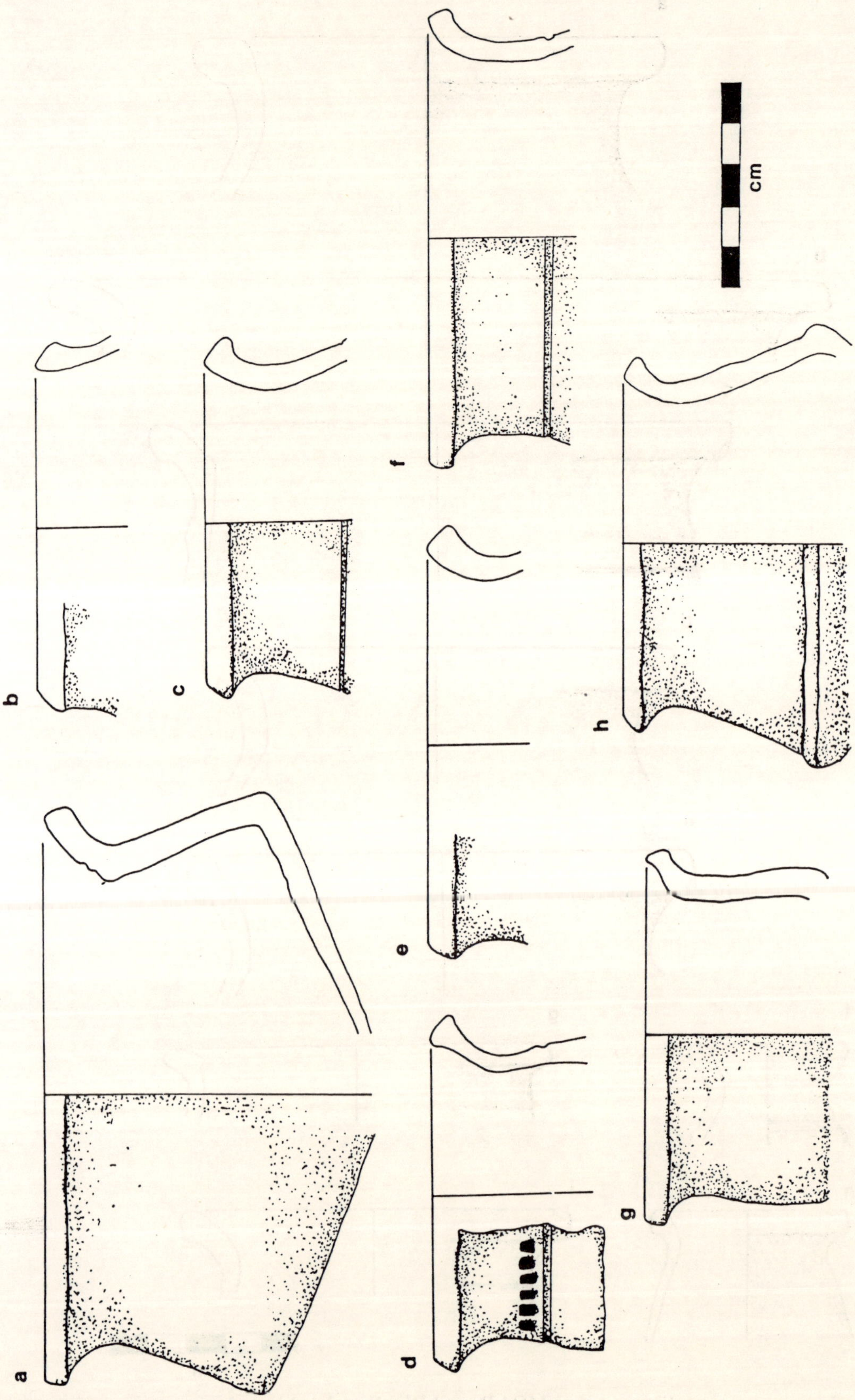

Figure A.6 NMQ1 Straight Rim Restricted Vessels

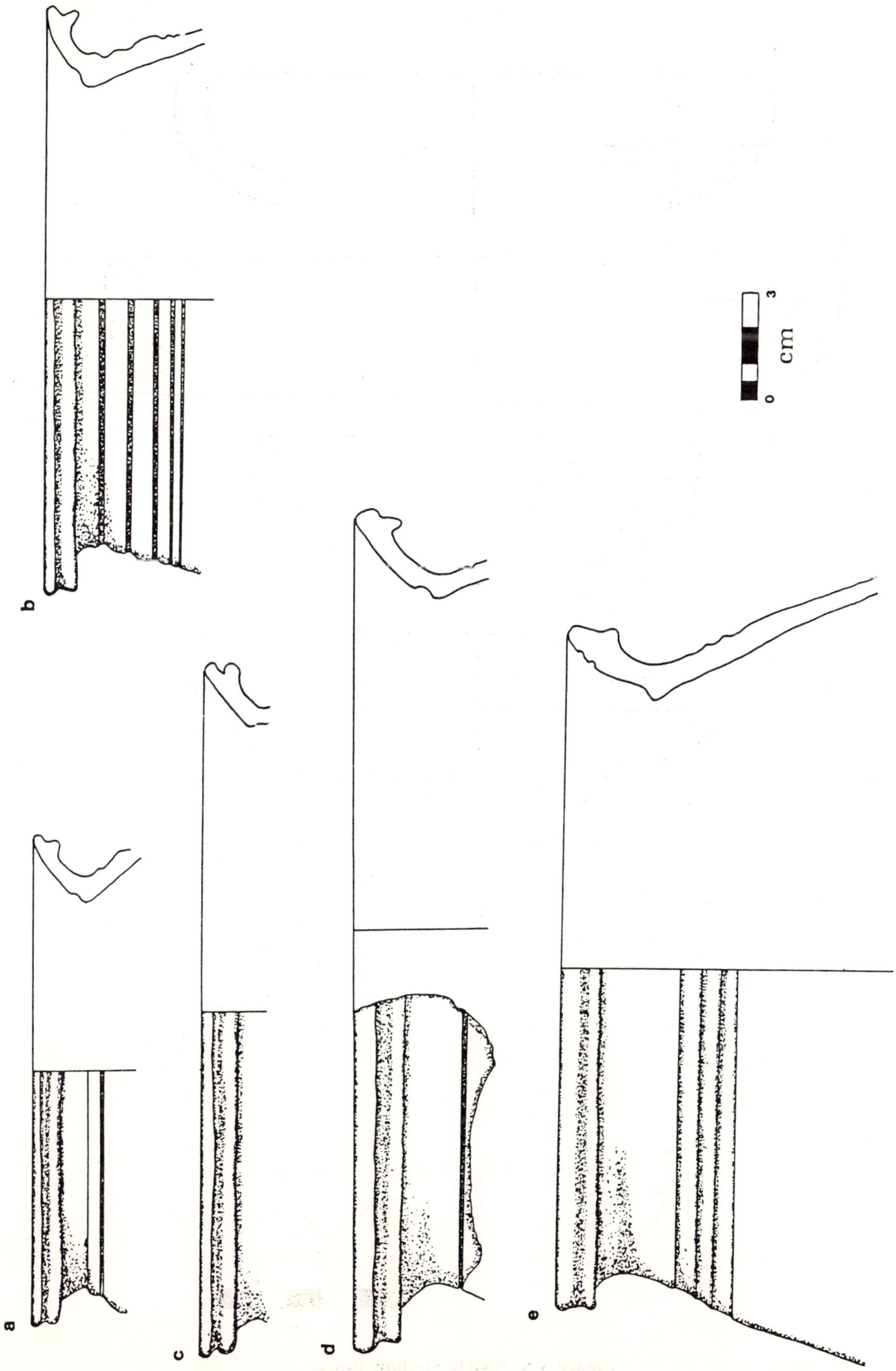

Figure A.7 NMQ1 Flange Rim Restricted Vessels

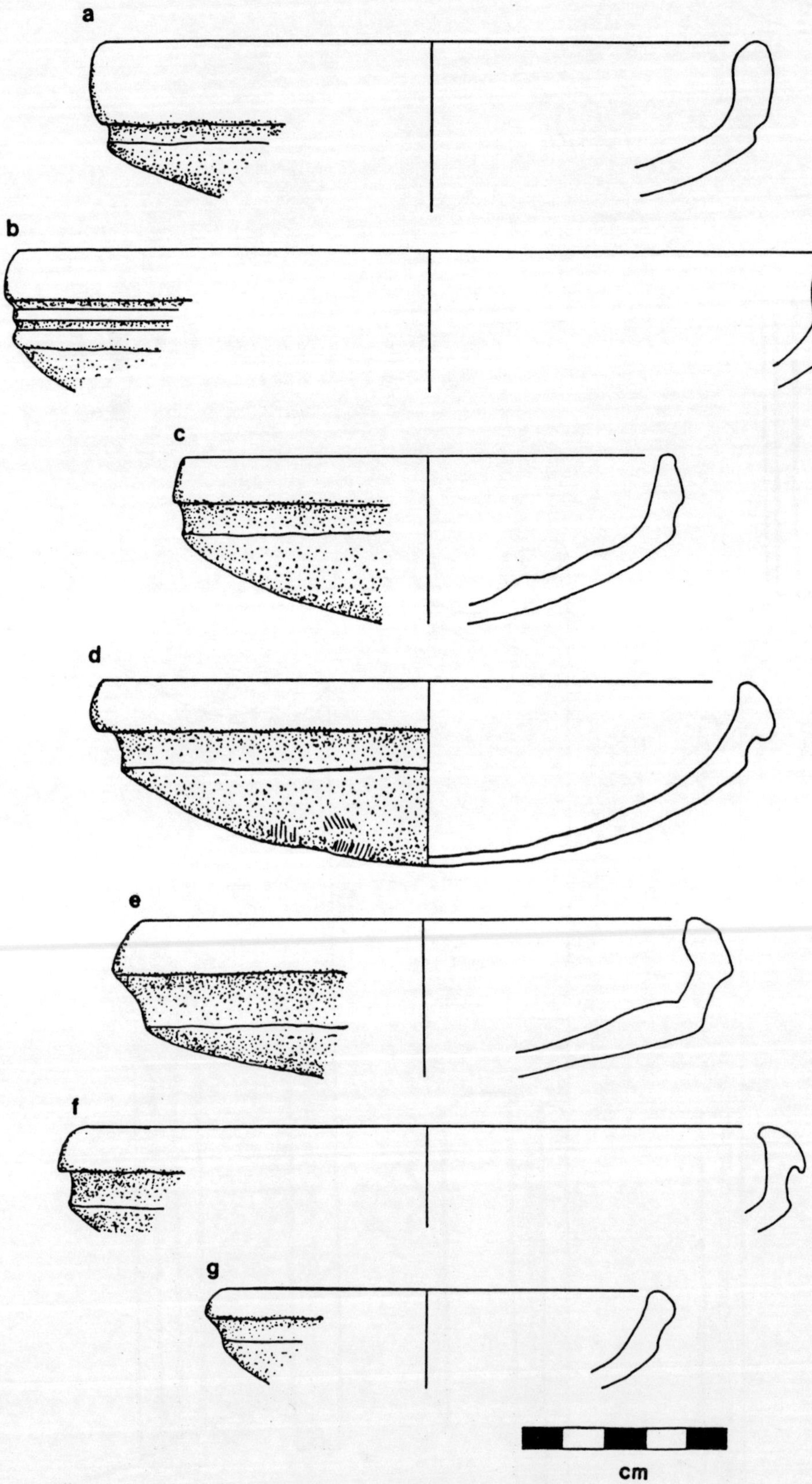

Figure A.8 NMQ2 Shallow Bowls

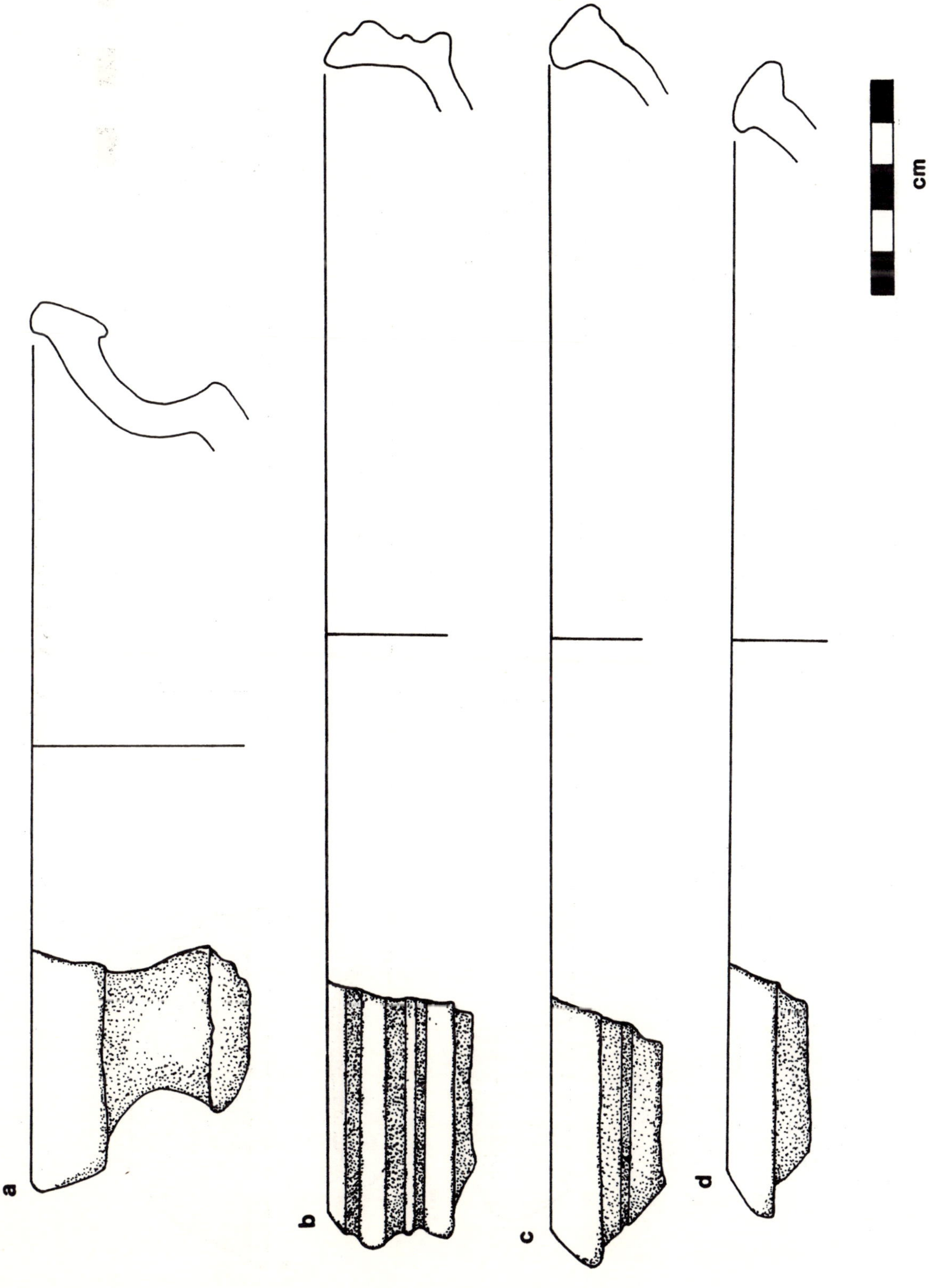

Figure A.9 NMQ2 Other Bowls

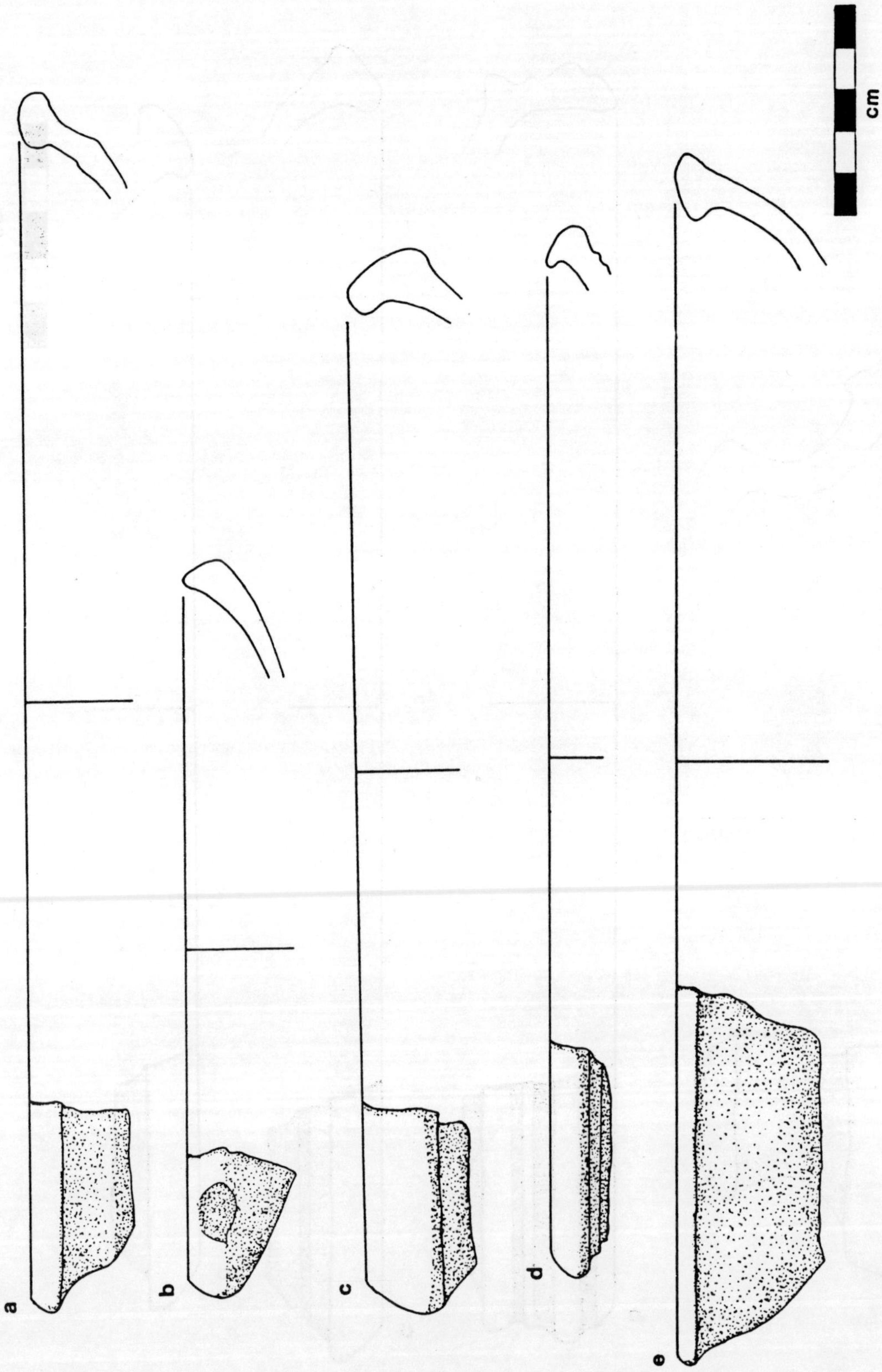

Figure A.10 NMQ2 Other Bowls

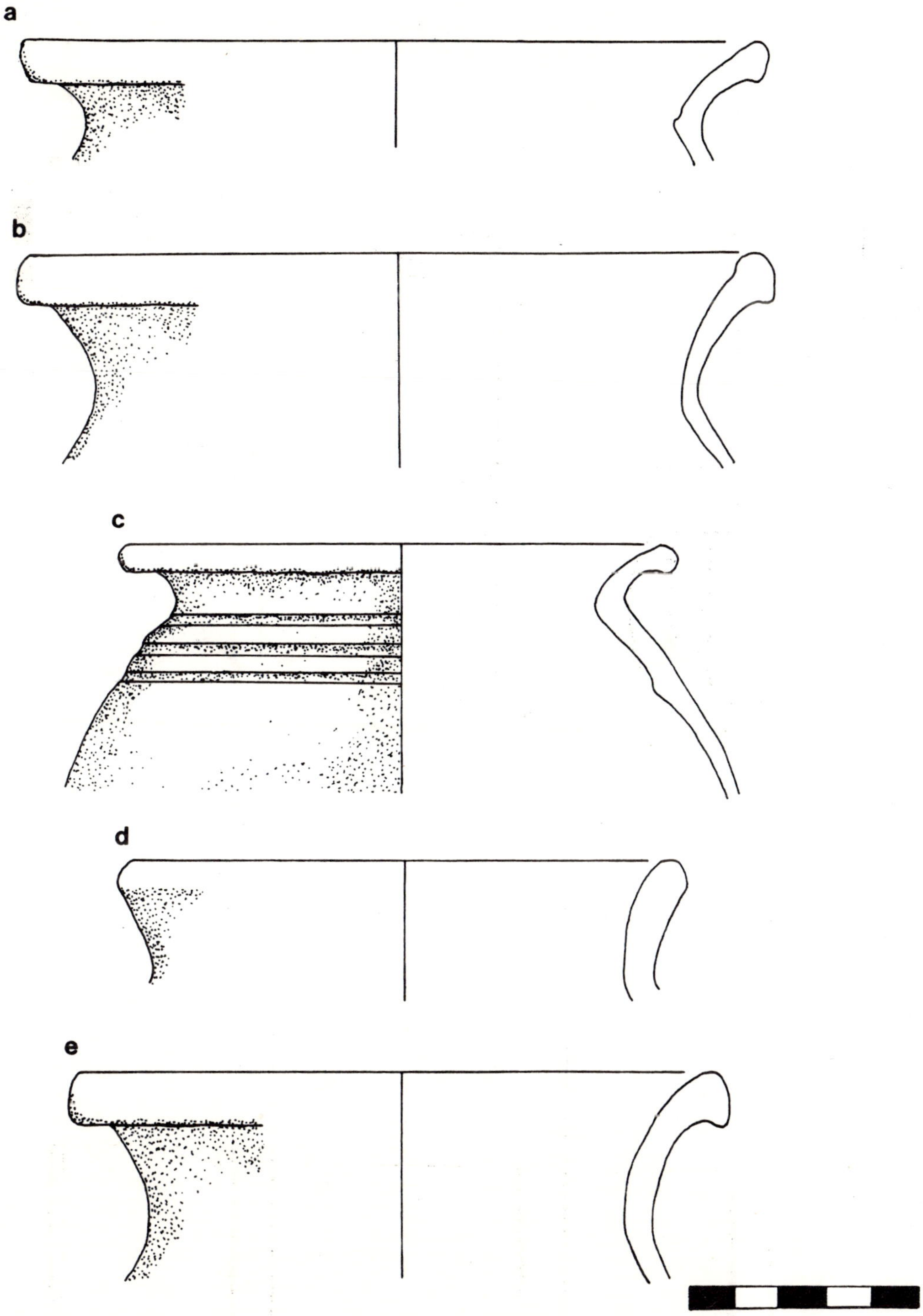

Figure A.11 NMQ2 Round Rim Restricted Vessels

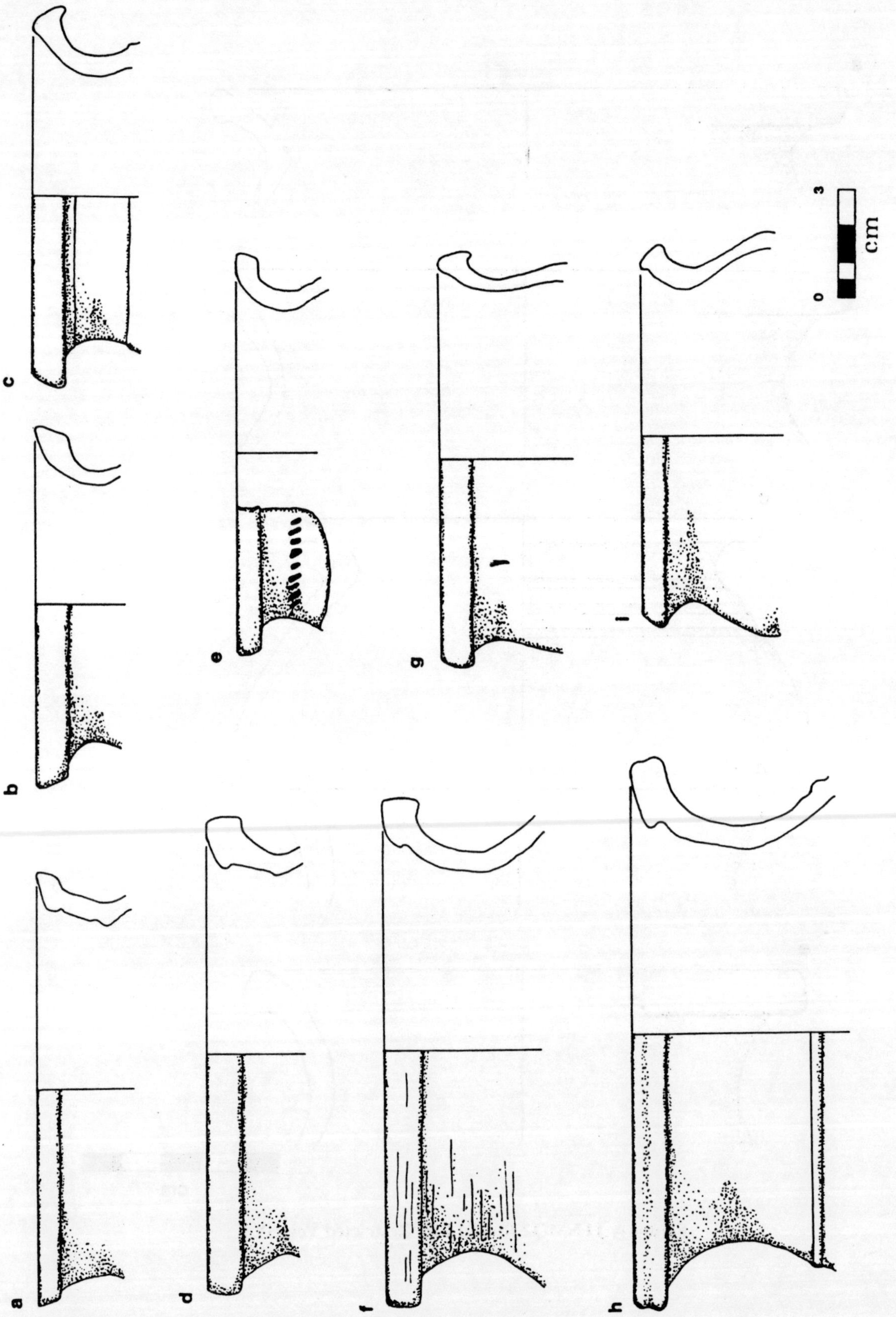

Figure A.12 NMQ2 Straight Rim Restricted Vessels

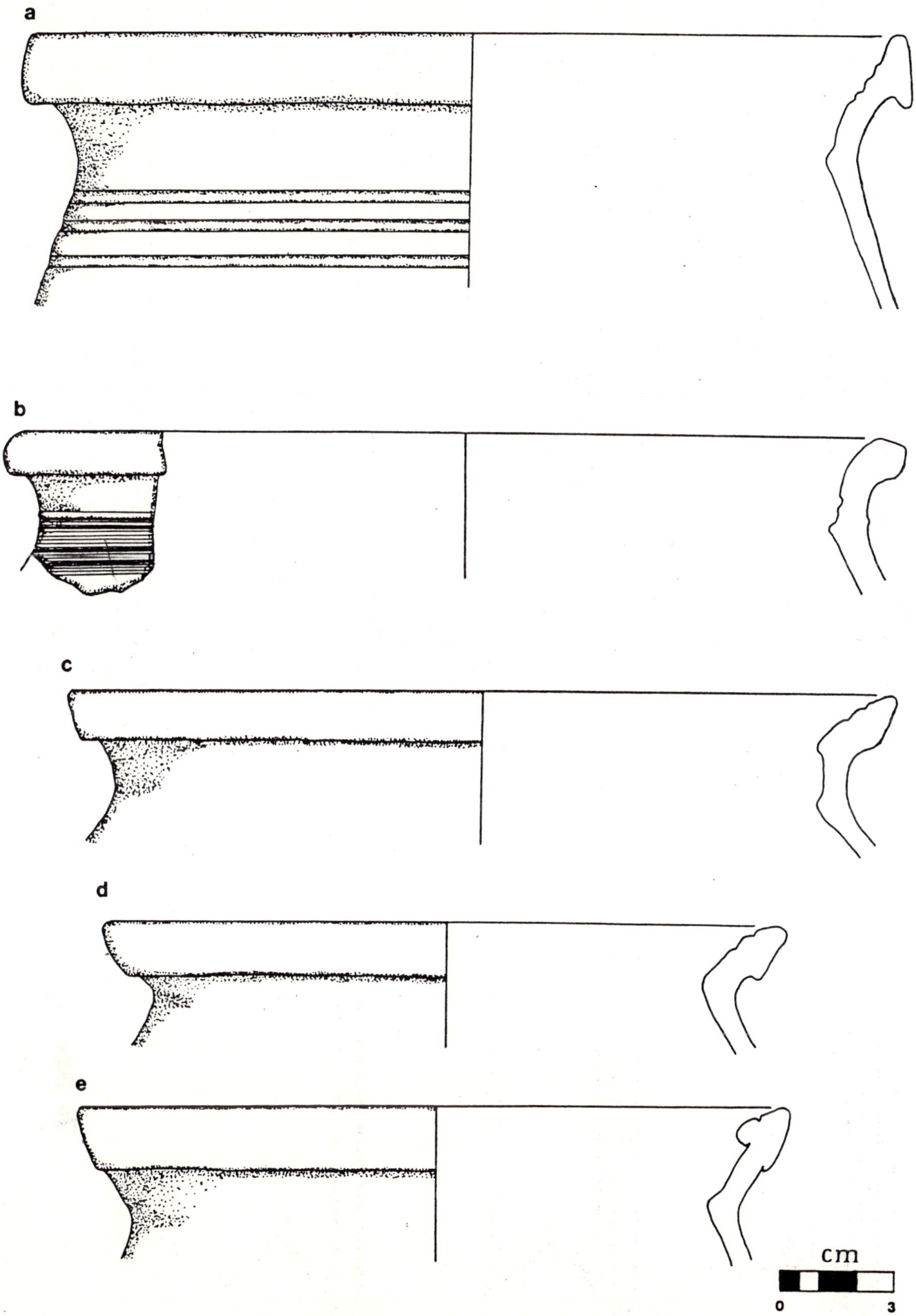

Figure A.13 NMQ2 Straight Rim Restricted Vessels

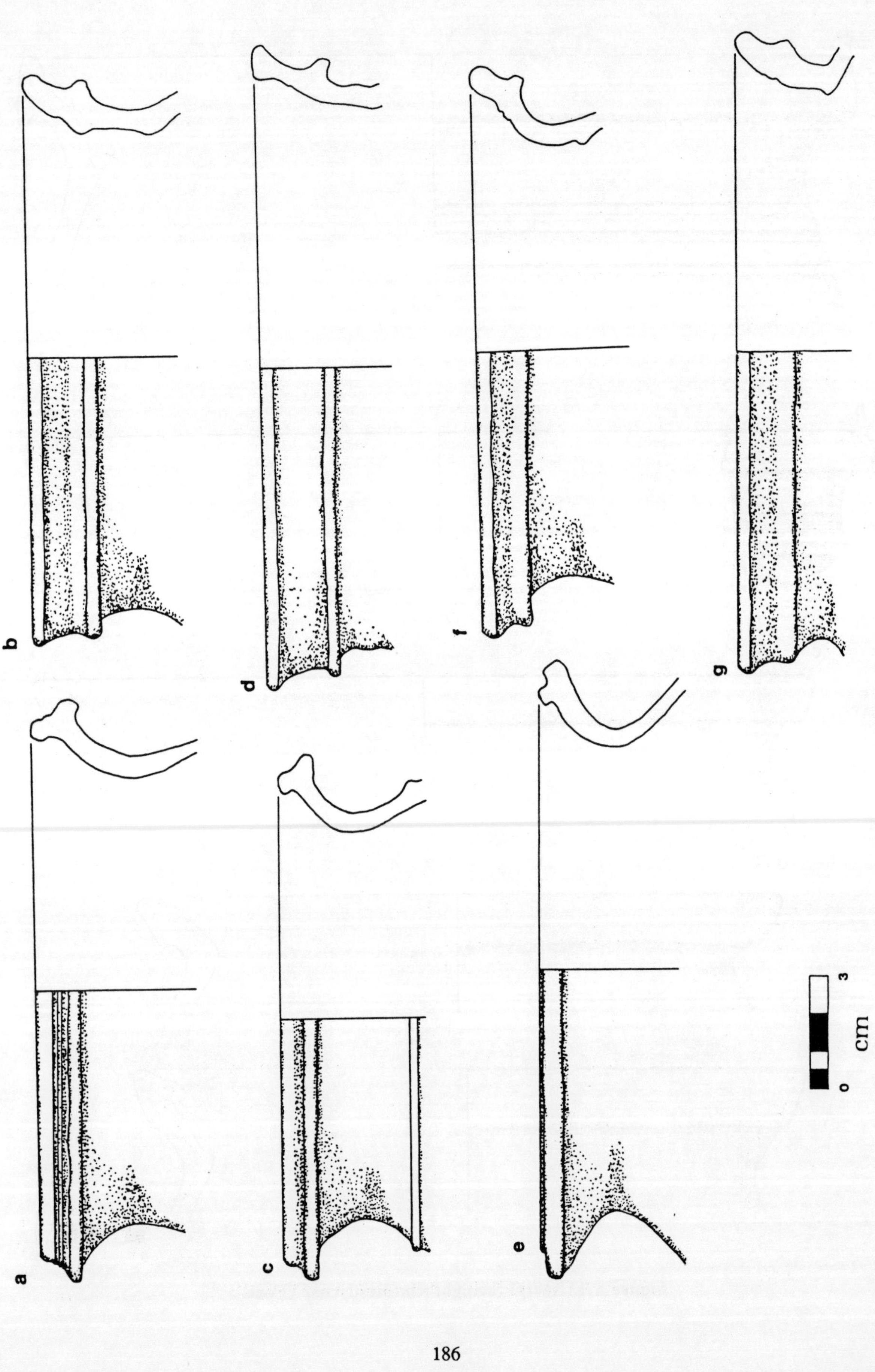

Figure A.14NMQ2 Flange Rim Restricted Vessels

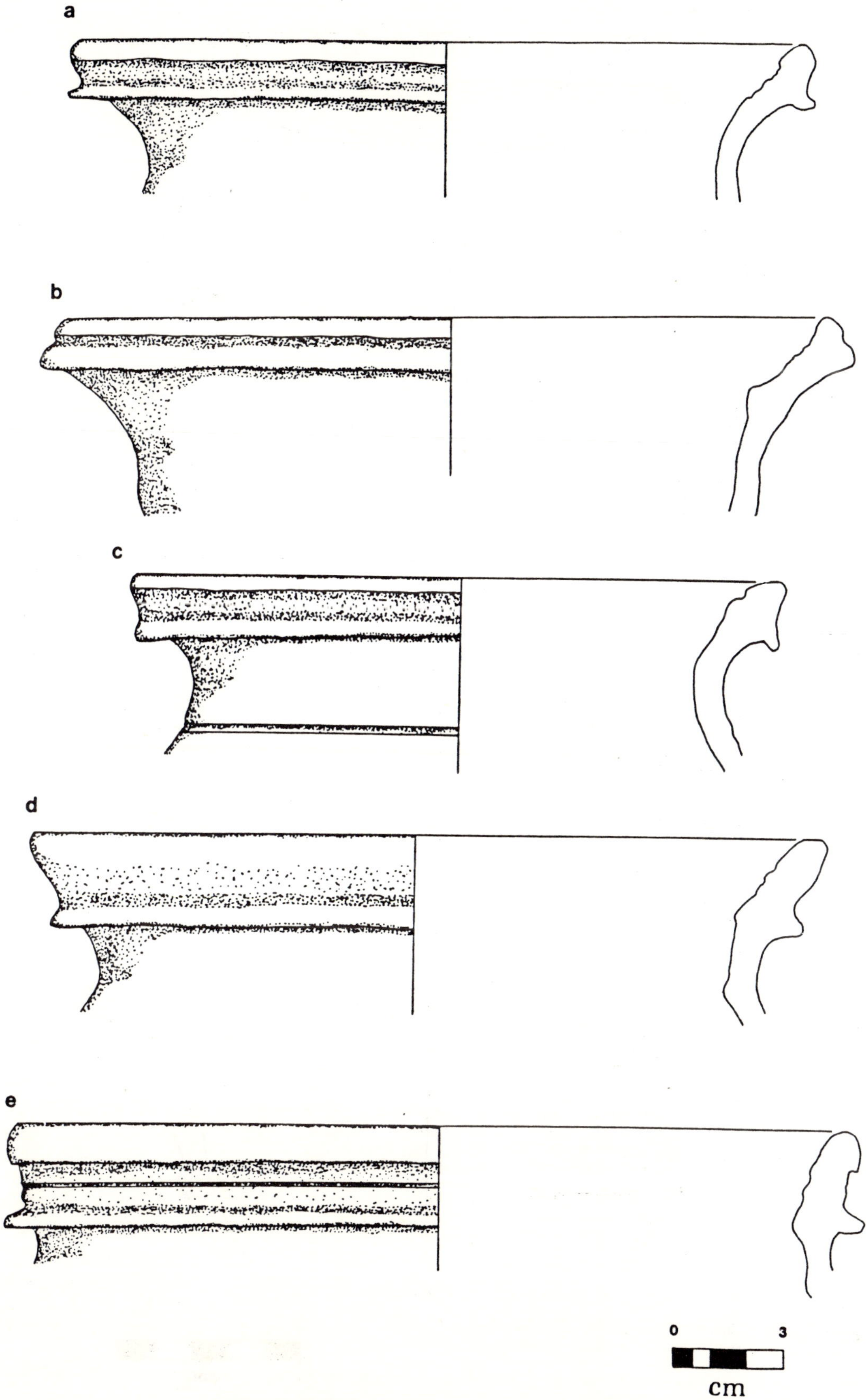

Figure A.15 NMQ2 Flange Rim Restricted Vessels

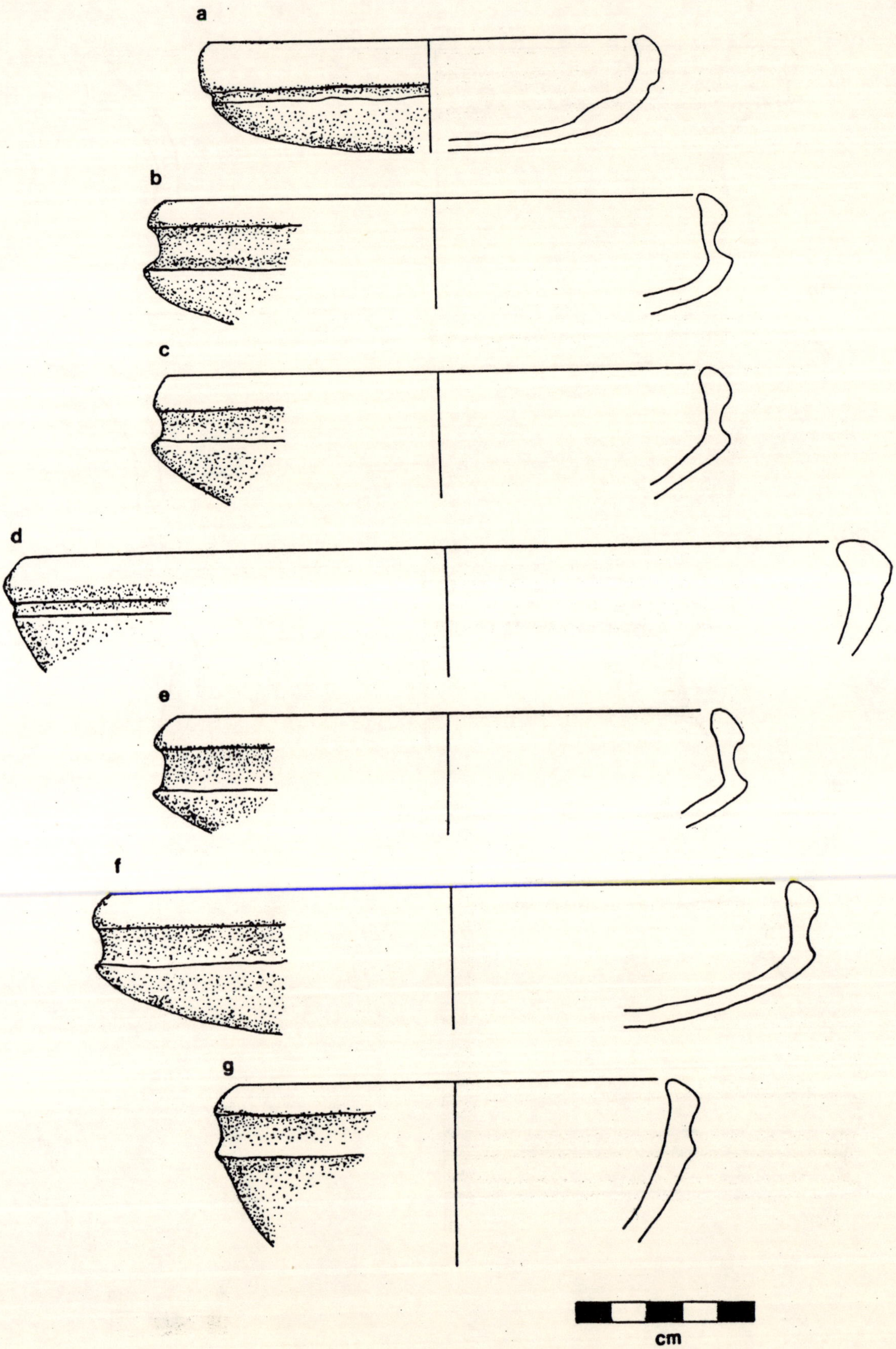

Figure A.16 NMQ3 Shallow Bowls

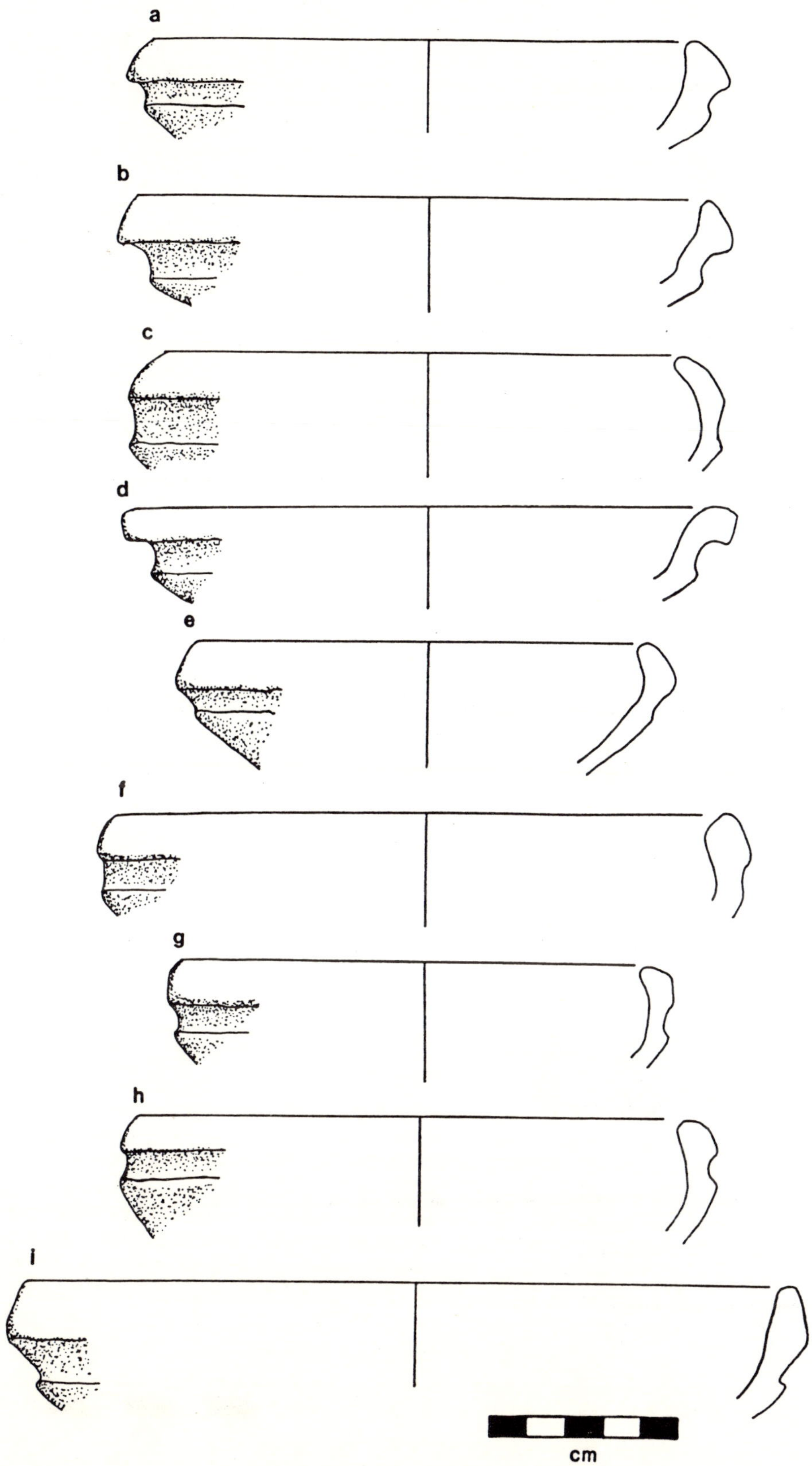

Figure A.17 NMQ3 Shallow Bowls

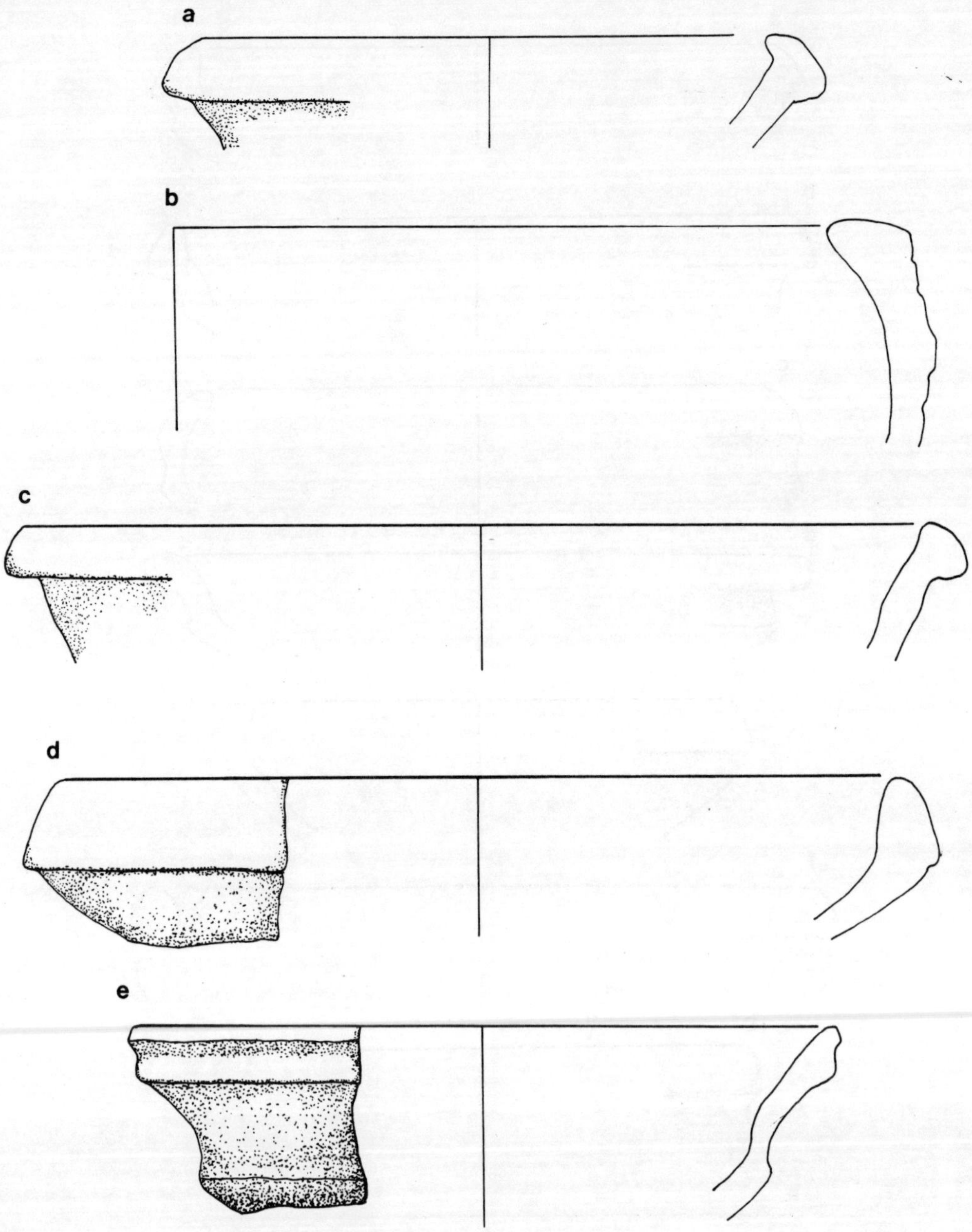

Figure A.18 NMQ3 Other Bowls

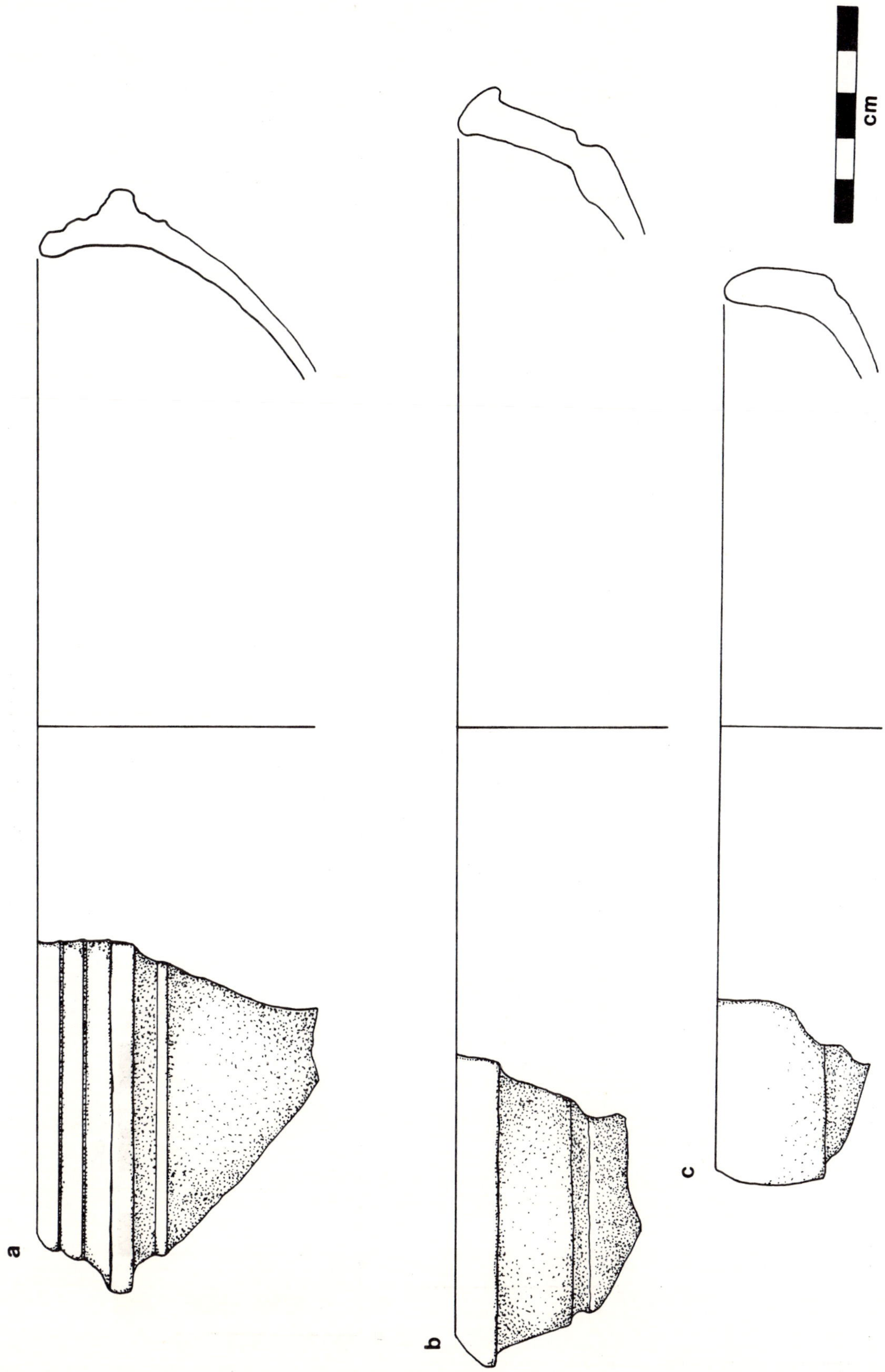

Figure A.19 NMQ3 Other Bowls

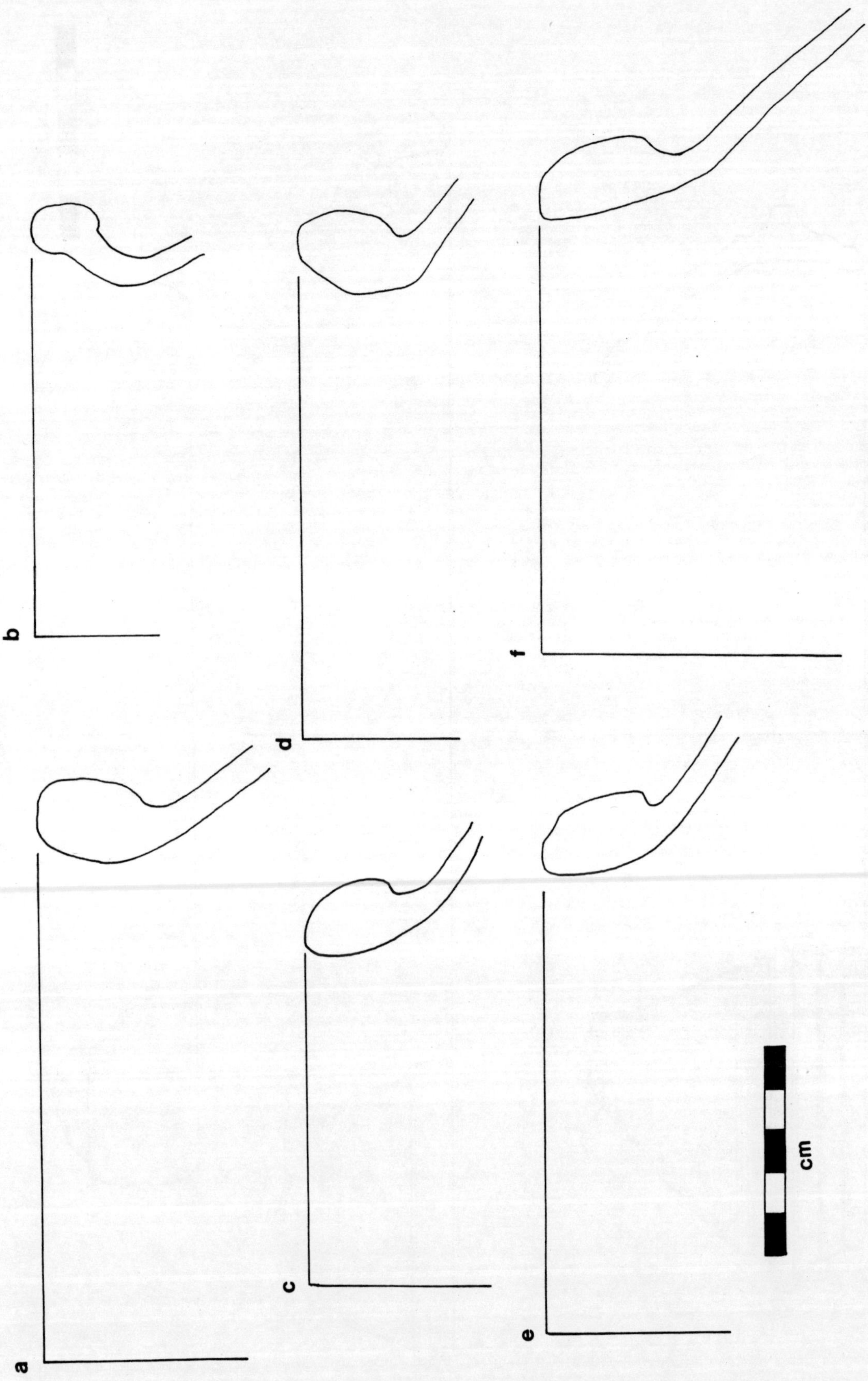

Figure A.20 NMQ3 Round Rim Restricted Vessels

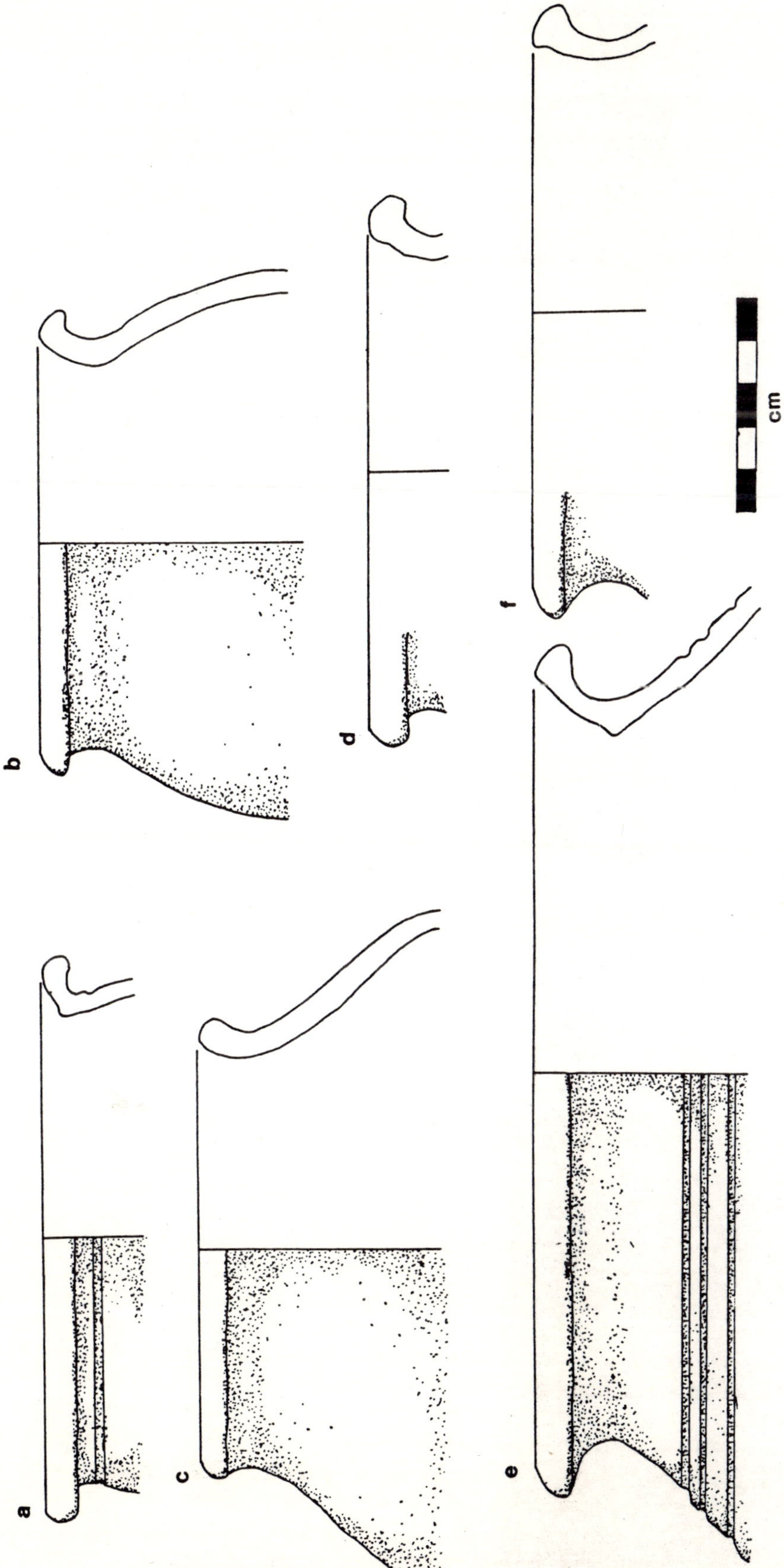

Figure A.21 NMQ3 Round Rim Restricted Vessels

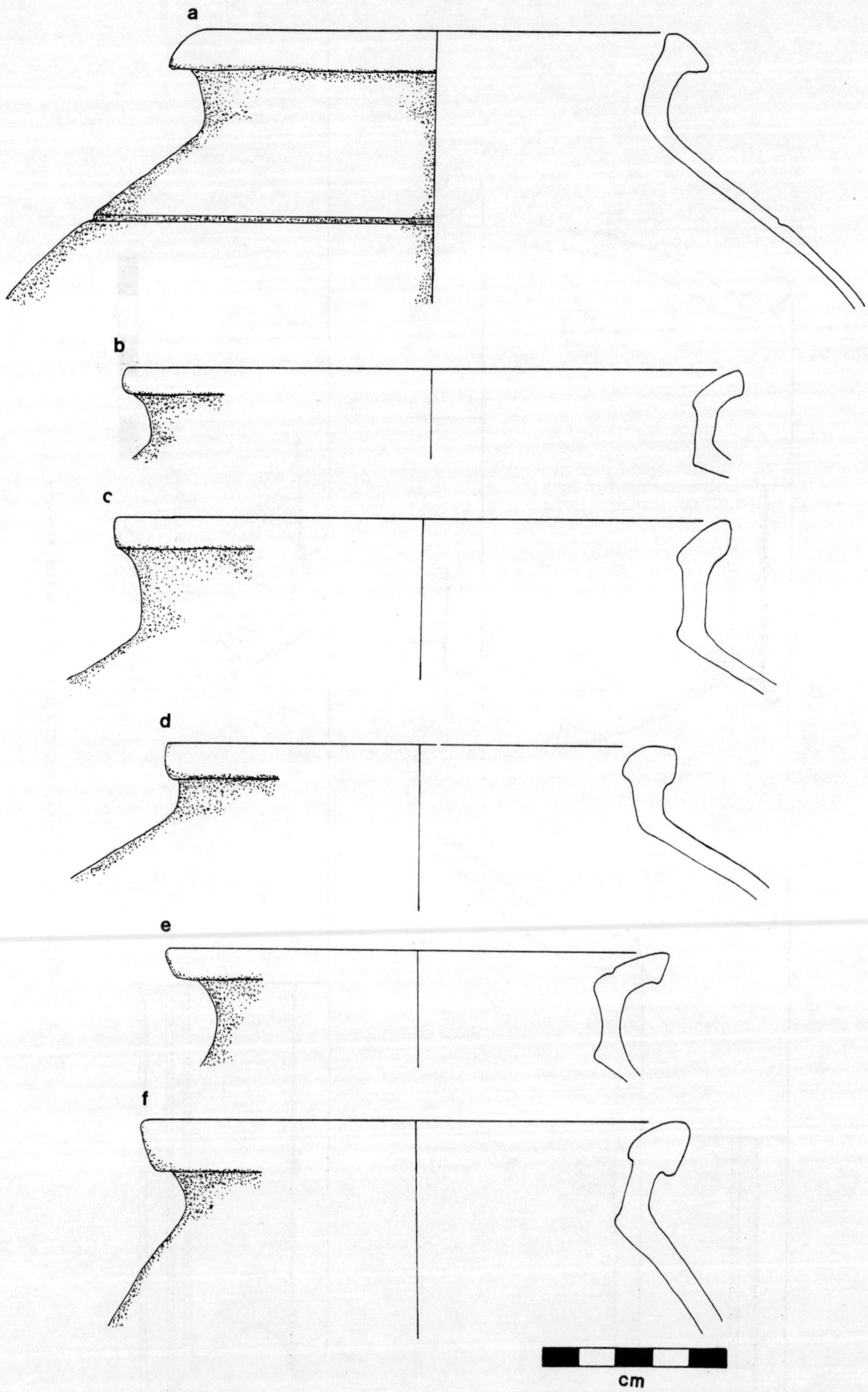

Figure A.22 NMQ3 Straight Rim Restricted Vessels

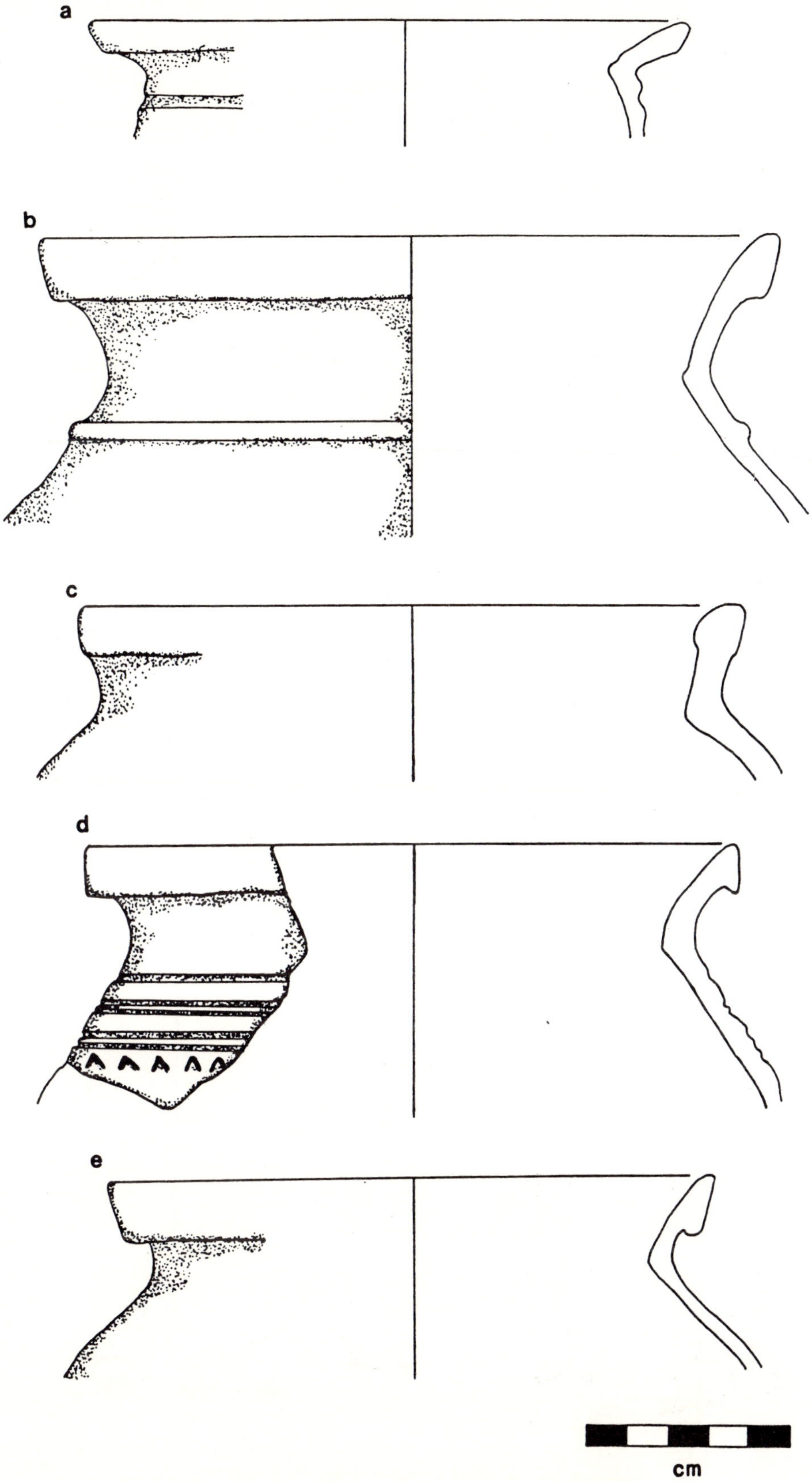

Figure A.23NMQ3 Straight Rim Restricted Vessels

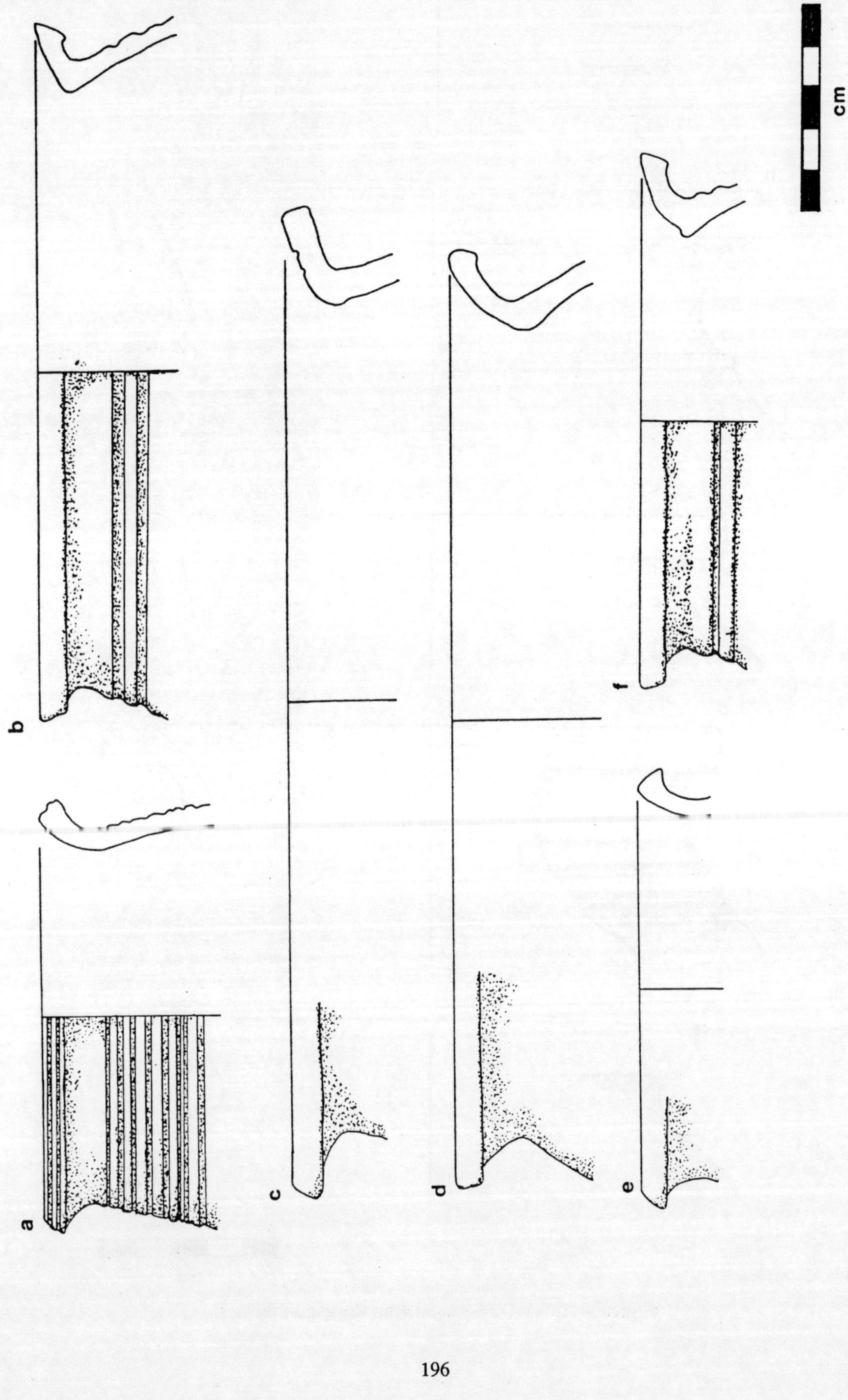

Figure A.24 NMQ3 Straight Rim Restricted Vessels

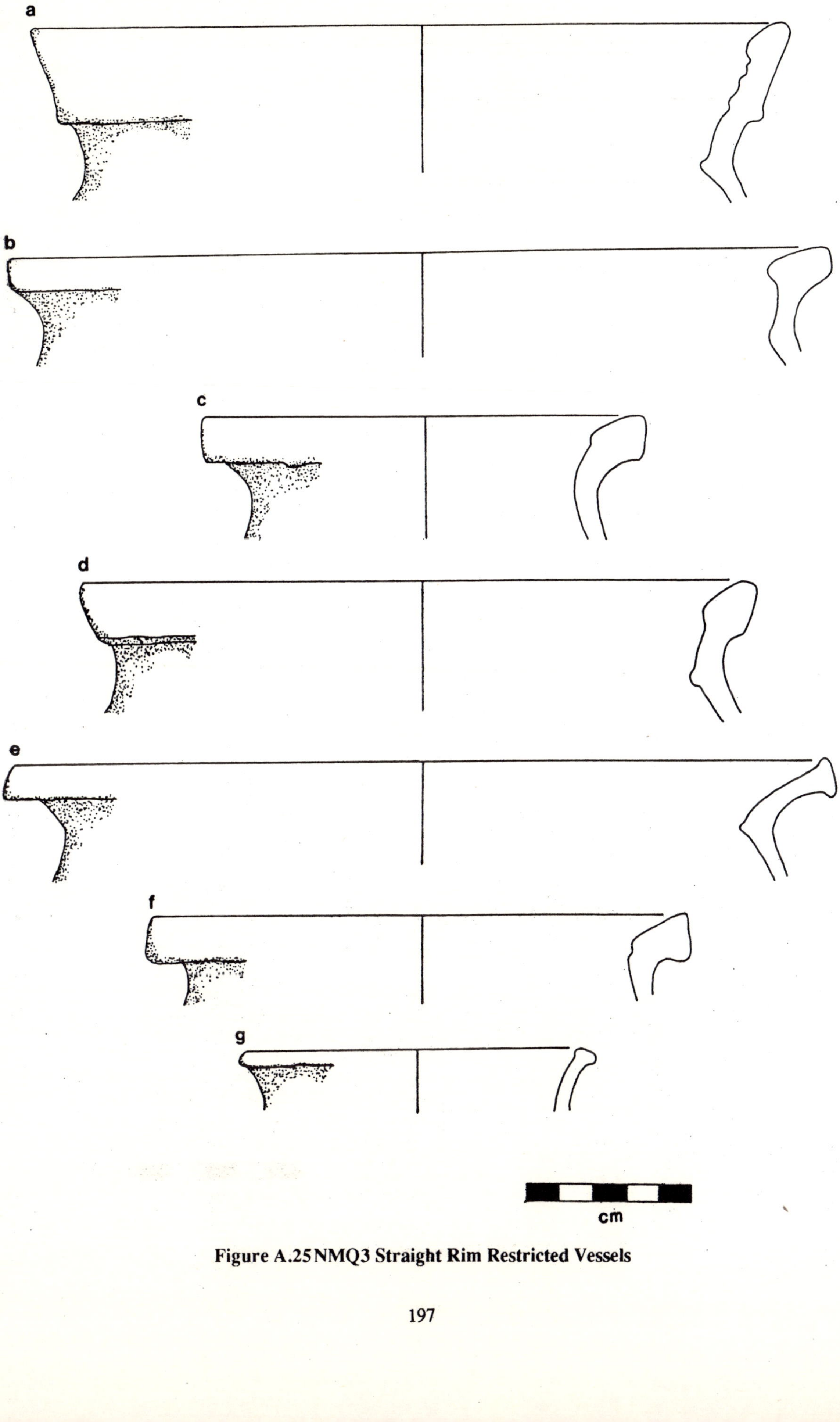

Figure A.25 NMQ3 Straight Rim Restricted Vessels

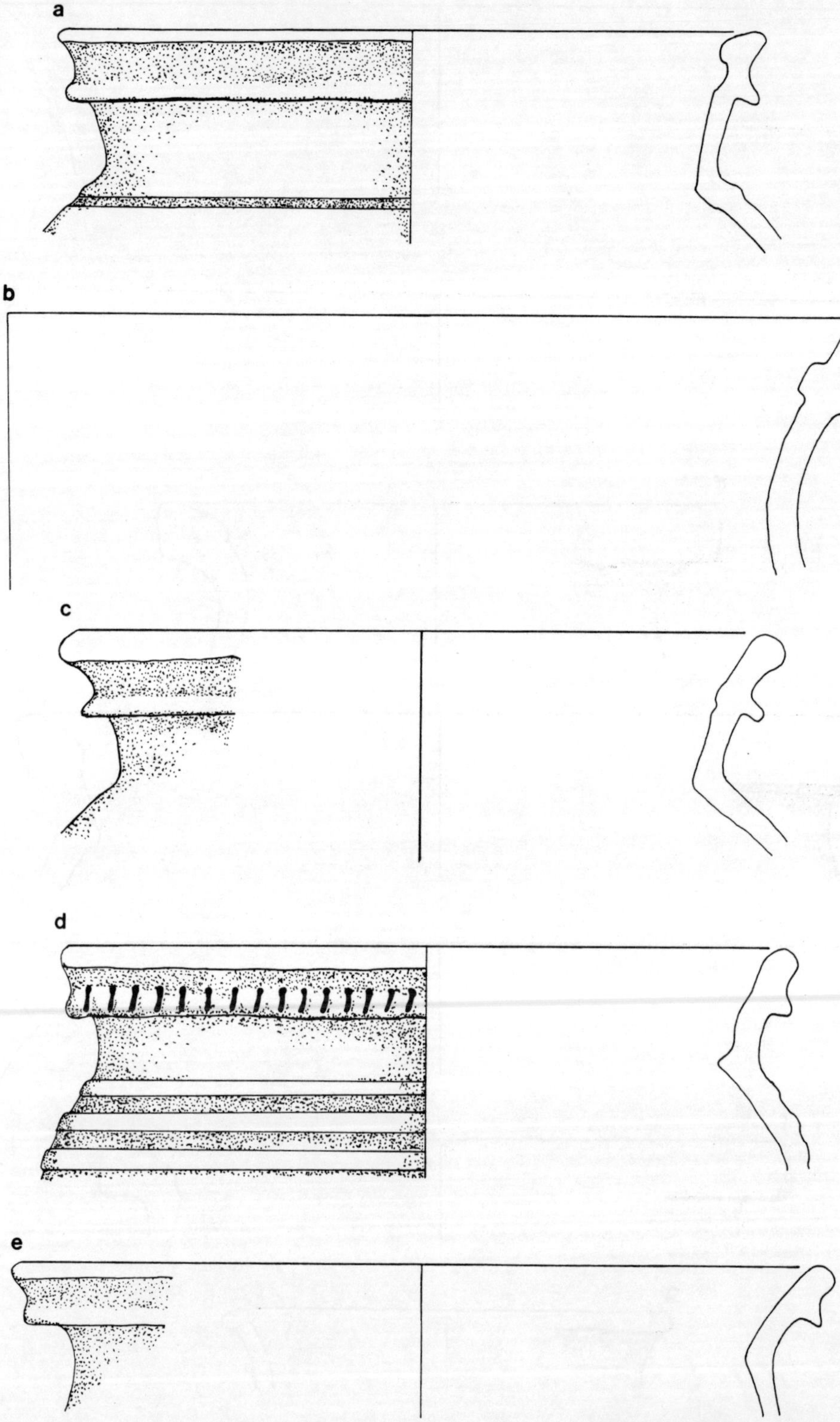

Figure A.26 NMQ3 Flange Rim Restricted Vessels

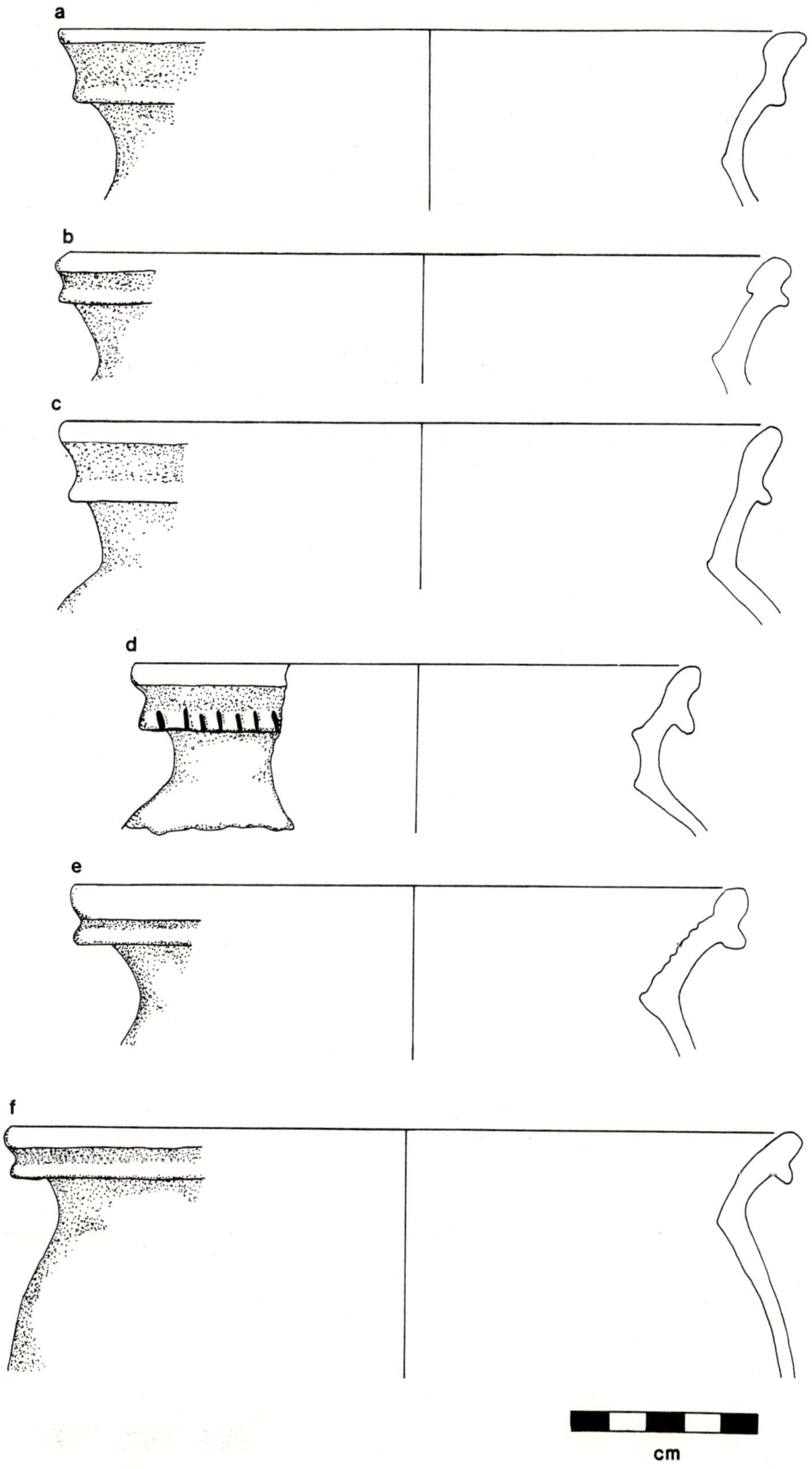

Figure A.27 NMQ3 Flange Rim Restricted Vessels

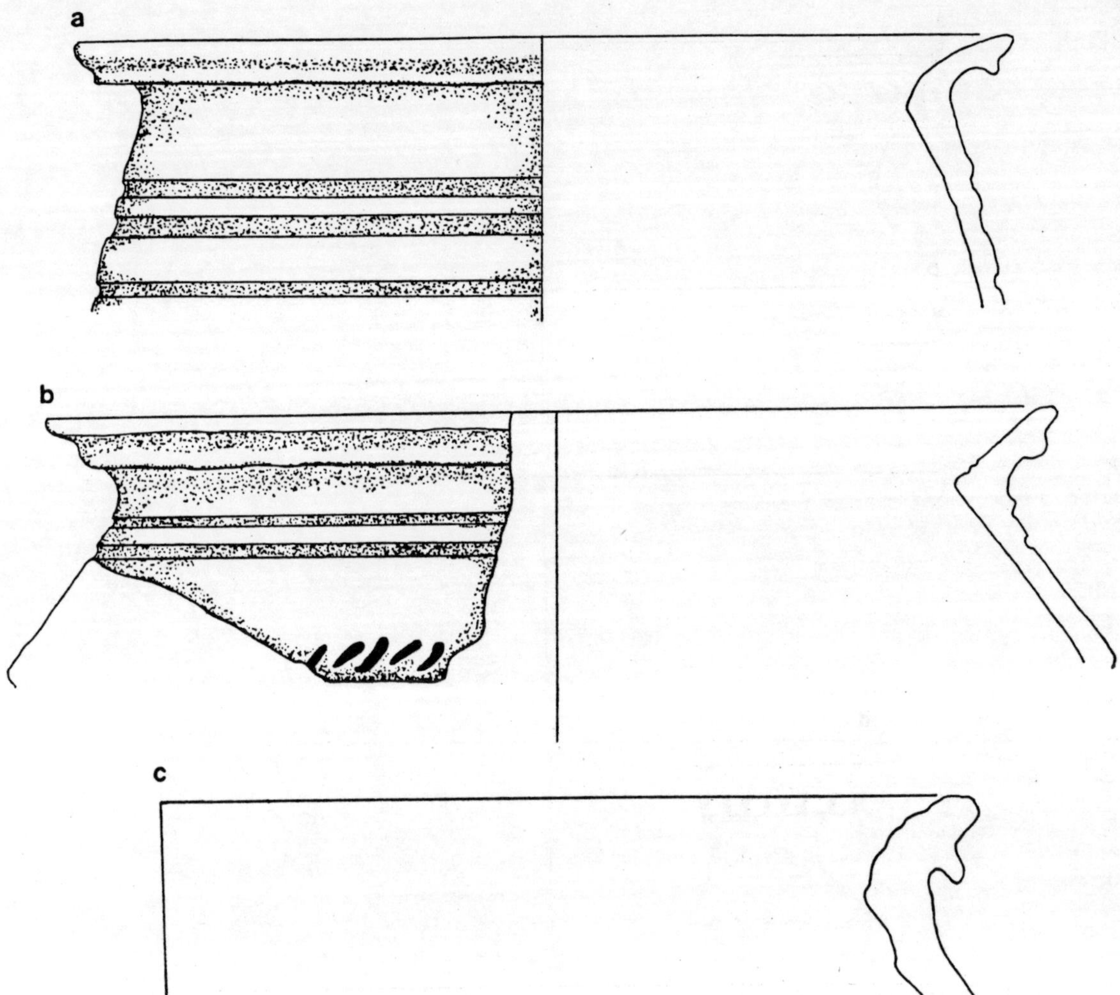

Figure A.28 NMQ3 Flange Rim Restricted Vessels

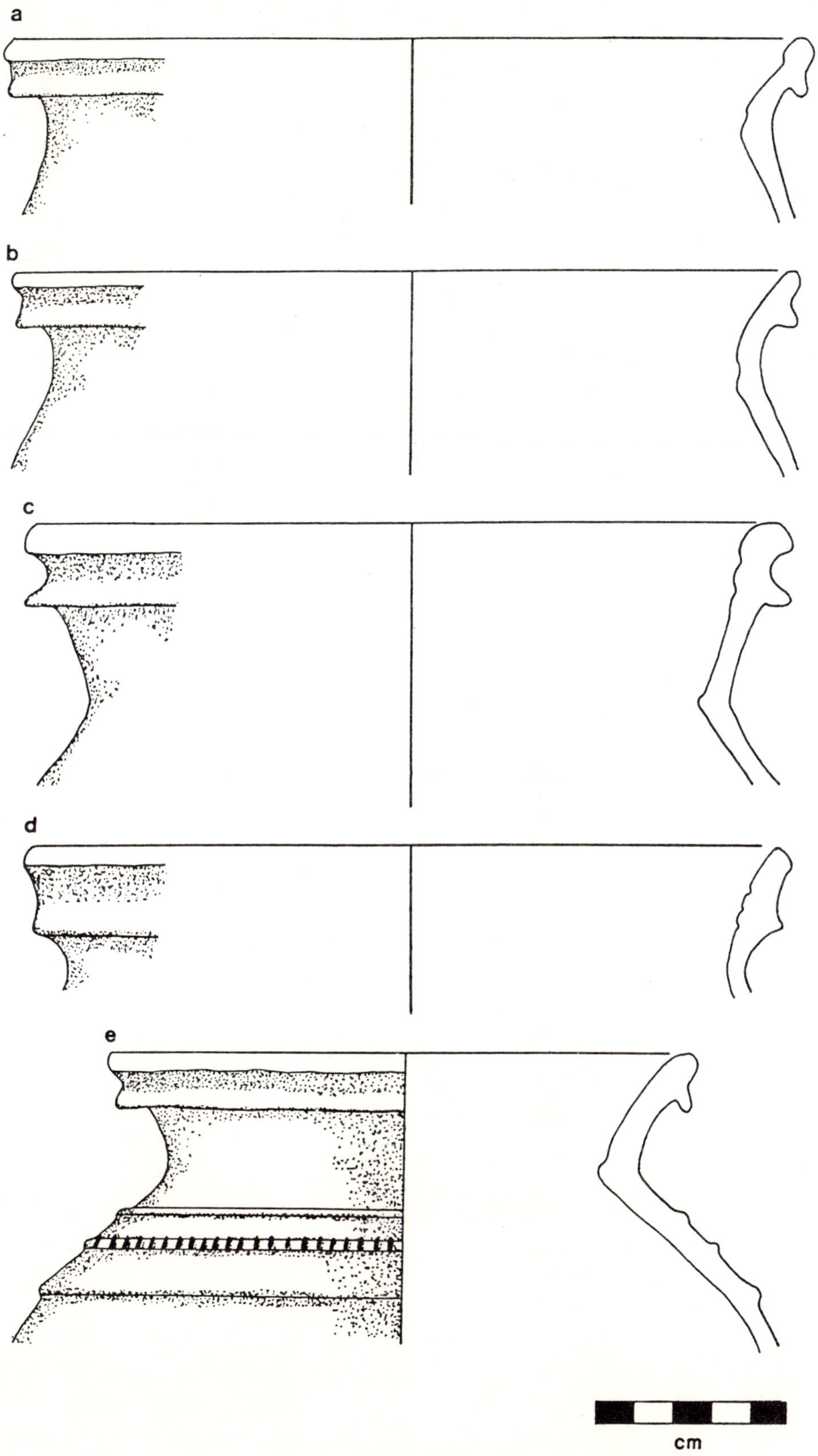

Figure A.29 NMQ3 Flange Rim Restricted Vessels

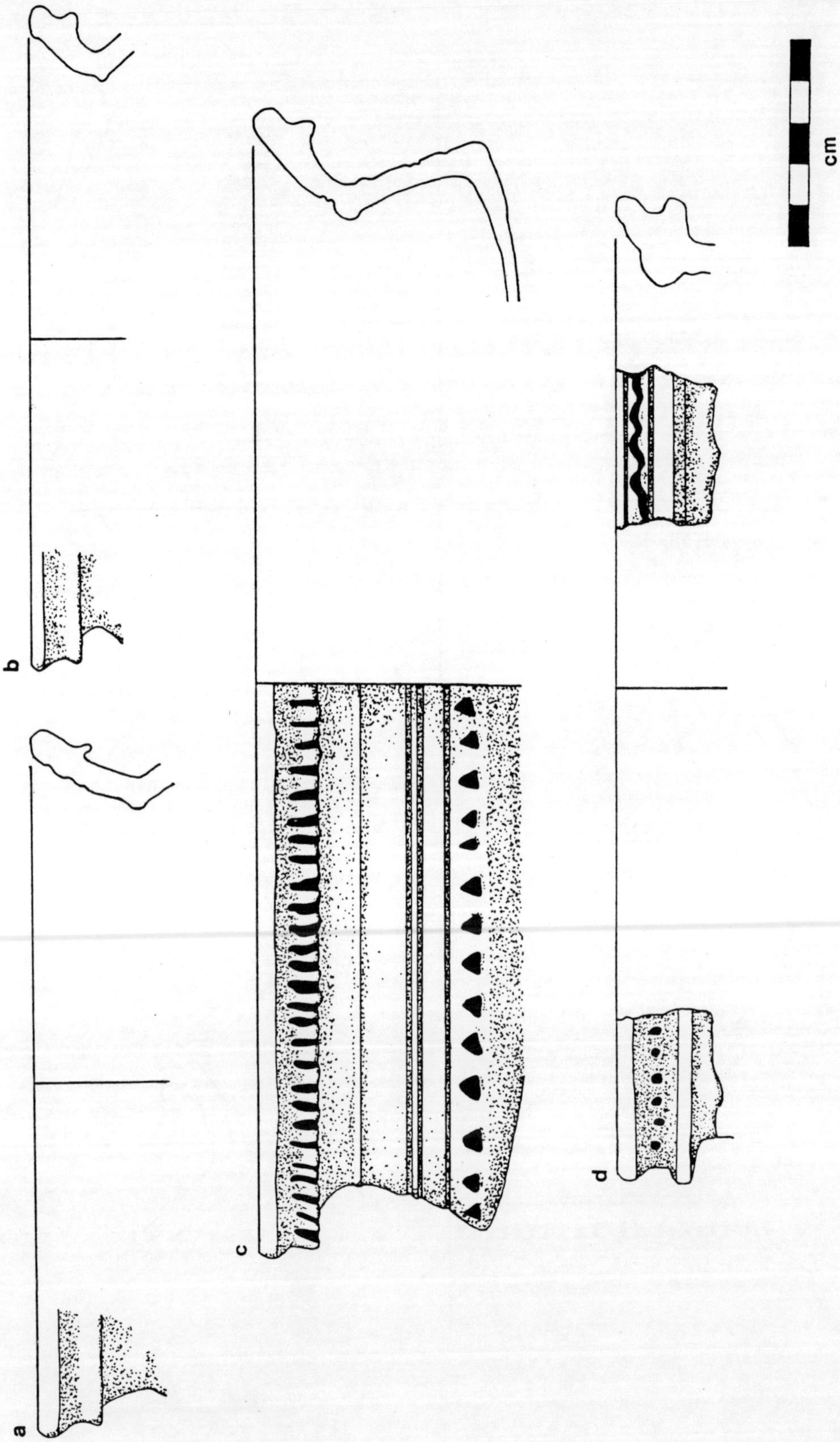

Figure A.30 NMQ3 Flange Rim Restricted Vessels

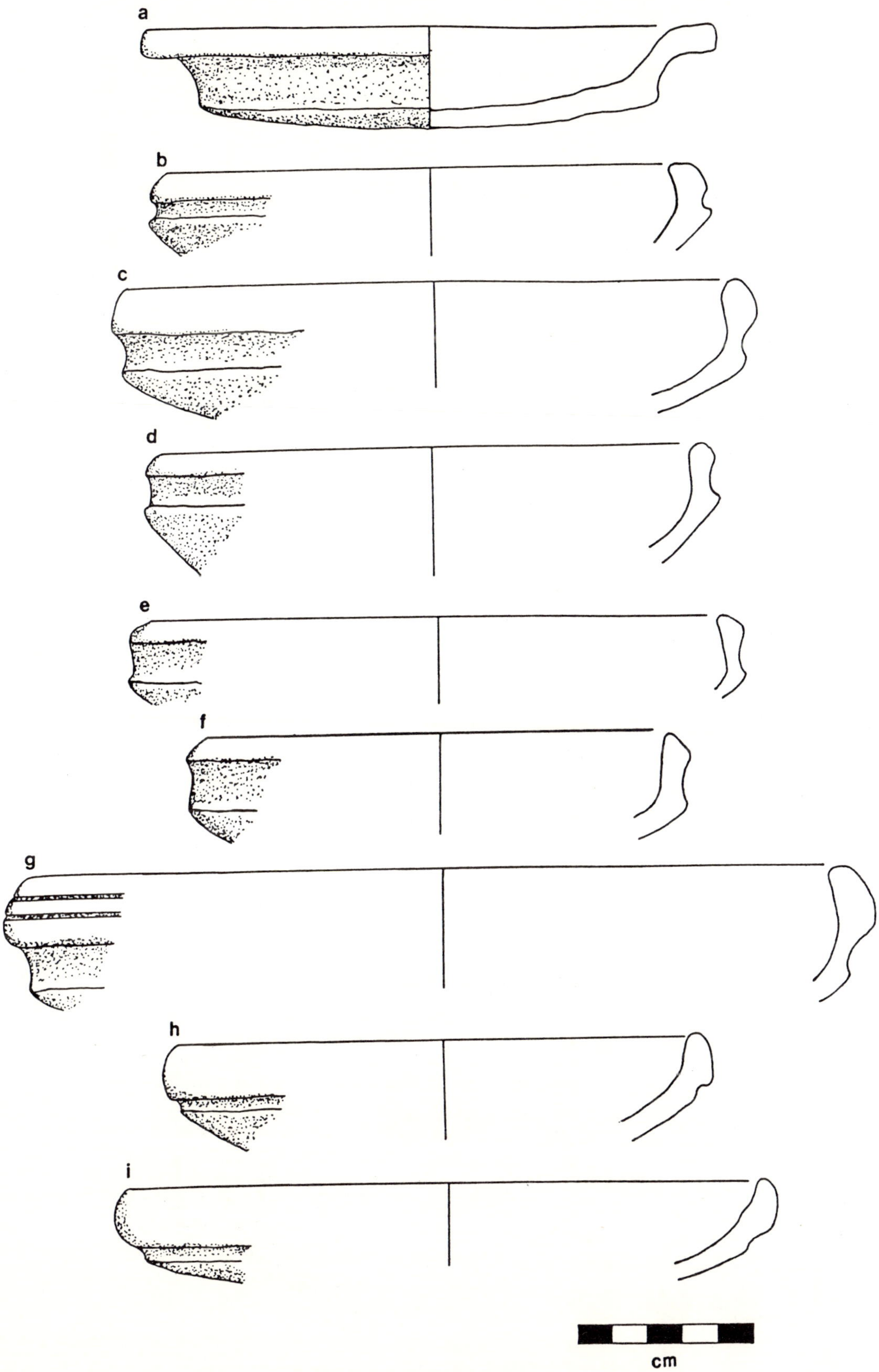

Figure A.31 NMQ4 Shallow Bowls

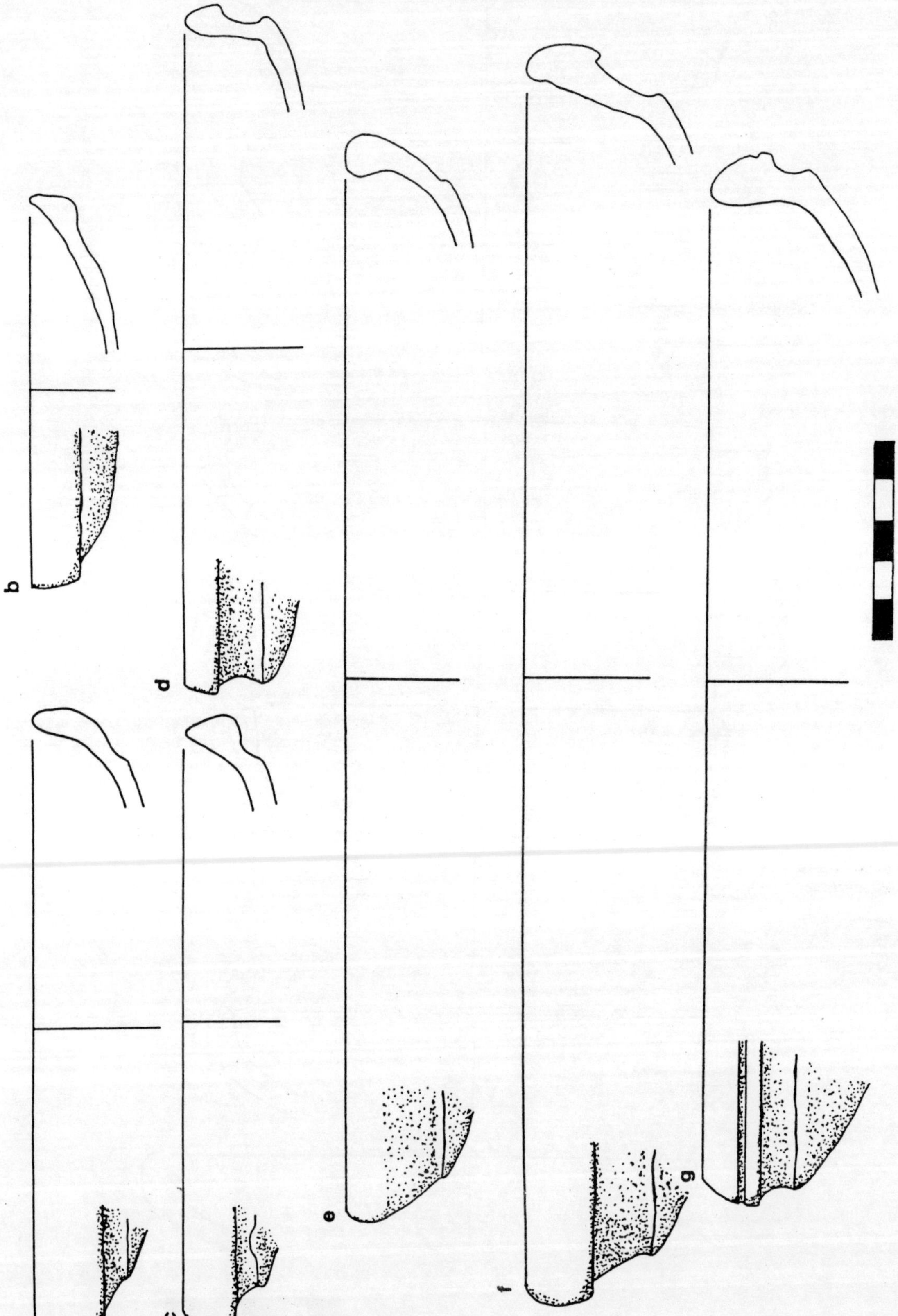

Figure A.32 NMQ4 Shallow Bowls

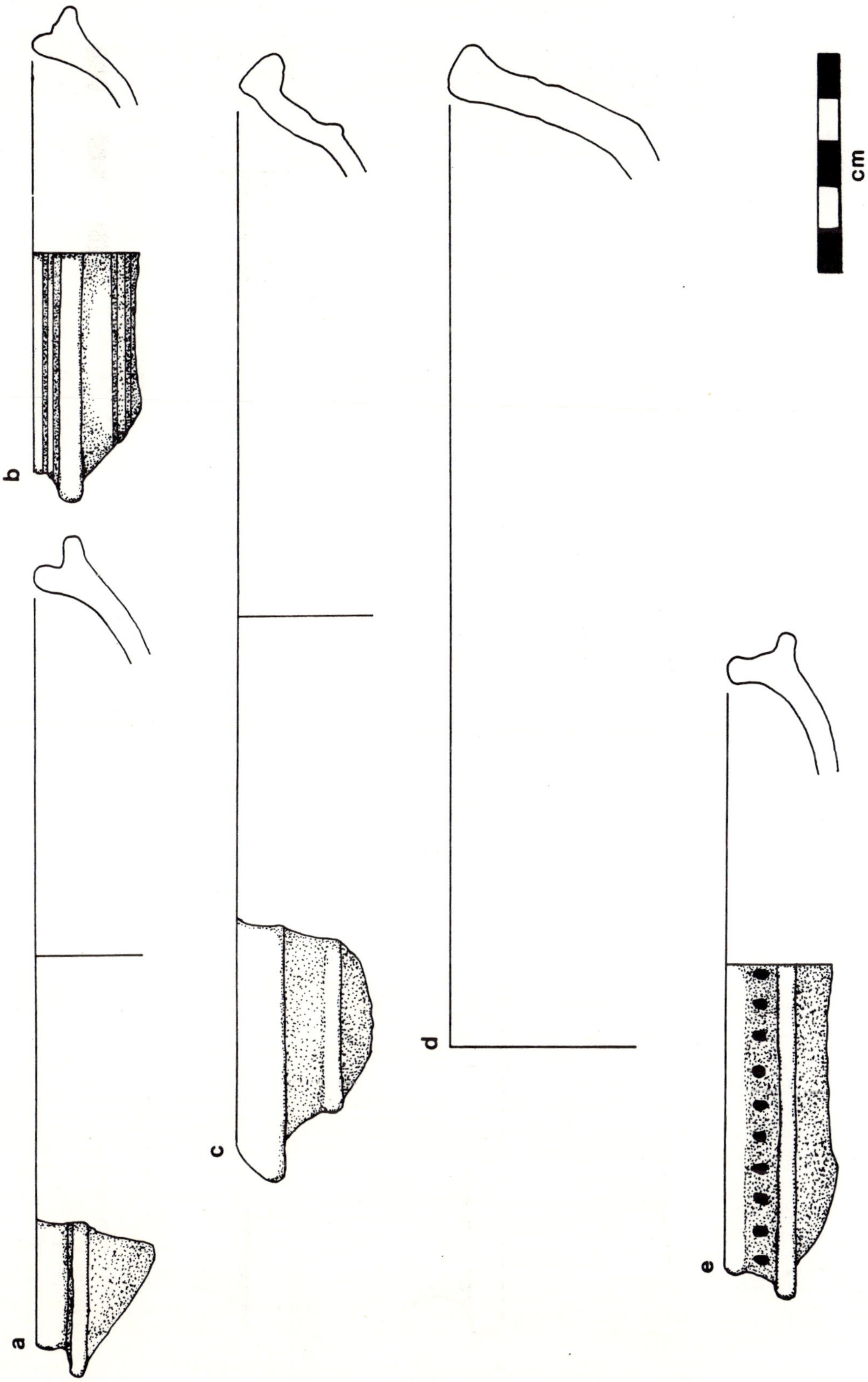

Figure A.33 NMQ4 Other Bowls

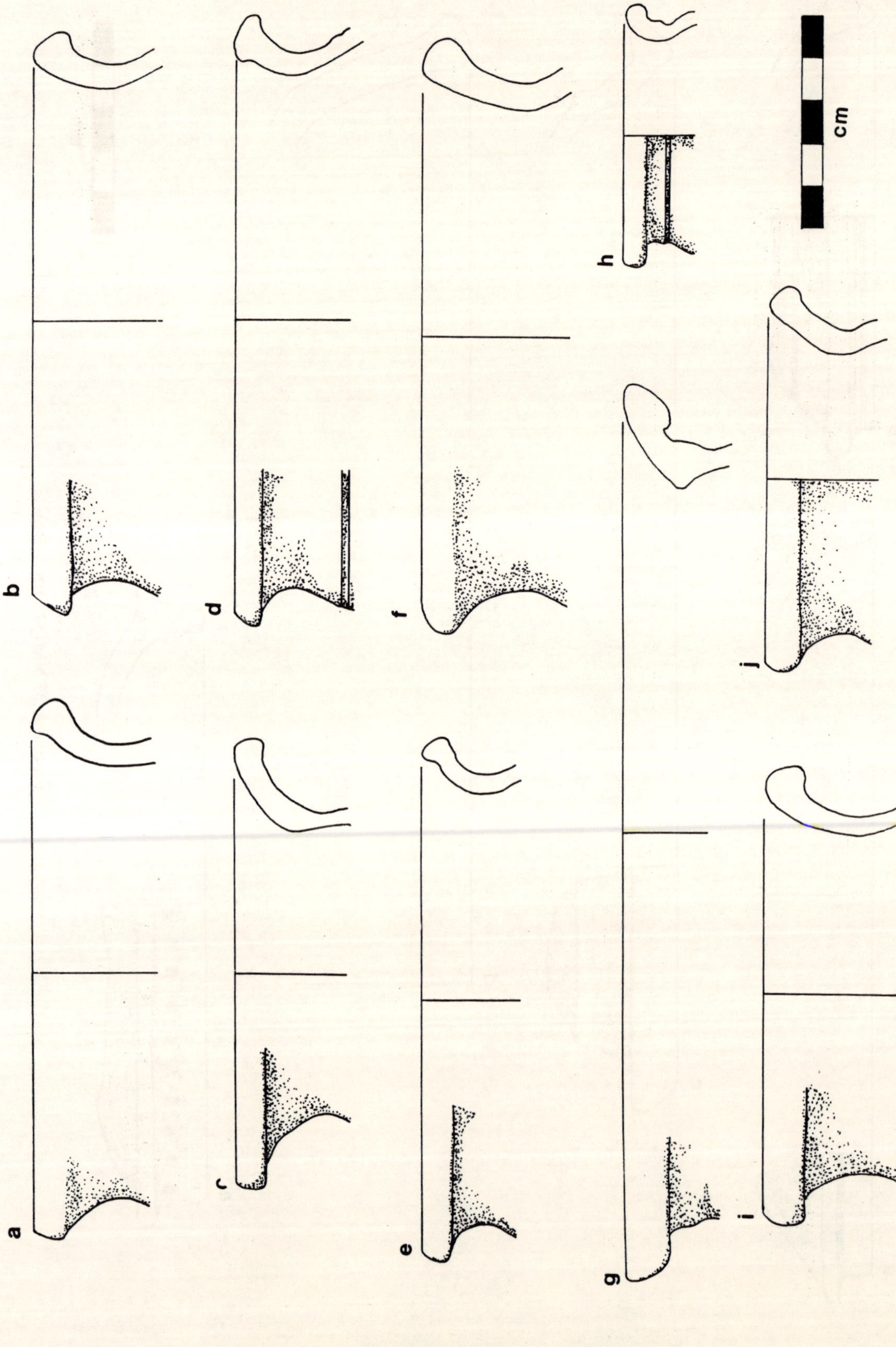

Figure A.34 NMQ4 Round Rim Restricted Vessels

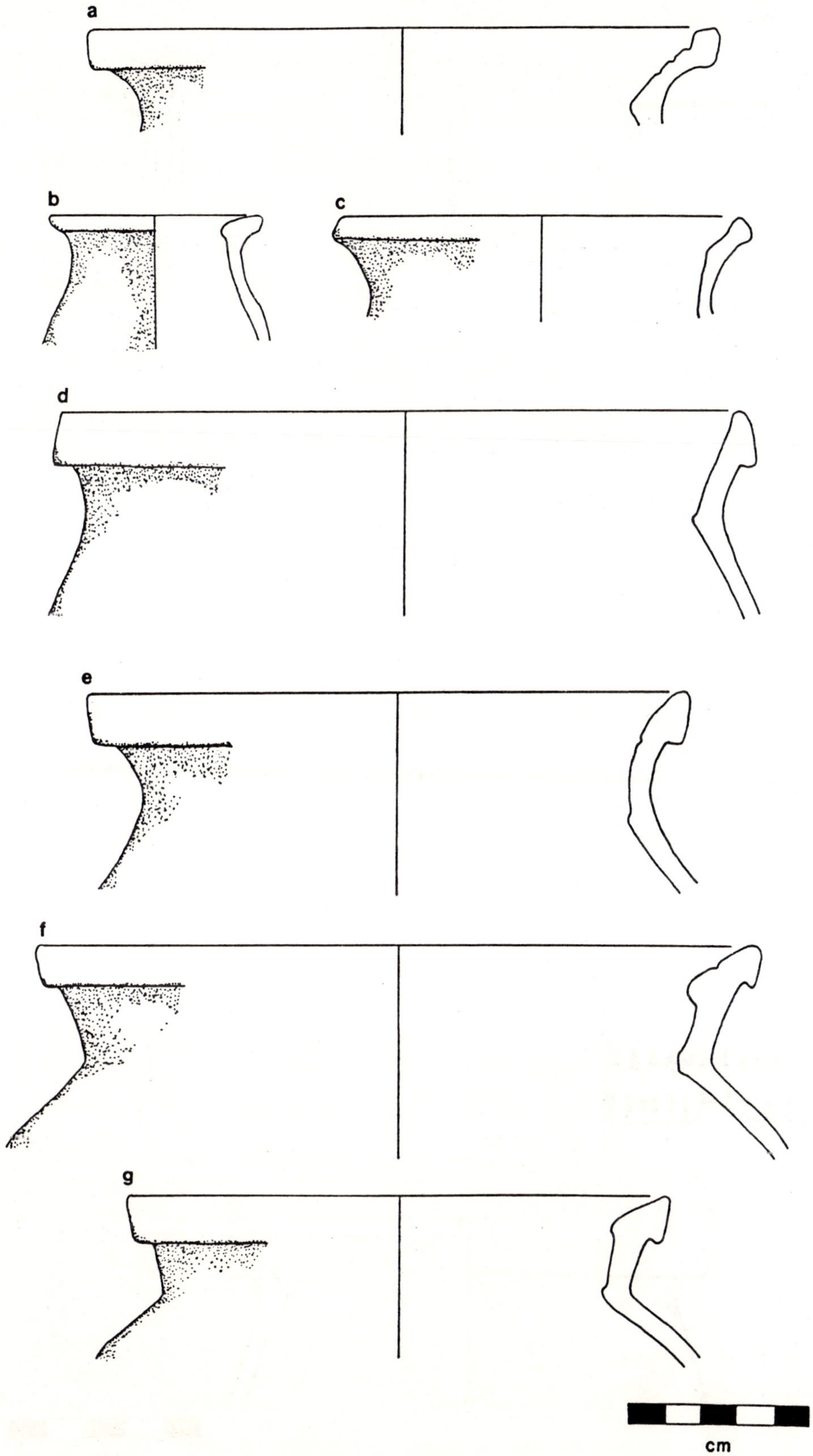

Figure A.35 NMQ4 Straight Rim Restricted Vessels

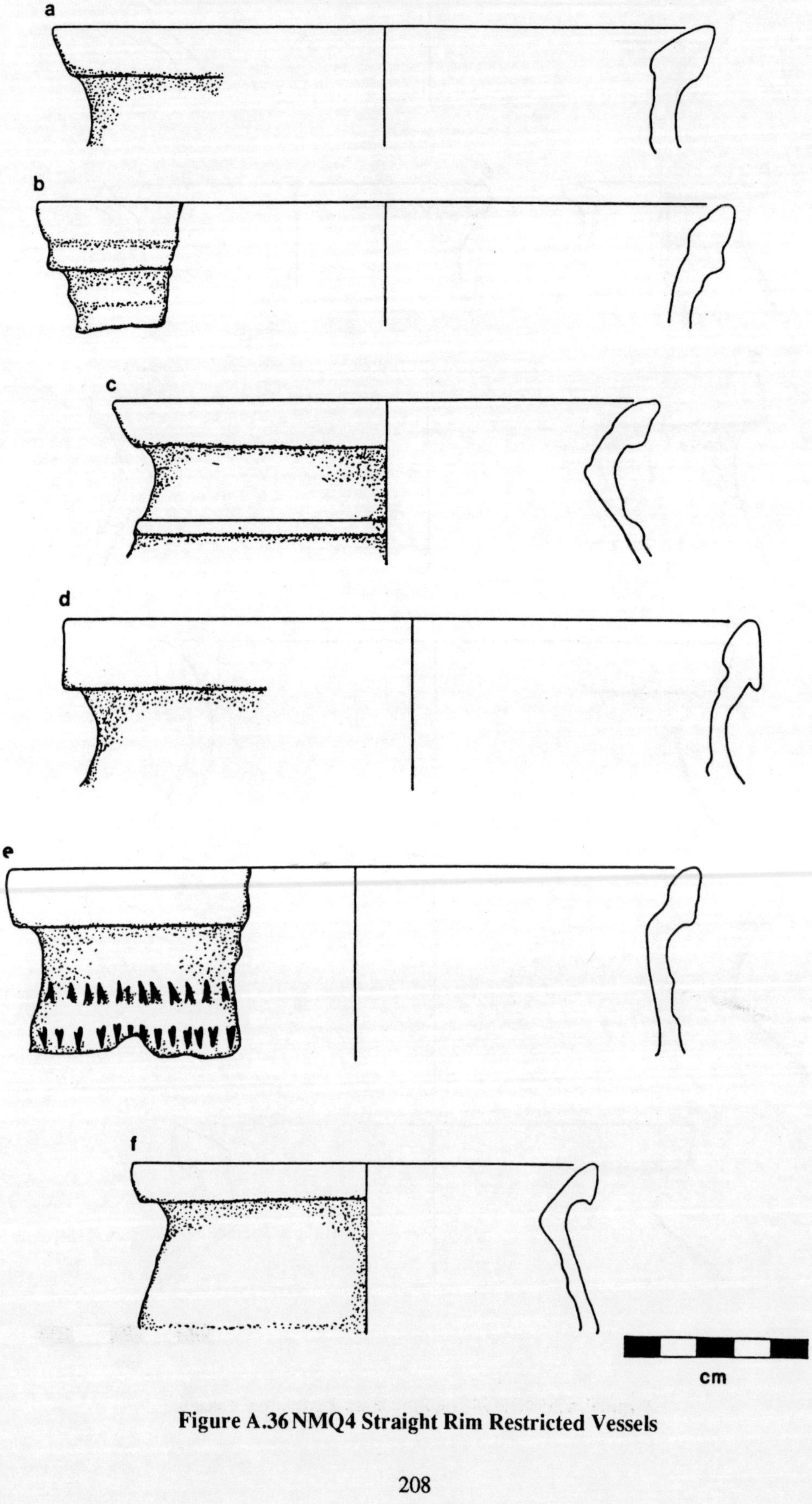

Figure A.36 NMQ4 Straight Rim Restricted Vessels

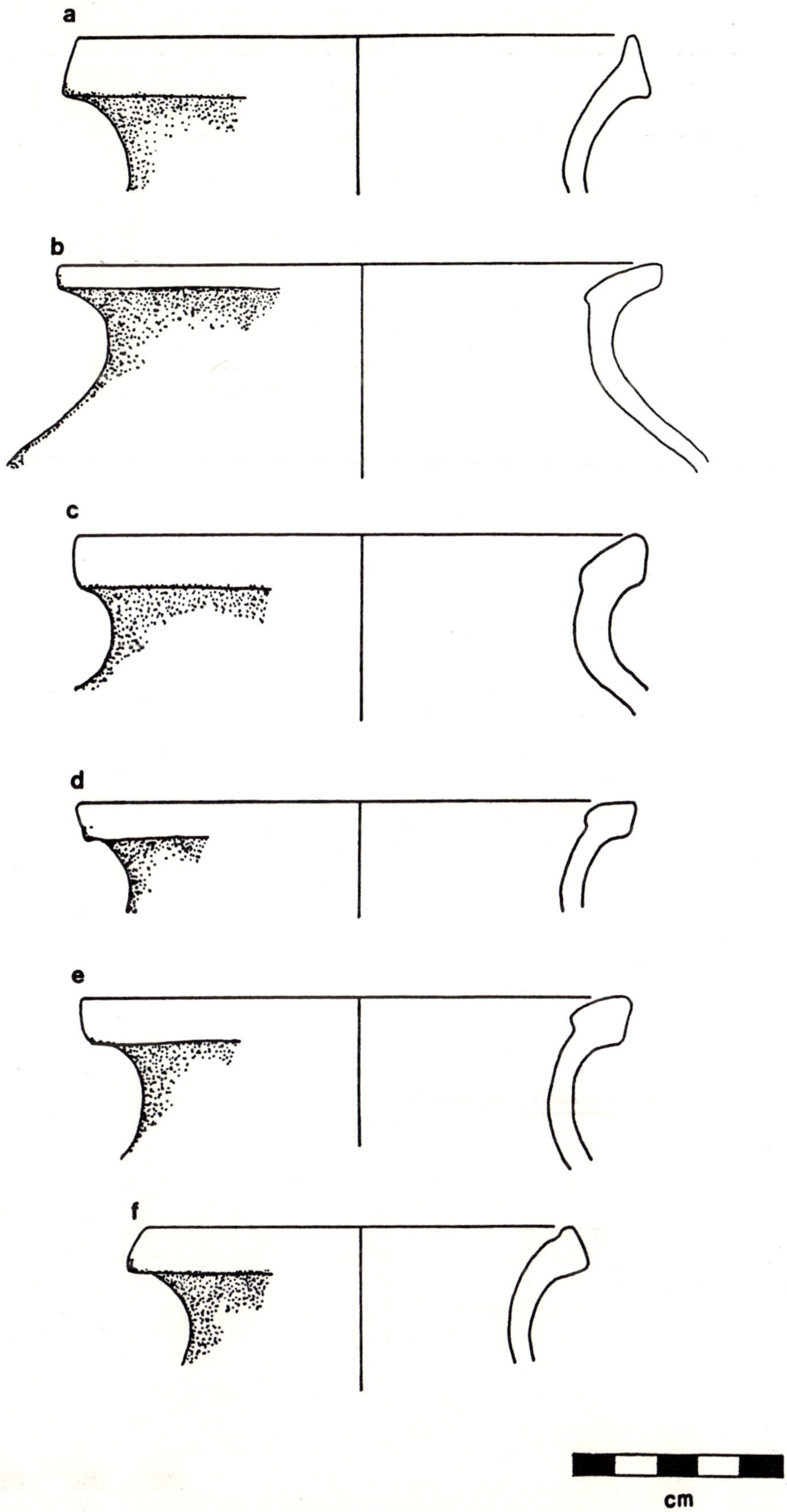

Figure A.37 NMQ4 Straight Rim Restricted Vessels

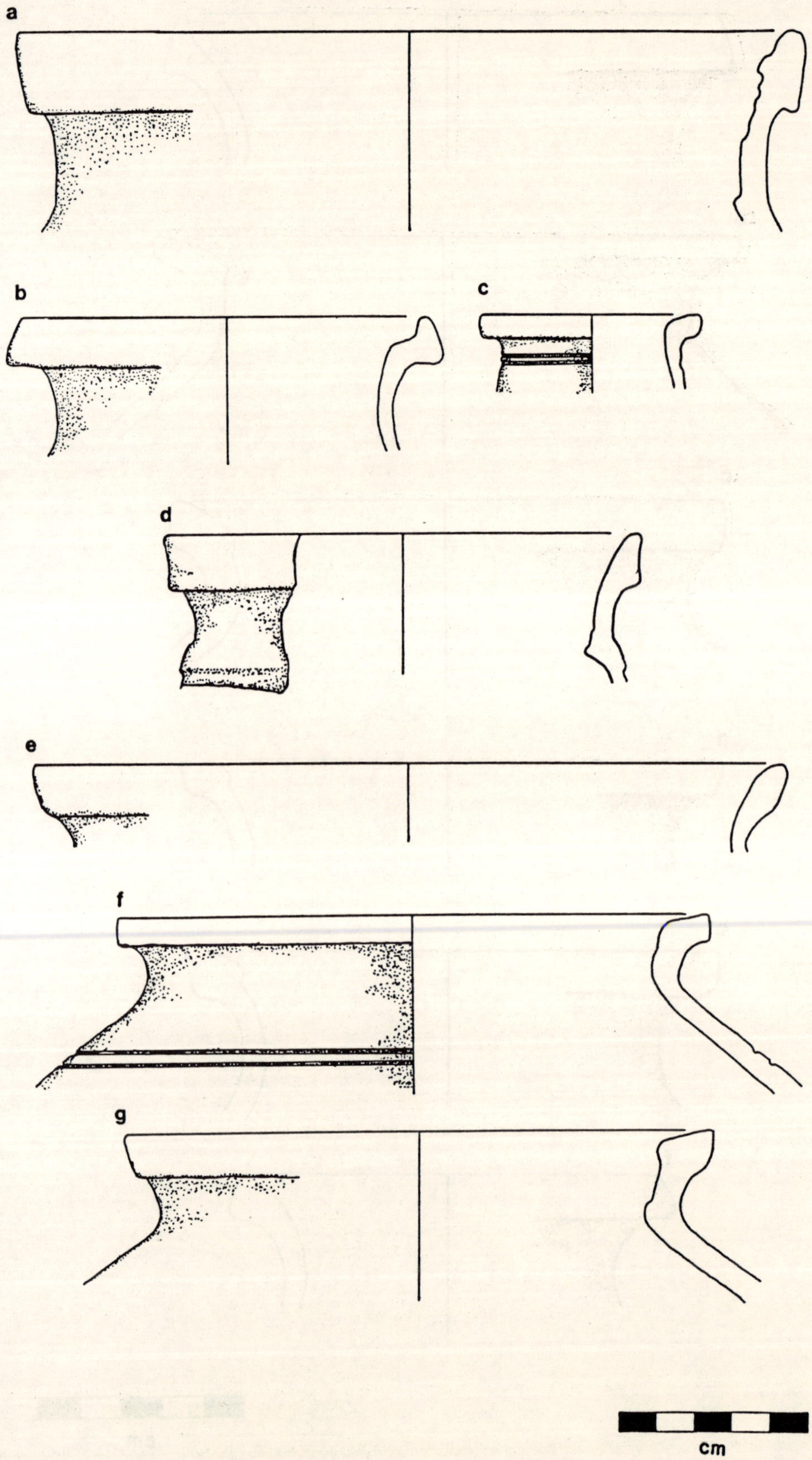

Figure A.38 NMQ4 Straight Rim Restricted Vessels

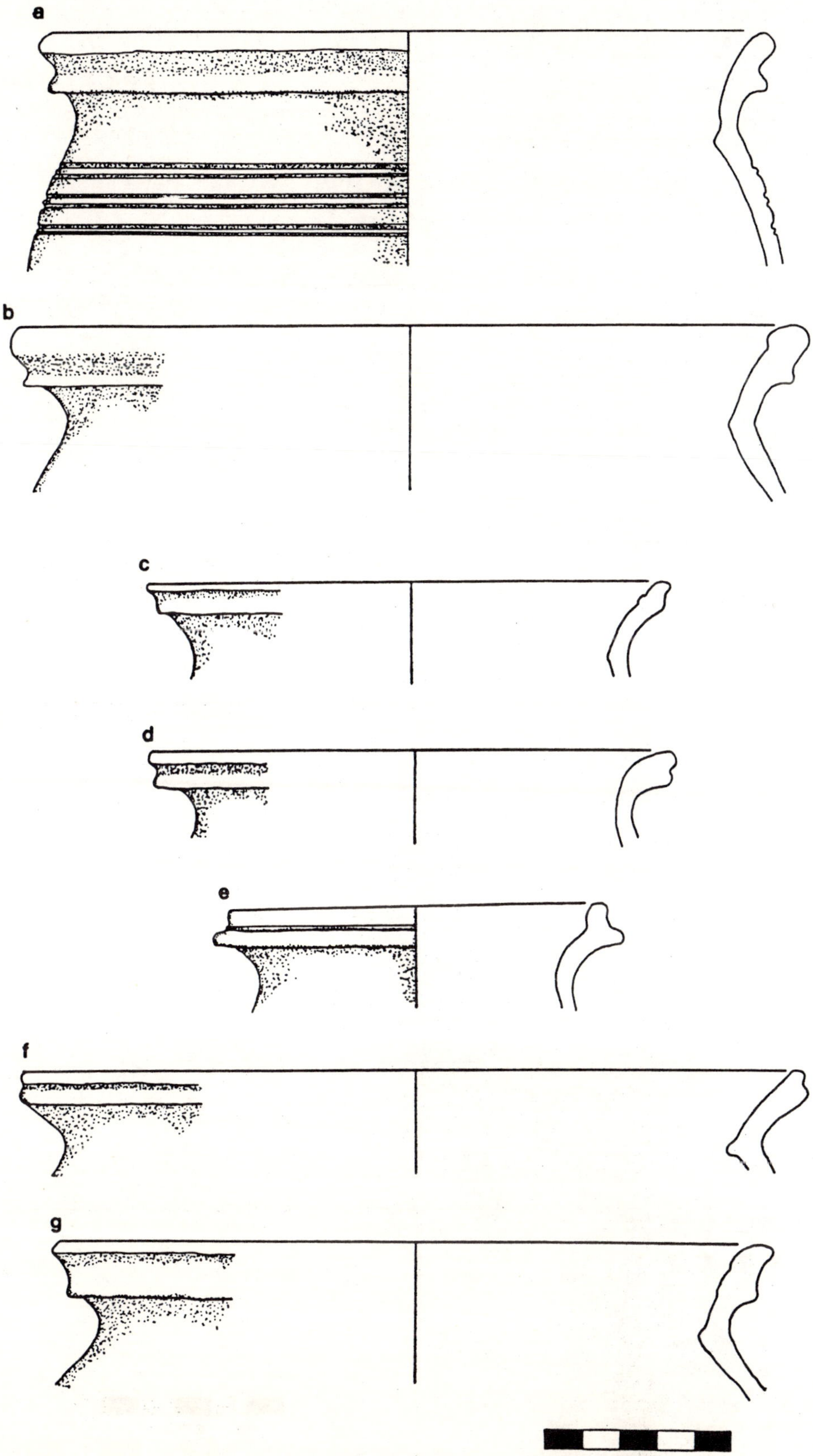

Figure A.39 NMQ4 Flange Rim Restricted Vessels

ä
b
c
d
e
f
g

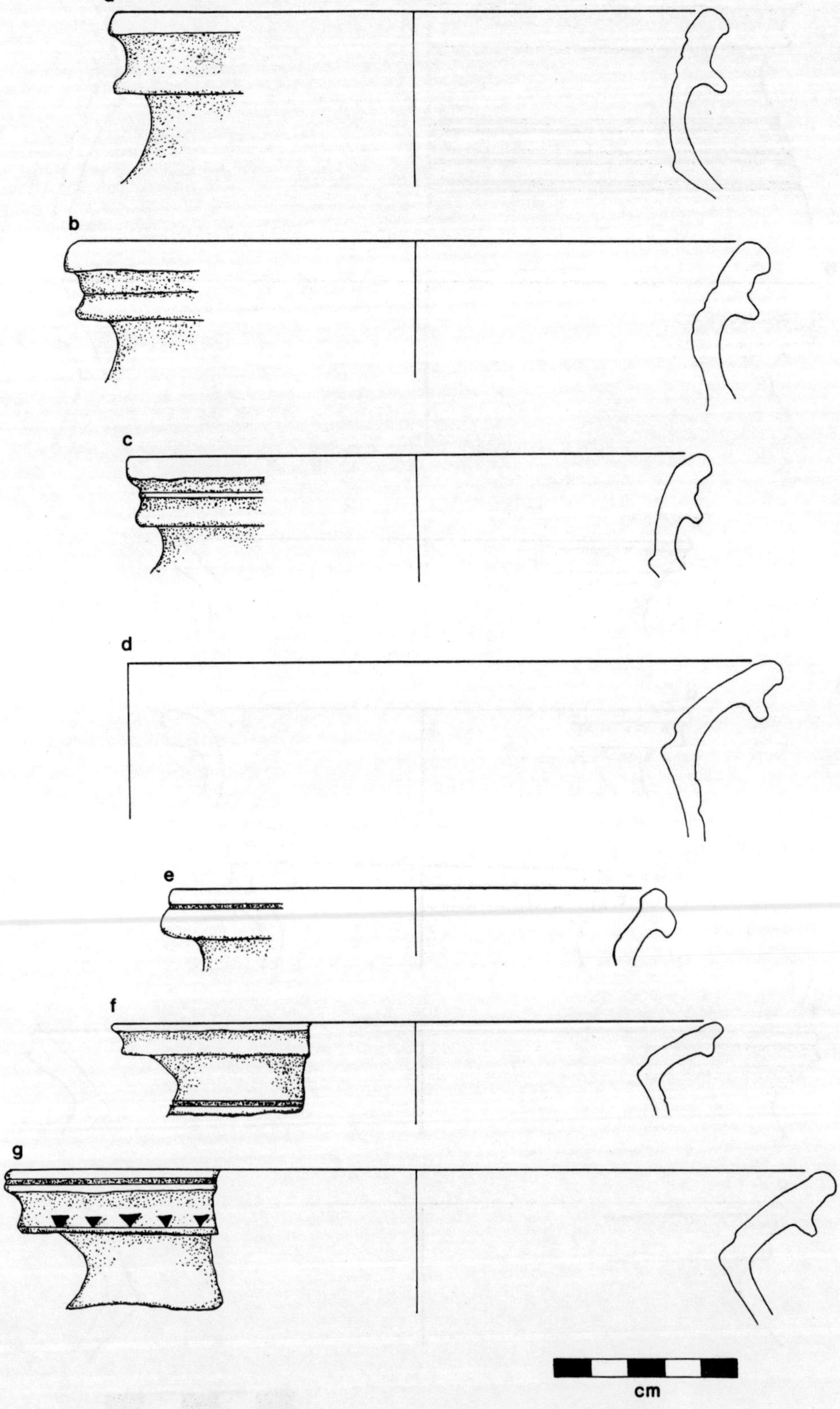

Figure A.40 NMQ4 Flange Rim Restricted Vessels

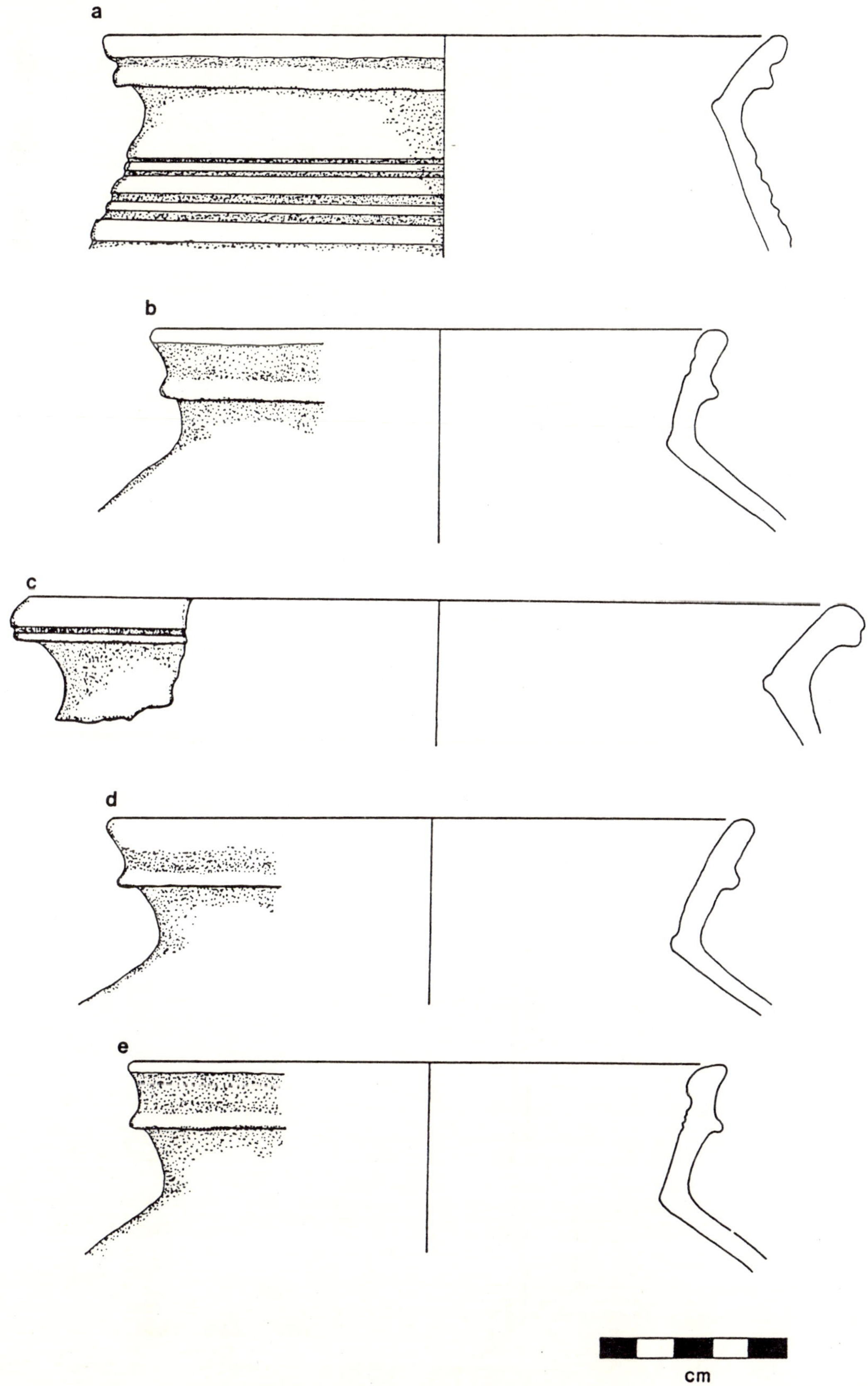

Figure A.41 NMQ4 Flange Rim Restricted Vessels

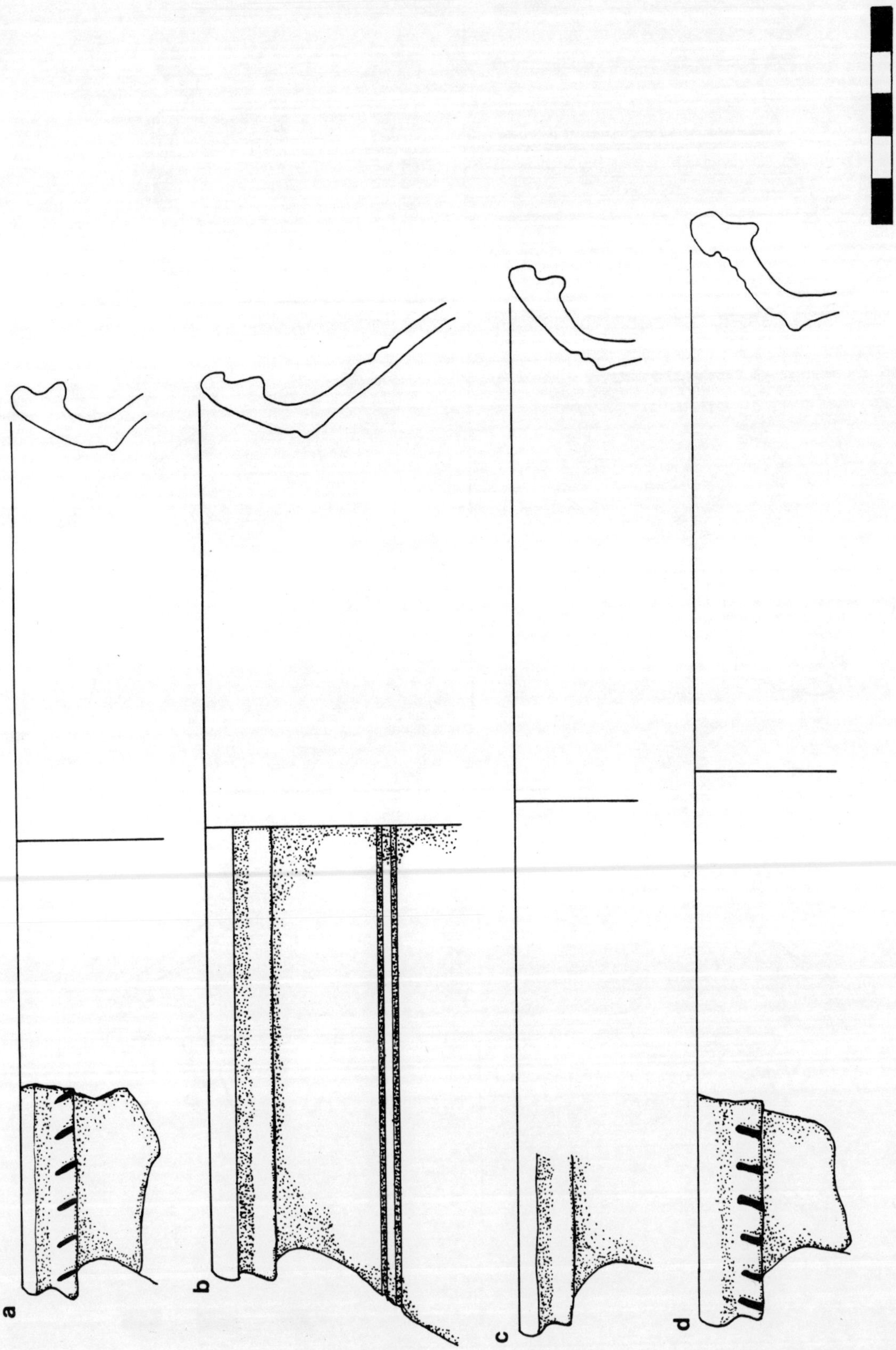

Figure A.42 NMQ4 Flange Rim Restricted Vessels

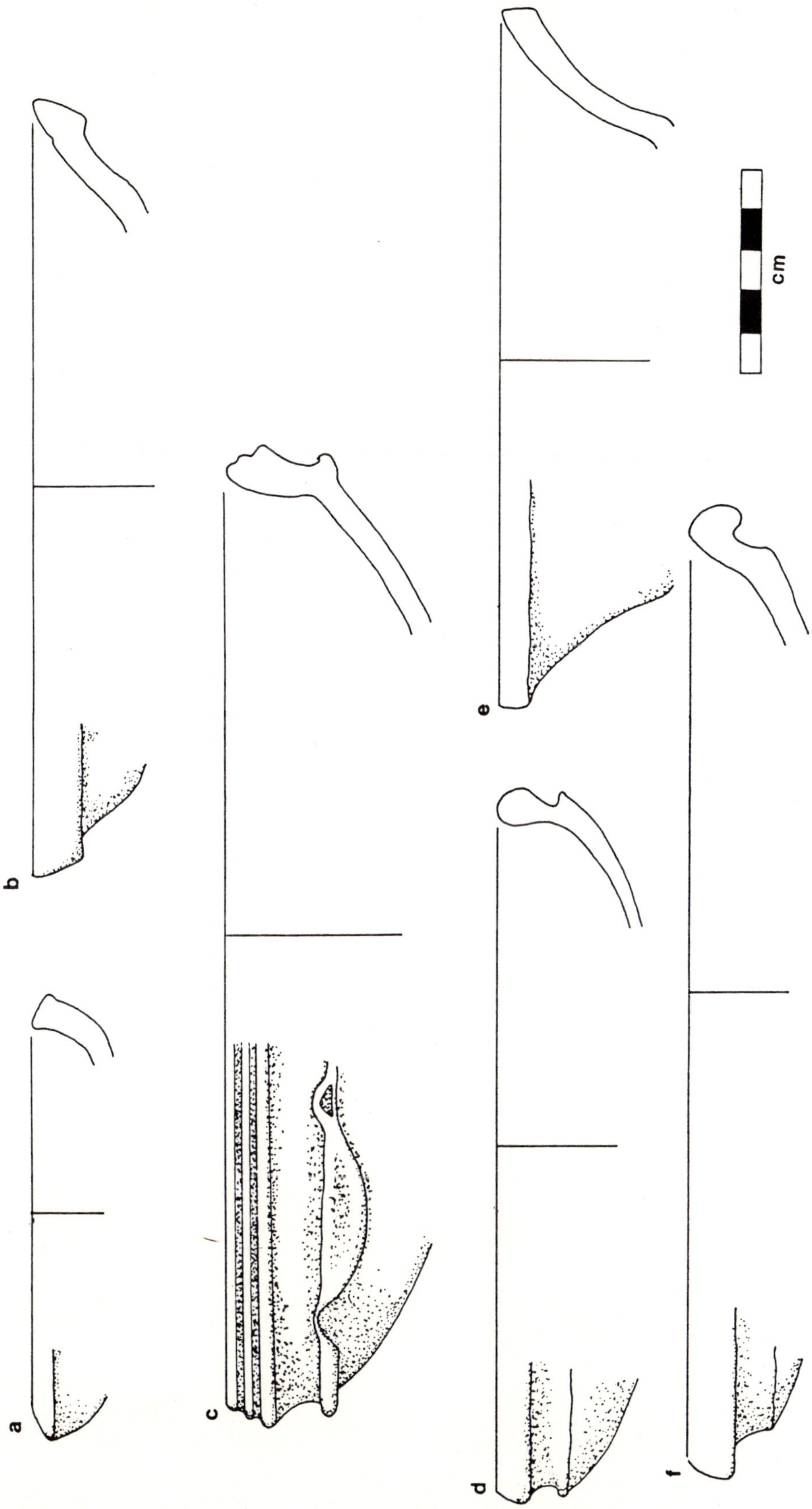

Figure A.43 NMQ5 Unrestricted Vessels

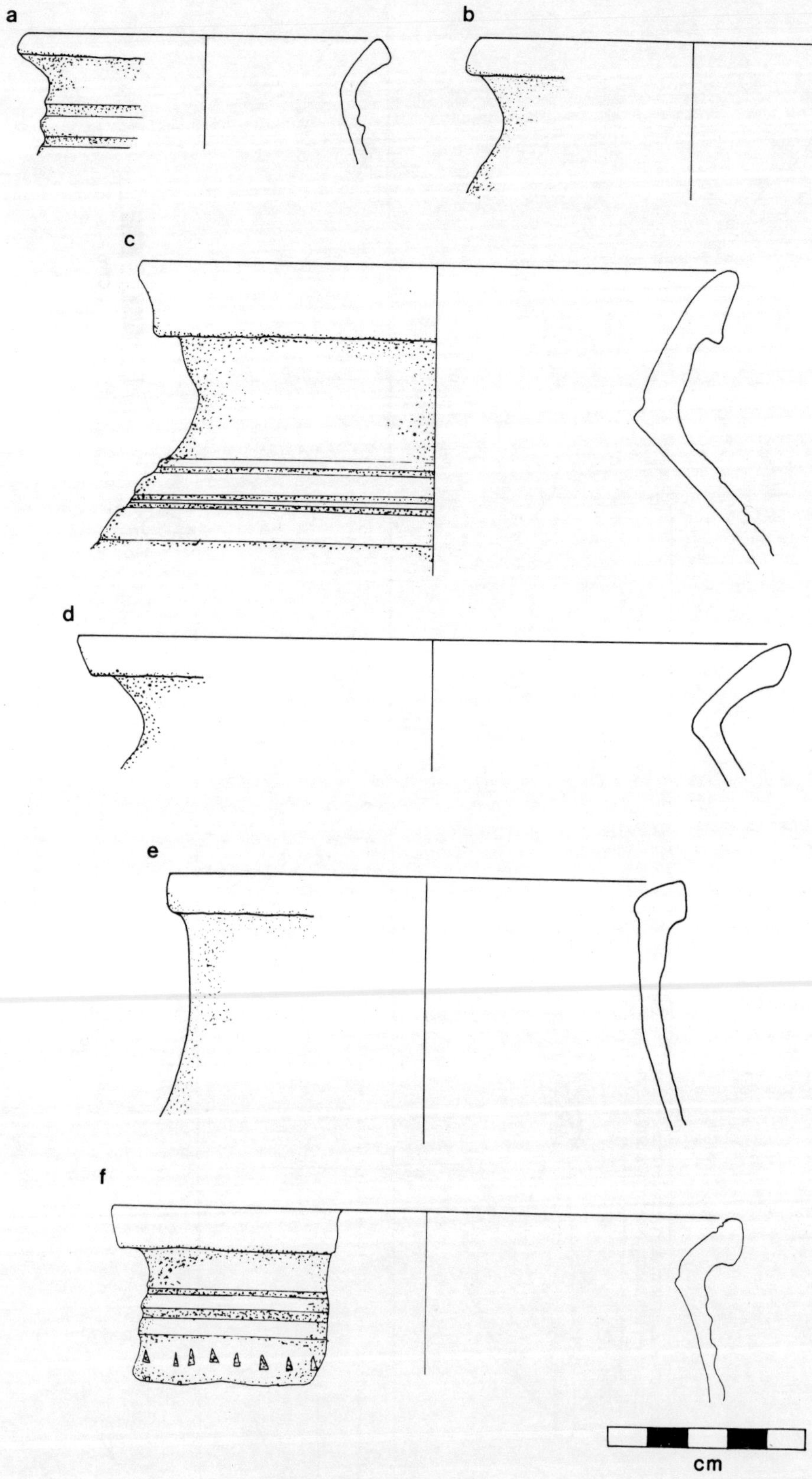

Figure A.44 NMQ5 Straight Rim Restricted Vessels

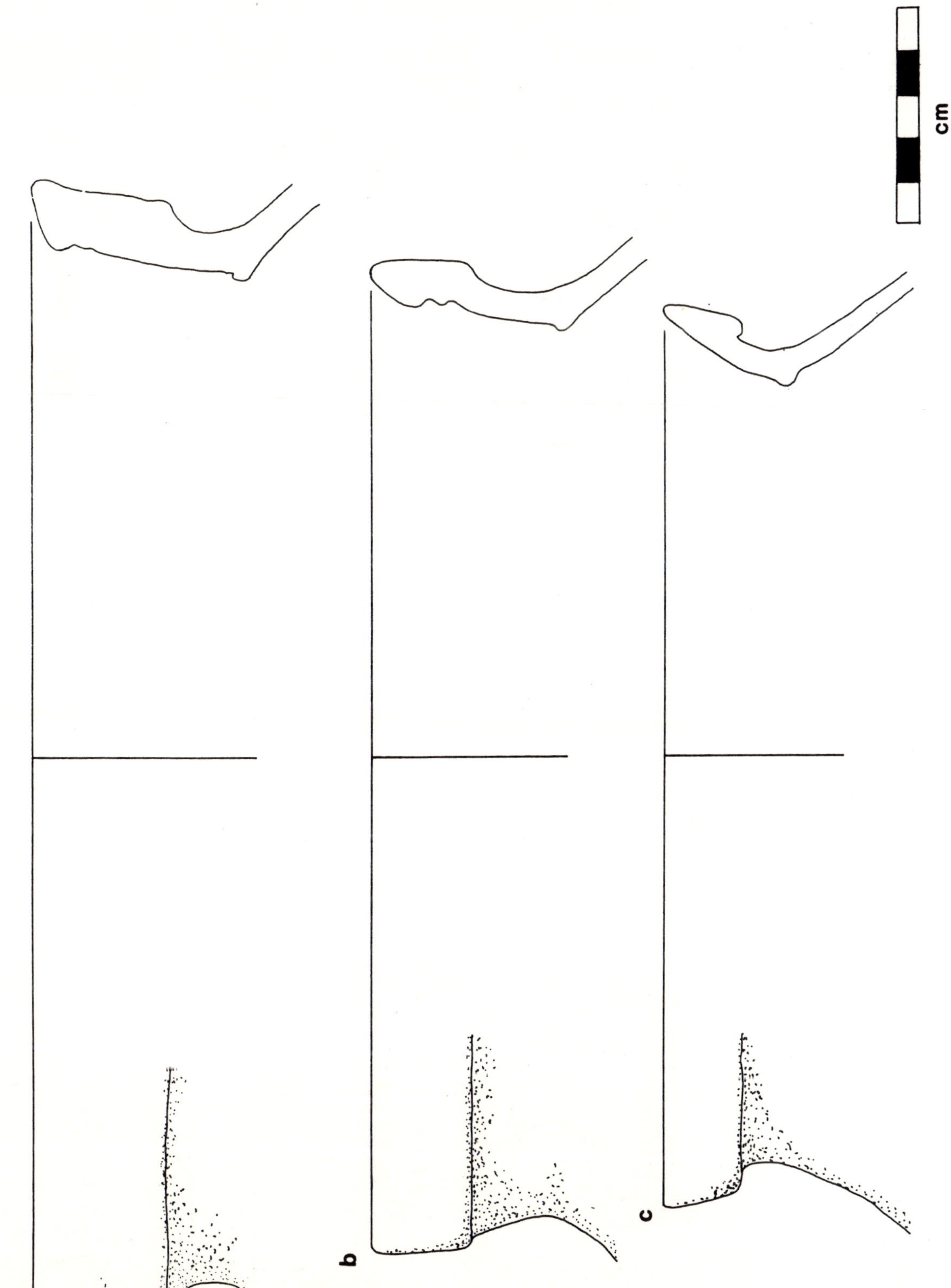

Figure A.45 NMQ5 Straight Rim Restricted Vessels

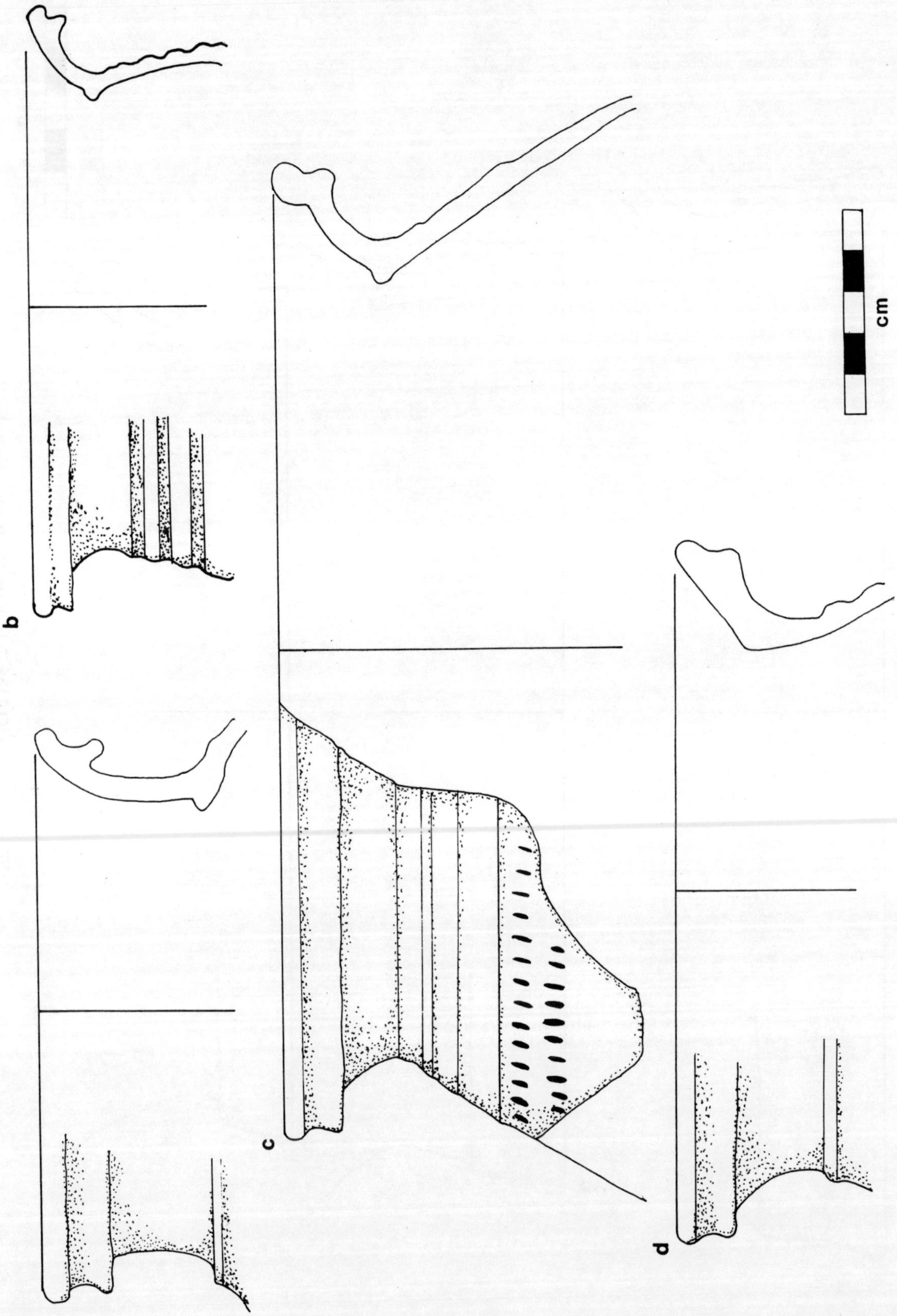

Figure A.46 NMQ5 Flange Rim Restricted Vessels

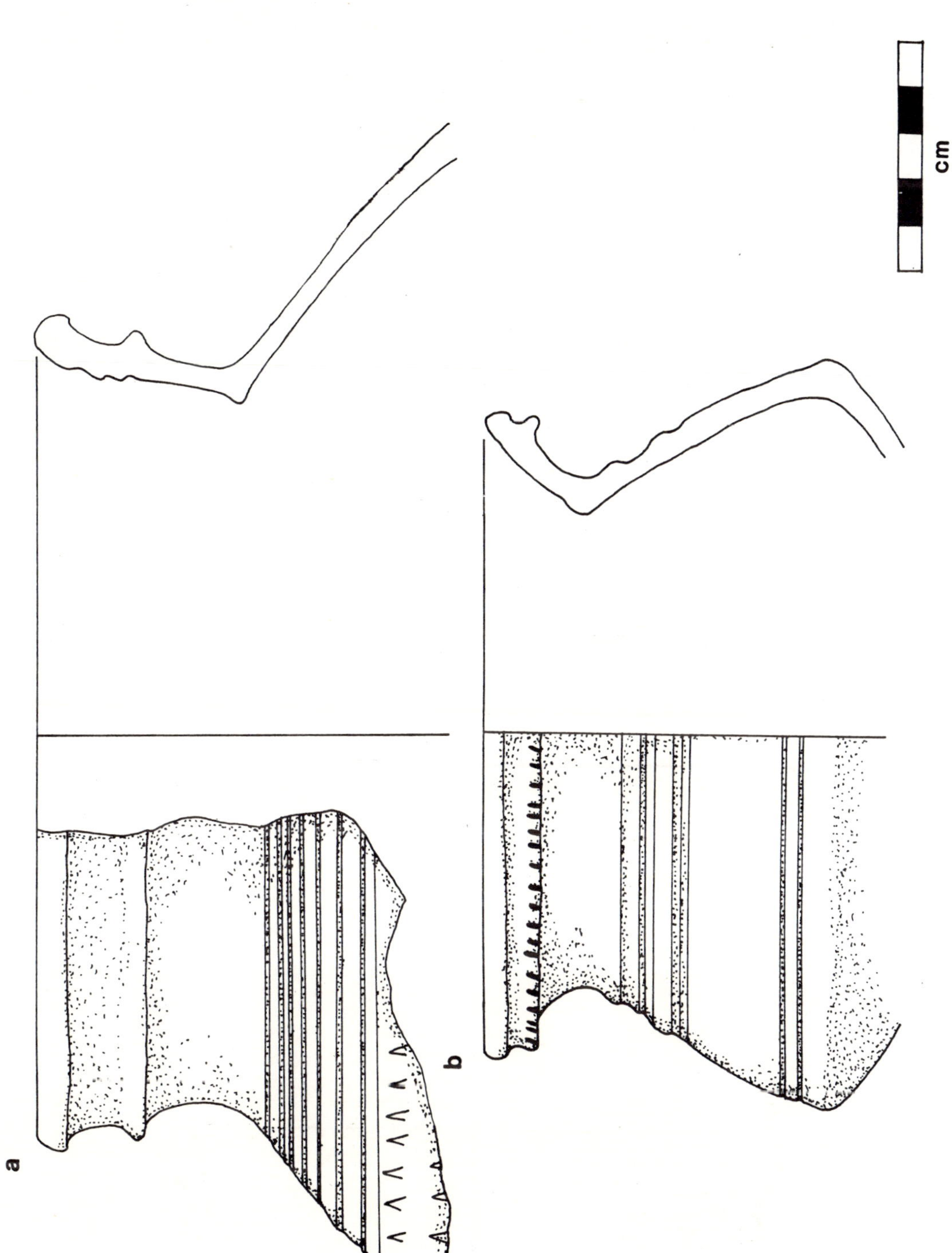

Figure A.47NMQ5 Flange Rim Restricted Vessels

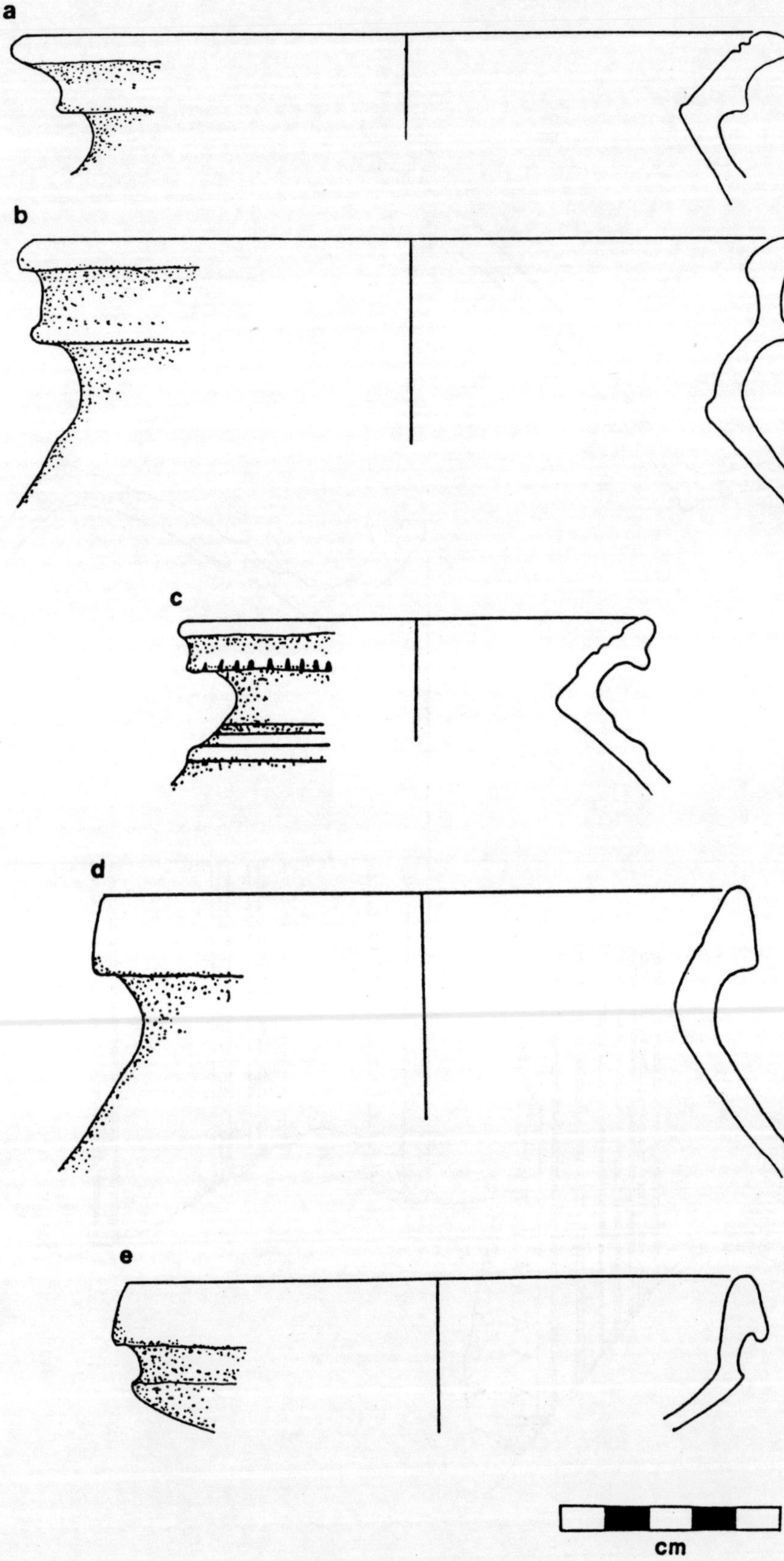

Figure A.48 NMQ6 Vessels

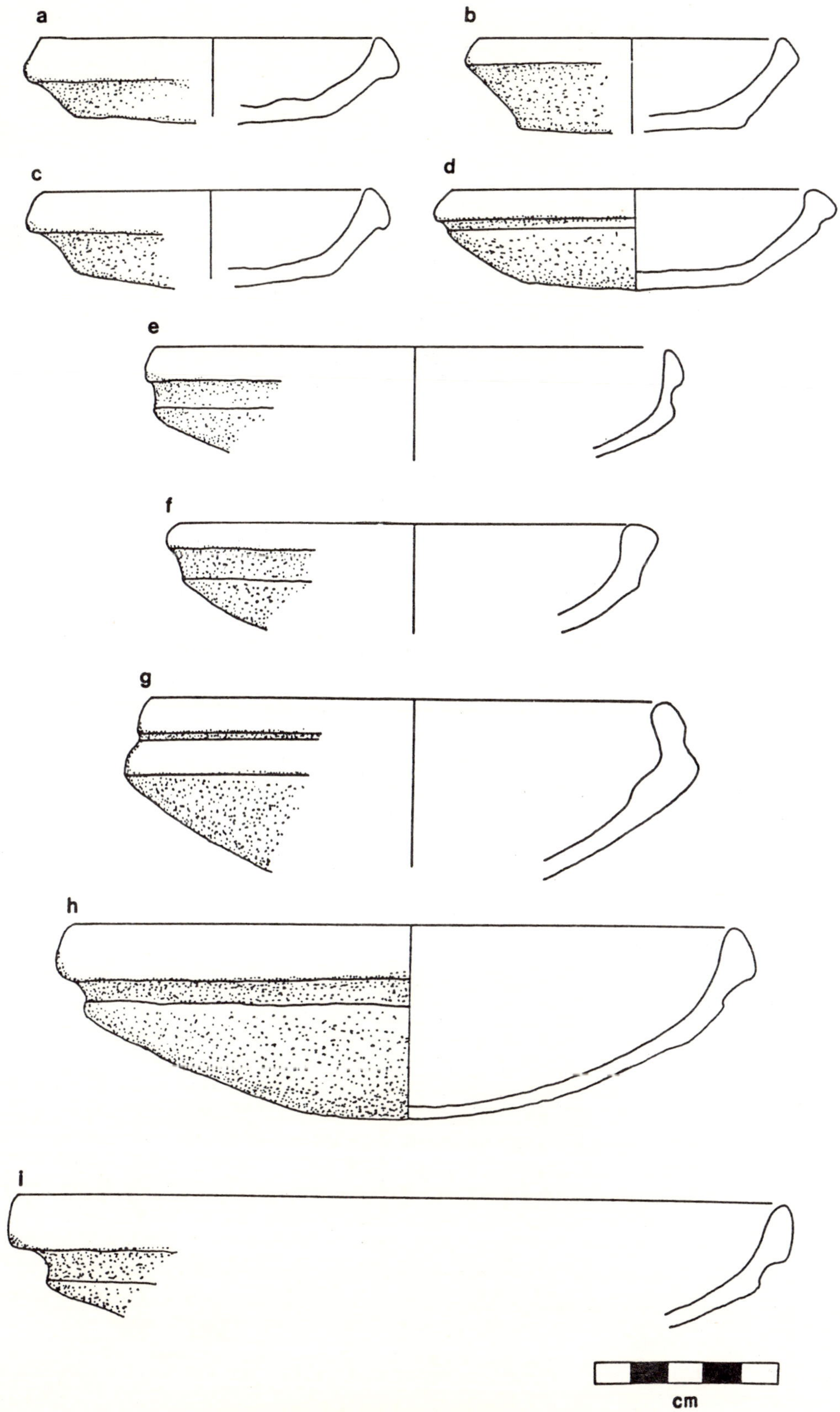

Figure A.49 NMQ7 Lamps and Shallow Bowls

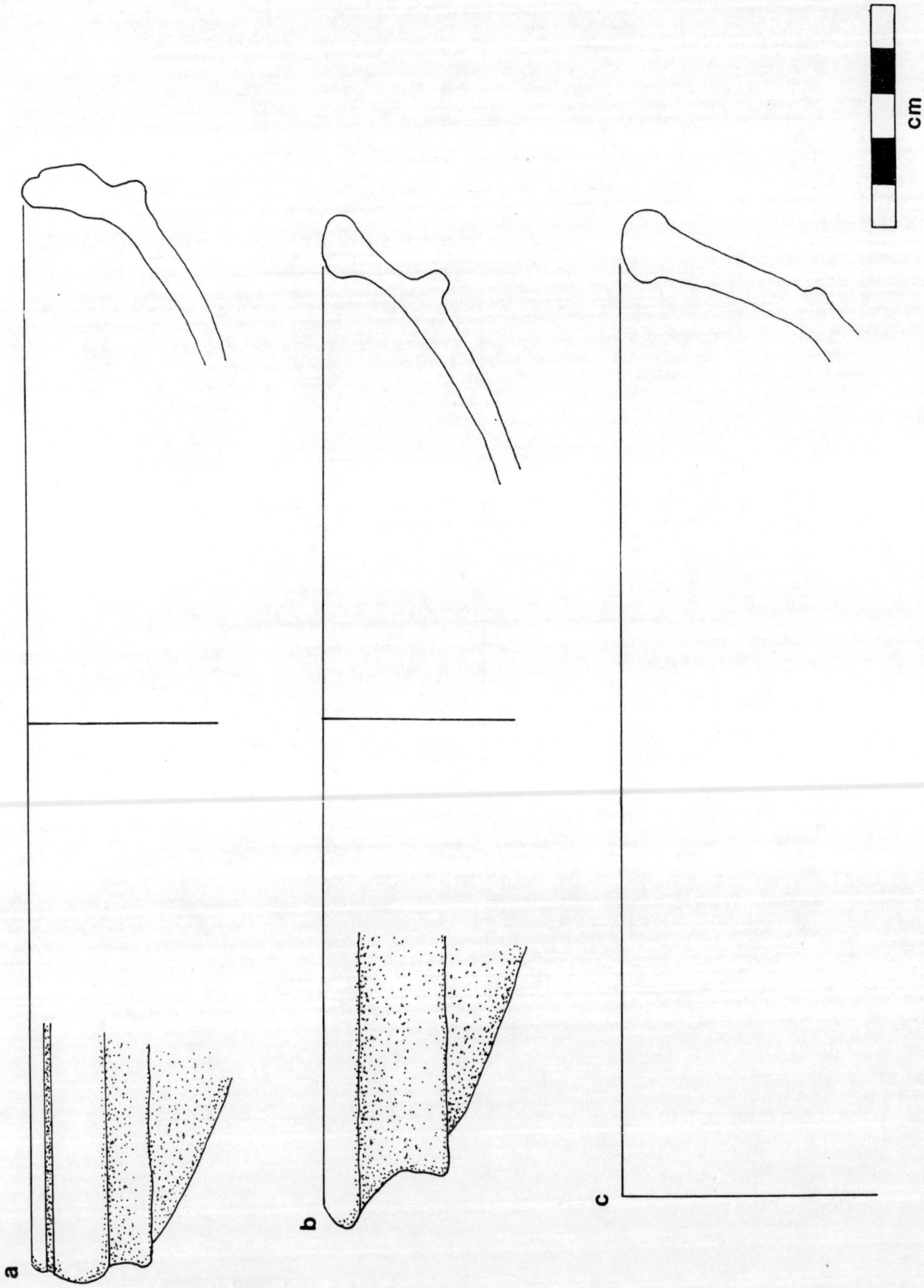

Figure A.50 NMQ7 Shallow Bowls

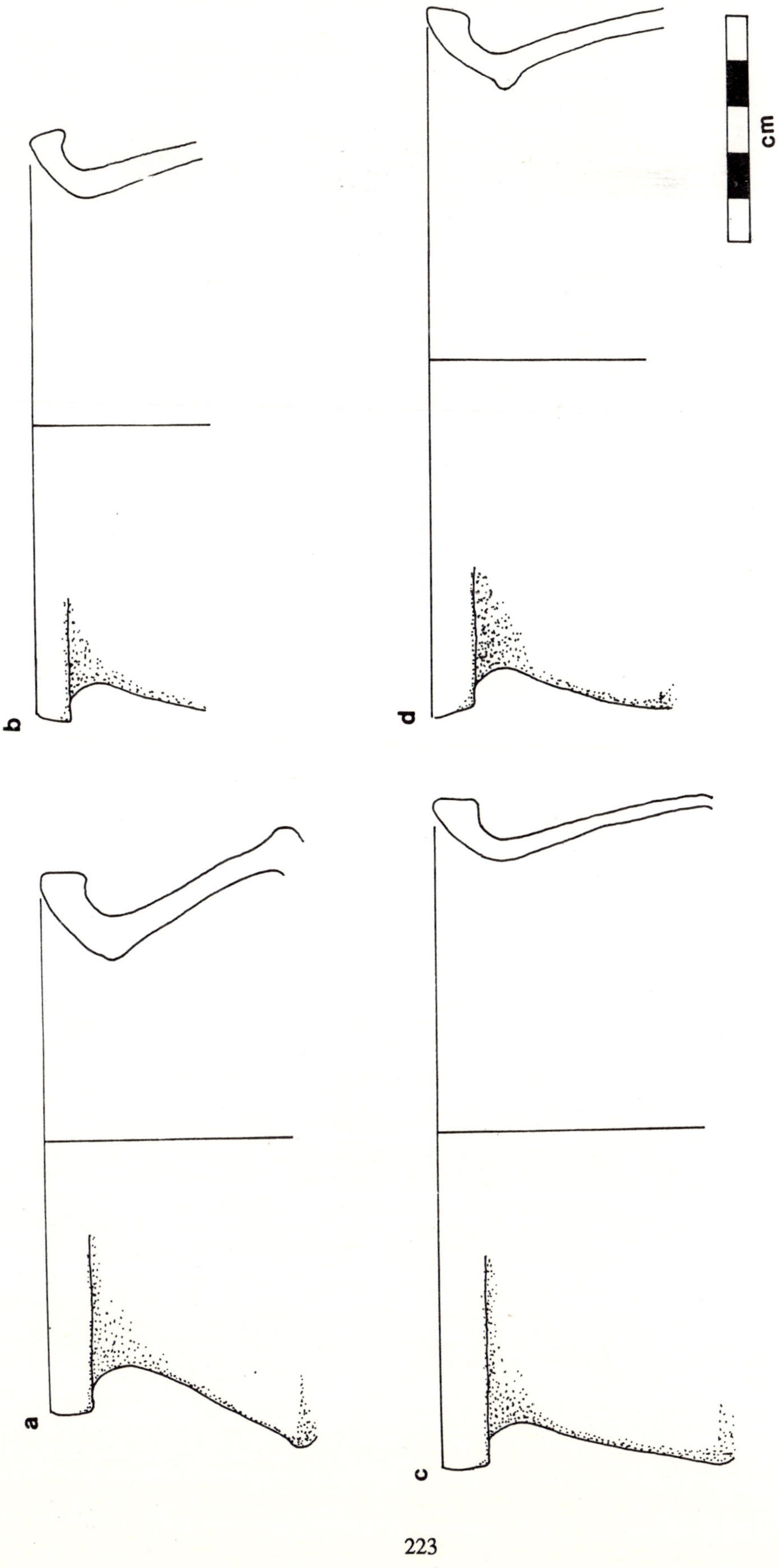

Figure A.51 NMQ7 Straight Rim Restricted Vessels

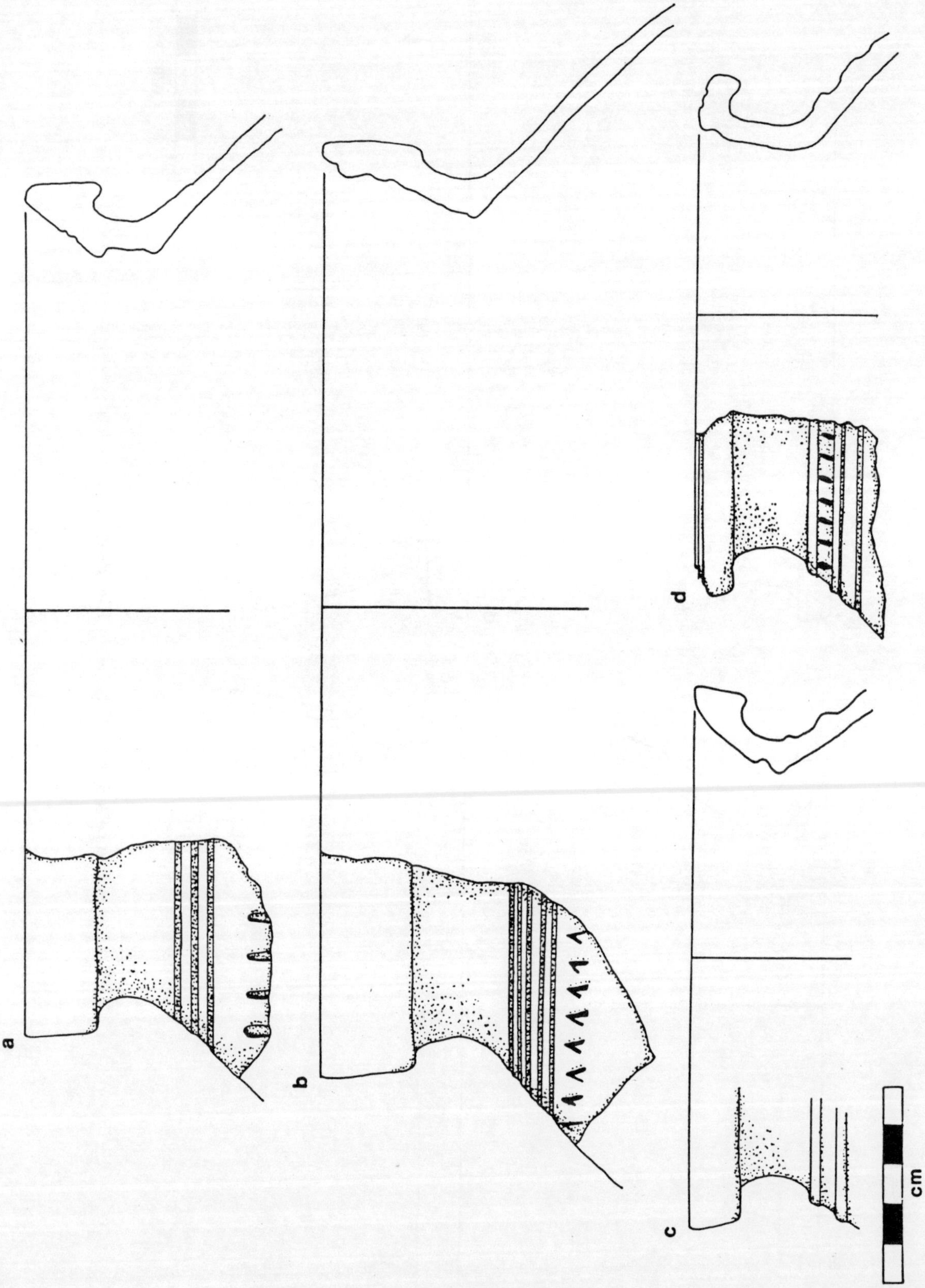

Figure A.52 NMQ7 Straight Rim Restricted Vessels

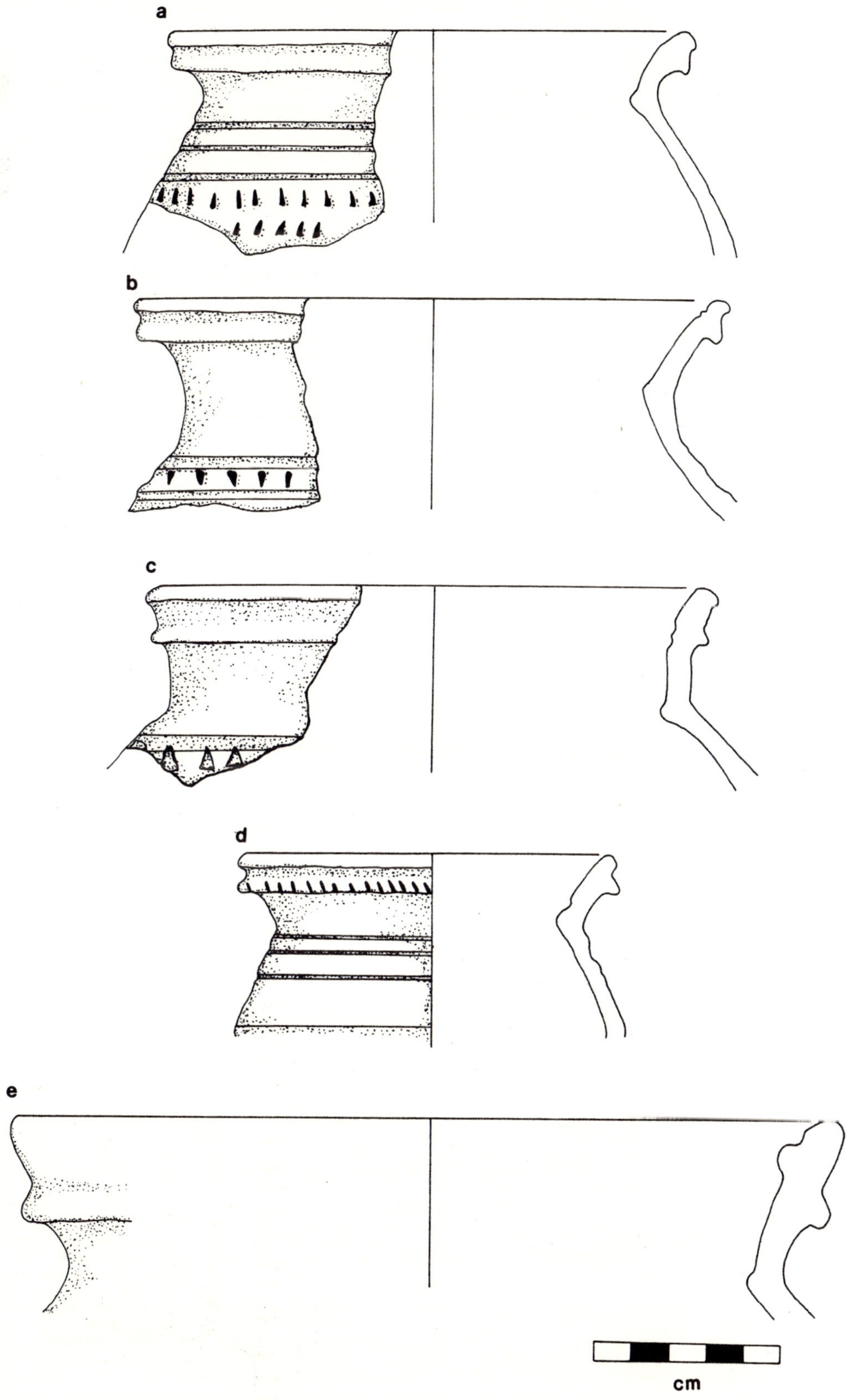

Figure A.53 NMQ7 Flange Rim Restricted Vessels

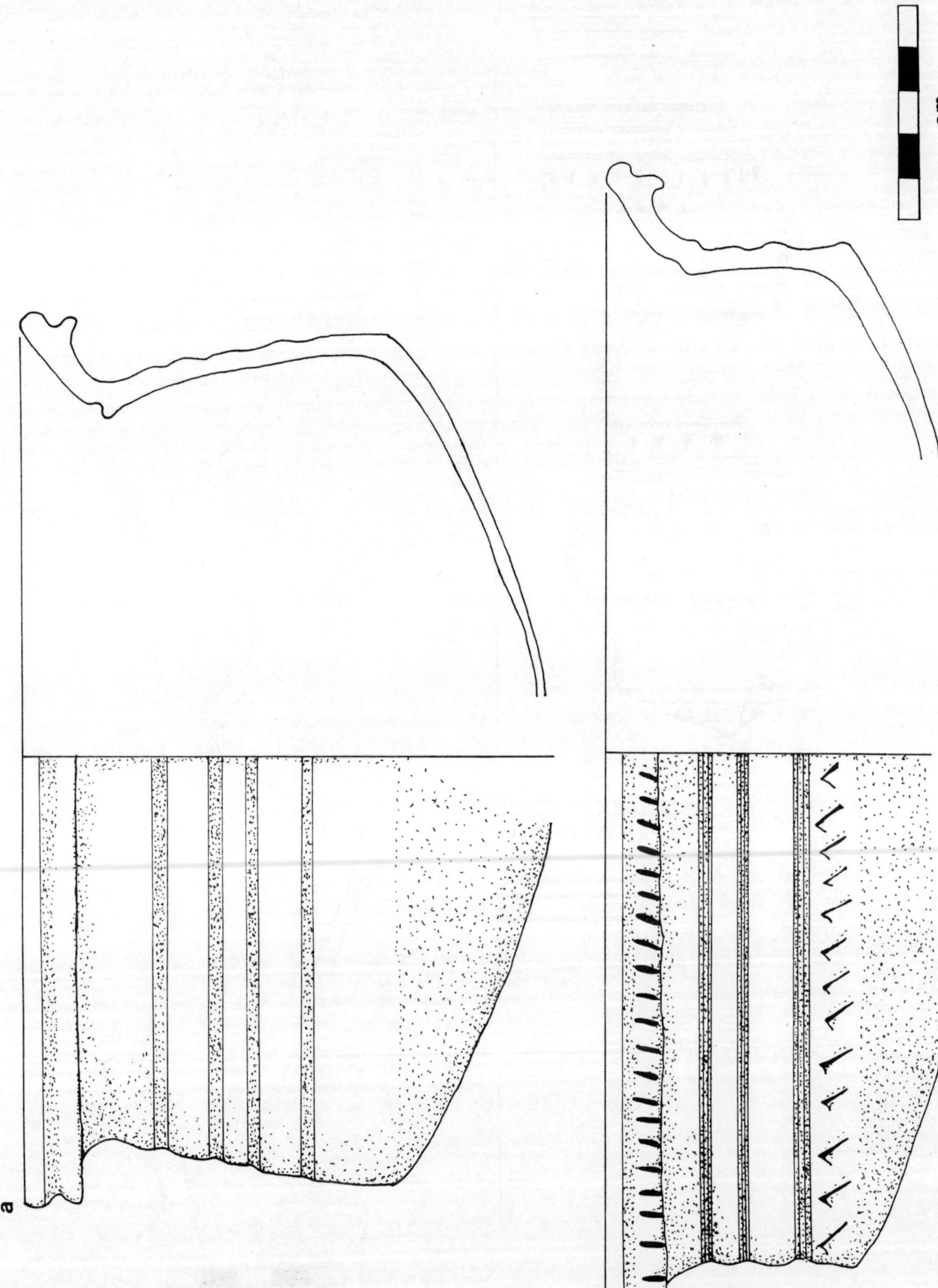

Figure A.54NMQ7 Flange Rim Restricted Vessels

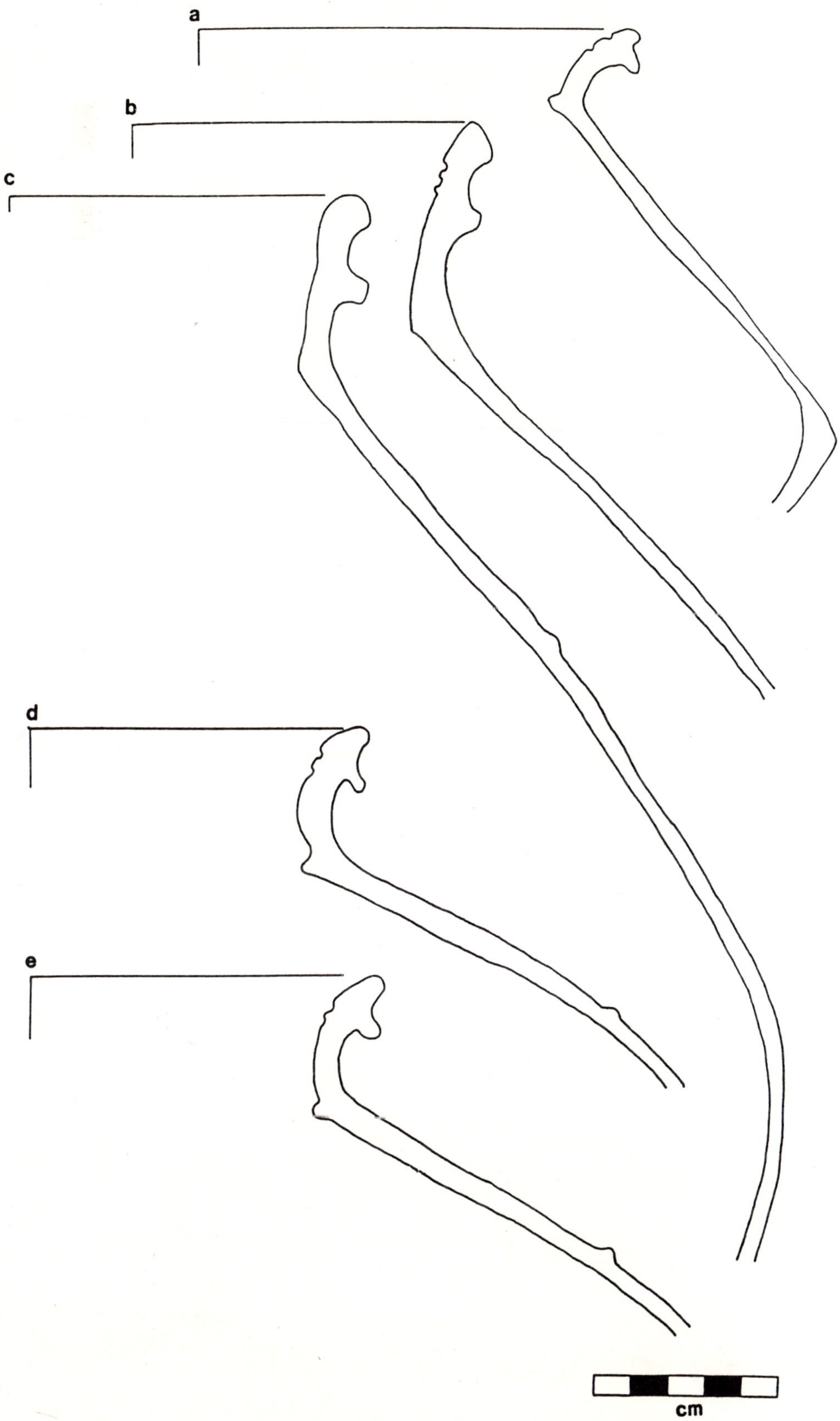

Figure A.55 NMQ7 Flange Rim Restricted Vessels

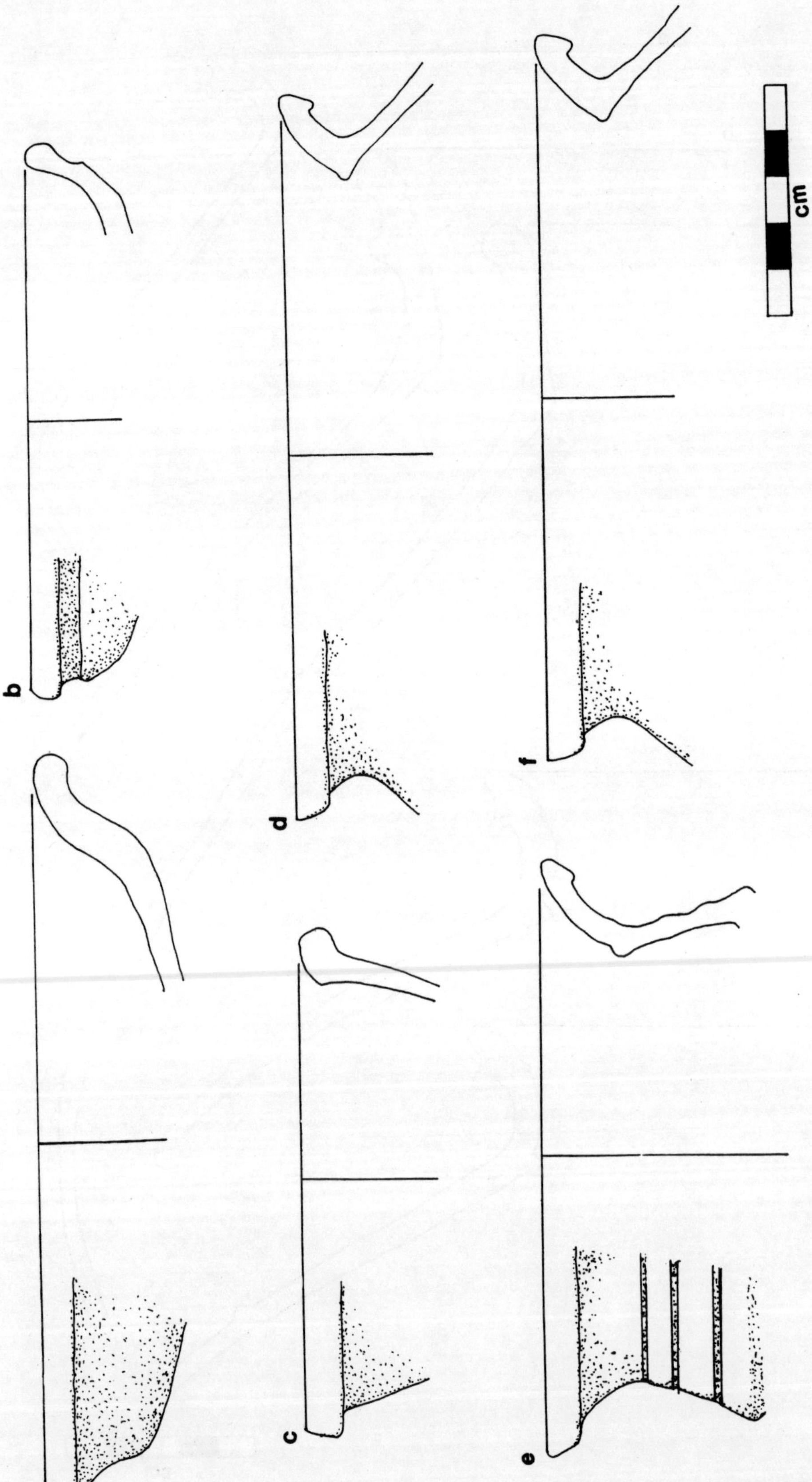

Figure A.56 NMQ8 Unrestricted Vessels and Straight Rim Restricted Vessels

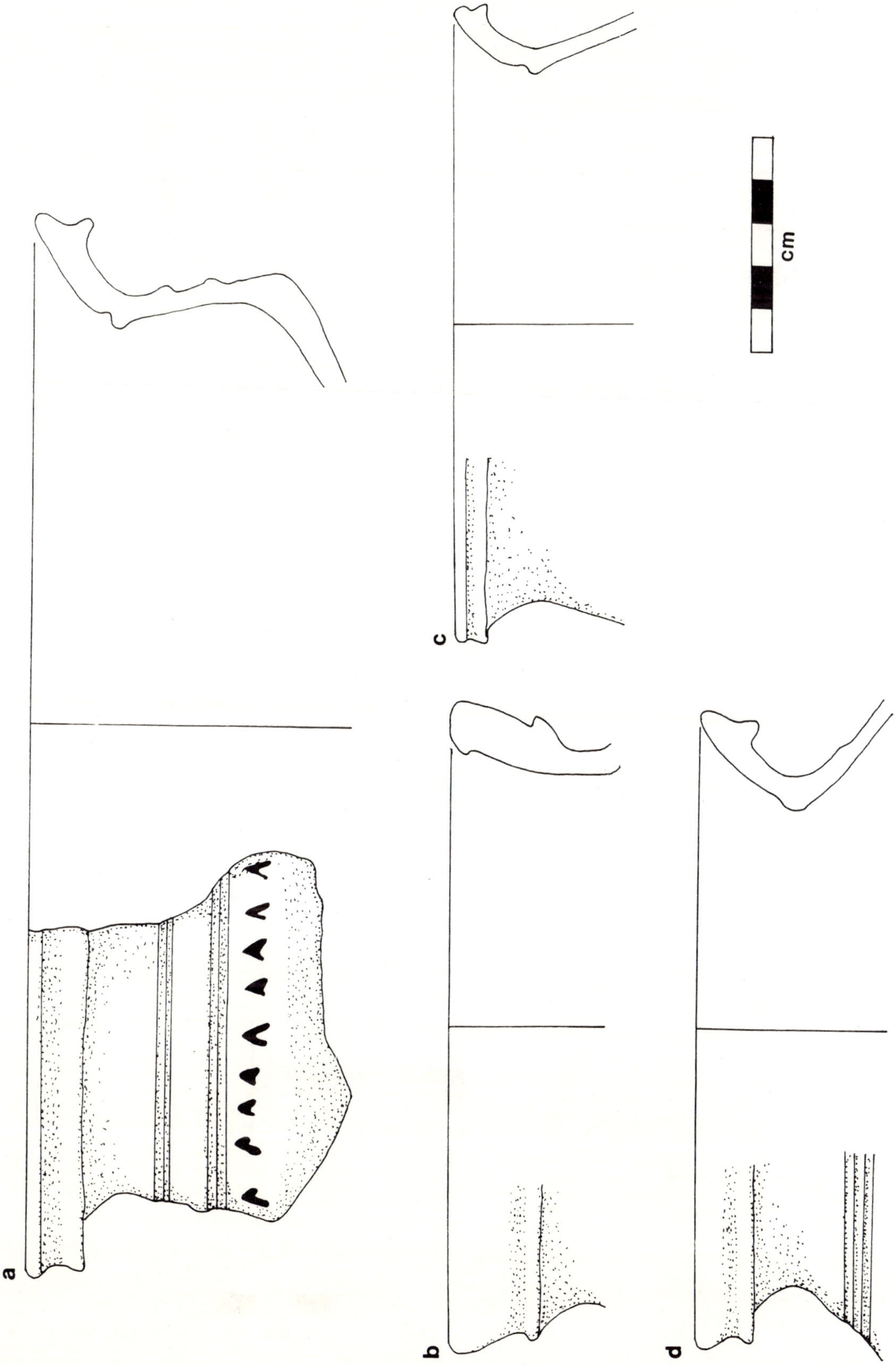

Figure A.57 NMQ8 Flange Rim Restricted Vessels

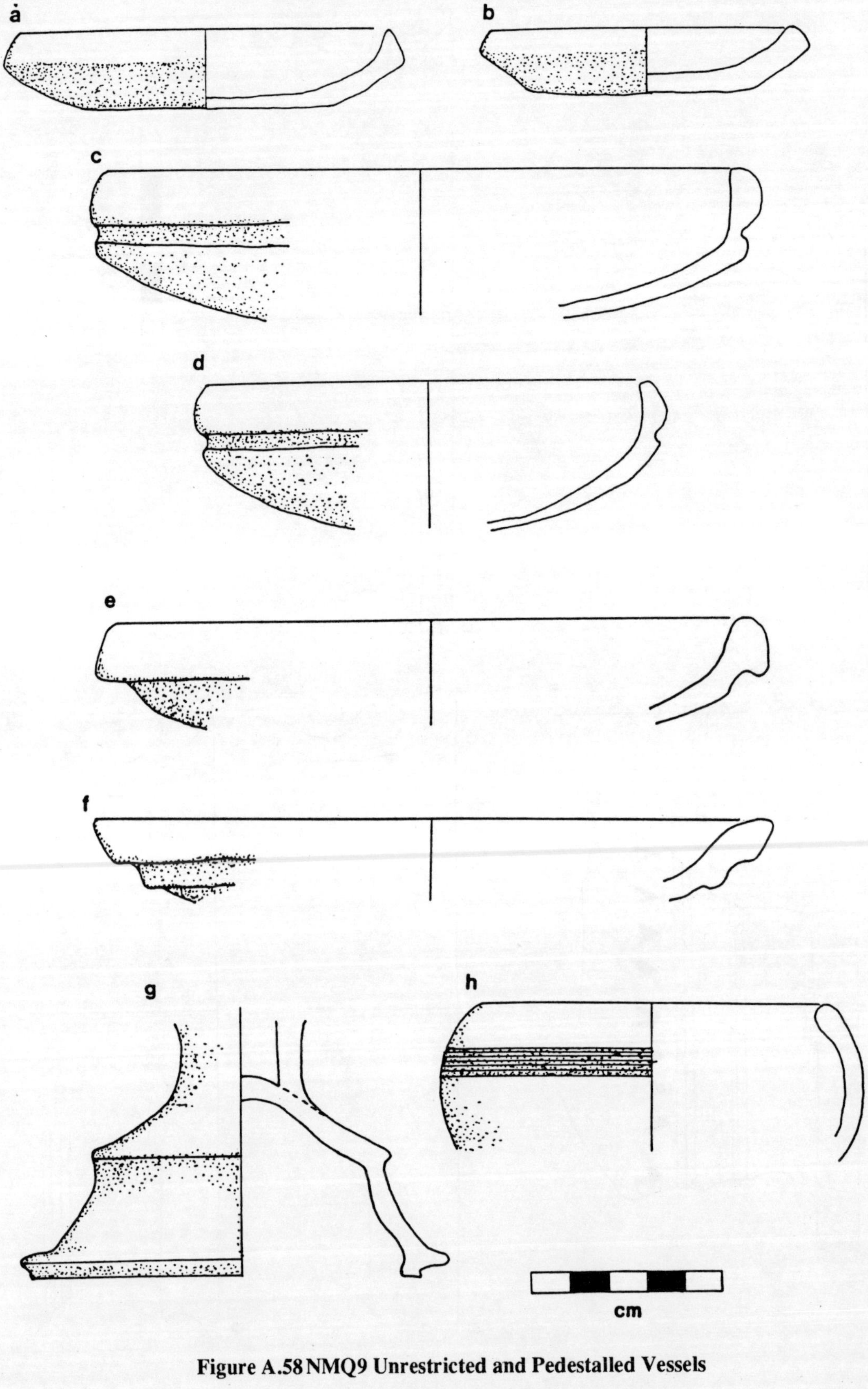

Figure A.58 NMQ9 Unrestricted and Pedestalled Vessels

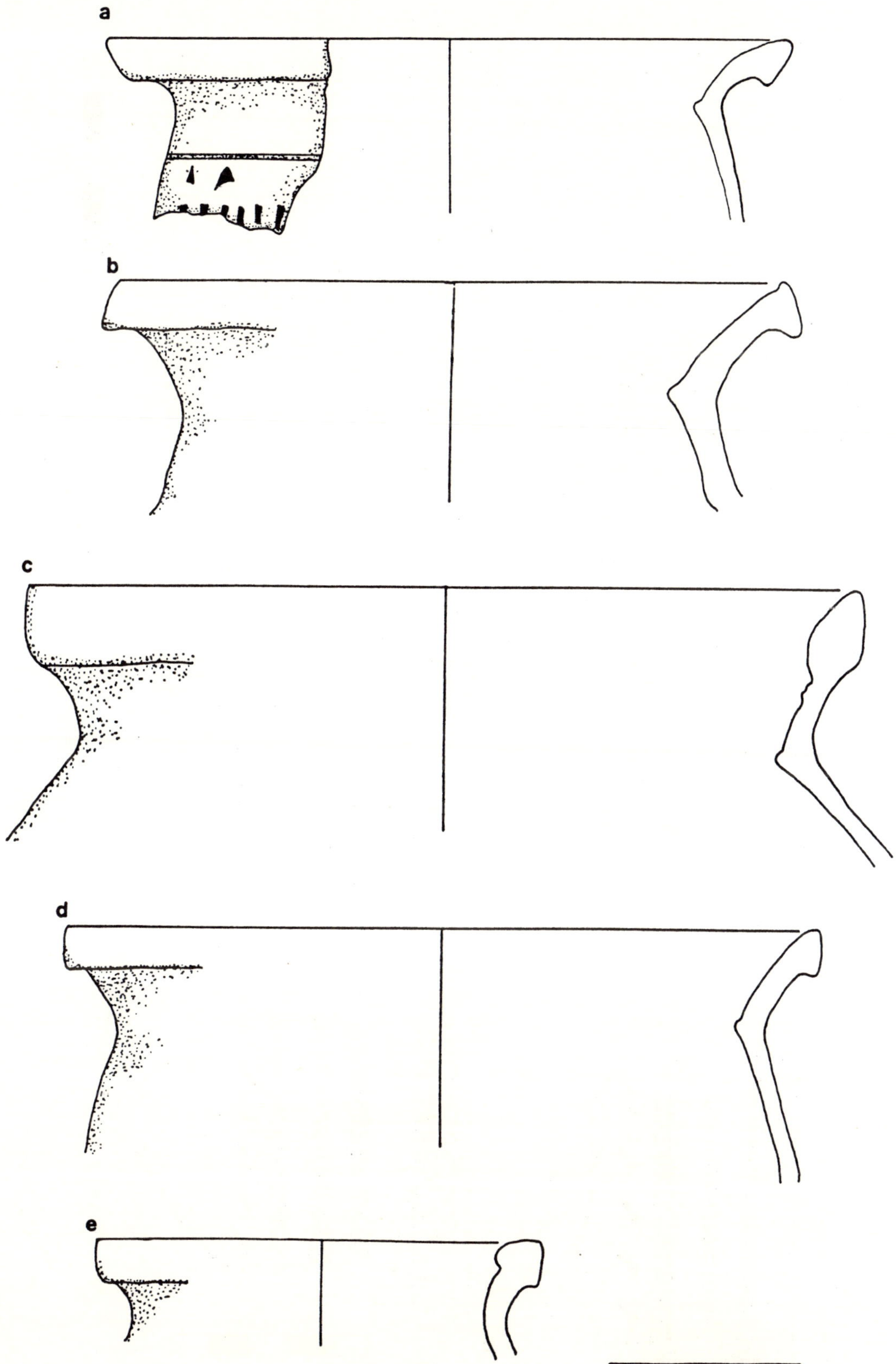

Figure A.59 NMQ9 Straight Rim Restricted Vessels

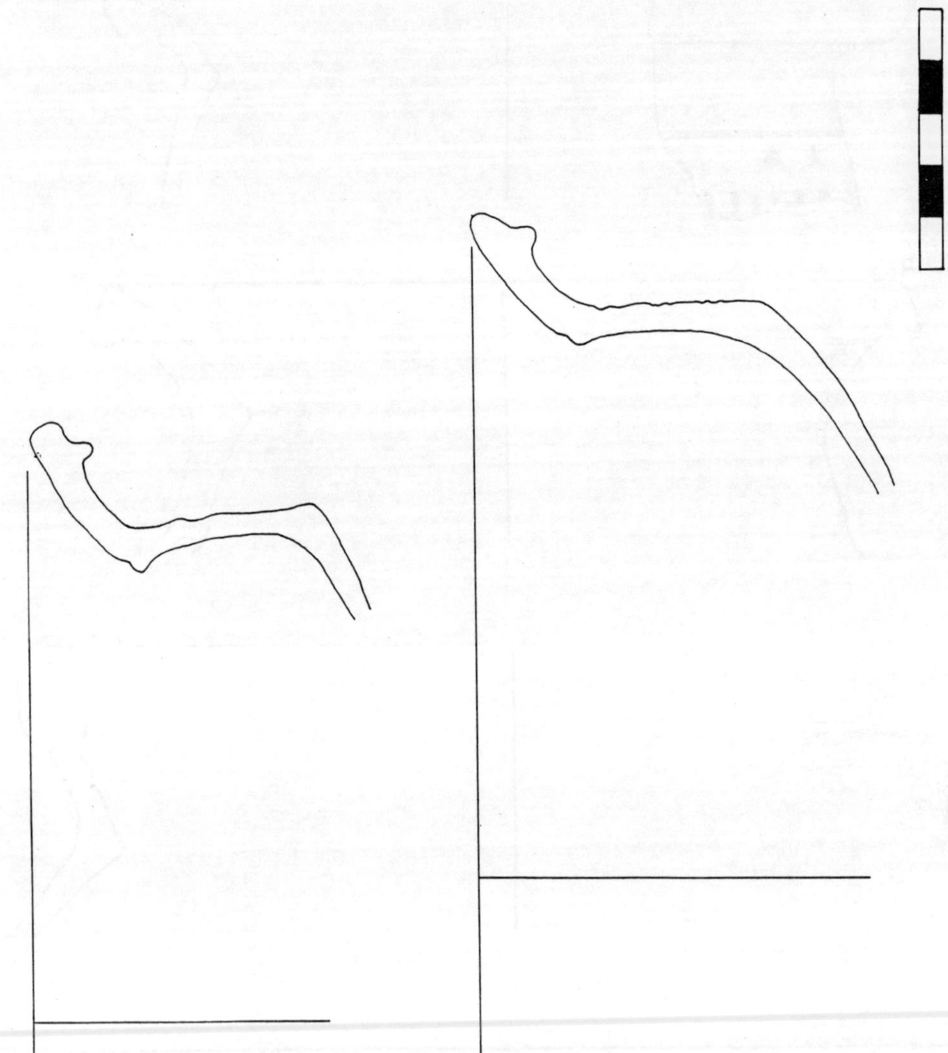

Figure A.60 NMQ9 Flange Rim Restricted Vessels

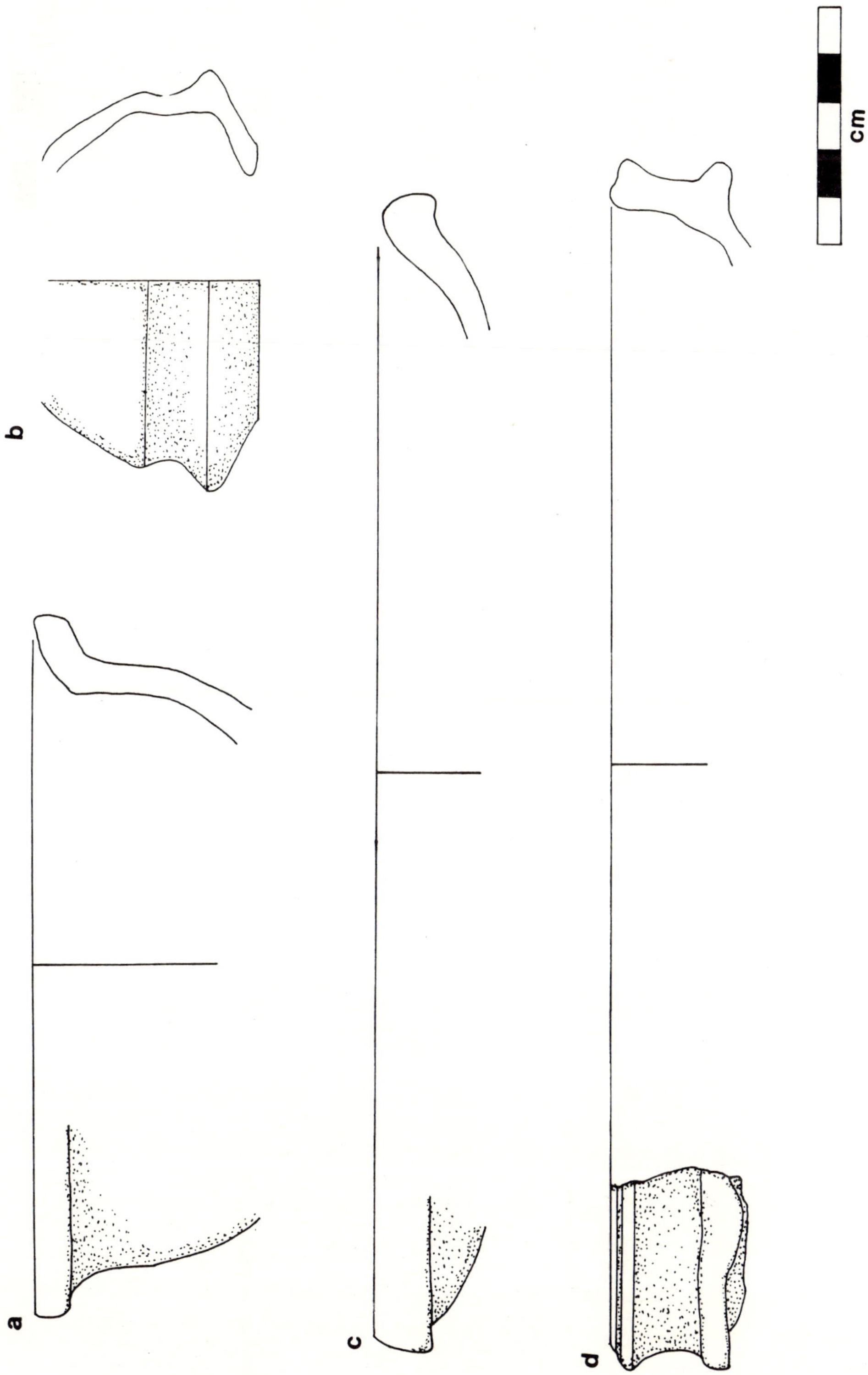

Figure A.61 NMQ10 Other Bowls and Conical Lid

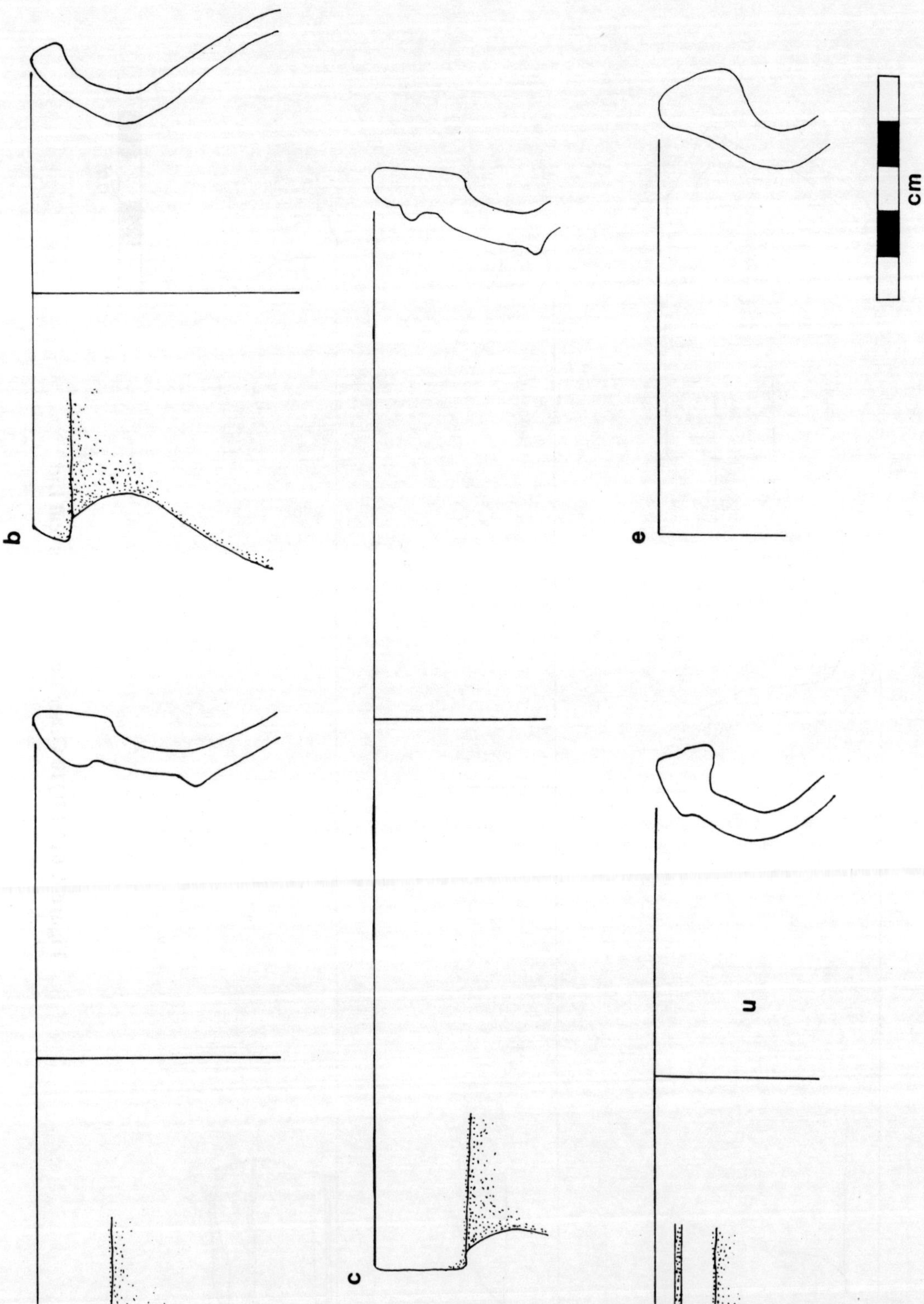

Figure A.62 NMQ10 Straight Rim Restricted Vessels

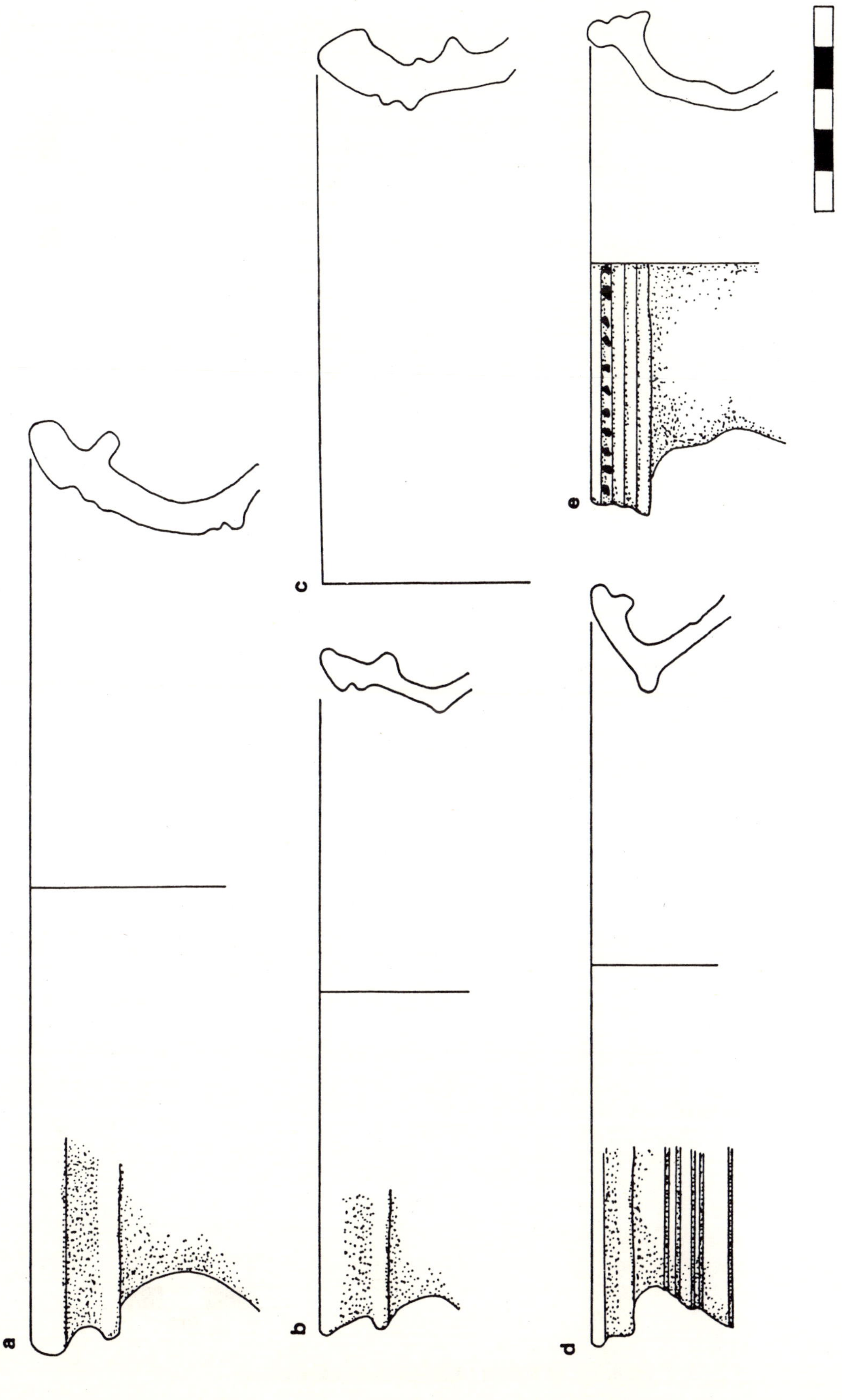

Figure A.63 NMQ10 Flange Rim Restricted Vessels

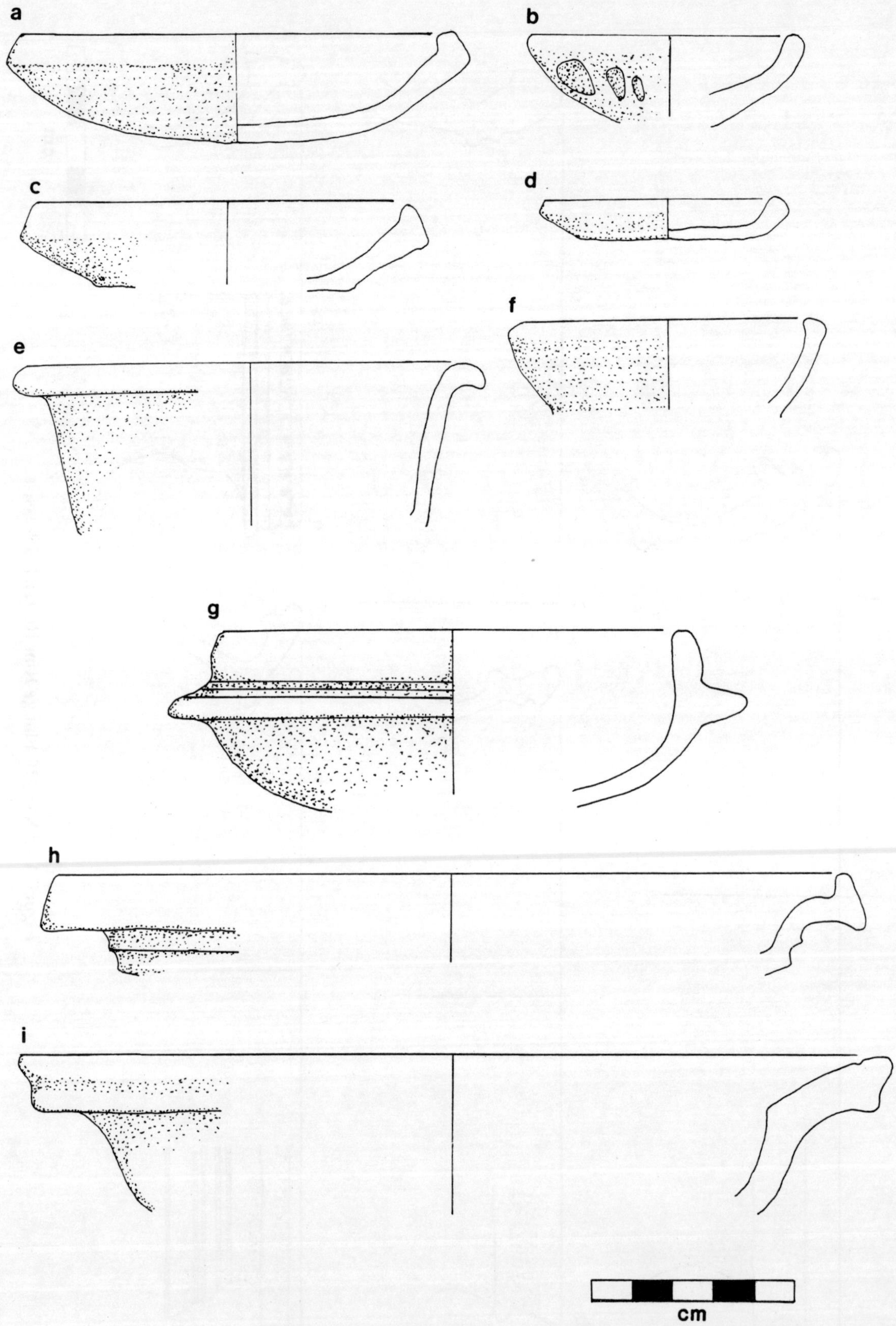

Figure A.64 NMQ12 Lamps and Other Bowls

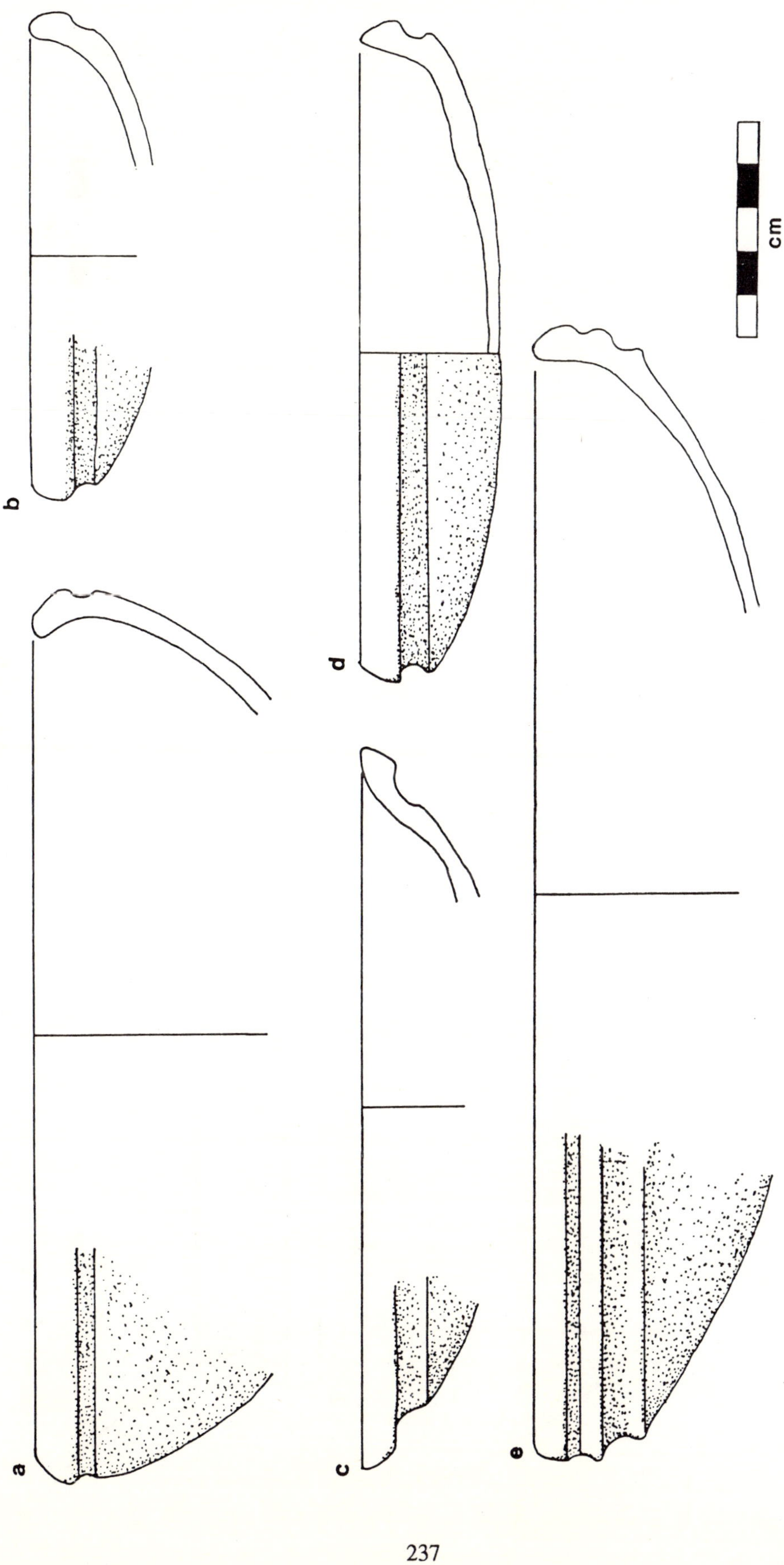

Figure A.65 NMQ12 Shallow Bowls

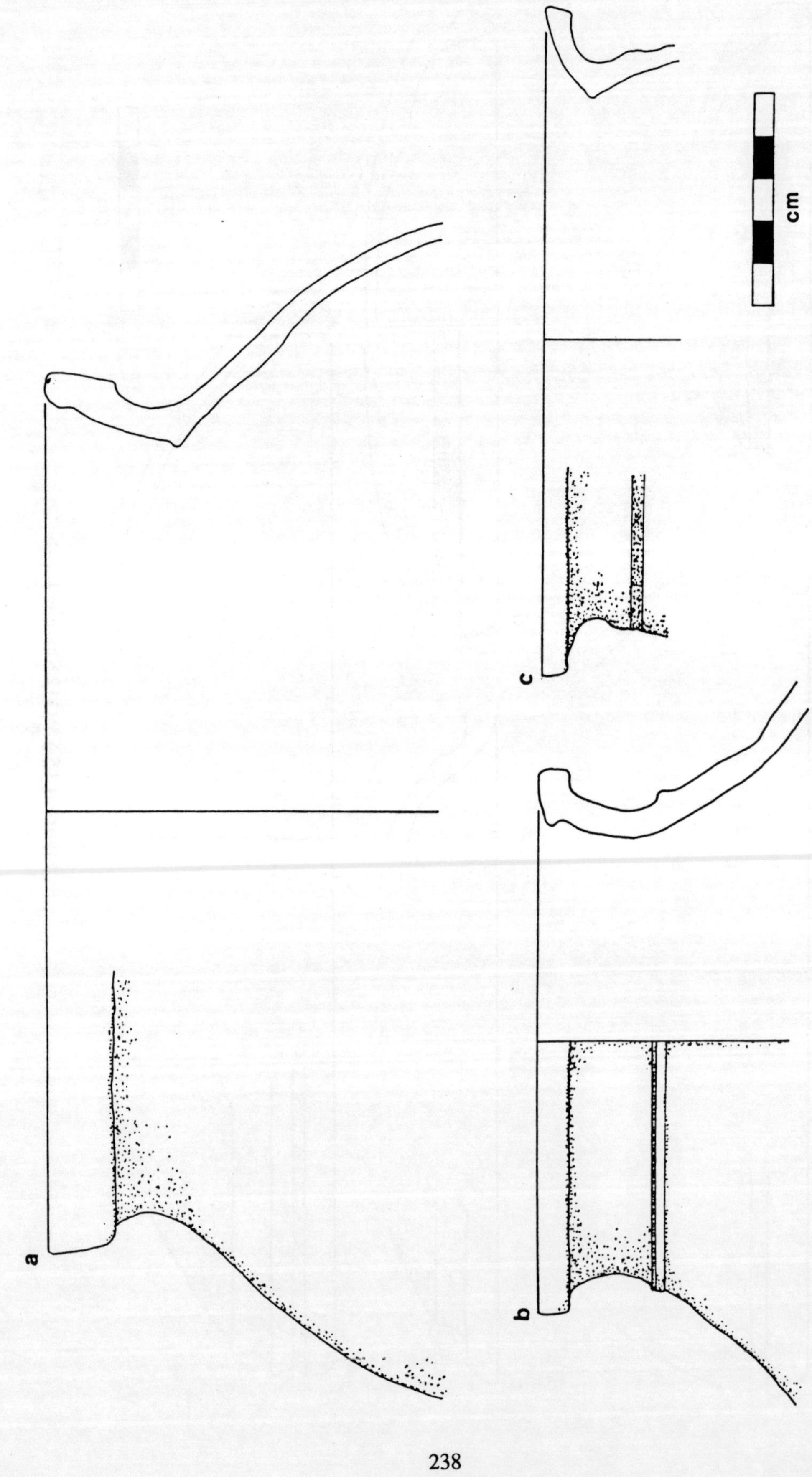

Figure A.66 NMQ12 Straight Rim Restricted Vessels

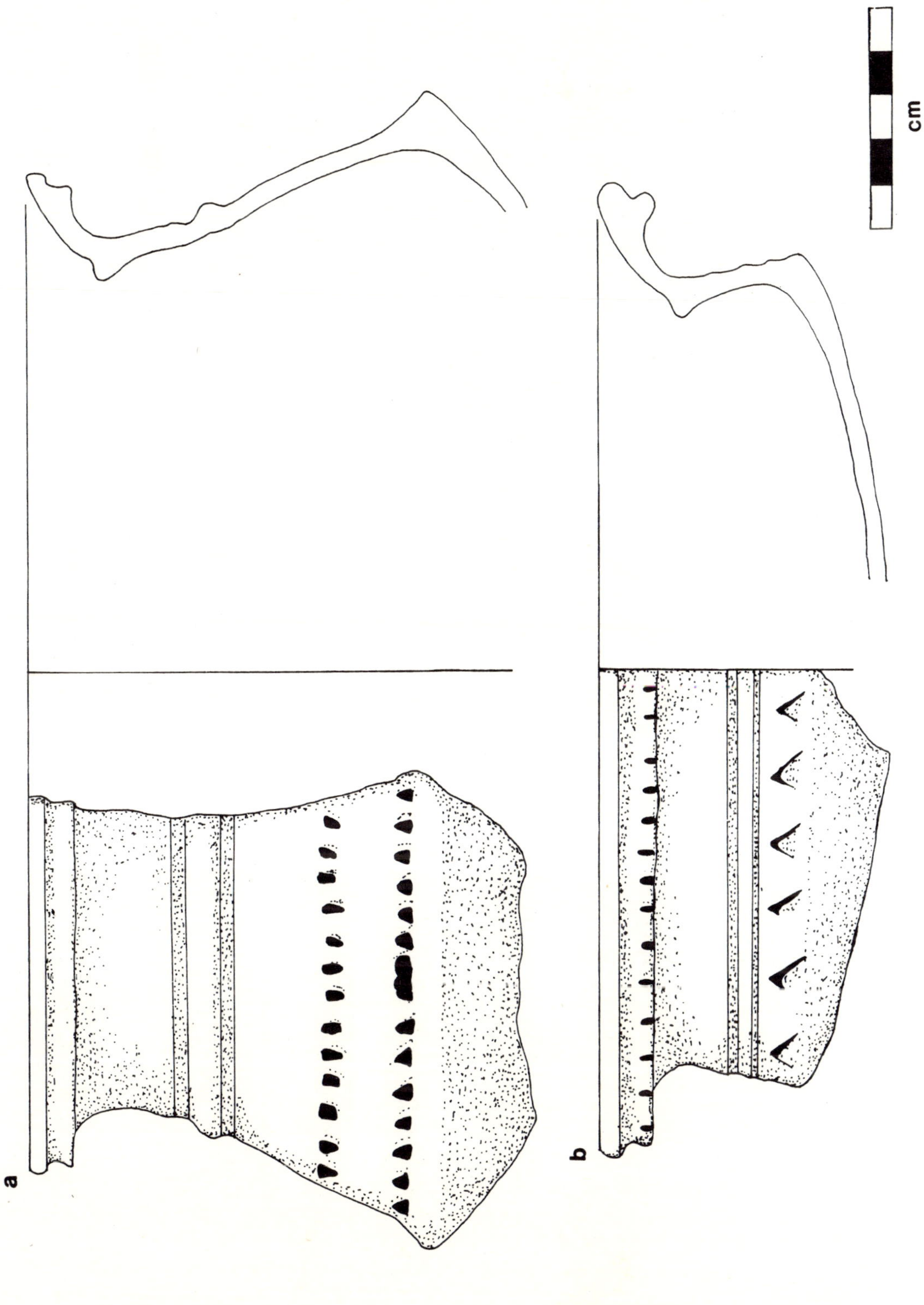

Figure A.67 NMQ12 Flange Rim Restricted Vessels

Index

Citations in the index refer to text only; appendixes are not indexed. Referenced figures are indicated by suffix 'f' after the page number.)